On Reading Books to Children

Parents and Teachers

Center for Improvement of Early Reading Achievement
CIERA

Steven A. Stahl, University of Georgia
Susan B. Neuman, Temple University
P. David Pearson, University of California, Berkeley
Series Editors

On Reading Books to Children

Parents and Teachers

Edited by

Anne van Kleeck
University of Georgia

Steven A. Stahl
Eurydice B. Bauer
University of Illinois

LAWRENCE ERLBAUM ASSOCIATES, PUBLISHERS
2003   Mahwah, New Jersey   London

Lawrence Erlbaum Associates, Inc., Publishers
10 Industrial Avenue
Mahwah, NJ 07430

Cover design by Kathryn Houghtaling Lacey

Library of Congress Cataloging-in-Publication Data

On reading books to children : parents and teachers / edited by Anne van
    Kleeck, Steven A. Stahl, Eurydice B. Bauer.
        p. cm.
    Includes bibliographical references and index.
    ISBN 0-8058-3968-2 (cloth)—ISBN 0-8058-3969-0 (paper)
    1. Oral reading. 2. Storytelling. 3. Children—Books and reading. I. Van
    Kleeck, Anne. II. Stahl, Steven A. III. Bauer, Eurydice B. (Eurydice
    Bochereau)

LB1573.5 .O62   2003
327.67´7—dc21
                                                                    2002073889
                                                                         CIP

Books published by Lawrence Erlbaum Associates are printed on acid-free
paper, and their bindings are chosen for strength and durability.

Printed in the United States of America
10 9 8 7 6 5 4 3 2 1

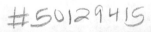

Contents

Preface

Anne van Kleeck
University of Georgia

Steven A. Stahl
University of Illinois

Divides between different groups of scholars seem to be common in literacy scholarship. The research on book sharing—a seemingly innocuous practice—is no exception. On the one hand, it is easy to presume that "everyone" knows how important it is to read to young preschool and school-aged children. Parents, or at least middle-class parents, seem to know: Adams (1990) suggests that her son received over 1,000 hours of exposure to print and stories prior to first grade. Teachers seem to know, and have been heard to tell parents that their failure to read to their child is a reason for the child's failure to learn to read. Policymakers also know the importance of storybook reading: as Teale (this volume) notes, the major literacy policy document of the 1980s, *Becoming a Nation of Readers*, concluded that "the single most important activity for building the knowledge required for eventual success in reading is reading aloud to children" (Anderson, Hiebert, Scott, & Wilkinson, 1985, p. 23).

While it may seem that book sharing is a panacea for reading difficulties and illiteracy, this conclusion has lately been called into question. Family book sharing with young preliterate and early literate children is by no means a universal practice across cultural, linguistic, and social lines. Where it is practiced, it may be negotiated in a variety of ways, many of which are quite different from those favored in middle-class White families. As such, interventions based on research among middle-class White families may be inappropriate, and hence less

effective, for families from other backgrounds. Furthermore, careful analysis of book sharing research raises the question of whether or not the practice is as effective in promoting print literacy as accepted wisdom suggests.

The traditional focus on book sharing is also very narrow. It ignores the fact that the young children of our time are growing up in a world in which multiple literacies have often become the norm.

The research on book sharing often endorses, either implicitly or explicitly, very particular cultural and political viewpoints. By focusing on the book sharing context itself, the traditional research on home and family literacy immediately biased itself toward cultural groups that valued and engaged in this particular practice, and who did so in a manner that closely matched the literacy practices of mainstream schools. Studies of book sharing's effect on the development of print literacy in school have tended to view the practices of mainstream-culture families as providing children with the most effective socialization for school literacy.

When these research-validated "effective practices" become the basis for interventions for children who are at risk for difficulty in developing print literacy and engaging in the literate practices of the classroom (e.g., Zevenbergen & Whitehurst, this volume), then the enterprise becomes political. That is, the focus on mainstream book sharing practices, which are assumed to best prepare the child for mainstream classroom practices, shape policy that dictates the "best" practices that will be taught to parents and teachers. This hegemonic approach has been resisted by recent efforts to consider literacy as a social practice and promote socioculturally appropriate interventions (e.g., Delgado-Gaitan, 1991; New, 2001). It has also prompted several contributors to this volume to question a variety of the assumptions underlying book sharing research (e.g., Anderson, Anderson, Lynch & Shapiro; Barrera & Bauer; Carrington & Luke; Teale).

The polarized view is that the problem boils down to either blaming families or blaming schools for children's literacy deficits. One school of thought claims that families are not providing the basic literacy practices and values that will facilitate their children's transition into school. The other holds that it is educators' outdated, culturally biased views of literacy that create the greatest barriers to scholastic achievement, particularly for those children who do not hail from white, middle-class, two-parent families (see Carrington & Luke, this volume).

But the divide between these two perspectives goes still deeper, to the question of "deficits." One group sees deficits in the child's basic knowledge about domains that are considered foundational to developing print literacy. This includes knowledge of print concepts, the alphabet and how it relates to spoken language, text and narrative construction, decontextualized or abstract language, the syntax and vocabulary of literate language, and so on.

The other group might go so far as to eschew the idea of "deficit" altogether (see Carrington & Luke, this volume). From this perspective, children's difficulties in achieving adequate literacy are seen to emanate from a mismatch—not between home and school cultures, but between the school's narrow view of literacy and the reality of multiple literacies in today's society; and between educators' notion of "family" and the more complex reality of modern family structure. As one might expect, this perspective calls for the development of new and more complex notions of family, community, and literacy.

We believe there is much value in both of these perspectives. It is critical that we become aware of the culturally shaped, and hence biased, assumptions of much book sharing research. We also need to further expand our research into other literacy activities and media that reflect the range of literacy practices characteristic of society today. But we also take the stance that much important knowledge has been learned from the traditional research in this field. Furthermore, we suggest that much remains to be clarified by critically questioning, with the greater clarity afforded by hindsight, what has been done thus far, and then figuring out how this line of research might be more effectively conducted in the future. Our understanding of how children can be effectively socialized to use books in ways that promote their school success does not have to, and should not, come at the price of insensitivity to the fact that such practices may not be appropriate to, and hence effective in, other cultural contexts.

What is needed is continuation of, and dialogue between, the two perspectives described herein. Clearly, more research is needed to illuminate the diversity of literacy practices in homes and schools. The assumptions underlying educational policies and practices must be made explicit, so that cultural biases can be acknowledged and notions of literacy expanded. At the same time, research on mainstream families and book sharing will continue to provide us with valuable information on what can be learned, and how it can be learned in this particular context. While an emphasis on book sharing sets aside the complexity of multiple literacies, this simplification may also bring into focus important mechanisms for the teaching and learning of print-based literacy.

Continuing research on a variety of cultural and linguistic groups might effectively build upon the excellent scholarship that is beginning to accrue, including work with Mexican-American families (e.g., Goldenberg, Reese, & Gallimore, 1992; Valdés, 1996; Vernon-Faegans, Hammer, Miccio, & Manlove, 2001), Puerto-Rican-American families (Volk & de Acosta, 2001), African-American families (e.g., Anderson-Yockel & Haynes, 1994; DeBaryshe, 1995; Gadsden, 1993; Heath, 1983), and Turkish and Surinamese Dutch families (Bus, Leseman, & Keultjes, 2000; Leseman & de Jong, 1998). Educators in preschools and elementary schools should integrate information about diversity in literacy practices into their understanding of what constitutes literacy, and into their notions about the variety of contexts and activities that might promote literacy development among children from diverse backgrounds. However, until all schools are effectively accommodating children from all cultural, linguistic, and social backgrounds at all levels in the educational system, it may be helpful to teach non-mainstream children to become bicultural with respect to literacy practices.

In acknowledging the need of literacy research to expand beyond book sharing, the implication is that book sharing is widely practiced in educational settings. Such is not the case, as Dickinson, McCabe, and Anastasopoulos (this volume) report, based on data from 133 preschool classrooms in the Boston area. Of their 166 observations, 66 classrooms did not engage in book reading at all. In the remaining 100 classrooms, the average time devoted to book sharing in a day was only about 10 minutes. On a composite score of several measures of the overall classroom environment, only 13% of the classrooms were rated as "strong" in their support of language, literacy, and curriculum, while 44% were rated as "low quality." We might wonder, then, how many children are even learning the most basic print-based literacy skills in mainstream educational institutions. Do findings of this nature reflect a lack of opportunities for children to learn the complex array of multiple literacies that they need to face today's world? We would guess they might, but research which defines literacy more broadly will be needed to verify this hunch.

Questions also arise regarding mainstream, middle-class families. While children from such backgrounds are somewhat less likely to have reading difficulties than their non-mainstream peers, many certainly do struggle in learning to read and write. Part of the reason may be that not all mainstream preschoolers receive the kind of socialization during book sharing that is associated with better print literacy achievement later on. In fact, the variation in the amount of book sharing discussions among White, middle-class parents is enormous (e.g., Martin & Reutzel, 1999; van Kleeck, Gillam, Hamilton, & McGrath, 1997), and the different styles found within this group are not all equally conducive to positive outcomes for children's language and literacy skills (Haden, Reese, & Fivush, 1996; Reese, Cox, Harte, & McAnally, this volume).

Listening to stories does improve children's reading, but not in all ways, for all children. The reality is that storybook reading is not as powerful an influence on children's reading as has been claimed. Meyer and colleagues first found this out while analyzing the data from a longitudinal study of children's reading (Meyer, Stahl, Wardrop, & Linn, 1994). They correlated reports of parents reading to children and observations of teachers reading to children with a variety of reading achievement measures. Not only did they fail to find correlations significantly different from zero, but most of the correlations were negative. They speculated that many of their measures were print-specific, and that time spent reading to children may have usurped some of the time normally devoted to print-related instruction.

Further, they discovered that theirs was not the only study that had found such effects (see Stahl, this volume). Scarborough and Dobrich (1994), in their meta-analysis of storybook reading studies, found that storybook reading had disappointingly small effects on reading achievement, acounting for only 8% of the variance. Bus, van IJzendoorn, and Pellegrini (1995), who used somewhat different techniques to analyze their data, nonetheless found results similar to those of Scarborough and Dobrich. These smaller-than-expected (but statistically reliable) effects suggest that the reality of reading to children is more complex than the optimists propose. Instead, some of the effects of reading to children which are explored in this volume might:

- Be stronger on measures of vocabulary (deTemple & Snow) than on measures of word recognition (Stahl).
- Depend on the style of reading by the parent (Reese, Cox, Harte, & McAnally) or the teacher (Dickinson & McCabe).
- Relate to the emotional bonding between parent and child (Bus).
- Be different among parents and children from different cultures (Anderson, Anderson, Lynch, & Shapiro; Barrera & Bauer) or children with language delays (van Kleeck & Vander Woude).

In short, simply reading to children will not, in itself, cure or prevent children's reading problems.

We try, in this volume, to integrate chapters on the effects and limitations of book sharing with children with chapters discussing promising programs involving storybook reading. Thus, we have included chapters by Morrow and Brittain and by Teale on primary grade teachers reading aloud to children, by Zevenbergen and Whitehurst on their long-term research on dialogic reading, and by McKeown and Beck on their new research on the Text Talk program.

The last section of this volume, entitled "Where Do We Go From Here?", opens with a chapter by van Kleeck that tries to place book sharing within the larger context of emergent literacy, by deconstructing the global manner in which the effects of adults reading with children have often been viewed. Van Kleeck suggests that in order to get a nuanced view of the effects of book sharing, we need to examine how adults read, what text they read, and how and when we measure the effects of book sharing. Pellegrini and Galda suggest looking at the *context* of book sharing, to see how it fits into a larger model of social relations. Yaden is similarly concerned with context, but suggests using dynamic systems analysis to understand the connections and disconnections between parent and child, and how these might relate to learning.

The research literature on reading stories to children is a rich one. We certainly could have included more chapters, reflecting more lines of research. We perhaps could have even added another volume. But we also hope that the ideas set forth in this volume will stimulate new lines of research as well as refinements of current methods, yielding far richer findings in this small but important arena of literacy development.

REFERENCES

Adams, M. (1990). *Beginning to read: Thinking and learning about print*. Cambridge, MA: MIT Press.

Anderson, R., Heibert, E., Scott, J., & Wilkinson, I. A. G. (1985). *Becoming a nation of readers: The report of the Commission on Reading*. Washington, DC: The National Institute of Education.

Anderson-Yockel, J., & Haynes, W. O. (1994). Joint book-reading strategies in working-class African American and White mother–toddler dyads. *Journal of Speech and Hearing Research, 37*, 583–593.

Bus, A. G., Leseman, P. P., & Keultjes, P. (2000). Joint book reading across cultures: A comparison of Surinamese-Dutch, Turkish-Dutch, and Dutch parent–child dyads. *Journal of Language Research, 32*(1), 53–76.

Bus, A. G., van IJzendoorn, M. H., & Pellegrini, A. D. (1995). Joint book reading makes for success in learning to read: A meta-analysis on intergenerational transmission of literacy. *Review of Educational Research, 65*(1), 1–21.

DeBaryshe, B. D. (1995). Maternal belief systems: Linchpin in the home reading process. *Journal of Applied Developmental Psychology, 16*, 1–20.

Delgado-Gaitan, C. (1991). Involving parents in the schools: A process of empowerment. *American Journal of Education, 100*, 20–47.

Gadsden, V. L. (1993). Literacy, education, and identity among African-Americans: The communal nature of learning. *Urban Education, 27*(4), 352–369.

Goldenberg, C., Reese, L., & Gallimore, R. (1992). Effects of literacy materials from school on Latino children's home experiences and early reading achievement. *American Journal of Education, 100*, 497–536.

Haden, C. A., Reese, E., & Fivush, R. (1996). Mother's extratextual comments during storybook reading: Stylistic differences over time and across texts. *Discourse Processes, 21*, 135–169.

Heath, S. B. (1983). *Ways with words: Language, life, and work in communities and classrooms*. New York: Cambridge University Press.

Leseman, P. P. M., & de Jong, P. F. (1998). Home literacy: Opportunity, instruction, cooperation and social-emotional quality predicting early reading achievement. *Reading Research Quarterly, 33*(3), 294–318.

Martin, L. E., & Reutzel, D. R. (1999). Sharing books: Examining how and why mothers deviate from the print. *Reading Research and Instruction, 39*(1), 39–70.

Meyer, L. A., Stahl, S. A., Wardrop, J. L., & Linn, R. L. (1994). Effects of reading storybooks aloud to children. *Journal of Educational Research, 88*(2), 69–85.

New, R. S. (2001). Early literacy and developmentally appropriate practices: Rethinking the paradigm. In S. B. Neuman & D. K. Dickinson (Eds.), *Handbook of early literacy development* (pp. 245–262). New York: Guilford Press.

Scarborough, H. S., & Dobrich, W. (1994). On the efficacy of reading to preschoolers. *Developmental Review, 14*, 245–302.

Valdés, G. (1996). *Con respeto: Bridging the distances between culturally diverse families and schools.* New York: Teachers College Press.

van Kleeck, A., Gillam, R., Hamilton, L., & McGrath, C. (1997). The relationship between middle-class parents' book-sharing discussion and their preschoolers' abstract language development. *Journal of Speech-Language-Hearing Research, 40*, 1261–1271.

Vernon-Feagans, L., Hammer, C., Miccio, A., & Manlove, E. (2001). Early language literacy skills in low-income African American and Hispanic children. In S. B. Neuman & D. K. Dickinson (Eds.), *Handbook of early literacy development* (pp. 192–210). New York: Guilford Press.

Volk, D., & de Acosta, M. (2001). "Many differing ladders, many ways to climb…": Literacy events in the bilingual classrooms, homes, and community of three Puerto Rican kindergartners. *Journal of Early Childhood Literacy, 1*(2), 193–224.

I
Book Sharing in Families

1

Social-Emotional Requisites for Learning to Read

Adriana G. Bus
Leiden University

My interest in the question of how book reading affects young children's reading development goes back to my experiences as a reading specialist in an Amsterdam inner-city neighborhood. The low level of reading accomplishment in this neighborhood made me realize that one cannot become a conventional reader by systematic reading instruction alone. Despite a strong emphasis on phonics and extra practice for children who lagged behind, I saw the majority of these immigrant and low-income Dutch children get bogged down in the lower levels of reading accomplishment.

I hypothesized that the contributions of the home—and probably the inter-relationship between home and school—should be taken into account when one is examining the roots of literacy. I began to study parent–preschooler book reading, thinking that this activity might be an important incentive for learning to read. There are, of course, other literacy-related activities that contribute to children's literacy development; however, book reading seems to be one of the most influential "natural," literacy-related family activities (Bus, van IJzendoorn, & Pellegrini, 1995). This chapter discusses the outcomes of a series of studies in which I closely examined various aspects of parent–preschooler storybook readings. The studies' results suggest one possible explanation of how book reading supports children's literacy development during both the pre-school and elementary stages.

A SOCIAL-EMOTIONAL BASE FOR CHILDREN'S ENGAGEMENT IN BOOK READING

The first studies assumed that children's interest in books and joint reading is rooted in social context, rather than in a biologically endowed trait for exploration of uncharted territories stimulating their development (e.g., Crain-Thoreson & Dale, 1992). I felt this affinity with the social construction hypothesis because simply reading a text aloud seemed an insufficient method for starting a process in which children learn about reading by sharing books with their parents, particularly in the beginning stages of book reading.

As long as children are unfamiliar with the structure of stories and the manner in which they are phrased, they may need their parents' help to bridge the gap between their own world and that presented in the book. It therefore seemed plausible to me that the benefits of book reading would strongly depend on how parents supported their children. I hypothesized that children needed support from an adult who was sensitive to their motives and understandings. Parents might need to find ways to immerse their child in books by capitalizing on the child's personal interests and motives (cf. Baker, Scher, & Mackler, 1997; Dickinson & Tabors, 1991; Snow, Barnes, Chandler, Goodman, & Hemphill, 1991).

To test these assumptions I tried to compose groups of parents who differed in their ability to support their child sensitively in complex learning situations. Because the quality of the parent–child attachment relationship seemed an excellent criterion by which to determine the extent of parents' sensitivity and supportiveness, I started a research program that compared the book reading experiences of parent–child pairs who had a secure attachment relationship with those of pairs having an insecure one (Bus, 1994, 2000, 2001; Bus & van IJzendoorn, 1988, 1992, 1995, 1997; Bus, Belsky, van IJzendoorn, & Crnik, 1997).

Attachment categories represent children's mental representations of their interactions with their parents. Children develop these representations on the basis of experience. They anticipate that the parent's future behavior will be similar to the past interactions on which the child's representations are based. Secure parents who have generally responded to their child in a sensitive and supportive way thus strengthen the child's expectation that they will continue to do so in the future. An insecure relationship, on the other hand, implies that parents are less sensitive to their children's needs; consequently the children have not developed trust in the parent's support in unknown and often somewhat frightening situations.

Hypothesizing that book reading depends on the parental ability to engage children in books, the frequency and quality of book reading sessions may differ as a function of this measure of the parent–child relationship. Assuming that insecure parents are less able to respond to and support their children in complex situations, I hypothesized that a positive history of interactive experience with the parent (experienced by the so-called "securely attached" children) would foster more frequent and more productive book reading interaction, while the negative interactions experienced by the "insecurely attached" children would limit the occurrence of book reading and its learning potential.

I expected that the insecure pairs would have disciplining problems and that the children would often be distracted. Because of their prior negative experiences, such children might not expect much from the interaction, and consequently might refuse to listen. Their parents might not succeed in adapting the reading to their children's interests, motives, and understandings in order to lower the child's resistance to reading. The setting might not be stimulating for both parent and child. And as a result, these pairs might not share books as often as the securely attached pairs.

To test whether sensitive parental support, rather than the child's interest or disinterest (Crain-Toreson & Dale, 1992), could explain differences in children's book reading experiences and derivative learning, I started a series of studies in which I compared parent–child pairs that differed in the quality of their social-emotional relationships (Bus et al., 1997; Bus & van IJzendoorn, 1988, 1992, 1995, 1997).

MOTHER–CHILD ATTACHMENT SECURITY PREDICTS THE QUALITY AND QUANTITY OF BOOK READING

The outcomes of studies that test interaction patterns during book reading support the hypothesis that securely attached children show more interest in joint book reading than their insecurely attached counterparts. Comparing securely and insecurely attached mother–child pairs during joint book reading sessions, I repeatedly observed differences in the engagement and enjoyment levels of the children in these two groups.

Insecurely attached children appeared to be more often disengaged from their mothers or the book reading than securely attached children, as shown by measures of child attentiveness, maternal interventions to control the child's behavior, and child responsiveness (Bus et al., 1997; Bus & van IJzendoorn, 1988, 1992, 1995, 1997). From a cross-sectional study of interactive reading with 18-, 32-, and 66-month-old children (Bus & van IJzendoorn, 1988), for example, it appeared that the atmosphere surrounding the interaction of securely attached dyads was more positive than that around the insecurely attached pairs. There was less need for discipline in securely attached dyads; these children were less distracted than their insecurely attached peers.

Even in a group of 1-year-old infants with little book reading experience at best, children's interest in books still varied as a function of attachment security, suggesting that interactive experiences with the mother other than those involving books may also affect children's responses to book reading (Bus & van IJzendoorn, 1997). In this study I observed mothers and their 44- to 63-week-old infants in the university laboratory. Among other tasks, the mother–infant pairs shared a simple expository book with thematically ordered pictures typical for this age range: each page showed a farm setting, accompanied by a one-sentence text describing the events in the picture.

Similarly to other studies of book reading to babies (e.g., van Kleeck, Alexander, Vigil, & Templeton, 1996), we found that most maternal energy was devoted to getting and keeping the baby's attention and encouraging participation in the routine. However, the insecurely attached children were less attentive than the secure ones: they often looked at other objects in the environment or made attempts to escape from the mother's lap. Insecurely attached children responded less to the book content by referencing: they were less inclined to make animal sounds, touch the pictures (for example, caressing an animal picture), or make movements to represent a pictured object (like horse-riding in response to a picture of a horse). Their mothers were more inclined to control their behavior by putting an arm around the child, thus restricting the infant's movements, or by keeping the book out of reach.

If adults frequently fail to engage their children in book reading sessions, the children may remain dependent on the parent for understanding stories, rather than becoming actively engaged and eliciting book interactions. Books may not become an attractive parent–child activity, and joint book reading may not be established as a family routine. To test this hypothesis, another study (Bus & van IJzendoorn, 1992, 1995) was designed that explored the frequency of parent–preschooler book reading as a function of attachment security. I expected that the securely attached parent–child pairs would more often share a book than the insecurely attached pairs.

The mothers selected for this study differed in the frequency of reading books to their children. One group of mothers reported that their children never seemed to have enough of book reading; these mothers read books to their children one or more times a day, often at the child's request. The other group of mothers reported that joint book reading occurred at most a few times a week. A few mothers in this group admitted that they had stopped trying to read to their children out of frustration. One of these mothers, for instance, thought that another reading attempt in the university laboratory did not make sense, since her son showed so little interest in books. Subsequent observations confirmed that this child did not enjoy sharing a book with the mother. In fact, he turned nasty when his mother tried to immerse him in a picture storybook that other children of his age group seemed to like.

The findings of this study were in accordance with my expectation that attachment security related to the frequency of joint book reading. As expected, most of the frequently reading pairs were securely attached (73%), whereas only a minority of the infrequently reading pairs were securely attached (23%). This is a strong effect, taking into account that the assessment of parent–child attachment security was completely independent of book reading. An attachment researcher blind for the grouping based on reading frequency and not knowing how the mothers read to the children coded how the child responded to the parent in a so-called "strange situation," in which the child was reunited with the parent after a short separation in a strange environment.

Arguing strictly logically, the differences in attachment security may result from differences in book reading experiences. Positive interactive experiences during book reading sessions may help to develop basic trust in the mother's supportive presence. Although I can not exclude this interpretation, I do not consider it very plausible. Other results (Bus & van IJzendoorn, 1992) have revealed evidence for the hypothesis that the manner in which parents interact with their young children is deeply embedded in the parent's own biography.

Simply reading a text aloud is not in itself sufficient to encourage children to learn from being read to. My studies so far, all of which included an assessment of the parent–child attachment security, strongly suggest that the parent's supportive presence affected how a child would immerse in books. The studies yielded clear-cut evidence that the quality of the parent–child relationship had to be taken into account to explain why some children found being read to boring or unpleasant, while others loved it. Assuming that attention is critical for learning to take place, the former group may not have been internalizing much from the books.

In many studies of book reading it is assumed that certain didactic types of utterances during storybook reading may support children's learning from that reading (e.g., Dickinson, De Temple, Hirschler, & Smith, 1992; Heath, 1982; Reese & Cox, 1999). It is an adult who helps the child maneuver purposefully through a maze of text, illustrations, and unfamiliar vocabulary. However, the consistent correlation between book reading and attachment security suggests that there are other, emotional dimensions to book reading that may explain whether young children learn from the process. In subsequent studies I tried to better understand these dimensions.

CAPITALIZING ON THE CHILD'S PERSONAL INTERESTS AND MOTIVES

As long as children's linguistic knowledge is limited, adults have to find ways to make a book interesting in spite of such obstacles. In line with my finding that attachment security relates to book reading I did not expect that merely explaining a book's content would be an effective way to keep the child's interest. Numerous studies identified variability in potentially important types of utterances for children's story skills: e.g., discussing what has happened, why it happened, and which feelings the story may elicit (e.g., Reese & Cox, 1999; Whitehurst et al., 1988); however, knowing from my previous studies that the emotional level of parent–child interactions influenced the reading process, I now hypothesize that parental success in the early stages might largely depend on the creation of an interactional context that fostered children's engagement.

To engage a young reader in the world of the book, it is of the utmost importance that parents capitalize on intimate knowledge of their child's personal world; on familiar and meaningful settings, possessions and sensations; and on the language with which these are associated (Jones, 1996). Research has revealed numerous examples of caregivers changing the print or altering the text during book reading to make it more attractive to the child (e.g., Martin & Reutzel, 1999; van Kleeck et al., 1996). One of Martin and Reutzel's mothers, for instance, added a dog to a simple story, even though this animal was not mentioned in the original text, but was only present in one of the illustrations. Later on the mother explained that the child was very fond of dogs. The mother expected that inserting the dog into the story would make the text more exciting for the child.

A study involving 18-month-old Caucasian American boys (Bus et al., 1997), all very similar in age and book reading experiences, confirmed the hypothesis that parents who have an insecure relationship with their child are less likely to create an interactional context that fosters children's engagement. Profiles of interaction differed as a function of the attachment categories. Some insecurely attached children were inclined to be more unresponsive to book content and to be more distracted than the children from the secure group. The mothers in this study read from a book in which each page contained a short text accompanied by a series of pictures of babies making faces, crawling, staying, walking, playing, eating, drinking, being dressed or bathed, and sleeping.

Taking into account that most children in this age range have problems under-standing language, it makes more sense to focus their attention on appealing pictures, and on details that might make children aware of some events, than to read the text. Most mothers in the insecure group, however, were inclined to merely read the text, ignoring other ways to immerse the child in the book.

These mothers may have proceeded this way in order to terminate an unpro-ductive and unsatisfactory interaction with an unresponsive and distracted child. Looking at the sessions, one gets the impression that these children do not expect support and help from the mothers during reading. I often saw the children squirm out of their mothers' laps. The mothers, on the other hand, were unable to break through their children's negative expectations and sup-port them at the appropriate level of understanding. They limited themselves to holding their children tightly or telling them to sit and listen. Because of the lack of maternal support for their understanding and motivation, these insecure children may have been more unresponsive to the book content and more dis-tracted than other children.

Another group of insecurely attached children was superficially more en-gaged, but a better look at the sessions revealed several problems. The mothers initiated labeling routines to the same extent or even more often than secure mothers. However, these insecure mothers were also inclined to overstimulate and overcontrol. For instance, they did not allow the child to skip a page or part of it when he or she was bored or eager to explore another one. The mothers in-sisted on exploration of all details before a new page could be read.

Their children were not obviously disengaged but were less responsive than other children. They also differed from the rest by showing aggression towards the mother (pushing or hitting her) and by responding at a low level to the book (for example hitting the book). By encouraging book-orientation, these moth-ers may have been attempting to circumvent their children's aggressive re-sponses. I had the impression that because these mothers stressed dialogic reading so much, they may have provoked their children to express frustration through these behaviors.

This detailed study of parent–child interactions during book reading sessions supports the hypothesis that interactions are often awkward if the parent–child relationship is insecure. Overall, the in-depth study of differences in interaction suggests that less engagement by the children coincides with their mothers' in-ability to bridge the worlds of the young reader and the book. Secure parents may be more inclined to drift away from the official storyline by improvising dif-ferent main characters and events. A secure parent is careful to note the child's real-life interests where they occur in the picture, even if they bear little or no obvious relation to the story as a whole (Jones, 1996). Insecure parents, on the other hand, may be less inclined to tune in to the child by identifying visual content ("look, that's your ball") or linguistic coding ("see the baba lamb?") that would attract the young reader's attention. These speculations are in line with my observations, but go beyond the "hard" results so far.

HOW BOOK READING MATTERS FOR LITERACY-LEARNING PROCESSES

In more recent studies I have begun to explore how children's learning is tied up with their book reading experiences (de Jong & Bus, 2002; Bus, Sulzby, & Kaderavek, 2001). I discuss here the outcomes of a study focused on low-income mothers with limited education and their 2- to 3-year-old children (Bus et al., 2001). It tested what children dissimilar in their book reading history would internalize from a story after four interactive readings of the book. The age at which their mothers reported to have started reading to the children ranged from before the first to around the third birthday. Previous research has proved that emergent reading of favorite books is a sensitive measure for subtle differences in children's knowledge of a story's structure, phrasing, and written characteristics (e.g., Elster, 1998; Sulzby, 1985). Even emergent readings by very young children with speech-language impairment have some characteristics of written stories (Kaderavek & Sulzby, 2000).

Children differed in their ability to reconstruct a cohesive story that included the location, the characters, the problem, the attempts to solve the problem, and the resolution (cf. Neuman, 1996). Insofar as the preschoolers in this study produced a story-like emergent reading, they described the main character's attempt to solve his problem and the results of that attempt; after four re-readings of *Sam Vole and His Brothers* (Waddell & Firth, 1992), some children discussed how sad Sam becomes when he rummages alone through the garden, but noted that he feels happy again when he encounters his two big brothers. Hardly any child described either the setting (two big brothers who collect grass and nuts for Sam) or the main character's problem (Sam wants to show that he can collect things by himself).

When children began to reproduce facets of the story, then the phrasings of their emergent readings became more similar to the original text: i.e., their emergent readings included nouns, verbs, and whole phrases derived from the focal book. Through repeated readings the children internalized discourse structures (e.g., "all by myself," "slipping out of the house") and vocabulary (e.g., "meadow," "happily") typical of this book.

Not until children had been involved in book reading routines for a long time did they reach the more advanced levels of internalization. Two- and 3-year-old children in this study who had started book reading with their parents early (before 14 months) internalized more from the focal book after four re-readings than their later-starting peers. Apparently, internalization of a story's content and phrasing is not just rote memorization stimulated by the re-readings. Children use the knowledge of story structure and phrasing that they have acquired through previous experiences with books to make sense of new texts and internalize a story's structure and phrasing (cf. Purcell-Gates, 1988; Sénéchal, 1997; Sulzby, 1985; Sulzby & Zecker, 1991). Children who have internalized the chains of events and phrasings typical of storybooks are better prepared to recognize events and structures in new texts. MacNeil (1989), looking back at his own early book reading experiences, suggests that words and word patterns accumulate in layers; as the layers thicken, they govern all understanding and appreciation of language thenceforth.

Examination of correlations between characteristics of the interactive reading sessions and children's internalizations strengthened the hypothesis that parents should adapt their book reading styles to each child's level of book understanding. The amount of discussion decreased as children were involved in book reading for a longer period. In line with another study (Bus & van IJzendoorn, 1995), the more experienced children needed fewer explanations and less verbal support during the reading of text. That is, they were interested in the story without needing much extratextual support. The interactions of mother–child dyads with longer book reading experience focused more on making inferences. These mothers initiated discussions about the main characters' motives. In other words, the discussions became more complex as children knew more about stories—knowledge accumulated as a result of previous book reading experiences.

Consistent with the assumption that reading promotes the understanding of basic storybook concepts, which in turn facilitates the understanding of new books, a child's history of book reading with their parents seems to determine the extent to which they will internalize a story's structure and language from repeated readings. When parents began book reading sessions with their children at an early age, those children internalized more information from repeated readings of a book. Over time and with guided practice, preschoolers begin to notice similarities between chains of events and phrasings of events and emotions in the present story and in previously read stories. In addition to internalization of the story's structure and language, one may expect that older and more experienced children would also internalize vocabulary and features of the written text (cf. de Jong & Bus, 2002; Murray, Stahl, & Ivey, 1996).

CONCLUSION

Children do not learn simply from their parents reading a text aloud. Particularly in the youngest age groups, stories may not be attractive by themselves. The series of studies described here supports the assumption that a child's interest in books and joint reading is rooted in adults' ability to engage the child, rather than in some biologically endowed trait urging children to explore uncharted territories and stimulate their own development (e.g., Crain-Thoreson & Dale, 1992). As the parent–child relationship becomes more secure, children derive more enjoyment from being read to and become more engaged during these sessions (Bus et al., 1997; Bus & van IJzendoorn, 1988, 1995, 1997). This result was replicated several times, among various age groups.

The finding that parent–child attachment relates to the quality and quantity of book reading suggests that parents add something of their own to book readings in order to make them more exciting for their children. This is particularly true with very young children, for whom books are hard to understand and not enjoyable as such. Children's commitment and learning depends on the parental ability to bridge the child's world and the world of the book by using their intimate knowledge of the child's personal experiences, of familiar and meaningful settings, possessions and sensations, and of the language with which these sensations are associated. More secure parents seem to know better how to adapt the pictures and text that will interest their child, even though their book reading sessions may look very similar to those of less-secure parents. With very young children (1- to 2-year-olds), even drastic adaptations may be required in order to immerse the child in a reading, when text is part of the book. Parents may ignore the focal story and create new stories for their own children; a disproportionate amount of adult speech time may be devoted to details from the pictures that have little to do with the printed story that accompanies them (cf. Jones, 1996; Martin & Reutzel, 1999).

I doubt that there is a strong basis for promoting specific styles (such as non-immediate talk) for reading books to the very young (cf. Dickinson & Tabors, 1991). Speculations, extensions and inferences are, of course, part of many discussions surrounding parent–child readings. But there is no evidence that the growth of early literacy skills is particularly fostered by challenging discursive-language abilities. Research suggests that parental style reflects the extent to which book reading has become a routine, and children begin to understand stories without much support (Bus et al., 2001). The amount of parent–child interaction during book reading, for instance, decreases as preschoolers grow older and more experienced (e.g., Bus et al., 2001; Bus & van

IJzendoorn, 1995). Supportive interactions are required during the transition from looking at pictures to understanding a story's structure and phrasing. Once children have built up basic conceptions of stories by sharing books with their parents, they may be able to internalize the structure and phrasing of new stories just by listening to read-alouds.

Some researchers believe that children's learning from book reading may not become manifest until late elementary school, when they begin to read stories and other texts on their own (Leseman & de Jong, 2001; van Kleeck, Gillam, Hamilton, & McGrath, 1997; Whitehurst et al., 1999). Another hypothesis holds that vocabulary and story understanding affect beginning reading skills, as well (e.g., Bus, 2001). The internalization of stories' phrasing and vocabulary may make text more transparent and predictable, and in this way may contribute to the transition from emergent to conventional reading. Furthermore, book reading may affect knowledge of the written form of text and words, and thus support beginning reading skills. Kindergartners internalize physical features of the book and of print when they become more proficient in understanding stories. Mapping out effects of book reading in a group of 5- to 6-year-olds has revealed internalization of features of written text, as well (de Jong & Bus, 2002).

The bottom line of the results is that the process of learning to understand books in the early stages of reading development strongly depends on the social-emotional qualities of the parent–child interaction. Parents raise children's interest in books by the way in which they mediate stories. The emotional qualities of reading sessions seem more important than content-related aspects such as inference, active participation by the child, or quantity of discussion. This is true at least as long as children are relatively inexperienced, as were the children in the studies I have discussed here in this chapter. Given that many parents have problems bridging the gap between the world of their young child and that of books, the admonition "read to your child" perhaps should not be taken too literally.

REFERENCES

Baker, L., Scher, D., & Mackler, K. (1997). Home and family influences on motivation for reading. *Educational Psychologist, 32,* 69–82.

Bus, A. G. (1994). The role of social context in emergent literacy. In E. M. H. Assink (Ed.), *Literacy acquisition and social context* (pp. 9–24). New York: Harvester Wheatsheaf.

Bus, A. G. (2000). Book reading through the lens of attachment theory. In L. Verhoeven & C. Snow (Eds.), *Creating a world of engaged readers* (pp. 39–54). Mahwah, NJ: Lawrence Erlbaum Associates.

Bus, A. G. (2001). Early book reading experience in the family: A route to literacy. In S. Neuman & D. Dickinson (Eds.), *Handbook of research in early literacy* (pp. 179–191). New York: Guilford Press.

Bus, A. G., Belsky, J., van IJzendoorn, M. H., & Crnik, K. (1997). Attachment and bookreading patterns: A study of mothers, fathers, and their toddlers. *Early Childhood Research Quarterly, 12,* 81–98.

Bus, A. G., Sulzby, E., & Kaderavek, J. (2001). *Parent–child reading, emergent reading, and speech-language impairment.* Manuscript in preparation.

Bus, A. G., & van IJzendoorn, M. H. (1988). Mother-child interactions, attachment, and emergent literacy: A cross-sectional study. *Child Development, 59,* 1262–1273.

Bus, A. G., & van IJzendoorn, M. H. (1992). Patterns of attachment in frequently and infrequently reading dyads. *Journal of Genetic Psychology, 153,* 395–403.

Bus, A. G., & van IJzendoorn, M. H. (1995). Mothers reading to their three year olds: The role of mother–child attachment security in becoming literate. *Reading Research Quarterly, 40,* 998–1015.

Bus, A. G., & van IJzendoorn, M. H. (1997). Affective dimension of mother–infant picturebook reading. *Journal of School Psychology, 35,* 47–60.

Bus, A. G., van IJzendoorn, M. H., & Pellegrini, A. D. (1995). Joint book reading makes for success in learning to read. A meta-analysis on intergenerational transmission of literacy. *Review of Educational Research, 65,* 1–21.

Crain-Thoreson, C., & Dale, P. S. (1992). Do early talkers become early readers? Linguistic precocity, preschool language, and emergent literacy. *Developmental Psychology, 28,* 421–429.

de Jong, P., & Bus, A. G. (2002). Quality of book reading matters for emergent readers: An experiment with the same book in a regular or electronic format. *Journal of Educational Psychology, 94,* 145–155.

Dickinson, D. K., & Tabors, P. O. (1991). Early literacy: Linkages between home, school and literacy achievement at five. *Journal of Research in Childhood Education, 6,* 30–46.

Dickinson, D. K., De Temple, J. M., Hirschler, J., & Smith, M. W. (1992). Book reading with preschoolers: Co-construction of text at home and at school. *Early Childhood Research Quarterly, 7,* 323–346.

Elster, C. A. (1998). Influences of text and pictures on shared and emergent readings. *Research in the Teaching of English, 32,* 43–78.

Heath, S. B. (1982). What no bedtime story means: Narrative skills at home and school. *Language in Society, 11,* 49–76.

Jones, R. (1996). *Emerging patterns of literacy. A multi-disciplinary perspective.* London: Routledge.

Kaderavek, J. N., & Sulzby, E. (2000). Narrative production by children with and without specific language impairment: Oral narratives and emergent readings. *Journal of Speech, Language, and Hearing Research, 43,* 34–49.

Leseman, P., & de Jong, P. (2001). Lasting effects of home literacy on reading achievement in school. *Journal of School Psychology, 39,* 389–414.

MacNeil, R. (1989). *Wordstruck: A memoir.* New York: Penguin Books.

Martin, L. E., & Reutzel, D. R. (1999). Sharing books: Examining how and why mothers deviate from the print. *Reading Research and Instruction, 39,* 39–70.

Murray, B. A., Stahl, S. A., & Ivey, M. G. (1996). Developing phoneme awareness through alphabet books. *Reading and Writing: An Interdisciplinary Journal, 8,* 307–322.

Neuman, S. B. (1996). Children engaging in storybook reading: The influence of access to print resources, opportunity, and parental interaction. *Early Childhood Research Quarterly, 11,* 495–514.

Purcell-Gates, V. (1988). Lexical and syntactic knowledge of written narative held by well-read-to kindergartners and second graders. *Research in the Teaching of English, 22,* 128–160.

Reese, E., & Cox, A. (1999). Quality of adult book reading affects children's emergent literacy. *Developmental Psychology, 35,* 20–28.

Sénéchal, M. (1997). The differential effect of storybook reading on preschoolers' acquisition of expressive and receptive vocabulary. *Journal of Child Language, 24,* 123–138.

Snow, C. E., Barnes, W. E., Chandler, J., Goodman, I. F., & Hemphill, L. (1991). *Unfulfilled expectations: Home and school influences on literacy.* Cambridge, MA: Harvard University Press.

Sulzby, E. (1985). Children's emergent reading of favorite storybooks. A developmental study. *Reading Research Quarterly, 20,* 458–479.

Sulzby, E., & Zecker, L. B. (1991). The oral monologue as a form of emergent reading. In A. McCabe & C. Peterson (Eds.), *Developing narrative structure* (pp. 175–213). Mahwah, NJ: Lawrence Erlbaum Associates.

van Kleeck, A., Alexander, E. I., Vigil, A., & Templeton, D. E. (1996). Verbally modelling thinking for infants: Middle-class mothers' presentation of information structures during book sharing. *Journal of Research in Childhood Education, 10,* 101–113.

van Kleeck, A., Gillam, R. B., Hamilton, L., & McGrath, C. (1997). The relationship between middle-class parents' book-sharing discussion and their preschoolers' abstract language development. *Journal of Speech, Language, and Hearing Research, 40,* 1261–1271.

Waddell, M., & Firth, B. (1992). *Sam Vole and his brothers.* Cambridge: Cablewick Press.

Whitehurst, G. J., Falco, F. L., Lonigan, C., Fischel, J. E., DeBaryshe, B. D., Valdez-Menchaca, M. C., & Caulfield, M. (1988). Accelerating language development through picture-book reading. *Developmental Psychology, 24,* 552–558.

Whitehurst, G. J., Zevenbergen, A. A., Crone, D. A., Schultz, M. D., Velting, O. N., & Fischel, J. E. (1999). Outcomes of emergent literacy intervention from Head Start through second grade. *Journal of Educational Psychology, 91,* 261–272.

2

Learning Words From Books

Jeanne De Temple
Catherine E. Snow
Harvard University

Looking at and reading books with young children is widely recommended as a contribution to children's school readiness and as preparation for learning to read. No doubt there are multiple paths by which such experiences contribute to children's development during the preschool period—including the positive affective consequences of having an adult's full attention; opportunities for becoming familiar with the conventions of text and the organization of books in various genres; exposure to print leading to knowledge of letters and numbers; opportunities to develop phonological awareness from books focusing on rhyme and word play; exposure to culturally valued information; and engagement in linguistically relatively complex conversations. In this chapter, though, we focus on examining the potential of shared book reading to contribute to a very specific, and, we argue, crucial aspect of preschool development: children's vocabulary.

Our goal is not to provide a comprehensive review of the sizeable body of research which has shown empirical links between book reading experiences and vocabulary (e.g., Beals, De Temple, & Dickinson, 1994; Sénéchal, LeFevre, Hudson, & Lawson, 1996; Sénéchal, LeFevre, Thomas, & Daley, 1998). Rather, it is to link analyses of interaction during book reading and the particular affordances of book reading to the body of research on the nature and course of children's vocabulary development.

Vocabulary development is a key challenge during the preschool period, and indeed throughout childhood and adolescence (Nagy & Herman, 1987). Vocabulary size is highly correlated to reading ability, via mechanisms that probably shift from the preschool to the adolescence period (Anderson & Freebody, 1981). High correlations between the vocabularies of preschool-aged children and their early reading progress no doubt reflect in part the correlation of vocabulary size with other factors that promote literacy development, such as knowledge about concepts of literacy, capacity to engage in phonological analysis of words (Walley, 1993), and greater world knowledge. The correlation of vocabulary with reading later in a child's school years probably reflects the fact that wide and intensive reading is the only way for children to learn many relatively infrequent words—thus, only good and avid readers have optimal opportunities to expand their vocabularies (Elley, 1989). Of course, knowing more words also enables comprehension (e.g., Stahl & Fairbanks, 1986), which in turn is prerequisite to the capacity for learning new words from reading.

Vocabulary knowledge is wildly variable among normally developing children, with estimated vocabulary sizes of first-graders varying by a factor of five (Shibles, 1959). This variation is strongly related to density of oral language exposure (e.g., Huttenlocher, Haight, Bryk, Selzer, & Lyons, 1991), which in turn is strongly related to social class (Hart & Risley, 1995). Vocabulary relates to reading skill (and amount of time spent reading) in school-age children (Chall, 1987), and in the preschool period relates to being read to interactively.[1]

As a background to discussing the basic claim of this chapter, that book reading with preschoolers can be a major stimulus for vocabulary development, we first review briefly some of the conclusions drawn from research on child language development about the nature of vocabulary learning in preschoolers.

WHAT DO WE KNOW ABOUT VOCABULARY ACQUISITION FROM BIRTH TO AGE 5?

The early language acquisition of hundreds of children, learning several dozen different languages, has now been described. We know there is considerable variability in the course of language development, reflecting differences among children, the settings in which they learn to talk, and language structures. Thus,

---

[1]The title of this chapter reveals the assumption underlying this analysis of the association between reading and vocabulary: Reading has an impact on vocabulary. Like Stanovich (1986), we recognize that the nature of the association is bidirectional. Children with greater vocabularies probably enjoy reading more, have a better understanding of content, and are able to draw on a wider array of reading material, thereby reading more and increasing their vocabularies. Young children with greater vocabularies may be more engaged or attentive while being read to and they may request book reading more than those with smaller vocabularies. Mothers and children with greater vocabularies may engage in more interesting or complex conversations about books, thus exposing the child to new words.

the brief sketch of vocabulary acquisition that we present here is of necessity simplified and incomplete.

Time Course

Children typically speak their first recognizable words at about 1 year of age, and typically acquire their first 25 to 50 words relatively slowly, and with great effort, often losing earlier-learned forms as new forms emerge. These early words may be pronounced correctly, or in ways that are greatly simplified (e.g., *baba* for "blanket," "baby," "bottle," and/or "booboo"). Early words are often used in semantically unconventional ways (e.g., using *dog* only for the family dog, or, conversely, using it for all four-legged animals), and the communicative meanings expressed by early words are quite limited when compared to those expressed only a few months later. Thus, for example, nouns might be used for naming in the context of reading a particular book or for requesting favored objects, but not for referring to those same objects with other communicative purposes.

Typically, it is sometime between the ages of 18 and 28 months when children move beyond the early word period, in which words are acquired one by one, into a period referred to as the "vocabulary spurt." At this point, lexical acquisition suddenly becomes more rapid (going from a new word every few days to several new words a day) and systematic (words become more conventional in meaning, more regular in pronunciation, and seem to be related to one another within a semantic system). For children learning English, Dutch, Spanish, and certain other, less-studied languages, this vocabulary spurt is normally characterized by a sudden increase in the percentage of common nouns that children know (Fenson et al., 1994). Speakers of languages such as Korean, Japanese, and Hungarian may focus more on verbs during the spurt, for reasons that have to do with language structure and characteristics of parent–child interaction. It is interesting to note how picture books designed for very young children in the English-speaking world reflect (and perhaps enhance) the noun bias by offering many pictures of objects. Such a strong noun focus may be atypical in picture books designed for young Korean and Japanese speakers, who are themselves more focused on learning verbs (Gopnik & Choi, 1995).

Facilitating Word Learning

A long line of research with English-speaking children has robustly demonstrated that children learn nouns in the context of joint attention, that is, when mother and child are both looking at or manipulating an object, and the mother provides a name for it (Tomasello & Farrar, 1986). Conversely, though, verbs seem to be learned in the context of impending, rather than current, action (e.g., a mother, saying of an unsteady tower of blocks, "watch out, it's going to fall," creates a context for learning the verb *fall*; Tomasello, 1995). Part of the reason why vocabulary development is so rapid under conditions of rich input is that preschool-aged children have robust capacities for social analysis, which enable them to figure out adults' likely referents even when the connection between word and referent is not straightforward or immediately apparent (Tomasello & Barton, 1994).

As already noted, language input is a major predictor of speed of vocabulary acquisition. Children who hear more words per unit of time learn more words. Within the limits of amount of speech ever addressed to children in the real world, the relationship seems to hold. Part of the density effect is presumably mediated by frequency—we know that children normally need several exposures to a word in order to learn it. Young children learn their first words from among those that are most frequent in their language environments (Hart, 1991), although older children with larger vocabularies can learn words from fewer exposures.

In addition, perceptual salience influences word learning. Thus, words presented in isolation, words that are stressed, words in brief utterances, and words in initial or final position within utterances are most likely to become part of the child's vocabulary. Words are also more easily learned if they are presented in the exaggerated prosody and stress patterns typical of child-directed speech (Golinkoff, Hirsh-Pasek, Bailey, & Wenger, 1992).

Words that have high affective value are also more easily learned. For example, children's early words typically include the names of important persons, and words used to request or mark enjoyable activities (e.g., *peek-a-boo*; Ninio & Snow, 1996). Later on, words embedded in highly valued narratives or activities are more easily acquired (Snow & Goldfield, 1983).

As children's vocabularies grow, word learning becomes easier. This is largely because of the paradigm effect—children come to understand paradigmatic relationships among words, and can then quickly learn new words that fill slots in their paradigms. Thus, after children have mastered *red, green, yellow, blue, black,* and *white,* the more infrequent color words like *purple, orange,* and *pink* become learnable. Children who know the names of 15 dinosaur species can more easily learn a new dinosaur name than children who know no dinosaur names at all.

The paradigm effect is one aspect of the facilitative effect of semantic embeddedness. Words heard in semantically rich linguistic contexts are learned better. Semantic support might derive from physical contexts (using a word in conjunction with a picture that clarifies its meaning) or linguistically informative contexts (e.g., saying "I was enraged, I was really angry, I have never been so mad"). Weizman and Snow (2001) showed that maternal use of low-frequency lexical items in rich semantic contexts predicted later vocabulary growth more strongly than these items' use in lean or uninformative contexts (see the following section for examples from book reading interactions). Similarly, contexts drawing on detailed world knowledge can be helpful (e.g., if the task were to learn the nonce word *maxillosaurus*, the dinosaur maven could benefit from a sentence like "the maxillosaurus resembles the stegosaurus in size, but unlike the stegosaurus it had pointed teeth and a huge jaw, because it was a meat eater.").

Word learning is not an all-or-nothing process. Children can start to establish a lexical item in their memory after one or two exposures, in a process called fast-mapping; but full specification of the item's phonology, meaning, and usage may require many exposures (Carey, 1978; Clark, 1973, 1993). Occasional re-exposure will also be required in order to retain words by consolidating memory traces (Nagy & Scott, 2000).

Finally, because "knowing a word" means knowing its phonological, semantic, and syntactic properties in detail, passive exposure supports learning less effectively than do opportunities to use the word (Nagy & Scott, 2000). Thus, environments that support word learning permit children to engage in conversations with adults, during which the children find opportunities to use words that they are in the process of acquiring.

HOW MIGHT BOOK READING PROMOTE VOCABULARY ACQUISITION EVEN MORE EFFICIENTLY?

We turn now to consider the features of book reading interactions that have been described in our own research and that of others, and to consider how those interactions that have been described as effective or high-quality might be influencing vocabulary. Many researchers have analyzed conversations around book reading in order to identify the features or aspects of those conversations that effectively support children's language and literacy development (e.g., Ninio, 1983; Ninio & Bruner, 1978; Snow & Ninio, 1986). In some cases, these features have even been incorporated into intervention programs, which in turn have shown effects on children's development (Lombard, 1994; Whitehurst et al., 1994). There is, fortunately, considerable convergence among the various findings on the question of which interactive features are facilitative. Here, we briefly present a description of these facilitative features of or approaches to book reading, together with a summary of the research findings that suggest that these features are, indeed, effective. (Many of these enhanced book reading styles are discussed in greater detail by their originators in other chapters of this volume.) We also discuss—somewhat more speculatively—how each feature or strategy might contribute specifically to children's vocabulary development. Future research will, we hope, subject these speculations to rigorous empirical study.

Non-Immediate Talk During Book Reading

Non-immediate talk is that talk produced by mother or child which goes beyond the information contained in text or illustrations to make predictions; to make connections to the child's past experiences, other books, or the real world; to draw inferences, analyze information, or discuss the meaning of words and offer explanations. In the Home School Study of Language and Literacy Development (Snow, 1991), mothers' use of this type of talk while reading to their preschool-aged children was found to relate to their children's later performance on measures of vocabulary, story comprehension, definitions, and emergent literacy (De Temple, 1994, 1991).

One component of non-immediate talk is the discussion of vocabulary—for example, explanations of word meaning. Non-immediate talk creates opportunities for children to understand and use the somewhat more sophisticated vocabulary required for envoicing evaluative reactions to the book, discussing characters' internal states, making predictions concerning the next episode, and so on. These kinds of talk inevitably introduce relatively complex vocabulary.

In the following interaction, 3-year-old Laval's mother points to a picture while reading the picture book *The Very Hungry Caterpillar* (Carle, 1966), and asks him to produce the appropriate label. But when he's unable to do so she provides two non-immediate utterances, one that offers a defining feature of the desired word and another that suggests an evaluative element ("real hot").

Example 1. Laval, Age 39 Months
(Source: New Chance Observational Study)

Mother: What's that? [pointing to the sun]
Child: [shrugs]
Mother: What's that? What make you hot?
Child: I don't know. Huh?
Mother: What make you hot?

Child: [shrugs]
Mother: The sun don't make you hot?
Child: Mmhm. [nods]
Mother: It make you real hot? [nodding]
Child: Mmhm. [nods]

By contrast, Jamil and his mother engage in a rote type of interaction ("recitation style") while reading a substantial portion of the same book. However, upon completion of the text the mother focuses on real-world information (that caterpillars turn into butterflies) and the rare vocabulary word *cocoon;* both of these were classified as non-immediate talk. She not only draws attention to the purpose of the cocoon (i.e., what caterpillars live in) but also requires a standard pronunciation of the target word, making sure her son has learned the new word.

Example 2. Jamil, Age 57 Months
(Source: New Chance Observational Study)

Child: He built a small house.
Mother: Called a cocoon.
Child: Called a cocoon.
Mother: Around himself.
Child: Around himself.
Mother: He stayed inside.
Child: He stayed inside.
Mother: For more than two weeks.
Child: For more than two weeks.
Mother: Then he nibbled a hole.
Child: Then he nibble a hole.
Mother: In the cocoon.
Child: In the cocoon.
Mother: Pushed his way out and.
Child: Pushed his way out and.
Mother: He was a beautiful butterfly!
Child: He was a beautiful butterfly!
Mother: So what the cocoon turn into? I mean excuse me. What do caterpillars turn to?
Child: Butterflies!
Mother: Right. What do they live in?

Child: A butterfly house. Um, this. [points to cocoon]
Mother: What is that called?
Child: A cula.
Mother: A cocoon!
Child: A cocoon.
Mother: Okay.

The following example shows how reading an expository book about elephants (Hoffman, 1983), provided by the experimenter, provides a unique, rich opportunity for Domingo and his mother to discuss a topic that is remote from their day-to-day experience. Their discussion includes vocabulary words such as *tusk, ivory,* and *herd,* embedded in evaluative comments and connections to the child's life, which are classified as non-immediate because they go beyond the information in the text.

Example 3. Domingo, Age 5;11 Years
(Source: Home School Study of Language
and Literacy Development)

Mother: That's a tusk see? It's white. Know what Domingo?
Child: Hmm?
Mother: Hunters kill these elephants for that.
Child: Why?
Mother: Because they want it for, um, well, they use it for different things I think um some museums buy them and I don't know about museums but I know that they kill the for this white um.
Child: There's no tusk on these elephants though.
Mother: See? That one's bigger so some of them die because of that. That is sad.
Child: I wish there was not such things as hunters and guns.
Mother: I know it me too. Oh there's a herd. That's a lot of them. See how they walk?
Child: Ma here's ones that's dead.
Mother: I don't think he's dead! Well we'll find out. "They use their tusks to dig." Oh see he's digging a hole! "They use their tusks to dig for salt...."
Child: Hmm.
Mother: Let's look and see if there's another page you might like. It's ivory! The tusks are made of ivory. And they can make things

with these tusks and that's why some animals, they die, hunters kill them.

Child: No wonder why they have hunters.

Mother: Yeah that's sad.

Child: I'm never gonna be a hunter when I grow up.

Mother: Oh thank God I'm glad.

In classroom situations where teachers read to groups of children, it may appear to be more difficult to ask the open-ended questions characteristic of non-immediate talk. It also seems likely that the benefit of non-immediate talk would be lost without the opportunity for individual verbal participation. However, in the classrooms of 4-year-olds in the Home School Study of Language and Literacy, the amount of non-immediate talk used by the teachers while reading to the group was strongly associated with the receptive vocabulary scores of our target children (Beals et al., 1994).

Dickinson and Smith (1994) identified the importance of a particular type of non-immediate talk during group book readings in the preschool classroom. Child-involved analytic talk, which refers to analysis, prediction, and vocabulary utterances by both the teacher and children, was observed during book reading. Four-year-olds exposed to a high proportion of child-involved analytic talk during group book reading in preschool had higher kindergarten vocabulary scores, even when controlling for total amount of book-related talk. Child-involved analytic talk, like non-immediate talk during book reading at home, and like dialogic book reading talk, can be presumed to promote vocabulary development by presenting words in a rich semantic context, and by promoting children's use of novel lexical items. In a study of 4-year-olds from low-income families, Wasik and Bond (2001) found that even in group settings, book-presented words increased vocabulary if the book reading was interactive and stimulated child talk, provided a rich semantic context for novel vocabulary items, and repeated the words often enough.

Book Reading Quality

Book Reading Quality is a global rating of reader performance that captures an element of the book reading experience not necessarily reflected in codings of the conversation that occurs during book reading. Book Reading Quality combines ratings of the reader on three point scales in each of the following areas: Reading Intonation, Reading Fluency, and Comfort Level. Readers who include little or no talk about the book may nonetheless successfully engage children through the use of an effective, animated, and lively reading style that demonstrates their own enjoyment and comprehension of the story. Conversely, a halting, awkward reading style with misplaced emphases may impede a child's comprehension or interest.

In a study of teen mothers from a welfare sample reading to their preschool-aged children, Book Reading Quality was associated with the mothers' educational level and with a rating of the child's home environment (HOME-SF; De Temple & Snow, 1998). Mothers who were rated higher on Book Reading Quality also used more non-immediate talk while reading (both the percent of talk that was coded as non-immediate and the number of non-immediate utterances).

Higher Book Reading Quality could be assumed to promote vocabulary development specifically by presenting new words from the text in more easily comprehensible, semantic contexts, and by heightening their salience through fluent and dramatic oral reading. Such a reading style provides access to high-quality phonological models of new words, and furthermore promotes child interest in being read to, thus increasing density of exposure.

Dialogic Reading

Whitehurst and his colleagues (Zeverbergen & Whitehurst, this volume) describe a method of reading aloud to young children that is designed to enhance their language development. This approach is particularly applicable to early intervention programs for children at risk of academic failure, because such programs have well-established techniques for teaching parents and other caregivers how to implement the method. *Dialogic reading* is based on three theoretical principles: encouraging the child to become an active learner during book reading (e.g., asking the child questions), providing feedback that models more sophisticated language (e.g., expansions), and finally, challenging the child's knowledge and skills by raising the conversation to a level just above their ability (e.g., asking about characteristics of an object for which they already know the label).

In experimental studies, the preschool-aged children of middle-class mothers who were trained to use dialogic reading techniques did, in fact, score higher on measures of expressive language than the children of untrained mothers (Whitehurst et al., 1988), though unfortunately these positive effects did not extend to receptive vocabulary as tested using the PPVT (Dunn & Dunn, 1981).

Further experimental studies focusing on children in low-SES families at risk for academic failure involved training daycare teachers in the use of dialogic reading to groups of children (Whitehurst et al., 1994). Children with teachers who used the technique scored higher on measures of both expressive and receptive vocabulary than children in the control groups. Those children whose parents *and* teachers were part of the experiment displayed the greatest language skill on these measures.

Another powerful test of the effectiveness of dialogic reading was implemented by Lim (1999; see also www.wri-edu.org/bookplay); she worked with Korean-immigrant families whose children were losing their spoken Korean as the family language gradually shifted to English. Lim taught dialogic reading techniques to the parents of these families in Korean, and provided Korean books for them to read with their children. The children in the experimental group showed significant improvements in their oral productive and receptive Korean skills, even though the book reading sessions constituted their major source of exposure. The length of time that the parents reported being engaged in Korean book reading was related to the gains made by the children.

The impact of dialogic reading can be related to a number of the vocabulary development principles listed in the first section of this chapter. Dialogic reading provides richer semantic contexts for novel words, tends to last longer than straight reading—thus giving children denser exposure to the book vocabulary, and promotes children's use of novel lexical items.

Comprehender-Style Book Readings

Several studies describing naturally occurring styles of reading to young children distinguish the styles of mothers called "describers," who focus on description (similar to immediate talk, which may involve simply labeling or describing pictures), from those they call "comprehenders," who focus on story meaning (similar to non-immediate talk, which may include inferences and interpretation of the story). These different styles are associated with children's language skills. Children of middle-class mothers using the "comprehender" style had higher vocabulary scores than children whose mothers favored the "descriptor" style focusing on labels; both maternal styles and child vocabulary differences remained consistent over the course of the longitudinal study (Haden, Reese, & Fivush, 1996).

Reese and Cox (1999) used an experimental design to investigate the effect of book reading style on preschoolers' emergent literacy skills, including vocabulary. They isolated three styles: describer, comprehender, and performance-oriented (in which the reader discusses the story after the reading). Their results indicate that children's initial vocabulary skills are an important factor in determining the effect of reading style on vocabulary growth. Those children with lower initial PPVT scores showed more growth on the posttest if they were in the describer group, whereas those with higher initial scores seemed to benefit most from the performance-oriented style of reading.

These findings conform with what we would expect from our brief review of vocabulary development. Younger children (those still focused on acquiring nouns) benefit from the more noun-oriented describer style, whereas linguistically more advanced children benefit from the discussion associated with a comprehension focus, during which they are exposed to more sophisticated vocabulary and have opportunities to use novel words themselves.

Instructive and Helpful Interactions

Weizman and Snow (2001; see also Weizman, 1995) performed an analysis of the types of talk that surround the use of rare or sophisticated vocabulary items in book reading, as well as other interactive settings. They found that the incidence of interactions characterized as instructive or helpful (i.e., interactions in which information about the meaning of the word was available, and during which the child's attention and learning were scaffolded) explained as much variance in vocabulary outcomes as did the density of sophisticated words. Examples of these instructive and helpful interactions display how talk supported vocabulary learning:

Example 4. Five-Year-Old Child and His Mother Reading *What Next, Baby Bear!* (Murphy, 1983), Coded as Instructive and Highly Scaffolded (Source: Home School Study of Language and Literacy Development)

Child: I want to have … what are those? Those are those are little little um volcanoes?

Mother: Little *volcanoes?* Well yeah. Kind of. They're *craters.*

Child: *Craters?*

Mother: Yeah.

Child: And the fire comes out of it?

Mother: No. They just look like *volcanoes* but they're not.

Child: Yeah they're on the moon.

Mother: Yeah.

Child: Big things like when they have a round thing? That's the *volcano*.
Mother: Mmhm.

Example 5. Five-Year-Old and His Mother Reading
What Next, Baby Bear!, Coded as Helpful, Not Scaffolded
(Source: Home School Study of Language
and Literacy Development)

Mother: What next, baby bear! We've read some of these other Pied Piper
           books. I guess not this one but they have other bear stories.
           There's that Christmas bear one?
Child: Yeah! We have it.
Mother: They had a story about the bear that couldn't *hibernate*. He woke
           up in the middle of the winter and then a guy comes to his door.
           Yeah all dressed in red and he's cold and the bear lets him in the
           house in his cave and the bear plays guitar and he feeds the guy.
           Then he goes for a ride with the guy up in the sky.
Child: That's Santa Claus.

These examples demonstrate that book reading constitutes a context within
which quite unusual words can be introduced, their meaning can be more easily
explained because of pictorial and textual support, and the child's attention to
the words and their referents can be effectively scaffolded.

Repeated Readings of the Same Book

Snow and Goldfield (1983) described changes in the nature of conversation between a single mother and her child during successive readings of a particular
book. They documented that lexical items used by the mother during earlier
discussions of a particular page or picture were often adopted by the child during later discussions, particularly if those words had been repeated by the child
when first used by the mother. The child was also more likely to acquire items
for use if they had been used more than once by the mother, that is, if a particular picture was discussed several times and the same words were used in discussing it every time.

These findings relate clearly to the principles of lexical acquisition discussed
previously—namely, that repetition and children's active use of novel lexical
items promote their acquisition. This study also highlights one of the unique
features of book reading interactions—that they allow parent–child dyads to revisit the same topics of conversation several times, and to rely on information

brought up during previous encounters to enrich their discussions. Topics recur while looking at books in a much more reliable way than they do in other interactive settings, such as playing with toys or engaging in mealtime conversations.

IS GOOD BOOK READING CRUCIAL TO VOCABULARY DEVELOPMENT?

We have presented analyses here that in some cases show the direct effects of particular book reading features on vocabulary, and in other cases can be hypothesized to invoke demonstrated principles of good vocabulary development. Given the many other positive effects of well-designed book reading interactions on children's development, it may be worthwhile to tweak these interactions in order to ensure positive effects on vocabulary, as well. Nonetheless, we must admit that preschool-aged children might be exposed to all the features that promote large vocabularies without ever experiencing book-reading interactions. Although this situation is unlikely to arise in a literate culture, a variety of other factors besides book reading do clearly contribute to vocabulary development. For example, families that engage in mealtime conversations which include interesting topics and extended discourse—particularly past event narratives and explanations—promote their children's lexical development (Weizman & Snow, 2001). Attendance at a preschool that provides access to cognitively challenging talk during science activities, field trips, and snacktime also promotes vocabulary (Dickinson & Tabors, 2001). Opportunities for pretend play at preschool and incidence of fantasy during pretend play with one's mother also relate to vocabulary outcomes (Katz, 2001). Thus, we are not arguing that book reading is indispensable to vocabulary development; simply that it provides a particularly efficient and effective context for supporting vocabulary. In the following section we discuss some issues that arise around the unique potential of book reading interactions to foster vocabulary development.

Paradoxical Rare Word Effect

One of the particular reasons why book reading promotes vocabulary is that it contributes relatively rare, sophisticated words to interactions. Normal spoken interaction tends to rely on the repeated use of a relatively small set of words (Hayes & Ahrens, 1988), whereas written texts are lexically more varied. And of course books written for young children can introduce topics that would rarely emerge in quotidian conversation (such as the African elephants discussed in Example 3), and the associated rare lexical items. Thus, one would expect that reading books which include rare words, and using those words in the context of conversation about the text, would promote vocabulary development.

In a series of analyses of conversations between low-income mothers and their preschool-aged children, collected in the context of the Home–School Study of Language and Literacy Development, the incidence of rare words (those beyond the 3,000 most common root words of English) was analyzed and related to child vocabulary outcomes. Paradoxically, the use of rare words while playing with toys or during mealtimes consistently showed a more robust relationship to child outcomes than the use of rare words during book reading (Beals & Tabors, 1995; Weizman & Snow, 2001). Why should this effect have emerged?

While collecting data for this study, we provided books for mothers and children to read, thus artificially limiting variation across the families in the number and type of rare words they would encounter. Although our analyses focused on the use of rare words in conversation, not just while reading aloud, the homogeneity across the families in the stock of available rare words no doubt truncated variation in the predictor variable for this setting a good deal more than it did for other conversational settings, where variability in conversational topics and frequency of rare words was enormous. Thus, an investigation of the effect of encounters with rare words during book reading on children's vocabulary really requires allowing parents freedom to select their own books, and should take into account factors such as frequency of reading, frequency of re-reading particular books, and the nature of the interaction surrounding each novel word encountered. While a great deal of research has been carried out on the nature and effect of book reading interactions, little specific attention has been paid to the use of rare words in those interactions, outside the studies cited earlier.

Books as Lexical Reservoirs

When considering vocabulary as a developmental outcome, particularly in light of the relationship between vocabulary and literacy development, our attention naturally turns to children growing up in low-income families, especially those at extremely high risk of reading difficulties. Such children are being raised by parents who themselves may have limited literacy skills, and who thus are likely to have restricted vocabularies (Hart & Risley, 1995). Furthermore, such children may well be attending Head Start or other early education programs, or spending time in daycare settings within which the adult caretakers also have limited literacy skills and oral vocabularies. Can reading (or looking at) books enhance the lexical quality of interactions with preschoolers within such family or group-care settings?

In principle, well-selected books should be able to compensate to some extent for the language limitations of adults. Books provide a structured presentation of a richer vocabulary and span content areas that might never emerge in casual conversation (see Hayes & Ahrens, 1988). They also are available for frequent re-readings, thus enhancing children's opportunities to enrich and consolidate their understanding of new word meanings. However, the language and literacy skills of the adults are not irrelevant, and might themselves benefit from exposure to modeled reading of the children's books, in which the correct pronunciation and meaning of less-frequent words are conveyed (see, e.g., the positive effects of parent training documented in Jordan, Porche, & Snow, 2000). However, research is needed into the ways in which less literate adults use books with children and into the best methods for promoting styles of book reading that exploit opportunities for lexical development.

Book Selection

There has been relatively little work done on the differential impact of different sorts of books, or of books with different lexical inventories. How important is it to have the "right books" available for young children, to select books that introduce particular vocabulary words? How can parents or preschool educators make informed decisions about which words they should focus on and which books provide optimal vocabulary exposure?

As an illustration of book-specific word learning, we present some sample discussions about a particular illustration in the book *What Next, Baby Bear!* (Murphy, 1983). This illustration prompted many readers to focus on a rare word (*strainer*). The fictional character places a strainer on his head as part of a spacesuit for his pretend play. Although the word "strainer" is never used in the text, readers used this illustration to draw attention to the concept.

Example 6a

Mother: Look at what he's got for a space helmet! Silly bear!
Child: That's for macaroni!
Mother: I know, it's a strainer.

Example 6b

Mother: See that strainer? Drain the spaghetti with that huh?

Example 6c

Child: That's not a space helmet.
Mother: What is it?
Child: A bowl.
Mother: Right. It's a strainer. I think it's got another word for it too. I don't remember though.

Example 6d.

Mother: Is that a space helmet really?
Child: No.
Mother: What is it really?
Child: The thing that you wash.
Mother: That you wash, right. You put spaghetti in it when you're getting the water out right?
Child: Mhm.
Mother: A colander.
Child: Colander.

It is worth noting that the words *strainer* and *colander,* while relatively infrequent, are not really very sophisticated or complex in their meaning. Thus, the conversations here focus on identifying the right name for the pictured object, and clarifying the defining function of the object—straining spaghetti—in contrast with its pictured use as a helmet. Conversations about other, slightly more complex lexical items, display more attention to the nuances of the target word's meaning, as displayed in some of the examples presented previously.

Text Versus Conversation

We have primarily focused on the conversations that occur during book reading with preschoolers, reflecting the tendency for adults interacting with young children to read books with relatively little text, and to devote more time to the discussions than to reading aloud. These book reading conversations are not universal, however, even with young children; in some cultures and families the text itself is quite central, and conversation consists primarily of getting children to repeat the text verbatim (Tabors & De Temple, 1998; McNaughton, 1995). And with older children, it is more likely that longer texts will be read aloud, perhaps with little or no elaborative conversation (De Temple, 1994).

Further research is needed to discover the degree to which such variations might make a difference in vocabulary development.

We know that children reading at the fourth-grade level and above can learn new vocabulary items simply from reading, as long as they do not encounter too many unknown words in a text, and as long as the context provides some information about word meaning. But we have encountered no studies that would cast light on the degree to which prereaders or early readers can simply pick up word meanings from being read to, without conversational interaction that highlights the words to be learned, enriches the information available about those words, and provides children with opportunities to use the words themselves. Again, this is an area ripe for further research.

CONCLUSION

We have chosen to focus this chapter rather specifically on the potential impact of book reading for preschoolers' vocabulary development. We of course acknowledge the importance of other book reading effects, but note that vocabulary development is both central in preparing children for success at school and highly susceptible to the impact of a well-designed environment. As expectations for literacy achievement in the early school years rise, it thus becomes increasingly urgent to think about how to design preschoolers' home and school environments in order to ensure optimal literacy development. We believe that the contribution of book reading interactions to this effort is well worth ongoing investigation.

REFERENCES

Anderson, R. C., & Freebody, P. (1981). Vocabulary knowledge. In J. T. Guthrie (Ed.), *Comprehension and teaching: Research reviews* (pp. 77–117). Newark, DE: IRA.

Beals, D. E., DeTemple, J. M., & Dickinson, D. K. (1994). Talking and listening that support early literacy development of children from low-income families. In D. K. Dickinson (Ed.), *Bridges to literacy: Children, families and schools* (pp. 19–40). Cambridge, MA: Blackwell.

Beals, D., & Tabors, P. (1995). Arboretum, bureaucratic, and carbohydrates: Preschoolers' exposure to rare vocabulary at home. *First Language, 15,* 57–76.

Carey, S. (1978). The child as word learner. In M. Halle, J. Bresnan, & G. Miller (Eds.), *Linguistic theory and psychological reality* (pp. 264–293). Cambridge, MA: MIT Press.

Carle, E. (1966). *The very hungry caterpillar.* New York: Philomel.

Chall, J. (1987). Two vocabularies for reading: Recognition and meaning. In M. G. McKeown & M. E. Curtis (Eds.), *The nature of vocabulary acquisition.* Mahwah, NJ: Lawrence Erlbaum Associates.

Clark, E. V. (1973). What's in a word? On the child's acquisition of semantics in his first language. In T. E. Moore (Ed.), *Cognitive development and the acquisition of language* (pp. 65–110). New York: Academic Press.

Clark, E. V. (1993). *The lexicon in acquisition.* Cambridge: Cambridge University Press.

De Temple, J. M. (1991). Family talk: Sources of support for the development of decontextualized language skills. *Journal of Research in Childhood Education, 6,* 11–19.

De Temple, J. M. (1994). *Book reading styles of low-income mothers with preschoolers and children's later literacy skills.* Unpublished doctoral dissertation, Harvard University, Cambridge, MA.

De Temple, J. M., & Snow, C. E. (1998). Mother–child interactions related to the emergence of literacy. In M. J. Zaslow & C. A. Eldred (Eds.), *Parenting behavior in a sample of young mothers in poverty: Results of the new chance observational study* (pp. 114–169). New York: Manpower Demonstration Research Corporation.

Dickinson, D. K., & Tabors, P. O. (2001). *Beginning literacy with language: Young children learning at home and school.* Baltimore: Brookes.

Dickinson, D. K., & Smith, M. (1994). Long-term effects of preschool teachers' book reading on low-income children's vocabulary and story comprehension. *Reading Research Quarterly, 29,* 105–122.

Dunn, L. M., & Dunn, L. M. (1981). *Peabody Picture Vocabulary Test–Revised.* Circle Pines, MN: American Guidance Service.

Elley, W. B. (1989). Vocabulary acquisition from stories. *Reading Research Quarterly, 24,* 174–187.

Fenson, L., Dale, P. S., Reznick, J. S., Bates, E., Thal, D. J., & Pethnick, S. J. (1994). Variability in early communicative development. *Monographs of the Society for Research in Child Development, 59* (5, Serial No. 242).

Golinkoff, R. M., Hirsh-Pasek, K., Bailey, L. M., & Wenger, N. R. (1992). Young children and adults use lexical principles to learn new nouns. *Developmental Psychology, 28*(1), 99–108.

Gopnik, A., & Choi, S. (1995). Names, relational words, and cognitive development in English and Korean speakers: Nouns are not always learned before verbs. In M. Tomasello & W. Merriman (Eds.), *Beyond names for things: Young children's acquisition of verbs* (pp. 63–80). Mahwah, NJ: Lawrence Erlbaum Associates.

Haden, C. A., Reese, E., & Fivush, R. (1996). Mothers' extratextual comments during storybook reading: Stylistic differences over time and across texts. *Discourse Processes, 21,* 135–169.

Hart, B. (1991). Input frequency and children's first words. *First Language, 11,* 289–300.

Hart, B., & Risley T. R. (1995). *Meaningful differences in the everyday experience of young American children.* Baltimore: Brookes.

Hayes, D., & Ahrens, M. (1988). Vocabulary simplification for children: A special case of "motherese"? *Journal of Child Language, 15,* 395–410.

Hoffman, M. (1983). *Animals in the wild: Elephant.* London: Belitha.

Huttenlocher, J., Haight, W., Bryk, A., Seltzer, M., & Lyons, T. (1991). Early vocabulary growth: Relation to language input and gender. *Developmental Psychology, 27,* 236–244.

Jordan, G., Porche, M., & Snow, C. E. (2000). Project EASE: Easing children's transition to kindergarten literacy through planned parent involvement. *Reading Research Quarterly, 35,* 524–546.

Katz, J. (2001). "You'll just have to pretend the door": Playing at home. In D. Dickinson & P. O. Tabors (Eds.), *Beginning literacy with language: Young children learning at home and school.* Baltimore: Brookes.

Lim, Y. S. (1999). *Facilitating young Korean children's language development through parent training picture book interaction.* Unpublished dissertation, University of Washington, Seattle.

Lombard, A. D. (1994). *Success begins at home: The past, present, and future of a home intervention program for preschool youngsters.* Guilford, CT: Dushkin.

McNaughton, S. (1995). *Patterns of emergent literacy: Processes of development and transition.* New York: Oxford University Press.

Murphy, J. (1983). *What next, baby bear!* New York: Dial.

Nagy, W., & Herman, P. (1987). Breadth and depth of vocabulary knowledge: Implications for acquisition and instruction. In M. G. McKeown & M. E. Curtis (Eds.), *The nature of vocabulary acquisition.* Mahwah, NJ: Lawrence Erlbaum Associates.

Nagy, W. E., & Scott, J. A. (2000). Vocabulary processes. In M. L. Kamil, P. B. Mosenthal, P. D. Pearson, & R. Barr (Eds.), *Handbook of reading research* (Vol. 3, pp. 269–284). Mahwah, NJ: Lawrence Erlbaum Associates.

Ninio, A. (1983). Joint book-reading as a multiple vocabulary acquisition device. *Developmental Psychology, 19,* 445–451.

Ninio, A., & Bruner, J. S. (1978). The achievement and antecedents of labeling. *Journal of Child Language, 5,* 1–15.

Ninio, A., & Snow, C. E. (1996). *Pragmatic development.* Boulder, CO: Westview.

Reese, E., & Cox, A. (1999). Quality of adult book reading affects children's emergent literacy. *Developmental Psychology, 35*(1), 20–28.

Sénéchal, M., LeFevre, J. A, Hudson, E., & Lawson, P. (1996). Knowledge of picture-books as a predictor of young children's vocabulary development. *Journal of Educational Psychology, 88,* 520–536.

Sénéchal, M., LeFevre, J. A., Thomas, E., & Daley, K. (1998). Differential effects of home literacy experiences on the development of oral and written language. *Reading Research Quarterly, 32,* 96–116.

Shibles, B. H. (1959). How many words does a first grade child know? *Elementary English, 31,* 42–47.

Snow, C. E. (1991, Fall/Winter). The theoretical basis for relationships between language and literacy development. *Journal of Research in Childhood Education, 6,* 5–10.

Snow, C. E., & Goldfield, B. (1983). Turn the page please: Situation-specific language acquisition. *Journal of Child Language, 10,* 551–569.

Snow, C. E., & Ninio, A. (1986). The contracts of literacy: What children learn from learning to read books. In W. Teale & E. Sulzby (Eds.), *Emergent literacy: Writing and reading* (pp. 116–137). Norwood, NJ: Ablex.

Stahl, S. A., & Fairbanks, M. M. (1986). The effects of vocabulary instruction: A model-based meta-analysis. *Review of Educational Research, 56,* 72–110.

Stanovich, K. (1986). Matthew effects in reading: Some consequences of individual differences in the acquisition of literacy. *Reading Research Quarterly, 21,* 360–407.

Tabors, P. O., & De Temple, J. M. (1998). "But ain't no nasty word": Mothers' use of recitation style in picture book reading. In A. Koc, E. Taylan, A. Ozsoy, & A. Kuntay (Eds.), *Perspectives on language acquisition: Selected papers from the Seventh International Congress of Child Language Development* (pp. 325–336). Istanbul: Boğaziçi University Printhouse.

Tomasello, M. (1995). Pragmatic contexts for early verb learning. In M. Tomasello & W. Merriman (Eds.), *Beyond names for things: Young children's acquisition of verbs* (pp. 115–146). Mahwah, NJ: Lawrence Erlbaum Associates.

Tomasello, M., & Barton, M. (1994). Learning words in nonostensive contexts. *Developmental Psychology, 30,* 639–650.

Tomasello, M., & Farrar M. J. (1986). Joint attention and early language. *Child Development, 57,* 1454–1463.

Walley, A. C. (1993). The role of vocabulary development in children's spoken word recognition and segmentation ability. *Development Review, 13*(3), 286–350.

Wasik, B. A., & Bond, M. A. (2001). Beyond the pages of a book: Interactive book reading and language development in a preschool classroom. *Journal of Educational Psychology, 93,* 243–250.

Weizman, Z. O. (1995). *Sophistication in maternal vocabulary input at home: Does it effect low-income children's vocabulary, literacy and language success at school?* Unpublished doctoral dissertation, Harvard University, Cambridge, MA.

Weizman, Z. O., & Snow, C. E. (2001). Lexical input as related to children's vocabulary acquisition: Effects of sophisticated exposure and support for meaning. *Developmental Psychology 37,* 265–279.

Whitehurst, G. J., Arnold, D. H., Epstein, J. N., Angell, A. L., Smith, M., & Fischel, J. E. (1994). A picture book reading intervention in daycare and home for children from low-income families. *Developmental Psychology, 30,* 679–689.

Whitehurst, G. J., Falco, F., Lonigan, C. J., Fischel, J. E., DeBaryshe, B. C., Valdez-Menchaca, M. C., & Caulfield, M. (1988). Accelerating language development through picture-book reading. *Developmental Psychology, 24,* 552–558.

3

Diversity in Adults' Styles of Reading Books to Children

Elaine Reese
Adell Cox
Diana Harte
Helena McAnally
University of Otago

[C]hildren are, by virtue of being human, deeply involved in social contexts—in social interaction with others, observation of others, and use of socio-cultural tools, skills and perspectives.

—Rogoff, 1990 (p. 208)

Perhaps the most important sociocultural tool that a child can have in Western society is literacy, a skill that can only be learned through social interaction. Consequently, it is widely accepted not only that children should be read to, but also that such readings will benefit their emergent literacy skills (e.g., Whitehurst & Lonigan, 1998). *Emergent literacy* refers to the knowledge children have about literacy prior to formal schooling. Relevant skills include knowledge about the conventions of print, letter identification, vocabulary, and story skills, as well as an awareness of the conventions and purposes of book reading (e.g., Snow & Dickinson, 1991). All of these skills are potentially learned through shared book reading (Bus, van IJzendoorn, & Pellegrini, 1995; Scarborough & Dobrich, 1994; Wells, 1985; Whitehurst & Lonigan, 1998), as well as other storytelling activities (e.g., Beals, De Temple, & Dickinson, 1994;

Low & Durkin, 2001; Reese, 1995). The frequency of shared book reading during the preschool years purportedly accounts for about 8% of the variance in children's later literacy achievement; this effect decreases in strength as children's literacy skills increase (Bus et al., 1995; Scarborough & Dobrich, 1994).

Although the percentage of total variance in emergent literacy that is accounted for by shared book reading appears small, researchers argue that shared book reading is still a potentially important contributor to later achievement (e.g., Bus et al., 1995; Lonigan, 1994; Stahl, this volume; Whitehurst & Lonigan, 1998). Wells (1985), for example, found that differences in achievement during the early years of schooling could be attributed to differences in literacy knowledge at the time of entry into school. In particular, the frequency of joint book reading with preschoolers was significantly associated with a knowledge-of-literacy test at age 5 and a reading comprehension test at age 7. Based on their review of the literature, Whitehurst and Lonigan (1998) proposed that shared book reading contributes indirectly to children's school achievement, primarily by enhancing their oral language skills and literacy knowledge. These same authors also emphasize the importance of book reading quality, as well as quantity.

This view is in keeping with an apprenticeship model of cognitive development (Vygotsky, 1978; Rogoff, 1990), in which adult scaffolding of children's early interactions eventually results in children's independent cognitive skills. In a book reading situation, for example, the adult may engage the child by asking him or her to turn pages or label pictures; as the child becomes proficient at this activity, the adult may require him to read simple words, until eventually the child can read the book alone. Vygotsky (1978) referred to the difference between a child's actual and potential abilities with support as the "zone of proximal development" (ZPD), and argued that any scaffolding provided by adults should be consistent with the child's abilities. A preschool child, for example, will not benefit from the text of a story unless it is read aloud to her. If, however, the words in the book are beyond the child's comprehension even when read aloud, then the book reading cannot be expected to benefit the child. Consequently, for book reading to be beneficial, both the style of the reader and the level of the book must be within the ZPD of the child to whom the story is read (cf. Lonigan & Whitehurst, 1998).

This chapter has three goals. The first is to provide an overview of the descriptive and experimental work to date on adults' book reading styles with preschoolers. The second is to present our own research on book reading interactions between New Zealand adults and preschoolers. In the first study of ours that we describe, we examined naturally occurring book reading interactions between New Zealand mothers and their preschoolers in the home. In our second study, we experimentally manipulated these naturally occurring book reading styles as a first step in establishing the effects of different reading styles on children's literacy. Our third and final section discusses methods for increasing the external validity of experimental studies, in order to lay the groundwork for future large-scale book reading interventions that could be used in the home and the preschool. We begin with a review of the existing research on the quality of shared book reading.

SHARED BOOK READING AT HOME AND PRESCHOOL

It may not be reading to children per se that is beneficial, but the way in which children are read to that exerts beneficial effects on their literacy-related abilities. Adults differ widely in the choice of reading styles that they adopt with young children. Heath (1982) was one of the first researchers to note this variation. Some of the parents in her study adopted a higher level interactive style in which they focused on story meaning, affective responses, and links to the child's own experiences. Others used a lower level interaction style that primarily consisted of labeling and describing pictures, or discouraged interaction in general and instead engaged strictly in a reading of the text. These styles appeared to vary by class, with middle-class White families adopting the higher level style and working-class White families adopting the lower level style.

Similarly, McNaughton (1995) observed reading style differences as a function of culture. White New Zealand families of European descent, much like Heath's middle-class White families, tended to engage in a great deal of collaboration with their children during reading sessions, and focused on story meaning. Maori, Samoan, and especially Tongan New Zealand families instead favored a "tutorial" reading style, in which the goal was for the child to learn the text verbatim. This style was still interactive, but did not focus at all on meaning. Leseman and de Jong (1998) noted a similar reading style among Turkish and Surinamese immigrant families in the Netherlands. Critically, the instructional quality of mothers' reading style in this study—as measured by the proportion of high-level narrative techniques such as inferences and evaluations—positively predicted children's vocabulary and word decoding at age 7. These results were maintained even after controlling for children's language development at the start of the study, at age 4.

Diversity of adults' story reading styles is also evident *within* cultures. Pellegrini, Brody, and Sigel (1985) found that variations in parents' use of high-level comments during shared book reading were positively linked to their children's verbal IQ scores. Haden, Reese, and Fivush (1996) studied a group of White middle-class American mothers and their children from 3½ to 6 years of age. Upon their first reading of an unfamiliar text, mothers could be classified either as *describers* (similar to Heath's lower level style), *comprehenders* (similar to Heath's higher level style), or *collaborators* (a style that changed with children's development). Mothers were largely consistent in their styles over a 1½-year period. Moreover, maternal reading style was related to children's later literacy: Children of comprehender mothers scored higher on receptive vocabulary and story comprehension measures at age 6 than did the children of mothers reading in the other two styles. Children of collaborator mothers, in turn, scored higher on a letter recognition test than did the children of mothers in the other two groups. These results indicate that adult reading style is a stable construct, and reading style may be an important predictor of later literacy success. The findings are correlational, however, and the possibility still exists that children of mothers in these three groups initially differed in important ways.

In a preschool setting, Dickinson and Smith (1994) found that the reading styles of preschool teachers could also be divided into three categories: performance-oriented, co-constructive, and didactic-interactional. The performance-oriented styles emphasized dramatic reading, with few interruptions and an analytic discussion at the end of the reading that focused on story comprehension, definition of unusual words, and the relation of the book to children's experiences. Co-constructive styles tended to promote such analytic talk during the book reading, whereas the didactic-interactional style emphasized the child's recall by encouraging them to read along with the teacher. Thus, the co-constructive style is very similar to Haden et al.'s (1996) comprehender style, and the didactic-interactional style is similar to McNaughton's (1995) tutorial style. The performance-oriented style has not been found in the home setting to date. Dickinson and Smith (1994) found that children in the classrooms where analytical discussion occurred had better receptive vocabulary and story comprehension scores at the end of the year than children in classrooms with little analytic talk. This finding indicates that observed differences in teachers' reading styles may actually result in different outcomes for children's literacy skills; it maps quite nicely onto the links found in the home (Haden et al., 1996; Leseman & de Jong, 1998), with the higher level styles that focus on analytical discussions being beneficial in both settings.

THE EFFECTS OF ADULT BOOK READING STYLE ON EMERGENT LITERACY

It is important to remember that all of the aforementioned studies were correlational. These effects must be replicated experimentally before one can draw any firm conclusions about the effects of adult reading style on child literacy.

The effects of book reading style have been quite clearly established, however, in the realm of language development. Studies have shown that even simple interactions during book reading, such as asking children to point to pictures, are more beneficial than passive listening for 4-year-old children's vocabulary acquisition (Sénéchal, Thomas, & Monker, 1995). If this interaction is increased by questioning 3- to 4-year-olds about target words during book reading, then their expressive vocabulary benefits even more than their receptive vocabulary (Sénéchal, 1997). These experimental findings illustrate the benefits of interaction during book reading, but also suggest that different aspects of vocabulary are affected by different reading styles.

Another body of experimental work on the effects of book reading style has focused on a particular type of reading, called *dialogic reading* (e.g., Whitehurst, Falco, et al., 1988). Dialogic reading involves high levels of interaction between adult and child, with an emphasis on getting the child to answer open-ended questions and take more responsibility for storytelling over the course of repeated readings. With older preschoolers, dialogic reading incorporates higher level questions and links to the child's own experience.

In these studies, parents and/or preschool teachers are trained to read dialogically. Interventions take place over periods lasting from 6 weeks to 1 year. The children involved in dialogic reading are compared at pretest and posttest to children in control groups receiving naturally occurring reading only or non-reading activities, such as art projects. Whitehurst and colleagues have now amassed a large body of evidence showing that dialogic reading benefits children's language skills—especially their expressive vocabulary, and possibly their print skills (e.g., Whitehurst, Arnold, et al., 1994; Whitehurst, Epstein, et al., 1994; Whitehurst, Falco, et al., 1988). The benefits of dialogic reading seem to last for at least 1 year after the end of the intervention, although tests have so far failed to demonstrate an effect over a longer period of time (Whitehurst, Zevenbergen, et al., 1999).

Dialogic reading is undoubtedly beneficial for young children's expressive vocabulary skills. Past research, however, has not directly compared dialogic reading or similar styles with the other reading styles found in naturally occurring interactions between adults and children. Our own research is seeking to make this important comparison. Because literacy skills are diverse, it is possible that different styles of interaction may promote different skills. Dialogic reading is obviously beneficial for children's language abilities, but comprehender or performance-oriented styles may be more important for story comprehension.

The beneficial effects of dialogic reading may be especially great for younger preschoolers or less skilled older preschoolers. To date, the experimental research has only looked at younger and less skilled children (e.g., Hargrave &

Sénéchal, 2000). In contrast, correlational studies of older and more skilled pre-schoolers appear to indicate the benefits of higher level comprehender and per-formance-oriented styles, even for children's language development (Dickinson & Smith, 1994; Haden et al., 1996).

Study 1: Parent–Child Book Reading, New Zealand Style

Before we could embark on an experimental study of the effects of book reading styles in a New Zealand population, we first needed to establish the existence of varied book reading styles among New Zealand mothers and their children. McNaughton (1995) looked at this issue cross-culturally in New Zealand, but did not have a sufficient sample size to address the question of variability within individual cultures.

To accomplish this goal, we collected data on naturally occurring variations in book reading, beginning by looking at White New Zealand mothers of European ancestry and their preschool children. The tasks and analyses that we used were modeled after the Haden et al. (1996) study, but with a larger sample size and a cross-sectional design (see Harte, 1997, for full details). Twenty mothers and their 40-month-old children (10 boys and 10 girls), and another 20 mothers and their 58-month-old children (10 boys and 10 girls) were recruited from preschools and daycare centers. Families came from working- and middle-class neighborhoods, with mothers' education levels ranging from 10 to 19 years of schooling.

Female researchers visited each family three times in their homes. All visits were videotaped and audiotaped. In the first two sessions, which occurred 1 week apart, researchers provided mothers with an unfamiliar storybook: either *Hemi's Pet* (De Hamel, 1985) or *My Cat Maisie* (Allen, 1990). The order of these two texts across the two sessions was counterbalanced by children's age and gender. A third book, *Going for Fish* (Tarlton, 1990), was substituted in four cases where the mother or child was already familiar with one of the two standard texts. The two main experi-mental texts were similar in length, story structure, and number of illustrations (24 pages with 45 independent clauses and 28 pages with 60 independent clauses, re-spectively). Researchers asked mothers to read the books in their usual manner, but left the room during the story readings. In a third session, the researchers adminis-tered the Peabody Picture Vocabulary Test–Revised (PPVT-R; Dunn & Dunn, 1981) as a measure of children's language development.

Mothers' and children's extratextual comments during the readings were transcribed and coded with an adaptation of Haden et al.'s (1996) scheme. The main coding categories are shown in Table 3.1, and focus on distinctions be-tween lower level comments such as labeling and picture description and higher level comments, such as predictions and inferences. Note that each content

TABLE 3.1
Coding Maternal Utterances During Book Reading

Code	Description	Example
Labels	Labels request or provide character identification and labeling of objects, colors and animals.	*That is Andrew.* *What is this?*
Picture descriptions	Descriptions request or provide an explanation or elaboration of plot information beyond that given in the text, but focus on what has happened or is happening in the text, rather than on why it has happened.	*He's getting blue in the face* *What's he doing now?.*
Evaluations	Evaluations request or provide a judgement or state an individual's personal preference.	*This is a really good story.* *What did you think about that book?*
Inferences	Inferences request or provide predictions about what will happen in the story in addition to reasoning about mental states and causality in the story.	*What is he going to do with the dog?* *It must be morning.* *He's a bit sad.*
General knowledge	General knowledge utterances request or provide information about the real world, including definitions and counting routines.	*A guinea pig is a little fluffy animal.* *How many pets do you see?*
Whole book	Whole book comments request or provide title and author information or print concepts.	*It's called Hemi's Pet.* *How do you hold the book?*
Confirmation/ correction	Confirmations confirm the partner's previous utterance, often consisting of a repetition plus yes, right, or good. Corrections correct the partner's previous utterance.	*That's right, that's Hemi.* *No, that's the teacher.*
Personal experience	Personal experiences request or provide a connection between the child's experiences and the text.	*That looks like Grandma's cat.* *Who do you know called Andrew?*

category was divided into *provide* and *request* codes in order to assess the function of the utterance. The reliability of mother and child codes between two independent coders for 25% of the transcripts was 95.2%.

Like Haden et al. (1996), we then submitted the maternal codes to a cluster analysis procedure, in order to determine the existence of individual differences in mothers' reading styles. We chose the first reading session as the basis on which to assess maternal style in order to maximize comparability with the Haden et al. study, in which maternal style was also determined on the evidence from the dyads' first reading session.

The goal of cluster analysis is to classify individuals into categories on the basis of similarities and differences in a set of variables. Like Haden et al. (1996), we entered our conversation codes in the form of proportions of total talk. We also excluded from analysis four mothers who produced fewer than 10 comments during the course of their reading. The codes entered into the analysis for the remaining 36 mothers were as follows: provide labels, request labels, picture description, provide evaluations, request evaluations, whole book, confirmation/correction, provide inferences, request inferences, provide general knowledge, request general knowledge, and personal experience. The functional categories of "provide" and "request" were collapsed within content categories if the frequency of either code fell below 2%. We used Ward's hierarchical clustering method, which utilizes the squared Euclidean distance (the sum of the squared differences across all variables entered) to compare individuals and clusters of individuals (Anderberg, 1973; Norusis, 1988). The goal at each stage of clustering is to minimize the increment of the within-group error sum of squares by combining two like individuals. Eventually, all individuals are combined into a single cluster. Determination of the optimal number of clusters is made on both theoretical and practical grounds. Clusters should result in interpretable groups, but they should also be fairly equal in size, and the clusters should have formed at about the same Euclidean distance (i.e., at about the same point in the clustering process, indicating that the clusters contain individuals who are equally similar to each other).

Our analysis revealed two fairly equal clusters of individuals. Group 1 included 17 mothers and formed at a cluster distance level of 12; Group 2 consisted of 19 mothers and formed at a cluster distance level of 16. We then determined, via one-way ANOVAs, which variables differentiated the two groups of mothers (see Fig. 3.1).

Mothers in Group 1 requested more labels [$F(1,34) = 14.12, p < .01$]; provided more labels [$F(1,34) = 23.64, p < .01$]; provided and requested more picture descriptions [$F(1,34) = 6.36, p < .05$]; and requested more evaluations [$F(1,34) = 4.88, p < .05$] than mothers in Group 2. In contrast, mothers in Group 2 provided significantly more evaluations [$F(1,34) = 13.94, p < .01$] and inferences [$F(1,34) = 12.75, p < .01$] and requested and provided more personal experiences [$F(1,34) = 6.05, p < .05$] than mothers in Group 1. Based on these differences, we labeled the first group of mothers *describers* and the second

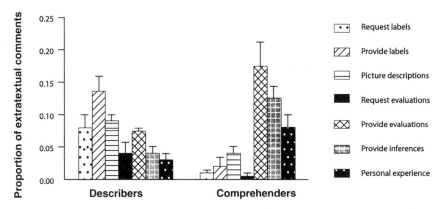

FIG. 3.1. New Zealand mothers' styles of storybook reading ($n = 36$).

group *comprehenders*. Describers spent a higher proportion of time labeling and describing the pictures and requesting evaluations from their children, whereas comprehenders spent a higher proportion of time providing high-level inferences and evaluations and requesting and providing personal experiences. The following examples illustrate the differences between these two styles in response to the same passage of text from *Hemi's Pet*. (The pictures on this page of the book show Hemi dressing his little sister Rata and then taking her into the kitchen for breakfast.) The passage runs as follows:

> The day of the pet show he washed her hands. He brushed her hair. He dressed her in her favourite dress. Mother said, "Look at Rata!" Dad said, "Where are you off to, love?" "I'm taking her to school," said Hemi. "I'm looking after her today."

Describer Mother and Child

Mother: There they are in the bathroom getting ready. Look, see he's brushing her hair and washing her hands. She's wearing that bright orange dress.

Child: Brushing, brush and washing her face.

Mother: Yep, look, someone's making toast in the kitchen.

Comprehender Mother and Child

Mother: Mmmm. Oh, look they've got a Weet-bix packet there. They must have that for breakfast too.

Child: (pointing) You don't eat that with a foon [spoon].

Mother: Yeah. Oh, she's having her cup of tea there, they might have finished their Weet-bix.

Child: And then they have some toast.

Mother: Yeah, toast and Marmite.

Notice how the describer mother engages in a rich description of the pictures, but does not go beyond this to make any inferences about the pictures or the text. The comprehender mother also describes the pictures ("look they've got a Weet-bix packet there"; "she's having her cup of tea there") but she does so in the context of drawing inferences. She first notes for the child that if the Weet-bix packet is on the table, it must be because that's the kind of cereal the family in the book has for breakfast, just like the child's own family. She also provides the child with the information that if the mother is having her cup of tea, she must have already finished her cereal, because tea-drinking usually occurs after the meal.

Analyses were performed on proportions of total talk. Mothers in the two reading styles did not differ in terms of their total extratextual talk [$F(1,34) = .00$, n.s.], but only in the quality of that talk. Neither did the children from the two groups differ in their total extratextual talk [$F(1,34) = .03$, n.s.]. Thus, we can be reasonably certain that mothers were not just behaving differently because their children were more or less responsive during the reading.

Recall also that mothers read one of three different books with their children; critically, the choice of books was not associated with maternal style. Our chi-square analysis of maternal style as a function of the choice of the two main books found no association, [$\chi^2(1) = 1.19$, n.s.].

Somewhat surprisingly, maternal reading style was not associated with children's age. We might have expected the mothers of older children to be more likely to adopt a higher level comprehender style, but mothers of 40- and 58-month-old children were equally likely to be describers or comprehenders [$\chi^2(1) = 1.0$, n.s.]. The older children in this study did have much more advanced language skills than the younger children, with a mean PPVT-R raw score of 60.3 for 58-month-olds versus 38.4 for the 40-month-olds [$F(1,38) = 29.68$, $p < .01$]. Clearly the lack of maternal accommodation cannot be explained by an absence of developmental differences between the younger and older children in this study.

The results of our style analyses are highly consistent with those obtained in a study of American mothers (Haden et al., 1996), although there are also some important differences between the two cultures. The two styles we obtained, describer and comprehender, are similar to the describer and comprehender styles found in Haden et al. Among the describer mothers in Haden et al.'s study, with their 40-month-old children, 41% of comments consisted of labeling events or picture descriptions. Collapsing our own label and picture description categories, 30% of our describer mothers' talk consisted of such lower level comments, directed to their 40- and 58-month-old children.

The similarities are less apparent between the comprehender mothers from the two countries. American comprehender mothers were differentiated from their peers at the start of the study through their use of print knowledge comments (25%), similar to our whole book category. Our comprehender mothers, in contrast, were primarily differentiated from other mothers by their use of inferences (18%), another high-level category.

Greater similarities were apparent between the New Zealand and American comprehender mothers by the time the American children reached 58 months, at which point their mothers' use of higher level inferences had increased to around 18% of total talk. We did not note the existence of a third (collaborator) style analogous to that found among the American mothers. This style was marked by mothers' initial responsiveness to their children in the form of confirmations, but was also distinguished by the greatest change in maternal style as children got older. Over time, mothers reading in the collaborator style decreased their use of confirmations, but increased their use of higher level inferences. In contrast, the American describer mothers were highly consistent over time, like our New Zealand mothers of both describer and comprehender styles. Thus, our finding of an absence of accommodation by New Zealand mothers to their children's developmental levels could account for the absence of a collaborative style in our New Zealand sample. New Zealand mothers simply did not make any accommodation to their children's age or language levels—a critical feature of the collaborator style found with American mothers. Still, the distinction between mothers using higher level comments and those using a lower level style appears to hold in both cultures. Any cultural differences existed primarily in the *type* of higher level comment used at a particular age, and in the degree of accommodation to the child's developmental level.

Study 2: Effects of Different Adult Book-Reading Styles on Children's Language and Literacy

Our first study demonstrated naturally occurring book reading styles among White New Zealand mothers. The two dominant styles used, describer and comprehender, are similar to naturally occurring styles among White middle-class American mothers. The describer style is similar in demand level to the dialogic reading style defined by Whitehurst and colleagues (e.g., Whitehurst, Falco, et al., 1988), but may not engender as much interaction with the child as does the dialogic reading style. In our second study, we wanted to test the effects of these naturally occurring reading styles on children's language and literacy. Haden et al. (1996) previously demonstrated positive associations between the comprehender style and preschoolers' later receptive vocabulary and story comprehension, and Leseman and de Jong (1998) found a positive link between mothers' high-level commentary and children's later vocabulary and word decoding.

We also wished to compare these two home-based reading styles with the performance-oriented style, which appears to occur primarily in preschool classrooms (Dickinson & Smith, 1994), possibly because of the group reading context. The performance-oriented style consists of high-level commentary introducing the book, but few interruptions during the actual reading. At the end of the book, the teacher asks comprehension and evaluative questions. Performance-oriented reading has been more strongly associated with receptive vocabulary gains than have other preschool reading styles.

We assessed the relative effectiveness of these three reading styles among a group of 48 four-year-old children attending state-sponsored preschools in New Zealand (92% of the children were White New Zealanders of European descent; see Reese & Cox, 1999, for further methodological details). The children were pretested on vocabulary (Peabody Picture Vocabulary Test–Revised; Dunn & Dunn, 1981), print (adapted from Clay, 1979, and Jastak & Jastak, 1978), and story comprehension skills (Beals et al., 1994), and were then randomly assigned to participate in readings in one of these three styles over a 6-week period. Adult readers read a selection of narrative storybooks to the children individually, in the prescribed style, during two or three sessions per week, for a total of 32 readings. The children were then posttested by another adult researcher on vocabulary, print, and story comprehension skills, using forms different from those applied in the pretest whenever possible. Pre- and posttesting took place in the children's homes, whereas reading sessions were conducted in the preschools.

The reading styles were modeled after the naturally occurring styles found among parents and teachers in America and New Zealand. Each style consisted of five questions and five comments per book, but the styles differed in the type and placement of commentary. The describer style employed low-level descriptions and labels. The comprehender style used high-level inferences and predictions. The performance-oriented style introduced the characters and solicited predictions prior to reading, and then requested and provided inferences and evaluations after the reading. Thus, the describer and comprehender styles were similar in their placement of comments, but differed in demand level; the comprehender and performance-oriented styles were similar in demand level but differed in the placement of comments. Table 3.2 contains examples of the three styles as observed during readings of the book *Hemi's Pet*.

TABLE 3.2
Examples of the Three Experimental Book-Reading Styles During *Hemi's Pet*
(de Hamel, 1985)

Style	Commentary
Describer	There is Rata. (p. 2)
	What is that girl doing? (p. 3)
	How many windows are there on the building? (p. 6)
	Hemi and Rata are in the bathroom. (p. 8)
	What are Mum and Dad having for breakfast? (p. 10)
	Look at all the animals. (p. 12)
	What is the budgie looking at in its cage? (p. 14)
	The cat has got green eyes. (p. 16)
	The cat got a prize too. (p. 22)
	Where is the red ribbon? (p. 23)
Comprehender	Why doesn't Rata go to school every day? (p. 1)
	Hemi wishes he had a pet to take. (p. 3)
	Why do you think Hemi smiled? (p. 6)
	Why is Hemi making Rata look pretty? (p. 7)
	Hemi is taking Rata to school as his pet. (p. 10)
	The children have different pets. (p. 12)
	Do all pets have four legs? (p. 13)
	Some of the pets have fur, some have four legs and some have a tail, but not all of them. (p. 20)
	No one else had a pet like Rata so Hemi and Rata won a prize. (p. 21)
	Do you think Hemi liked having Rata for a pet? (p. 23)
Performance-oriented	(Before reading)
	This story is about a boy named Hemi and his little sister, Rata. One day there is a pet show at school. But Hemi doesn't have anything to take! His little sister wants to know what a pet is. Let's see what special pet Hemi decides to take to school.
	(After reading)
	Who was Hemi's pet?
	Why did Hemi take Rata to school as his pet?
	What sort of pets did the other children take to school?
	Do you think Rata made a good pet?
	What was your favorite pet in the story?

TABLE 3.3
Pretest and Adjusted Posttest Means (and Standard Deviations)
by Literacy Skill and Reading Style Condition

	Reading Style					
	Describer		Comprehender		Performance-Oriented	
Test Phase/Measure	Mean	SD	Mean	SD	Mean	SD
Pretest						
PPVT-R	57.62	(12.71)	55.56	(10.78)	55.12	(10.91)
Print	15.25	(6.16)	15.06	(6.94)	16.00	(6.32)
Comprehension	3.26	(2.10)	4.69	(2.09)	4.07	(1.57)
Posttest						
PPVT-R	83.00	(9.10)	42.69	(8.19)	40.99	(7.85)
Print	25.67	(3.82)	8.14	(3.44)	17.82	(3.29)
Comprehension	5.25	(2.79)	3.65	(2.51)	9.54	(2.40)

Note. Posttest means are adjusted for pretest and reading style by pretest interaction scores.

Children in the three groups did not differ on their pretest skills (see Table 3.3), and so were well-matched before the intervention. The three pretest skills were moderately intercorrelated, however, so we needed to control for all of the children's pretest skills in assessing the unique effect of reading style on their posttest performance (see Table 3.4). We also wanted to explore the possibility that interactions between reading style and children's pretest skills would be observable in the form of effects on posttest skills. In keeping with a Vygotskian perspective, we predicted that the effects of reading style would depend on the children's initial skill levels: Children with lower initial skill levels would benefit most from a describer style of reading, children with higher initial skill levels

TABLE 3.4
Correlations Among Pretest Emergent Literacy Skills

Pretest Skills	PPVT-R	Print	Comprehension
PPVT-R	—		
Print	.41*	—	
Comprehension	.57*	.47*	—

*$p < .01$

would benefit most from a performance-oriented style, and the effects of the comprehender style would fall somewhere in between.

We used a dummy variable regression procedure (Judd, McClelland, & Smith, 1996) to test these hypotheses. First, a pair of dummy variables was created for the reading style effect. Then interaction terms were created by multiplying each pretest skill with the reading style variables, resulting in one pair of dummy variables for each of the three interaction terms. The seven resulting terms (three pretest variables, one pair of style variables, three pairs of pretest x style variables) were entered in a separate regression analysis for each posttest skill. The unique predictive variance of each term was tested by entering it after the other six terms had been entered. Table 3.3 shows the posttest skills for each group, adjusted for these covariates. Table 3.5 shows the results of the regression analyses. There was a main effect of reading style on children's vocabulary and print skills. In both cases, the describer style had the greatest positive effects overall, in comparison to performance-oriented reading for vocabulary and in comparison to comprehender reading for print skills. Also note, however, that significant interactions were observed between reading style and pretest skills,

TABLE 3.5
Predicting Children's Emergent Literacy Skills

Variable	Post PPVT–R		Post Print		Post Comprehension	
	β	ΔR^2	β	ΔR^2	β	ΔR^2
Pretest PPVT–R	.44	.09**	.05	.00	.03	.00
Pretest Print	.02	.00	.82	.25***	.38	.07*
Pretest Comprehension	.50	.08**	.19	.01	.32	.03
Reading Style	−.89		−1.07		−.85	
	−1.00	.06*	.07	.03*	1.16	.03
Style × PPVT–R	.56		.71		1.30	
	1.70	.06*	.45	.02	−1.41	.04
Style × Print	.62		.26		.12	
	−.38	.03	.13	.01	.29	.01
Style × Comprehension	−.24		−.08		.57	
	−.42	.02	−.62	.03*	−.03	.02

Note. Beta weights were derived upon entry after all other terms.
*$p < .05$; **$p < .01$; ***$p < .001$.

for both vocabulary and print (see Table 3.6 for the slopes of children's posttest performance as a function of reading style and pretest skill). In the case of vocabulary, reading style interacted with prior vocabulary knowledge. Children with lower initial vocabulary levels benefited most from the describer style, while children with higher initial vocabulary levels benefited most from the performance-oriented style. This interaction was reversed for print skills. Children with lower initial comprehension skills benefited most from a performance-oriented style, whereas children with higher initial comprehension skills benefited most from a describer style. We did not show any effect of reading style on comprehension skills.

These results are interesting for several reasons. First, they support other studies that have found vocabulary gains—and to a lesser extent, print gains—resulting from a describer-like reading style (dialogic reading). Our study extended this finding to a naturally occurring reading style. But previous experimental work on dialogic reading has not investigated its effectiveness in comparison to other specific reading styles, nor has it examined interactions with children's skill level. Our results qualify the effects of describer-like reading styles, by noting that such styles are best for enhancing lower level children's vocabulary skills, and possibly higher level children's print skills. Thus, one style of reading cannot be considered "best" for all children. Instead, the effectiveness of a reading style appears to be highly dependent on children's initial skill level and on the particular skill being fostered.

CONCLUSION

This chapter has addressed the first two goals of our ongoing research program. The first goal was to establish the existence of naturally occurring reading styles in a New Zealand population. We demonstrated that White New Zealand

TABLE 3.6
Slopes of Posttest Performance as a Function of Reading Style and Pretest Skill

	Posttest Skills (× Pretest Skills)	
Styles	PPVT-R (× PPVT-R)	Print (× Comprehension)
Describer	−.10	2.13
Comprehender	.61	.51
Performance-oriented	.90	−.63

mothers are similar to White American mothers in adopting a higher level or lower level style of book reading with their children. Most of the White New Zealand mothers took on a highly interactive style with their children, regardless of demand level. However, these mothers did not adopt different styles as a function of their children's age or language level. We then conducted an experimental test of these two reading styles in comparison with performance-oriented reading, which is also interactive but does not interrupt the text during reading, and which may be more appropriate in a preschool setting, where large-group reading may be a necessity. In accordance with our predictions, the describer style of reading was found to be beneficial for lower level children's vocabulary skills, whereas the performance-oriented style was beneficial for higher level children's vocabulary. This finding underscores the need for New Zealand parents to accommodate their reading style to their child's language and literacy levels. Perhaps increasing parents' awareness of their children's language and emergent literacy capacities would be a first step in this direction.

This strategy of drawing an experimental approach from the descriptive data seems promising. A possible next step would be to draw upon within-culture descriptive studies of the reading styles of Maori, Samoan, and Tongan New Zealand families (McNaughton, 1995) and then experimentally compare their tutorial style to other naturally occurring reading styles. It could be the case that the tutorial style, although not predicted to benefit children's vocabulary skills, will foster the development of story memory skills.

Like some other experimental research (e.g., Phillips, Norris, Mason, & Kerr, 1990), we failed to find that manipulation of reading style showed any effect on children's story skills. Yet reading styles are linked to children's story comprehension in the correlational research (Dickinson & Smith, 1994; Haden et al., 1996). Perhaps story comprehension is a harder skill to foster than vocabulary or print because it is more general, and depends on children's knowledge base. Longer, more intensive interventions may be required before an effect is observed.

Another limitation of our experimental study was our restriction to cognitive outcomes for the child. Shared book reading potentially has *affective* benefits for children, as well. In particular, researchers have found that mothers' use of emotional language during book reading predicts aspects of children's emotional development (e.g., Denham & Auerbach, 1995; Garner, Carlson Jones, Gaddy, & Rennie, 1997).

These studies are only a first step in comparing the relative effectiveness of different reading styles. The inclusion of a non-reading control group would help us assess whether children benefit from these reading styles in comparison to receiving no extra reading. It is possible that taking children out of the ordinary preschool curriculum has its disadvantages, as well as advantages. In addition, a direct comparison of the performance-oriented style to dialogic reading is warranted. The styles used in our studies were experimentally pure, but some of the critical elements of the dialogic style—such as repeated readings that encourage increasing interaction on the part of children, and the linking of the story with the child's personal experience—may have been lost in the purification process. Moreover, individual reading is not a possibility for a real-life intervention in a preschool setting. In fact, even group readings with up to five children are difficult to maintain in the absence of parent support. Whitehurst, Arnold, et al. (1994) noted that most preschools failed to continue small-group reading after their intervention ended. Small-group readings are critical to the success of dialogic reading programs, and performance-oriented reading offers an attractive alternative for its ease of implementation, especially among older, more advanced children. We do not know if performance-oriented reading would demonstrate the same positive effects in a group situation, although Dickinson and Smith (1994) have found that it has correlational benefits in large-group settings.

On the basis of our findings, we would recommend caution in promoting one reading style above all others. Parents and preschool teachers should instead focus on expanding their reading repertoires to include a diverse array of styles, and on refining their ability to shift styles, depending on the type of book and the child's mood, level, and age. McNaughton (1995) has termed this ability "reading with dexterity." Such caution is especially important when we are working with children from a diverse range of cultures, with different reading styles. A culturally sensitive intervention would supplement, not supplant, families' preferred book reading style.

Engaging the child in active participation during book reading is almost always better than straight reading of the text (e.g., Sénéchal et al., 1995), but beyond that principle, the type of interaction is best varied from book to book, day to day, and child to child. As our observations of performance-oriented reading make clear, interaction does not always have to take place *during* the reading. For a rather extreme example, imagine reading a poem to a young child. We wouldn't stop after each line to ask the child a question, because doing so would destroy the aesthetic integrity of the poem and possibly obscure some of its salient features. We could still employ an interactive approach, however, by introducing the poem and then discussing it after the reading. Some of the more poetic storybooks might best be read in a performance-oriented, rather than a dialogic, style. Ultimately, we will most likely find that keeping the child *and* the reader interested is the most important predictor of benefits from shared book reading.

ACKNOWLEDGMENTS

We would like to acknowledge the assistance of a University of Otago Division of Sciences grant to Elaine Reese. We would also like to thank Nicola Brown, Cherie Harris, Katie Harrison, Jane Herbert, and Keryn Pratt for their assistance with data collection and scoring. Most of all, we are grateful to the families who participated in this research and to the children and teachers at Bayfield, Grants Braes, Jonathan Rhodes, Kelsey Yaralla, Helen Deem, and Richard Hudson kindergartens.

REFERENCES

Allen, P. (1990). *My cat Maisie*. Auckland, NZ: Hodder and Stoughton.

Anderberg, M. R. (1973). *Cluster analysis for applications*. New York: Harcourt Brace Jovanovich.

Beals, D. E., De Temple, J. M., & Dickinson, D. K. (1994). Talking and listening that support early literacy development of children from low-income families. In D. K. Dickinson (Ed.), *Bridges to literacy: Children, families, and schools* (pp. 19–40). Cambridge, MA: Blackwell.

Bus, A., van IJzendoorn, M. H., & Pellegrini, A. D. (1995). Joint book reading makes for success in learning to read: A meta-analysis on intergenerational transmission of literacy. *Review of Educational Research, 65*, 1–21.

Clay, M. (1979). *Reading: The patterning of complex behavior*. Auckland, NZ: Heinemann.

De Hamel, J. (1985). *Hemi's pet*. London, UK: Reed Methuen.

Denham, S. A., & Auerbach, S. (1995). Mother–child dialogue about emotions and preschoolers' emotional competence. *Genetic, Social, & General Psychology Monographs, 121*, 313–337.

Dickinson, D., & Smith, M. (1994). Long-term effects of preschool teachers' book readings on low-income children's vocabulary and story comprehension. *Reading Research Quarterly, 29*(2), 105–122.

Dunn, L. M., & Dunn, L. M. (1981). *Peabody Picture Vocabulary Test–Revised*. Circle Pines, MN: American Guidance Service.

Garner, P. W., Carlson Jones, D., Gaddy, G., & Rennie, K. (1997). Low-income mothers' conversations about emotions and their children's emotional competence. *Social Development, 6*, 37–52.

Haden, C. A., Reese, E., & Fivush, R. (1996). Mothers' extratextual comments during storybook reading: Stylistic differences over time and across texts. *Discourse Processes, 21*, 135–169.

Hargrave, A. C., & Sénéchal, M. (2000). A book reading intervention with preschool children who have limited vocabularies: The benefits of regular reading and dialogic reading. *Early Childhood Research Quarterly, 15*, 75–90.

Harte, D. (1997). *Maternal styles of storybook reading: A New Zealand study*. Unpublished master's thesis, University of Otago, Dunedin, NZ.

Heath, S. B. (1982). What no bedtime story means: Narrative skills at home and school. *Language in Society, 11,* 49–76.

Jastak, J., & Jastak, S. (1978). *Wide-Range Achievement Test–Revised.* Wilmington, DE: Jastak & Associates.

Judd, C. M., McClelland, G. H., & Smith, E. R. (1996). Testing treatment by covariate interactions when treatment varies within subjects. *Psychological Methods, 1*(4), 366–378.

Leseman, P. P. M., & de Jong, P. F. (1998). Home literacy: Opportunity, instruction, cooperation and social-emotional quality predicting early reading achievement. *Reading Research Quarterly, 33,* 294–318.

Lonigan, C. J. (1994). Reading to preschoolers exposed: Is the emperor really naked? *Developmental Review, 14,* 303–323.

Lonigan, C. J., & Whitehurst, G. J. (1998). Relative efficacy of parent and teacher involvement in a shared-reading intervention for preschool children from low-income backgrounds. *Early Childhood Research Quarterly, 13,* 263–290.

Low, J., & Durkin, K. (2001). Individual differences and consistency in maternal talk style during joint story encoding and retrospection: Associations with children's long-term recall. *International Journal of Behavioral Development, 25,* 27–36.

McNaughton, S. (1995). *Patterns of emergent literacy.* New York: Oxford University Press.

Norusis, M. (1988). *Statistical Package for the Social Sciences/PC + V2.0.* Chicago: Statistical Package for the Social Sciences.

Pellegrini, A. D., Brody, G. H., & Sigel, I. E. (1985). Parents' book-reading habits with their children. *Journal of Educational Psychology, 77,* 332–340.

Phillips, L. M., Norris, S. P., Mason, J. M., & Kerr, B. M. (1990). Effect of early literacy intervention on kindergarten achievement. *Yearbook of the National Reading Conference, 39,* 199–207.

Reese, E. (1995). Predicting children's literacy from mother–child conversations. *Cognitive Development, 10,* 381–405.

Reese, E., & Cox, A. (1999). Quality of adult book reading affects children's emergent literacy. *Developmental Psychology, 35,* 20–28.

Rogoff, B. (1990). *Apprenticeship in thinking: Cognitive development in social context.* New York: Oxford University Press.

Scarborough, H., & Dobrich, W. (1994). On the efficacy of reading to preschoolers. *Developmental Review, 14,* 245–302.

Sénéchal, M. (1997). The differential effect of storybook reading on preschoolers' acquisition of expressive and receptive vocabulary. *Journal of Child Language, 24,* 123–138.

Sénéchal, M., Thomas, E., & Monker, J. (1995). Individual differences in 4-year-old children's acquisition of vocabulary during storybook reading. *Journal of Educational Psychology, 87*(2), 218–229.

Snow, C. E., & Dickinson, D. K. (1991). Skills that aren't basic in a new conception of literacy. In E. M. Jennings & A. C. Purves (Eds.), *Literate systems and individual lives: Perspectives on literacy and schooling* (pp. 179–191). New York: State University of New York Press.

Tarlton, J. (1990). *Going for fish.* Auckland, NZ: Ashton Scholastic.

Vygotsky, L. S. (1978). *Mind in society: The development of higher psychological processes.* (M. Cole, V. John-Steiner, S. Scribner, & E. Souberman, Eds.). Cambridge, MA: Harvard University Press.

Wells, G. (1985). Preschool literacy-related activities and success in school. In D. R. Olson, N. Torrance, & A. Hilyard (Eds), *Literacy, language and learning: The nature and consequences of reading and writing* (pp. 229–255). New York: Cambridge University Press.

Whitehurst, G. J., Arnold, D., Epstein J., Angell, A., Smith, M., & Fischel, J. (1994). A picture book reading intervention in daycare and home for children from low-income families. *Developmental Psychology, 30,* 679–689.

Whitehurst, G., Epstein, J., Angell, A., Payne, A., Crone, D., & Fischel, J. (1994). Outcomes of an emergent literacy intervention in Head Start. *Journal of Educational Psychology, 86,* 542–555.

Whitehurst, G. J., Falco, F. L., Lonigan, C., Fischel, J. E., DeBaryshe, B. D., Valdez-Menchaca, M. C., & Caulfield, M. (1988). Accelerating language development through picture book reading. *Developmental Psychology, 24,* 552–558.

Whitehurst, G. J., & Lonigan, C. J. (1998). Child development and emergent literacy. *Child Development, 69,* 848–872.

Whitehurst, G. J., Zevenbergen, A. A., Crone, D. A., Schultz, M. D., Velting, O. N., & Fischel, J. E. (1999). Outcomes of an emergent literacy intervention from Head Start through second grade. *Journal of Educational Psychology, 91,* 261–272.

4

Book Sharing
With Preschoolers
With Language Delays

Anne van Kleeck
University of Georgia

Judith Vander Woude
Calvin College

Shared book reading is a common activity in many homes, and is widely believed to support the development of children's literacy and language (see Bus, van IJzendoorn, & Pelligrini, 1995, and Scarborough & Dobrich, 1994, for different interpretations of the underlying causal relationship). Shared book reading often includes adult–child conversations about the book outside of the actual reading. Consequently, young children are expected to jointly construct meaning from a book's text, pictures, and the conversational support offered by parents (Bloome, 1983).

Constructing meaning from this array of sources may be difficult for children with language delays who are otherwise developmentally normal (e.g., no deficits in hearing, emotional factors, oral structure and function, or general intelligence). And yet book sharing experiences may be even more important for these children than they are for other children who are typically developing, for at least three reasons. First, book sharing is known to foster language development (cf. Bus, van IJzendoorn, & Pellegrini, 1995; Scarborough & Dobrich, 1994), and such children are by definition delayed in their oral language skills. Second, researchers have demonstrated that book sharing fosters preliteracy skills, and children with language delays also have documented deficits in many aspects of their preliteracy development. For example, compared to their age peers, these children have less knowledge about print (Boudreau & Hedberg, 1999; Gillam & Johnston, 1985; Terrell, 1994), poorer letter name knowledge (Boudreau & Hedberg, 1999), and poorer narrative skills (e.g., Craig & Evans, 1993; Crais, 1988; Liles, 1985a, 1985b, 1987; Liles & Purcell, 1987; MacLachlan & Chapman, 1988; Weismer, 1985). Third, book sharing with preschoolers fosters future reading achievement. Here again, preschoolers with language delays are at high risk for later reading and other academic difficulties, as documented by a large body of longitudinal and retrospective research (e.g., Aram & Nation, 1980; Aram, Ekelman, & Nation, 1984; Bishop & Adams, 1990; Catts, 1991; Garvey & Gordon, 1973; Korngold, Menyuk, Liebergott, & Chesnick, 1988; Menyuk & Chesnick, 1997; Padget, 1988; Rissman, Curtiss, & Tallal, 1990; Scarborough & Dobrich, 1990; Stark et al., 1984; Strominger & Bashir, 1977; Tallal, 1990). For all these reasons, shared book reading is frequently recommended as an intervention strategy for children with delayed language (Ratner, Parker, & Gardner, 1993; Schuele & van Kleeck, 1987; Snow, Scarborough, & Burns, 1999).

However, as research in this area of inquiry continues, it is becoming increasingly clear that it is not just the act of sharing books with preschoolers that is beneficial, but the way in which this interaction is conducted. Following this vein, scholars who conduct research on book sharing with preschoolers talk about the kinds of guidance, scaffolding, or mediation that parents provide for their children during this process. Mason (1990) defined mediation as "a protective umbrella of explanations, interpretations, and clarifications ... provided at the right moment by adults" (p. 2). Parents adjust this support as children's cognitive and linguistic abilities develop (e.g., Altwerger, Diehl-Faxon, Dockstader-Anderson, 1985; Bus & van IJzendoorn, 1988; DeLoache & DeMendoza, 1987; Dickinson, De Temple, Hirschler, & Smith, 1992; Murphy, 1978; Pellegrini, Brody, & Sigel, 1985; van Kleeck, Alexander, Vigil, & Templeton, 1996; van Kleeck, Vigil, & Beers, 1998). The mediation process helps children succeed in the process of book sharing, and gain new and higher level skills as, over time, parents "up the ante" to challenge their children. That is, the mediation changes over time to provide more challenge as children obtain higher skill levels.

We are just beginning to learn how children with language delays and their parents participate in this routine, highly linguistic activity. In this chapter, we first discuss two general findings that distinguish the book sharing interactions of parents of children with language delays from those of parents of preschoolers who are developing typically. The first general finding indicates that parents of children with language delays seem to carry more of the conversational load during shared reading. The second tells us that these parents tend to focus on lower levels of abstraction, and consequently use less decontextualized language during shared reading. We then go on to suggest a theoretical framework for understanding the nature of these interactions and how they compare to book sharing interactions with preschoolers who are developing typically.

Taken together, the results of the studies reviewed in this chapter suggest that reading books to children with language delays is not enough by itself. Instead, these children seem to benefit from specific conversational strategies that not only encourage their participation, but also expose them to input from different levels of abstraction. It seems that children gain different communicative skills via their experience with book sharing at different developmental levels.

BALANCE OF ADULT–CHILD PARTICIPATION IN SHARED BOOK READING

By the age of 3, children with typically developing language become active participants in book sharing conversations, as they do in general conversations, by speaking more frequently, asking more questions, and initiating more of the topics than they did previously (e.g., Goodsitt, Raitan, & Perlmutter, 1988; Snow, 1983; Snow & Goldfield, 1981). In contrast, at the age of 4, children with language delays continue to ask few questions and seldom initiate topics in book sharing interactions. The parents of preschool children with language delays also continue to talk more frequently than their children when discussing books, in comparison to the parents of children with typically developing language (Evans & Schmidt, 1991; Sigel & McGillicuddy-Delisi, 1984; Sulzby & Kaderavek, 1996). In this section, we first present the results of research on the balance of participation in the book sharing interactions of parents and their preschool children. These studies suggest that parents of preschool children with language delays may carry more than their share of the conversational load during book sharing—even as their children continue to develop their language abilities—than do parents of typically developing children. We then discuss intervention studies that address the benefits of teaching adults how to help their children with delayed language become more active participants in shared book reading conversations. Finally, we discuss the implications of these results and provide suggestions for future research on parent–child participation in shared book reading conversations.

Research on Balance of Participation

Evans and Schmidt (1991) observed differences in the balance of adult–child participation in the book-sharing conversations of two mother–child dyads: one including a child (3 years, 9 months) with delayed expressive language and average receptive language ability, and the other, including a language-matched child (2 years, 2 months) with typically developing language. Evans and Schmidt recorded these dyads reading the same book during nine sessions over a 5-month period. Even though there was no difference between the dyads in the total number of maternal utterances during book sharing, the mother of the child with delayed language initiated most of the conversational sequences, and her child asked questions infrequently, in comparison to the other mother and child. The mother of the child with delayed language also used more utterances to draw her child's attention to an object or event in the story, and used more questions and directives to elicit verbal responses from the child (e.g., "What is this?" or "Look again."). Evans and Schmidt suggested that the mother of the child with delayed language was responsible for maintaining the conversation, while the other mother and her child with typically developing language shared almost equal responsibility for their book-focused conversations.

Sulzby and Kaderavek (1996) found similar results when comparing two mother–child dyads, one including a child (4 years, 2 months) with delayed expressive language and average receptive language, and the other a language-matched child (3 years, 5 months) with typically developing language. They compared the conversations recorded during one book and one play interaction. Results indicated that the child with delayed language asked proportionally fewer questions (9% of the child's total number of utterances during book sharing) than the child with typically developing language (41% of their child's total number of utterances during book sharing). Conversely, the mother of the child with delayed language asked many more questions (61% of her total utterances during book sharing) than the mother of the child with typically developing language (12% of her total utterances during book sharing). Furthermore, compared to her language use during the play interaction, the mother of the child with delayed language reduced the length of her utterances in the book interaction, as measured by mean length of utterance (MLU), and increased her range of vocabulary, as measured by type-token ratio (TTR). The mother of the language-matched child with typically developing language did not demonstrate these differences between book and play interactions.

Pellegrini and colleagues (1985) compared the parent–child book sharing interactions of one group of 60 families whose children were broadly referred to as having "communication disabilities," with another group of 60 families whose children had no communication disabilities (cf. Sigel & McGillicuddy-Delisi, 1984). The children with communication disabilities were described as including those with speech sound production difficulties (called "phonological" delays) and/or language delays. No other information, such as severity of their disability or their level of comprehension abilities, was reported. Videotaped data included the mothers reading one book and the fathers reading another similar book with their children during the same session. Results showed that the parents of children with communicative disabilities initiated more conversational turns, asked more questions, and engaged in more nonverbal directives (e.g., patting the child, demonstrating a concept or restraining the child) than the parents of children with no communicative disabilities.

Although the study does not define how many children actually had language delays and how many had only speech delays, the results nonetheless support findings from the other studies reviewed in this section, suggesting that adults take on more responsibility for contributing to book sharing interactions with children who have language delays than they do with children who are developing typically.

Descriptive case studies also suggest that adults are primarily responsible for initiating and maintaining book sharing conversations with language-delayed children. In a study by Vander Woude (1998), four mothers and their children with histories of delayed language participated in four different book sharing routines: reading a familiar narrative book, a familiar expository book, an unfamiliar narrative book, and an unfamiliar expository book. The different genres represented the types of books that parents and children usually read (Goodsitt et al., 1988; Pellegrini, Perlmutter, Galda, & Brody, 1990).

The children selected for the case studies represented different age groups, as well as different severities and types of language delay. The two oldest children were Daniel (6 years, 6 months), who exhibited a moderate expressive language delay, and Jason (7 years, 0 months), who exhibited a moderate expressive and receptive language delay. The two younger children were Timothy (4 years, 0 months), who exhibited a severe receptive and moderate expressive language delay, and Karen (3 years, 11 months), who had a history of severe expressive language delay that had shown satisfactory improvement after intervention, as evidenced by her scores in the average range on standardized language tests. Results showed that all of the mothers controlled the book interactions by initiating more topics, speaking more often, and using longer utterances in their book discussions than did their children. Furthermore, the older children were at an age at which mothers of typically developing children often read books without inserting many comments or questions at all (Altwerger, Diehl-Faxon, & Dockstader-Anderson, 1985; Bus & van IJzendoorn, 1988; DeTemple, 2001; Goodsitt et al., 1988).

So why does it seem that parents of older children with language delays continue to carry more than their share of book conversations? In a discussion of why mothers of typically developing children talk less during book sharing as their children approach 5 years of age, DeTemple (2001) offered two explanations that may also explain why parents of children with language delays continue to use comments and questions at this stage. First, DeTemple proposed that early in a child's development mothers use conversations to check the child's understanding of a story. As the children near the age of 5, the mothers become more confident that their children can make sense of the story on their own, without needing to spend time talking about the main ideas or paraphrasing the text. Second, De Temple suggested that over time the children respond correctly to their mothers' questions more frequently; and consequently, the mothers do not need to spend as much time correcting or clarifying their children's responses. Both of these hypotheses fit well with the Vygotskian notion of skills first being other-regulated (that is, performed primarily by the member of the dyad who is more competent in that skill), then becoming increasingly self-regulated (that is, performed primarily by the dyad member who is learning the skill).

These hypotheses may also explain why mothers of older children with delayed language continue to talk frequently during shared book reading. Given the nature of language delays, their children may still need mediated assistance in order to understand the story. Furthermore, children with language delays often have difficulty responding correctly to their mothers' questions, and thus the mothers may need to continue spending time correcting or clarifying their children's answers.

Type of Language Delay and Balance of Participation

In addition to these differences between children with typically developing language and children with language delays, the *type* of language delay also appears to affect the balance of adult–child participation in book sharing conversations. Results of a study by Mogford-Bevan and Summersall (1997) suggest that children with both expressive and receptive language delays are less willing to engage in book interactions than children with expressive-only language delays. Their study included 11 children between the ages of 2 years, 6 months and 3 years, 9 months. Five of the children exhibited expressive-receptive language

delays, and 6 presented with expressive-only language delays. According to videotaped samples and parent interviews, when compared to children with expressive-only delays, children with expressive-receptive delays were more
disruptive when reading books, and needed constant encouragement to remain
engaged in book sharing (suggesting a heavier "conversational load" on their
parents).

Similarly, in the previously described study by Vander Woude (1998), the
two children with expressive-receptive language delays were less active participants in book sharing conversations than the two children with expressive-only
delays. The children with expressive-receptive delays used fewer utterances
and initiated fewer topics than the children with expressive-only delays. Additionally, compared to the mothers of children with expressive-only delays, the
parents of children with expressive and receptive delays used lengthier utterances during shared book reading dialogues.

It seems counterintuitive that mothers of children with less linguistic ability
would have longer utterance lengths; and indeed, other research has shown
that in general mothers' mean length of utterance is shorter with children with
receptive and expressive language delays than it is with children with expressive
delays only (Cunningham, Siegel, van der Spuy, Clark, & Bow, 1985). However, Cunningham and colleagues also found that a mother's ability to tune into
the child's linguistic ability by adjusting her mean length of utterance is dependent on how much the child participates in conversation. The greatest discrep-
ancies between children's and mothers' mean length of utterance were
observed among the dyads with the least communicative children. Although
additional studies with more subjects are needed to confirm this result, the children's poor conversational participation may explain the longer utterance
length found by Vander Woude (1998). Logically, this lack of participation
would make it very difficult for mothers to adjust to their child's level of linguistic ability.

Discussion of Parent–Child Participation Differences

These studies combine to suggest that parents of children with language delays
carry a greater portion of the conversational load during book sharing conversations than parents of language-matched children. Refining the distinction, parents of children with expressive and receptive language delays seem to carry a
greater portion of the conversational load than do parents of children with expressive-only language delays. However, additional investigations of larger
groups of children with language delays, carefully matched with both chrono-

logical age-mates and younger children who are language-age mates, are needed to corroborate these results.

Nevertheless, the results are supported by research carried out in other contexts than book sharing. Here as well, children with language delays are described as less assertive, less responsive, and less able to maintain topics than children with typically developing language (e.g., Bishop, Chan, Adams, Hartley, & Weir, 2000; Brinton, Fujiki, & Sonnenberg, 1988; Craig & Washington, 1993; Cross, Nienhuys, & Kirkman, 1985; Rosinski-McClendon & Newhoff, 1987; Siegel, Cunningham, & van der Spuy, 1979). Cross and her colleagues (1985) discussed how many of the adjustments that mothers make in spontaneous conversations (not during book-sharing contexts) with their children with language delays are probably explained by the fact that these children are less talkative and far less willing to engage in conversation than children with typically developing language. The researchers found that children with language delays not only produced less than half the number of utterances of other children in the same time period, but were also less responsive to their mothers' conversational contributions. Their mothers, on the other hand, asked more questions, in particular more "quiz" questions, to elicit conversation than their peers, and answered more of their own questions. Cross (1984) also suggested a relationship between other findings, such as the mothers' use of run-on sentences and a more rapid rate of speech, and the language-delayed children's lack of conversational participation.

An important question arises, of course, about whether the adjustments made by mothers to compensate for their children's relative lack of conversational participation are helpful to the children, or may in the long run contribute to further language difficulties. As Leonard (1998) notes,

> Even if the speech directed toward children with SLI [specific language impairment] is a direct and natural response to these children's apparent failure to converse in a typical manner, we cannot easily conclude that this speech plays no role in the children's problems with language. It is easy to see how a vicious cycle of nonoptimal interactions could be set in motion once the adult or peer perceives the child's limitations in language. The modifications made by the adult or peer might be an overcompensation or in some other way abnormal, which might in turn aggravate the child's language learning difficulties (p. 167).

There is one aspect of parental input during book sharing, however, that might have a positive influence on children's language development. The results reviewed in this section suggest that parents of children with language delays ask their children more questions and take more conversational turns during shared reading than parents of typically developing children. Thus, perhaps due to their children's lack of assertiveness, the parents of children with language delays continue—even as their children further develop linguistic skills—to provide input and multiple opportunities for their children to display their knowledge, by asking questions and initiating conversational turns. Studies have clearly shown that the amount of language input at home is significantly related to either the current rate or later levels of language development in typically developing children (Ellis & Wells, 1980; Hart & Risley, 1995; Huttenlocher, Haight, Bryk, Seltzer, & Lyons, 1991).

As Hart and Risley (1995) proposed, increased input provides a richer linguistic environment for children by exposing them "to a greater number of different words and expressions used to name and describe and to more prompts for practice; more practice should lead to more parent responses and approval" (p. 113–114). So it may be that the book sharing context benefits children with language delays because of the amount of focused interactive input provided in this context. But even here, a critical question remains about the positive benefit to children with language delays of increased linguistic input during book sharing. Is more talk beneficial if the child is not increasing his or her level of participation in the conversation? In other words, it may be the case that increased talk by the adult may not benefit the child unless the increase in adult talk is accompanied by an increase in child talk and hence in the amount of conversational participation. Indeed, it is possible that too much adult talk might actually make a child with language delays feel overwhelmed, and therefore actually decrease her or his level of participation, with the possibility of negative effects on development. And indeed, as we discuss in the next section, results of several intervention studies suggest that teaching adults to encourage their children's participation in book sharing by increasing their input in specific ways (e.g., asking more open-ended questions and expanding the child's utterances) may help children to be more active participants in book sharing conversation and may ultimately accelerate their language development.

Intervention Research: Teaching Parents Strategies for Book Sharing Conversations

Four studies on teaching adults strategies for sharing books with children with language delays have shown promising results. Dale and colleagues (Dale, Crain-Thoreson, Notari-Syverson, & Cole, 1996) compared the effects of two parental instructional programs on the language gains of 33 preschool children with mild to moderate language delays. One was a "dialogic" book reading program developed by Whitehurst and colleagues (1988), which teaches parents how to ask more open-ended and wh-questions, how to respond to children's questions with other questions that continue the topic, and how to expand and extend children's utterances. The other was a "conversational" program without the book sharing component. The conversational program, like the dialogic book reading program, promoted a responsive style of interaction. However, the dialogic program increased the mothers' use of wh-questions, open-ended questions, imitation, and expansions more than its conversational counterpart. Additionally, regardless of the type of program, children with moderate language delays showed increased verbal engagement and vocabulary growth, while the children with more mild language delays gained in sentence length, as measured by mean length of utterance (MLU).

Crain-Thoreson and Dale (1999) used a modified version of the dialogic program, in which they also taught parents to give their language-delayed children additional time to respond. The study included 32 children with a mean age of 4 years, 3 months, and moderate receptive and expressive language delays. They were assigned to one of three groups: a parent group with one-on-one shared book reading, a staff member group with one-on-one instruction, and another staff member group without one-on-one instruction. In all three groups, children showed increased participation and improved lexical diversity in the book sharing conversations when parents and staff members gave the children additional time to respond, increased their acknowledgements of the children's utterances, and decreased the number of information statements and who/what questions that typically encourage simple one-word responses. The children in this study did not significantly increase their vocabulary skills on standardized measures; however, they did have a lower MLU than the group in the study by Dale et al. (1996) described earlier.

McNeill and Fowler (1999) analyzed the effects of teaching the mothers of five children with language delays (ages 52 to 63 months) conversational strategies such as using praise, expanding the children's utterances, asking open-ended questions, and using extended pauses that give the children time to initiate a turn. The mothers were observed over a period of 9 weeks. Four of them consistently used the new strategies, and their children likewise increased their participation in the book sharing conversations. On the other hand, the one remaining mother did not maintain the new strategies throughout the intervention, and her child did not increase his participation. One interesting finding of this study is that as three of the mothers learned to praise their children's responses and initiations in the first week, the mothers also spontaneously began to use more open-ended questions and expand their children's utterances. Although the sample size was small, these results suggest that simply teaching parents to praise their children with language delays more frequently may help them fully engage the children in book sharing conversations.

Another study by Hargrave and Sénéchal (2000) looked at the effects of pre-school teachers' use of a dialogic reading intervention based on a model from Whitehurst and colleagues (1988). One group of teachers used this intervention in their classrooms, while another group used their customary style of shared reading. The researchers then looked at the effect of the intervention on the vocabulary gains of children with limited vocabularies. Both groups read every day for 4 weeks. The study included 36 children between the ages of 3 and 5 years, with an average age of 4 years, 1 month. As a group, the children's expressive vocabulary skills showed an average delay of 13 months. Results showed that even though the children in both groups increased their expressive vocabulary skills, the children whose teachers used the dialogic reading method made significantly greater gains on both a standardized test of expressive vocabulary and a test of the vocabulary used in the books the teachers had read. It is important to note, however, that the authors did not present other data on the children's cognitive and language skills. Thus, it is not possible to determine if the children in the study were only language-delayed or if their limited expressive vocabulary skills were related to complicating factors such as cognitive, emotional, or hearing impairments. Nonetheless, this study supports the idea of a relationship between adults' use of dialogic strategies during shared reading and children's expressive vocabulary development.

It may be possible that Crain-Thoreson and Dale (1999) would have found similar results to Hargrave and Sénéchal (2000) had they used standardized tests that were sensitive enough to detect the vocabulary growth that might have occurred during short periods of intervention. Pre- and posttests of vocabulary from the actual books read, as used by Hargrave and Sénéchal (2000), may have also detected this development more accurately.

Taken together, the comparative and intervention studies suggest that parents of children with language delays continue to provide support over time, just to encourage their children's participation in the conversation. They provide this encouragement by asking more questions and talking more, and, as intervention studies show, may more productively encourage participation by praising their children's communicative efforts and expanding the few initiative efforts that the children seem to make. Crain-Thoreson and Dale's (1999) study, in particular, seems to suggest that language-delayed children's efforts to participate need to be mediated by parents for an extended period of time before the children can actually begin to carry more of the balance of the conversation, as do children with typically developing language. Furthermore, it seems that, given the nature of parent–child interaction, the changing of established parental patterns of interaction helps dyads move beyond the kinds of interactional relationships that may be adversely influenced by language-delayed children's less responsive conversational style.

Future Research on Balance of Participation

These studies point to directions for future research. Researchers should measure gains in conversational participation (both initiations and responses), in addition to measuring gains on various language and literacy skills, since children's conversational participation may be foundational to setting up the kinds of interactions that foster language and literacy development. As Dale and his colleagues (1996) and Crain-Thoreson and Dale (1999) suggested, initial gains in conversational skills might be precursors to later gains in language development. So, children may make gains in the amount and/or appropriateness of their conversational participation as a result of a book sharing intervention, yet not make any gains on language or literacy measures until further intervention is conducted or more time has passed.

It should be kept in mind, however, that research on typically developing children indicates that as these children get closer to school age, their mothers engage in more reading and less dialogue about the books than they do with younger preschoolers (De Temple, 2001; Goodsitt et al., 1988). Mothers generally increase their amount of reading and decrease their amount of talk about the book as their children grow older. These kinds of developmental trends need to be kept in mind when designing interventions for children with language delays. Since such children may pass through the developmental stages more slowly, their parents may need to be encouraged to continue dialogues longer than they think appropriate, based on the child's age. We would expect children with language delays to be late in arriving at a stage where they could listen to text without a great deal of conversational scaffolding from their parents.

In addition to looking at parent–child conversations involving children older than preschool age, we should also investigate how parents and younger children (before the age of 3) who are "at risk" for language delays participate in book sharing conversations. Because delayed language is seldom identified in children before the age of 3, we know very little about how younger children who are "at risk" for language delays interact with their parents in book sharing conversations. Such research may lead to the development of more effective interventions, focusing on participation strategies implemented at an earlier developmental stage.

Finally, as previously mentioned, we should determine whether a greater amount of adult input leads to a higher level of conversational participation from children during book sharing. If not, one might suspect that the adult's "bombardment" has little impact on the linguistic practice the children are getting in this context. It may also be that some parents are better than others at eliciting their children's participation. And indeed, Bus suggests that children who have an insecure parent–child attachment relationship—characterized by less parental sensitivity to their needs—are likely to be less engaged and become more frustrated with shared reading activities (see Bus, this volume). An insecure parent has difficulty adapting text and providing supportive discussion to fit the child's interests and understanding, which, in turn, makes it difficult for the insecurely attached child to engage in the shared reading conversations. Although to date this phenomenon has not been studied among children with language delays, it is possible that some parents and their children with language delays have less secure attachments, which might, in part, explain the nature of the book sharing conversations we have described so far.

One study of spontaneous mother–child interaction (not during book sharing), however, suggests that not all mothers of children with language delays interact on the basis of insecure attachments. Cross and her colleagues (1985) compared 10 mothers' talk to their language-delayed preschoolers with their talk to younger siblings who had the same language ability, and found 11 significant differences. If we assume that a mother is unlikely to have an insecure attachment with her older child and a secure attachment with her younger one, these differences suggest that the child's language delay is likely the reason for the differences in maternal input to two children with otherwise similar language abilities. As we discuss in the next section, however, the adjustments may include more than improving the balance of parent–child participation. They may also include adjusting the level of abstract language in these conversations to meet the needs of the child.

ABSTRACT LANGUAGE CONTENT OF BOOK SHARING CONVERSATIONS

Book sharing is an ideal activity for developing children's understanding and use of language. Nevertheless, it is important to note that just reading to a child in the home environment does not ensure later literacy skills, nor does it appear that any kind of discussion about the book is adequate by itself (Heath, 1982, 1983; Wells, 1985). Both Heath's and Wells' research indicates that the type of language used in book sharing conversations had a significant effect on children's subsequent literacy development. Of particular importance is the concrete to abstract dimension of parents' or other adults' language, which is variously referred to in the literature as *abstract language* (e.g., Blank, Rose, & Berlin, 1978; van Kleeck, 1995; van Kleeck, Gillam, Hamilton, & McGrath, 1997), *decontextualized language* (e.g., Denny, 1991; Heath, 1982, 1983; Snow & Ninio, 1986), *distancing strategies* (e.g., Sigel & McGillicuddy-Delisi, 1984) and *nonimmediate language* (e.g., De Temple, 1990). Regardless of the term, such language places greater representational demands on children, who have to "use mental representation to transcend the observable present" (Sigel & McGillicuddy-Delisi, 1984, p. 75). It has often been associated with a *literate mode of thought* (e.g., Olson, 1989), which supports literacy development and general academic success during the middle elementary-school years (e.g., Blank, 1982; Donaldson, 1978; Snow, 1991).

The highest levels of cognitive demand that are placed on children during book sharing involve inferencing and reasoning about the information (e.g., De Temple & Snow, 1996; Sigel & McGillicuddy-Delisi, 1984; Sorsby & Martlew, 1991; van Kleeck et al., 1997). Engaging children in more abstract reasoning about the content of books is believed to help them deal in more sophisticated ways with the information presented in books. For instance, inferencing and reasoning are skills that will be particularly helpful later on when the school curriculum shifts from "learning to read" to "reading to learn," at around the third or fourth grade (e.g., Heath, 1982, 1983).

Many parents in print-rich homes begin to socialize their children from a very young age—even before the children themselves can talk—into cultural practices that require taking meaning from texts (e.g., van Kleeck, Alexander, Vigil, & Templeton, 1996). Children are led into thinking about how and why events take place in stories, to relate the events in books to experiences in their own lives, and to make judgments about events occurring in books. In a sense then, many preschoolers from print-rich homes learn to derive from books meaning that goes beyond the actual information presented in the text itself. This all occurs regularly before children have even begun the process of learning to read independently.

Given this background, we will first discuss the levels of abstraction present in book-sharing conversations with children with language delays and then describe the strategies that parents use to engage these children in conversations at higher levels of abstraction. Results of this growing body of research suggest that parents do not engage children with language delays in book sharing conversations with higher level, more abstract language as frequently as parents of children with typically developing language.

Language Delay and Levels of Abstraction

Armstrong and Pruett (2000) compared the levels of abstraction found in caregivers' input during their book sharing with 10 children: five with language delays and five with typically developing language. All children were between the ages of 3 years, 6 months and 4 years, 1 month. The researchers then transcribed and coded the same four levels of abstraction that van Kleeck and colleagues (1997) had used in a study with typically developing children (see van Kleeck, this volume, pp. 273–274). Results showed that the caregivers of children with language delays focused more than 50% of their utterances on the lowest level of abstraction (primarily labeling), while caregivers of typically developing children focused only 15% of their total utterances on this lowest level. In addition, caregivers of children with language delays used fewer utterances at the highest level of abstraction (4% of total utterances) than did the caregivers of typically developing children (16% of total utterances).

The tendency of adults to limit their input to lower levels of abstraction may be an accommodation to the lower levels of vocabulary typical of children with language delays (e.g., Rice & Bode, 1993; Watkins, Rice, & Molz, 1993). Ezell and Justice (1998) illustrated this possibility in a study that indicated a relationship between children's expressive vocabulary and the parents' rate of questions about print or pictures. They studied the frequency of such parental questions during shared book readings with twelve 3- to 5-year-old children with language delays. Parents of children with weaker expressive vocabulary skills asked more questions about pictures than parents of children with stronger skills. Ezell and Justice suggested that parents of children with delayed language primarily used book sharing conversations to stimulate and teach vocabulary.

This notion is further supported by the results of a study by Evans and Wodar (1997), who found that parents of preschool children with specific language impairments knew more about their children's vocabulary development and were better able to predict their children's receptive vocabulary scores than were two other groups of parents—parents of typically developing children of the same age and parents of younger typically developing children who were at the same language-development age. Thus, it seems reasonable to conclude that parents of children with language delays seem to know that their children need additional practice labeling the vocabulary in books.

Vander Woude (1998) also found proportionally high levels of labeling in four case studies, as described in the previous section. An analysis of both the mothers' and the children's utterances showed that the two 4-year-old children and their mothers spent a greater percentage of their time at lower levels of abstraction (83% of total text-related utterances) than the two 6- to 7-year-old children and their mothers (55% of total text-related utterances), across four different book reading sessions. When using language at lower levels of abstraction, all four dyads most frequently labeled items in the books, especially when reading familiar expository books.

Given the nature of expository books, it is not surprising that these books would elicit frequent labeling. Expository books often focus on presenting vocabulary related to a single concept (Pappas, 1993). For instance, they may describe parts of castles, descriptions of different animals, or characteristics of dinosaurs. What is remarkable, however, is the amount of time that parents and children with delayed language were found to spend on labeling when reading highly familiar books. Among typically developing children, frequent labeling is characteristic of book sharing at a much younger age, around 2 years old. Furthermore, children with typically developing language and their parents label items less frequently when reading familiar books, either expository or narrative (Goodsitt et al., 1988). These parents, like those in the study by Ezell and Justice (1998), seemed to use book reading as a vehicle for teaching vocabulary, rather than for having the child rehearse vocabulary that was already known.

Parents of children with language delays also seem to focus on lower levels of abstraction for a longer period of time, in spite of their children's linguistic gains. Vander Woude and Koole (2000) returned 1 year later to the same four families described in Vander Woude's 1998 study. They video-recorded the mothers reading two familiar and two unfamiliar books to their children with language delays. All four mothers and their children used approximately the same proportions of lower and higher levels of abstraction a year later across all four books, even though the children displayed increased receptive and/or expressive language skills in their standardized test results. This result was surprising, since a longitudinal study by van Kleeck et al. (1998) showed a clear increase in parents' use of higher levels of abstraction as typically developing children grew from 2 to 3 and then 4 years of age. It might be, however, that such a developmental progression would be seen in mothers and children with language delays as well, if more dyads were studied.

Sigel and colleagues also found frequent use of lower levels of abstraction in their study, described in the previous section (see Pellegrini et al., 1985, and Sigel & McGillicuddy-Delisi, 1984). They compared parental interactions during shared book reading with two groups of children: 60 with communication disabilities and 60 without such disabilities. In addition to coding the frequency of participation, they also coded what they identified as *parental distancing strategies*. They coded three levels of abstraction: (a) low-level strategies such as labeling, observing, describing, and demonstrating; (b) intermediate-level strategies, such as sequencing, reproducing, and describing similarities and differences; and (c) high-level strategies, such as evaluating, inferring cause and effect, and resolving conflicts. Even though parents of children with communication disabilities used the same amount of intermediate- and higher-level strategies as the parents of children without communication disabilities, they still used significantly more low-level strategies than their counterparts.

A related study by DeTemple (2001) of conversations between 74 typically developing children and their mothers during home book reading revealed an association between a higher percentage of mothers' immediate talk—talk about events present in the child's environment—and children's lower scores on measures of early literacy, including story comprehension, receptive vocabulary, and emergent literacy tasks. The results of the studies by Sigel and his colleagues and DeTemple support the notion that parents adjust the level of abstraction in their book sharing conversations to suit their children's linguistic competence.

A study by Marvin and Wright (1997) compared literacy socialization in the homes of preschoolers with speech-language impairment or other disabilities, and those of children without impairment. They distributed surveys to 396 families of 3- to 5-year-olds in early childhood special education programs and their peer models (i.e., peers who were typically developing). Two hundred and thirty-nine surveys were returned, including 119 from families of children with speech-language impairments, 50 from families of peer models, and 20 from families of children with disabilities other than speech and language impairments. The vast majority of respondents were mothers (91%), although some fathers and grandmothers also replied. There was no difference among these groups in the amount of reading aloud to children that was reported, with nearly half of the families in each group reporting that they read aloud on a daily basis. Of particular interest to the present discussion is the finding that families of children with speech-language impairments reported asking their children significantly fewer questions similar to, "What will happen next?" Furthermore, while this was not statistically significant due to great variability, only 32% of the families of children with speech and language impairments reported asking why something happened, compared to 48% of the families of typically developing children. These findings suggest that families of children with speech-language impairments perceive, and hence report, that they are asking fewer questions at the higher levels of demand than the families of children with typical language development.

Although not focused on book sharing interactions, the results of a study by Parnell, Amerman, and Harting (1986) support the idea that children with language delays have greater difficulty with higher levels of abstraction. This study looked at the ability of children with language delays and their typically developing peers to respond to questions. The results showed that even though children with language delays seemed to develop a hierarchy of wh-questions similar to that of their typically developing peers, they had more difficulty responding to abstract questions about events or objects beyond their immediate environment. In particular, in comparison to their typically developing peers, the children with language delays had more difficulty providing accurate responses to "when" and "why" questions when the referents were not present. They could, however, provide correct answers if the referent was present in pictured or concrete form. Even though this study did not use questions in a book sharing context, the results suggest that children with language delays have difficulty using higher level mental representation across different contexts and may have to depend on information in the immediate context to respond appropriately.

Parental Strategies for Abstract Language Use

Even though parents of preschool children with language delays seem to focus most of their input at lower levels of abstraction, they nonetheless use discourse strategies for discussing information at higher levels of abstraction. These discourse strategies take advantage of the known-information question structure. By "known information questions," we are referring to questions that ask for information already known to the questioner. As such, they are not true information-seeking questions, but rather serve a pedagogical function, such has having children rehearse or verbally display their knowledge. Before we describe these strategies, however, it is important to understand how book sharing conversations are usually structured with known-information questions.

Book sharing conversations are frequently structured in *initiation* + *response* + *evaluation* (IRE) sequences, a pedagogical discourse sequence commonly used by classroom teachers (Mehan, 1979). Parents, like teachers, tend to use known-information questions to initiate or sustain a topic, and when parents repeatedly use known-information questions, they teach their children to display their knowledge in a manner often expected in academic settings. Heath (1989) and Scollon and Scollon (1981) discuss this as the "verbal display of knowledge." Known-information or "test" questions abound in the book reading context of middle-class children from print-rich backgrounds, and help socialize them into cultural rules for displaying knowledge that will figure predominantly in the classroom settings they will later encounter.

In this section, we discuss two of the spontaneous discourse strategies that have emerged from research on book sharing with preschoolers with language delays: (a) asking questions that embed the lexical information the child needs in order to successfully respond to known-information questions; and (b) reducing the level of abstract language in successive questioning sequences. During book sharing interactions, parents appear to use these strategies spontaneously and intuitively to enhance their children's communicative success.

Use of Embedded Lexical Information. Parents of young, typically developing children adjust the types of book sharing questions they ask to accommodate their children's developing linguistic abilities. For example, a study by van Kleeck, Vander Woude, McDonald, and Vigil (in preparation) showed that when typically developing children were between 6 and 18 months of age, their mothers primarily used where-questions and yes–no questions when labeling during book sharing. For example, questions like "Where is the bear?" or "Is that a bear?" contain the name of the item ("bear") and consequently embed the lexical content within the utterance. Embedded questions or comments do not require retrieval of specific lexical items. The child merely needs to point or respond with a "yes" or "no." In contrast, when the mother points to a bear and asks a question with non-embedded information (e.g., "What is that?"), the child is first expected to process the question and then independently generate the lexical item. Later, when children are around 18 months old, mothers of typically developing children begin using many more non-embedded questions (see Table 4.1 for examples of embedded and non-embedded questions). The mothers intuitively appeared to supply less support as their children became more able to produce the desired answers.

A study by van Kleeck and Vander Woude (1999) suggested that the parents of older preschool children with delayed language frequently continued to embed lexical information in questions during book sharing conversations. The study compared two 3-year, 11-month-old children with expressive language delays with two typically developing children matched for age, gender, and nonverbal cognition. We looked at mothers' book sharing interactions in four ways: (a) maternal questions and comments with and without embedded lexical information; (b) levels of abstraction in maternal questions and comments (see van Kleeck, this volume, pp. 273–274, Table 13.1); (c) percentage of embedded utterances at lower and higher levels of abstraction; and (d) the percentage of embedded and non-embedded questions and comments that could be categorized as "problematic" or "smooth" interaction sequences. We defined as "prob-

TABLE 4.1
Embedded and Non-Embedded Utterances

Sequences With Embedded Utterances	Non-Embedded Questions		
1. Where Questions	1.	M:	What's that?
M: Where's his shadow?		C:	Moon.
C: (points)			
2. Yes–No Questions	2.	M:	What's happening in this scene?
M: Is that a dog?		C:	There's a scout and there's an Ewok. Threepio is up on the tree and here's all the other other Ewoks.
C: Mmhm.			
3. Declarative Comments	3.	M:	And what's about to happen?
M: See, the flower has a shadow.		C:	The-him control bunker is about to blow up.
C: (nods)		M:	Mhmm

lematic" those sequences in which the mother repaired her child's response, rephrased her own response, or received no response from the child where one was required. We defined as "smooth" those sequences which were not problematic. In other words, smooth sequences were characterized by children's responses that immediately satisfied parents' preconceived notions of correct answers to their questions (see Table 4.2 for examples).

The parents of the two children with delayed language used many more questions and comments with embedded lexical information (67%) than did the parents of the two children with typically developing language (35%). Furthermore, although all the parents provided input at all four levels of abstraction, the parents of the children with delayed language used proportionally more utterances at lower levels of abstraction (86%) than did the parents of the typically developing children (70%).

All of the parents embedded information in their utterances across all levels, but in differing proportions. The parents of the children with typically developing language used embedded information at higher levels (50%) more frequently than at lower levels (27%), as seen in the first three excerpts below. In contrast, the parents of the children with delayed language frequently used embedded information in their questions and comments at both lower (71%) and

TABLE 4.2
Examples of Problematic and Smooth Conversational Sequences

Problematic Sequences

---

(1) Dad (D) repeats his question after John (J) does not respond to his first question.

   D: Whose clothes are they, John?

   J: (1.0)

   D: Whose clothes?

(2) Mom (M) questions Patrick's (P) answer when reading a familiar storybook.

   M: You think the cat's gonna eat the mouse?

   P: (nods)

   M: Does it?

   P: (nods)

Smooth Sequences

---

(1) Dad (D) and Joey (J) are discussing a character in a familiar book.

   D: Do you remember her name?

   J: Treena

   D: Treena.

(2) Mom (M) and James (J) are discussing an event in a familiar book.

   M: Varoom! Leia's bike...

   J: Exploded!

   M: Exploded!

---

higher levels (77%). Examples of embedded information at lower levels of abstraction are shown in the last two of these excerpts:

1. D: He's gonna have trouble finding it, huh?
    C: (Nods head)
2. M: You think the cat's gonna eat the mouse?
    C: (Nods head)
    M: It could?
    C: (Nods)
3. M: He was the first one to be found because he wasn't a very good hider.
    C: Yeah.

4. M: You see the fish?
   C: Fish.
5. M: Do you see a shadow now?
   C: (Points)

This evidence suggests that children with delayed language may need support across both lower and higher levels of abstraction to co-construct successful conversation. Interestingly, more than 40% of the utterances with no embedded information were problematic for the parents and children with language delay, yet fewer than 10% of these utterances were problematic for the parents and children with typically developing language. In contrast, less than 16% of the utterances with embedded information were problematic for both groups. In other words, the children with delayed language were able to respond at rates similar to the children with typically developing language when the parents embedded information in their utterances, although we need to remember that they were not asked as many questions at higher levels of abstraction.

Crowe (2000) also suggested that mothers of children with language delays frequently use embedded questions to help their children manage the linguistic demands of shared book reading conversations. The conversations of five parents and their 3-year-old children with language delays who read the same storybook three times in 1 week were analyzed for different levels of abstraction. The conversations were transcribed and the mothers' questions were coded as "yes-or-no" ("Do you see him?"), "tag" (Critter's getting dressed, isn't he?"), "labeling" ("What/who is that?"), "description" ("What's happening here?") and "complex" ("Why did that happen?" or "What will happen next?"). The results varied across the five mothers. One mother simply read the text and never asked questions. The others used yes-or-no and tag questions most frequently, and labeling and descriptive questions less frequently. None of them used complex questions. Overall, the author suggested that the mothers reduced the linguistic demands on their children by using yes–no or tag questions along with nonverbal techniques such as pointing to the pictures.

In addition to reducing the amount of abstract input, the type of language delay also appears to affect parental use of embedded lexical information over time. The parents of children with expressive-receptive delays in the study by Vander Woude and Koole (2000) continued to use approximately the same proportion of embedded questions and comments for higher levels of abstraction (71% at Time 1 and 69% a year later), while the parents of children with expressive-only delays showed a substantial decline in embedded questions (81% at Time 1 and 50% a year later). This lack of change for the children with expressive-receptive delays occurred in spite of the children's gains in language abilities over the year. These results indicate that children with expressive-receptive delays may continue to have difficulty with non-embedded lexical questions at higher levels of abstraction, while the children with expressive-only delays may show less difficulty over time. Thus, parents of children with expressive and receptive delays may need to continue using embedded language to help their children successfully answer questions during shared reading dialogues.

Reducing the Level of Abstraction.   Not only do parents embed information or provide the correct answer when needed, they also seem to intuitively adjust their questions when their children are unable to respond to more abstract inquiries. Vander Woude (1998) reported that parents of children with language delays revised their initial questions with higher levels of abstract language to different questions with lower levels of abstraction that also referred to perceptually present information so that their children could respond successfully, as in the following excerpt, in which Jason and his mother are reading an unfamiliar narrative (*We're Going on a Bear Hunt* [Rosen & Oxenbury, 1989]):

1. M: Why do they have to keep going through it anyway?
2. J: [No response]
3. M: What kind of hunt are they on?
4. J: Hmm: [0.5 second pause] you say …
5. M: Looking for a …
6. M: I think it's a …
7. J: Bear.
8. M: It's a bear.
9. M: You're right.

Jason's mother used a higher level explanatory question in line 1. Jason did not respond, so she asked a less-abstract question in line 3, and then further lowered the cognitive demands in lines 5 and 6 by prompting the child to give a label. Jason answered in line 7 and his mother accepted that answer in lines 8 and 9. This excerpt exemplifies the interactional work that mothers do in order to help their children with language delays provide information, even at lower levels of abstraction.

Although more research with an increased number of participants—including both children with language delays and age-matched and language-matched typically developing children—is necessary to confirm the results, these studies suggest that parents discuss information differently with children with delayed language than they do with children with typically developing language. Given the linguistic demands of book sharing, it is possible that parents of children with language delays have learned over time to rely on these discourse strategies to co-construct a successful conversation.

Implications of Providing More Concrete Input to Children With Language Delays

As a group, these studies suggest that preschoolers with language delays are exposed to less abstract language than their age-mates during book sharing. Furthermore, although more longitudinal research is needed, it appears that parents who have children with both expressively and receptively delayed language may not increase their use of more abstract language over time, even though their children's language skills improve. In addition, it seems that parents and their 4- to 6-year-old children with language delays devote as much time to labeling or identifying pictures as do parents of typically developing 2-year-old children.

On the positive side, these results suggest that parents of older children with language delays are sensitive to their children's need for more vocabulary stimulation. They seem to realize that their children may need more practice in this area before they are ready for questions at higher levels of abstraction. On the negative side, however, these children may receive far less high-level abstract language input than their peers before they enter school.

The implication is not encouraging. As stated previously, research suggests that early socialization focused on abstract language development supports overall literacy development and academic success during the middle elementary school years. Furthermore, recall that the frequency of parental input across both lower and higher levels of linguistic abstraction has been associated with later abstract language gains among typically developing children (van Kleeck et al., 1997). Thus, although children with language delays may benefit from additional labeling practice, they may have less practice constructing more abstract information, such as the "how" and "why" of stories and their characters.

EXPLAINING THE FINDINGS: TWO THEORETICAL PERSPECTIVES

The overall finding of parental use of less abstract language when sharing books with language-delayed children may have two different explanations. One possibility, as suggested by the research on the balance of book sharing participation that was reviewed in the first section of this chapter, may be that parents of children with language delays are primarily discussing books at lower levels of abstraction in order to encourage their children, who tend to be passive and non-responsive, to participate more frequently in the book sharing interaction. In other words, parents of children with language delays seem to compensate for their children's less responsive discursive style by taking more turns themselves, reducing the level of abstraction, and providing answers to their own questions when these are necessary to sustain the conversation. From this perspective, the discourse features and amount of maternal input during book sharing, as well as the level of abstraction of that input, might all be explained by the children's relative lack of conversational participation.

Another possibility is that these parents are, by their language adjustments, showing sensitivity to their children's linguistic and (perhaps subtle) cognitive deficits. These two explanations are not necessarily mutually exclusive. Children with language delays may be less responsive to language at higher levels of abstraction because they have cognitive deficits that preclude them from effectively comprehending and using abstract language. In this sense then, their parents may be making very reasonable adjustments based on their children's abilities (or disabilities). This also means, however, that over time these children get less practice than their peers on the very skills in which they are weaker. While the adjustment may be reasonable and adaptive in some respects, it may also have the impact of further delaying the development of these children's abstract language abilities.

Let us provide further background on this possibility. *Specific language delay* is defined as a linguistic deficit in spite of typically developing nonverbal cognitive abilities. Nonetheless, there is substantial evidence that this definition may be too broad, since widely used nonverbal cognitive tests are heavily focused on visual perception of static figures, shapes, and designs at the earlier testing levels (Johnston, 1982; Kamhi, Minor, & Mauer, 1990). Included here are such classic tests as the Leiter International Performance Scale (1979), the Wechsler Intelligence Scale for Children–Revised (Psychological Corporation, 1974), The Test of Nonverbal Intelligence (Brown, Sherbenou, & Johnsen, 1982), and the Columbia Mental Maturity Scale (Burgemeister, Blum, & Lorge, 1972) as well as their more recent editions. In spite of the ability of preschoolers with language delays to display cognitive abilities within the normal range on tests such as these, the empirical evidence documents other kinds of cognitive deficits. We know, for example, that as a group these children exhibit deficits in symbolic play abilities, mental imagery, and some kinds of reasoning and problem-solving abilities (see Leonard, 1998, pp. 119–129, for a review of this research).

When children respond to more abstract language input during the preschool years, and do so even more during the school years, language is intimately related to and reflective of cognitive activity. In itself, abstract language use requires a variety of underlying cognitive skills (e.g., mental imagery, problem-solving, and reasoning). It is also possible that even if these children do not initially have subtle cognitive deficits, they may accrue them over time as a result of a language delay. As Johnston (1994) stated, "if language symbols are poorly controlled, there should be a cognitive consequence" (p. 109). And indeed, Leonard (1998) reviewed evidence that nonverbal cognitive abilities in children with language delays do decline over time, suggesting that language delay may lead to continuing cognitive consequences.

As such, we do not know why children with language delays seem to have problems with more abstract language during shared book reading. It may be due to their conversational reluctance (i.e., they do not learn well in a co-constructive sense because they do not participate enough); or it may be that their vocabulary delay keeps their parents too focused on simple levels of abstraction; or it may be a reflection of subtle cognitive deficits, in addition to their language delay.

In a sense, we are merely saying what other scholars have suggested (Bishop, 2000; Karmiloff-Smith, 1992): that most likely a combination of social and psychological factors explains the difficulties of children with delayed language. We further suggest that these factors may each play a more salient role at different points in the child's development. A model of this process of "movement" in children's learning over time, from social to psychological factors, was offered by van Kleeck (1994). As shown in her model in Fig. 13.1 (see van Kleeck, this volume, p. 287), social constructivist notions are most important for the early stages of development while psychological factors (i.e., mental representation) become more important over time.

A Vygotskian social constructivist perspective on learning and cognition, which emphasizes the importance of dialogue to the accrual of knowledge, may explain the participation balance and the content of the book sharing dialogues between parents and children with delayed language. Briefly explained, social constructivist theory emphasizes the importance of adult–child dialogue for creating a mutual understanding of language (Vygotsky, 1978). Central to this perspective is Vygotsky's concept of the "zone of proximal development," the idea that social interaction with adults allows children to learn by participating in activities just beyond their independent abilities. Over time, the interaction that best facilitates the child's thinking and language use occurs in this zone (Rogoff, 1990; Vygotsky, 1978).

Representational theory, on the other hand, claims that humans re-describe and re-present previously stored, implicit knowledge, in order to make it available for the development of conscious and reportable explicit knowledge within and across domains (see Karmiloff-Smith, 1992, for a full description of representational theory). To accomplish this, Karmiloff-Smith suggests using three recurrent phases of representation to describe how humans gain and use knowledge. In the first phase, children store mental representations from external stimuli, often sequential routines or events, as separate and entire entities, without changing their existing internal and stable representations. In the second phase, children work on re-describing and re-presenting internally stored mental representations while ignoring external stimuli, even if the external stimuli do not match internal representations. During this phase, children work on redefining the representation and making it simpler and more cognitively flexible by focusing on central features. This allows children to build theories, make analogies between like objects, and recall features automatically with greater speed. Finally, in the third phase, children adjust their stable internal representations to fit with external stimuli. The three phases are not age-related, but instead are reiterated as new knowledge is learned.

If the model in Fig. 13.1 is applied to adult–child participation in book sharing contexts, then during the first three phases of the upper portion of the model the adult controls the activity and provides considerable input within the child's zone of proximal development. The parent turns or helps turn the pages, physically directs the child's attention to objects and characters pictured in the book, and asks didactic questions that encourage language learning. Parents also model the expected behaviors for linguistically less able children (whether less able because they are younger and have less developed language, or because they have a language delay) by assuming the roles of both child and adult. Parents do this by first providing "hints," and finally by naturally answering the question themselves if the child is unable to answer.

This is the essence of *scaffolding*. When using scaffolding, parents assist their children by structuring and simplifying tasks to help their children learn (Bruner, 1983). Such scaffolding allows children to develop mental representations of the information, because in the book sharing context they are repeatedly exposed not only to particular information, but also to general ways of responding to certain types of questions and comments in an "error-free" context. The context is error-free in the sense that adults offer various kinds of supportive hints and prompts to help children respond when able, and simply fill in the appropriate response when children are unable to do so. We suggest that parents, as dialogic partners, adjust to their children's linguistic limitations by facilitating their children's involvement in book sharing conversations, as do parents of much younger children with typically developing language.

Figure 13.1 (van Kleeck, this volume, p. 287) also illustrates children's development of mental representations that enable them to anticipate and predict adults' behavior, first in specific events and then across events, which results in greater cognitive flexibility. In the last three phases of the model, parents continue to assist their children by introducing new contexts, planning and reviewing events, and helping children to self-monitor their new behavior. At the same time, children reorganize and cognitively simplify their internal representations so that they can form more abstract representations, such as categories or analogies. They are able to compare these internal representations with external observations and make corrections, if necessary. Finally, in this last phase they also learn to explain their knowledge and develop new hypotheses. The child is now in full control of the situation and can operate independently.

This model takes into account the bidirectional influences of adult and child behaviors. It exemplifies how parental input often just exceeds the level of the child's behavior. If the child does not have full and efficient mental representations of an event or linguistic behavior, then the parent provides more support. For instance, as described earlier in this chapter, De Temple (2001) reported that parents adjust the level of abstraction in their input to match the language and preliteracy skills of their children.

Studies of children with language delays consistently report a focus on lower levels of abstraction and more parental control of the book sharing situation. We suggest that children with language delays, particularly those with receptive-expressive language delays, seem to stay at lower levels of abstraction for a longer period of time than typically developing children, and thus require more adult support over time to help them reorganize and re-describe their internal mental representations for more efficient processing. These children seem to operate mainly within the early phases of the model, and as Bishop (2000) suggests, add bits of knowledge from external stimuli without cognitively reorganizing their mental representations across events.

We have discussed Vander Woude and Koole's (2000) finding that parents and their children with language delays continued to maintain the same balance of parent–child participation and focus on the same proportion of lower and higher levels of abstraction a full year later, in spite of documented increases in the children's language skills. Also, recall that parents of children with language delays used strategies such as embedding the higher level abstract language or reducing the level of abstraction in their questions to help their children succeed. These results suggest that children with language delays may develop specific and superficial knowledge of language, but continue to have immature methods for efficiently processing and applying that knowledge across different events. In other words, it seems, as Bishop (2000) suggested, that children with language delays continue to use ineffective methods for representing language.

CONCLUSION

Given the importance of abstract language input for children's subsequent literacy and academic development, we believe that future research should focus on interventions which facilitate adults' use of abstract language content, and encourage the increased participation of children with language delays.

It may be effective to train parents to use strategies such as praising, expanding, or cueing their children's responses at different levels of abstraction. However, it is clear that we need to learn much more about the different ways that children with delayed language develop early literacy before we can confidently make recommendations on how to promote their early literacy development. As Bishop (2000) stated, "We need to develop novel learning environments that go beyond the rather haphazard linguistic experiences that most children encounter. The latter kind of input might be adequate for a brain that is optimally organized for language learning, but not for the child with SLI [specific language impairment]" (p. 141). Future research should include comparative and intervention studies of larger groups of children, which determine the best developmental time to use different conversational strategies to encourage children's participation and communication, use labeling and descriptive-type questions, and teach parents and preschool teachers how to scaffold different levels of abstraction in their book sharing conversations. Overall, future research may help us find more effective ways to accelerate the language and preliteracy development of children with language delays, and help them further their academic achievement.

REFERENCES

Altwerger, A., Diehl-Faxon, J., & Dockstader-Anderson, K. (1985). Read-aloud events as meaning construction. *Language Arts, 62*, 476–484.

Aram, D., & Nation, J. (1980). Preschool language disorders and subsequent language and academic difficulties. *Journal of Communication Disorders, 13*, 229–241.

Aram, D., Ekelman, B., & Nation, J. (1984). Preschoolers with language disorders: Ten years later. *Journal of Speech and Hearing Research, 27*, 232–244.

Armstrong, M., & Pruett, A. (2000, November). *Shared reading: A comparison of children with language impairment and normal language abilities*. Paper presented at the convention of the American Speech-Language-Hearing Association, Washington, DC.

Bishop, D. V. M. (2000). How does the brain learn language? Insights from the study of children with and without language impairment. *Developmental Medicine and Child Neurology, 42,* 133–142.

Bishop, D. V. M., & Adams, C. (1990). A prospective study of the relationship between specific language impairment, phonological disorders, and reading retardation. *Journal of Child Psychology and Psychiatry, 21,* 1027–1050.

Bishop, D. V. M., Chan, J., Adams, C., Hartley, J., & Weir, F. (2000). Conversational responsiveness in specific language impairment: Evidence of disproportionate pragmatic difficulties in a subset of children. *Development and Psychopathology, 12,* 177–199.

Blank, M. (1982). Language and school failure: Some speculations about the relationship between oral and written language. In L. Feagans & D. Farran (Eds.), *The language of children reared in poverty* (pp. 75–93). New York: Academic Press.

Blank, M., Rose, S. A., & Berlin, L. J. (1978). *The language of learning: The preschool years.* New York: Grune & Stratton.

Bloome, D. (1983). Reading as a social process. *Advances in Reading and Language Research, 2,* 165–195.

Boudreau, D., & Hedberg, N. (1999). A comparison of early literacy skills in children with specific language impairment and their typically developing peers. *American Journal of Speech-Language Pathology, 8,* 249–260.

Brinton, B., Fujiki, M., & Sonnenberg, E. A. (1988). Responses to requests for clarification by linguistically normal and language-impaired children in conversation. *Journal of Speech and Hearing Disorders, 53*(4), 383–391.

Brown, L., Sherbenou, R., & Johnsen, S. (1982). *The Test of Nonverbal Intelligence.* Austin, TX: Pro-ed.

Bruner, J. (1983). *Child's talk.* New York: W. W. Norton.

Burgemeister, B., Blum, H., & Lorge, I. (1972). *The Columbia Mental Maturity Scale.* New York: Psychological Corporation.

Bus, A., & van IJzendoorn, M. (1988). Mother–child interactions, attachment, and emergent literacy: A cross-sectional study. *Child Development, 59,* 1262–1272.

Bus, A. G., van IJzendoorn, M. H., & Pellegrini, A. D. (1995). Joint book reading makes for success in learning to read: A meta-analysis on intergenerational transmission of literacy. *Review of Educational Research, 65,* 1–21.

Catts, H. (1991). Early identification of dyslexia: Evidence from a follow-up study of speech-language impaired children. *Annals of Dyslexia, 41,* 163–177.

Craig, H. K., & Evans, J. L. (1993). Pragmatics and SLI: Within-group variations in discourse behaviors. *Journal of Speech and Hearing Research, 36*(4), 777–789.

Craig, H. K., & Washington, J. A. (1993). Access behaviors of children with specific language impairment. *Journal of Speech and Hearing Research, 36*(2), 322–337.

Crain-Thoreson, C., & Dale, P. S. (1999). Enhancing linguistic performance: Parents and teachers as book reading partners for children with language delays. *Topics in Early Childhood Special Education, 19*(1), 28–39.

Crais, E. (1988, November). *Language/learning disabled children's storytelling compared with same-age and younger peers.* Paper presented at the convention of the American Speech-Language-Hearing Association, Boston, MA.

Cross, T. G. (1984). Habilitating the language-impaired child: Ideas from studies of parent–child interaction. *Topics in Language Disorders, 6,* 1–14.

Cross, T., Nienhuys, T., & Kirkman, M. (1985). Parent–child interaction with receptively disabled children: Some determinants of maternal speech style. In K. Nelson (Ed.), *Children's language* (Vol. 5, pp. 247–290). Mahwah, NJ: Lawrence Erlbaum Associates.

Crowe, L. (2000). Reading behaviors of mothers and their children with language impairment during repeated storybook reading. *Journal of Communication Disorders, 33,* 503–524.

Cunningham, C., Siegel, L., van der Spuy, H., Clark, M., & Bow, S. (1985). The behavioral and linguistic interactions of specifically language-delayed and normal boys with their mothers. *Child Development, 56,* 1389–1403.

Dale, P. S., Crain-Thoreson, C., Notari-Syverson, A., & Cole, K. (1996). Parent–child book reading as an intervention technique for young children with language delays. *Topics in Early Childhood Special Education, 16*(2), 213–235.

DeLoache, J., & DeMendoza, O. (1987). Joint picturebook interactions of mothers and 1-year-old children. *British Journal of Developmental Psychology, 5,* 111–123.

Denny, J. P. (1991). Rational thought in oral culture and literate decontextualization. In D. Olson & N. Torrance (Eds.), *Literacy and orality* (pp. 52–77). Cambridge, UK: Cambridge University Press.

DeTemple, J. (1990, April). *Contributions of book reading at home to decontextualized language skills.* Paper presented at the convention of the American Education Research Association, Boston, MA.

DeTemple, J. (2001). Parents and children reading books together. In D. K. Dickinson & P. O. Tabors (Eds.), *Beginning literacy with language* (pp. 31–51). Baltimore: Brookes.

DeTemple, J., & Snow, C. (1996). Styles of parent–child book-reading as related to mothers' views of literacy and children's literacy outcomes. In J. Shimron (Ed.), *Literacy and education: Essays in honor of Dina Feitelson* (pp. 63–84). Cresskill, NJ: Hampton Press.

Dickinson, D. K., De Temple, J., Hirschler, J., & Smith, M. (1992). Book reading with preschoolers: Co-construction of text at home and at school. *Early Childhood Research Quarterly, 7,* 323–346.

Donaldson, M. (1978). *Children's minds.* New York: Norton.

Ellis, R., & Wells, C. G. (1980). Enabling factors in adult–child discourse. *First Language, 1,* 46–62.

Evans, M. A., & Schmidt, F. (1991). Repeated maternal book reading with two children: Language-normal and language impaired. *First Language, 11,* 269–287.

Evans, M. A., & Wodar, S. (1997). Maternal sensitivity to vocabulary development in specific language-impaired and language-normal preschoolers. *Applied Psycholinguistics, 18,* 243–256.

Ezell, H., & Justice, L. (1998). A pilot investigation of parents' questions about print and pictures to preschoolers with language delay. *Child Language Teaching and Therapy, 14*(3), 273–278.

Garvey, M., & Gordon, N. (1973). A follow-up study of children with disorders of speech. *British Journal of Disorders of Communication, 8,* 17–28.

Gillam, R., & Johnston, J. (1985). Development of print awareness in language-disordered preschoolers. *Journal of Speech and Hearing Research, 28,* 521–526.

Goodsitt, J., Raitan, J. G., & Perlmutter, M. (1988). Interaction between mothers and preschool children when reading a novel and a familiar book. *International Journal of Behavioral Development, 11*(4), 489–505.

Hargrave, A. C., & Sénéchal, M. (2000). A book reading intervention with preschool children who have limited vocabularies: The benefits of regular reading and dialogic reading. *Early Childhood Research Quarterly, 15,* 75–90.

Hart, B., & Risley, T. R., (1995). *Meaningful differences in the everyday experiences of young American children.* Baltimore: Brookes.

Heath, S. B. (1982). What no bedtime story means: Narrative skills at home and school. *Language and Society, 2,* 49–76.

Heath, S. B. (1983). *Ways with words.* Cambridge: Cambridge University Press.

Heath, S. B. (1989). The learner as cultural member. In M. Rice & R. Scheifelbusch (Eds.), *The teachability of language.* Baltimore: Brookes.

Huttenlocher, J., Haight, W., Bryk, A., Seltzer, M., & Lyons, J. (1991). Early vocabulary growth: Relation to language input and gender. *Developmental Psychology, 27,* 236–248.

Johnston, J. (1982). Interpreting the Leiter IQ: Performance profiles of young normal and language-disordered children. *Journal of Speech and Hearing Research, 25,* 291–296.

Johnston, J. (1994). Cognitive abilities of children with language impairment. In R. V. Watkins & M. Rice (Eds.), *Specific language impairments in children* (pp. 107–121). Baltimore: Brookes.

Kamhi, A., Minor, J., & Mauer, D. (1990). Content and intratest performance profiles on the Columbia and the TONI. *Journal of Speech and Hearing Research, 33,* 1108–1116.

Karmiloff-Smith, A. (1992). *Beyond modularity: A developmental perspective on cognitive science.* Cambridge, MA: MIT Press.

Korngold, B., Menyuk, P., Liebergott, J., & Chesnick, M. (1988, June). *Early oral language as predictors of reading performance in first and second grade.* Paper presented at the Symposium in Child Language Disorders, Madison, WI.

Leiter International Performance Scale. (1979). Chicago: Stoelting.

Leonard, L. B. (1998). *Specific language impairment in children.* Cambridge, MA: MIT Press.

Liles, B. (1985a). Cohesion in the narratives of normal and language disordered children. *Journal of Speech and Hearing Research, 28,* 123–133.

Liles, B. (1985b). Production and comprehension of narrative discourse in normal and language disordered children. *Journal of Communication Disorders, 18,* 409–427.

Liles, B. (1987). Episode organization and cohesive conjunctives in narratives of child with and without language disorder. *Journal of Speech and Hearing Research, 30,* 185–196.

Liles, B., & Purcell, S. (1987). Departures in the spoken narratives of normal and language disordered children. *Applied Psycholinguistics, 8,* 185–202.

MacLachlan, B., & Chapman, R. (1988). Communication breakdowns in normal and language learning-disabled children's conversation and narration. *Journal of Speech and Hearing Disorders, 53,* 2–7.

Marvin, C., & Wright, D. (1997). Literacy socialization in the homes of preschool children. *Language, Speech, and Hearing Services in Schools, 28,* 154–163.

Mason, J. (1990). *Reading stories to preliterate children: A proposed connection to reading* (Technical Report No. 510). Champaign, IL: Center for the Study of Reading, University of Illinois at Urbana-Champaign.

McNeill, J. H., & Fowler, S. A. (1999). Let's talk: Encouraging mother–child conversations during story reading. *Journal of Early Intervention, 22,* 51–69.

Mehan, H. (1979). *Learning lessons.* Cambridge, MA: Harvard University Press.

Menyuk, P., & Chesnick, M. (1997). Metalinguistic skills, oral language knowledge, and reading. *Topics in Language Disorders, 17,* 75–87.

Mogford-Bevan, K. P., & Summersall, J. (1997). Emerging literacy in children with delayed speech and language development: Assessment and intervention. *Child Language Teaching & Therapy, 13*(2), 143–159.

Murphy, C. (1978). Pointing in the context of a shared activity. *Child Development, 49,* 371–380.

Olson, D. R. (1989). Literate thought. In C. Leong & B. Randhawa (Eds.), *Understanding literacy and cognition: Theory, research and application* (pp. 3–15). New York: Plenum.

Padget, S. Y. (1988). Speech-and-language-impaired three and four year olds: A five year follow-up study. In R. L. Masland & M. W. Masland (Eds.), *Preschool prevention of reading failure* (pp. 52–77). Timonium, MD: York Press.

Pappas, C. C. (1993). Is narrative "primary"? Some insights from kindergarteners' pretend readings of stories and information books. *Journal of Reading Behavior, 25,* 97–130.

Parnell, M. M., Amerman, J. D., & Harting, R. D. (1986). Responses of language-disordered children to wh-questions. *Language, Speech, and Hearing Services in Schools, 17,* 95–106.

Pellegrini, A. D., Brody, G. H., & Sigel, I. E. (1985). Parents' teaching strategies with their children: The effects of parental and child status variables. *Journal of Psycholinguistic Research, 14*(6), 509–521.

Pellegrini, A. D., Perlmutter, J. C., Galda, L., & Brody, G. H. (1990). Joint reading between Black Head Start children and their mothers. *Child Development, 61,* 51–67.

Psychological Corporation. (1974). *Wechsler Intelligence Scale for Children–Revised.* New York: Author.

Ratner, N. B., Parker, B., & Gardner, P. (1993). Joint book reading as a language scaffolding activity for communicatively impaired children. *Seminars in Speech and Language, 14*(4), 296–313.

Rice, M., & Bode, J. (1993). GAPS in the lexicon of children with specific language impairment. *First Language, 13,* 113–131.

Rissman, M., Curtiss, S., & Tallal, P. (1990). School placement outcomes of young language impaired children. *Journal of Speech Language Pathology and Audiology, 14,* 49–58.

Rogoff, B. (1990). *Apprenticeship in thinking: Cognitive development in social context.* New York: Oxford University Press.

Rosen, M., & Oxenbury, H. (1989). *We're going on a bear hunt.* New York: Simon & Schuster.

Rosinki-McClendon, M., & Newhoff, M. (1987). Conversational responsiveness and assertiveness in language-impaired children. *Language, Speech, and Hearing Services in Schools, 18,* 53–62.

Scarborough, H. S., & Dobrich, W. (1990). Development of children with early language delay. *Journal of Speech and Hearing Research, 33,* 70–83.

Scarborough, H. S., & Dobrich, W. (1994). On the efficacy of reading to preschoolers. *Developmental Review, 14,* 245–302.

Schuele, C. M., & van Kleeck, A. (1987). Precursors to literacy: Assessment & intervention. *Topics in Language Disorders, 7*(2), 32–44.

Scollon, R., & Scollon, S. B. (1981). Athabaskan–English interethnic communication. In R. Scollon & S. B. Scollon (Eds.), *Narrative, literacy, and face in interethnic communication* (pp. 259–290). Norwood, NJ: Ablex.

Siegel, L., Cunningham, C., & van der Spuy, H. (1979, April). *Interactions of language delayed and normal preschool children with their mothers.* Paper presented at the meetings of the Society for Research in Child Development, San Francisco, CA.

Sigel, I. E., & McGillicuddy-Delisi, A. V. (1984). Parents as teachers of their children: A distancing behavior model. In A. Pelligrini & T. Yawkey (Eds.), *The development of oral and written language in social contexts* (pp.71–92). Norwood, NJ: Ablex.

Snow, C. E. (1983). Literacy and language: Relationships during the preschool years. *Harvard Educational Review, 53*(2), 165–189.

Snow, C. E. (1991). The theoretical basis for relationships between language and literacy development. *Journal of Research in Childhood Education, 6,* 5–10.

Snow, C. E., & Goldfield, B. A. (1981). Building stories: The emergence of information structures from conversation. In D. Tannen (Ed.), *Analyzing discourse: Text and talk* (pp. 127–141). Washington, DC: Georgetown University Press.

Snow, C. E., & Ninio, A. (1986). The contracts of literacy: What children learn from learning to read books. In W. H. Teale & E. Sulzby (Eds.), *Emergent literacy: Writing and reading* (pp. 116–137). Norwood, NJ: Ablex.

Snow, C. E., Scarborough, H. S., & Burns, M. S. (1999). What speech-language pathologists need to know about early reading. *Topics in Language Disorders, 20*(1), 48–58.

Sorsby, A. J., & Martlew, M. (1991). Representational demands in mothers' talk to preschool children in two contexts: Picture book reading and a modeling task. *Journal of Child Language, 18,* 373–395.

Stark, R., Bernstein, L., Condino, R., Bender, M., Tallal, P., & Catts, H. (1984). Four-year follow-up study of language impaired children. *Annals of Dyslexia, 34,* 49–68.

Strominger, A., & Bashir, B. (1977, November). *A nine year follow-up of language disordered children.* Paper presented at the meeting of the American Speech and Hearing Association, Chicago, IL.

Sulzby, E., & Kaderavek, J. (1996). Parent–child language during storybook reading and toy play contexts: Case studies of normally developing and specific language impaired (SLI) children. *The National Reading Conference Yearbook, 45,* 257–269.

Tallal, P. (1990, March). *A follow-up study of children with language disorders.* Paper presented at the New York Orton Dyslexia Society, New York, NY.

Terrell, B. Y. (1994). Emergent literacy: In the beginning there was reading and writing. In D. N. Ripich & N. A. Creaghead (Eds.), *School discourse problems* (2nd ed., pp. 9–28). San Diego: Singular.

Vander Woude, J. (1998). *Co-construction of discourse between parents and their young children with specific language impairment during shared book reading events.* Unpublished doctoral dissertation, Wayne State University, Detroit, MI.

Vander Woude, J., & Koole, H. (2000, November). *"Why they do thats?" Abstract language in shared book reading.* Paper presented at the meeting of the American Speech-Language-Hearing Association, Washington, DC.

van Kleeck, A. (1994). Metalinguistic development. In G. Wallach & K. Butler (Eds.), *Language learning disabilities in school-age children and adolescents* (pp. 53–98). New York: Merrill.

van Kleeck, A. (1995). Emphasizing form and meaning separately in prereading and early reading instruction. *Topics in Language Disorders, 16*(1), 27–49.

van Kleeck, A., Alexander, E., Vigil, A., & Templeton, K. (1996). Modeling thinking for infants: Middle-class mothers' presentation of information structures during book-sharing. *Journal of Research in Childhood Education, 10*(2), 101–113.

van Kleeck, A., Gillam, R. B., Hamilton, L., & McGrath, C. (1997). The relationship between middle-class parents' book-sharing discussion and their preschoolers' abstract language development. *Journal of Speech Language Hearing Research, 40*(6), 1261–1271.

van Kleeck, A., & Vander Woude, J. (1999, November). *Conversations between parents and children with delayed language during book-sharing.* Paper presented at the meeting of the American Speech-Language-Hearing Association, San Francisco, CA.

van Kleeck, A., Vander Woude, J., McDonald, E., & Vigil, A. (in preparation). *An investigation of labeling routines: Mother–child interaction during book-sharing.* Unpublished manuscript.

van Kleeck, A., Vigil, A., & Beers, N. (1998, November). *A longitudinal study of maternal book-sharing emphasis on print from and print meaning with preschoolers.* Scientific technical presentation to the convention of the American Speech-Language-Hearing Association, San Antonio, TX.

Vygotsky, L. S. (1978). Mind in society: The development of higher psychological processes. (M. Cole, J. Scribner, E. Souberman, & V. John Steiner, Trans.).Oxford, England: Harvard University Press.

Watkins, R., Rice, M., & Molz, C. (1993). Verb use by language-impaired and normally developing children. *First Language, 37,* 133–143.

Weismer, S. E. (1985). Constructive comprehension abilities exhibited by language-disordered children. *Journal of Speech and Hearing Research, 28,* 175–184.

Wells, G. (1985). Preschool literacy-related activities and success in school. In D. Olson, N. Torrence, & A. Hildyard (Eds.), *Literacy, language and learning: The nature and consequences of reading and writing* (pp. 229–255). Cambridge: Cambridge University Press.

Whitehurst, G. J., Falco, F. L., Lonigan, C. J., Fischel, J. E., DeBaryshe, B., Valdez-Menchacha, M. C., & Caulfield, M. (1988). Accelerating language development through picture book reading. *Developmental Psychology, 24*(4), 552–559.

II
Storybook Reading
in the Classroom

5

A Framework for Examining Book Reading in Early Childhood Classrooms

David K. Dickinson
Lynch School of Education, Boston College

Allyssa McCabe
University of Massachusetts Lowell

Louisa Anastasopoulos
Educational Development Center, Newton, MA

How should we think about book reading in preschool classrooms? How are books being used in early childhood classrooms that serve low-income children? These are the twin questions—the ideal versus the real—that this chapter addresses. Despite the longstanding attention paid to reading, we believe that the view typical among researchers—ourselves included—has been piecemeal, either narrowly focusing on large-group reading or considering environmental aspects of book use. To help counteract this tendency, we propose a framework for examining book reading that encompasses what we see as the full range of features that one would ideally want to consider when examining book practices. Drawing on this framework, we report data suggesting that what is known about the value of books is not consistent with current practice, even in the relatively high-quality classrooms that Head Start provides for low-income children.

A QUICK TOUR OF PRIOR RESEARCH
ON BOOK READING

Book Reading in the Home

The impact of book reading in the home on children's language and literacy development has been a topic of active interest since at least the 1960s. While
there is some disagreement about the exact amount of impact (Bus, van
IJzendoorn, & Pellegrini, 1995; Scarborough & Dobrich, 1994), it is clear that
children benefit from living in homes where they are read to with some regularity. Early work established with some certainty that parent–child book reading
plays a contributive role in the development of children who read at an early age
(Clark, 1975; Durkin, 1966, 1974–1975). The specific contribution of book
reading to language development was subsequently identified by cross-sectional correlational research (Chomsky, 1972; Lonigan, Dyer, & Anthony,
1996; Raz & Bryant, 1990; Sénéchal, LeFevre, Thomas, & Daley, 1998), longitudinal research (Wells, 1985), and experimental intervention studies
(Whitehurst et al., 1987).

The Home-School Study of Language and Literacy Development, a longitudinal study of the development of language and literacy skills of children from
low-income homes, recently provided further evidence of the long-term impact
of book reading practices (DeTemple, 2001; Tabors, Snow, & Dickinson,
2001). Parental reports on children's book-related experiences (e.g., frequency
of book reading, library use, book ownership) accounted for significant variance
in regression models that controlled for demographic factors and predicted
end-of-kindergarten status. Reports of book reading and literacy support accounted for 23% of the variance in children's emergent literacy and 31% of the
variance in their receptive vocabulary. Growth models from kindergarten
through fourth grade indicate that the impact of these early experiences continued to be significant 4 years later (Roach & Snow, 2000).

The preponderance of evidence suggests that book reading influences language growth, but there is some reason to believe that phonological awareness
may also be affected. First, there is growing theoretical and empirical support for
the hypothesis that phonological awareness is spurred by language development (Goswami, 2001; Metsala, 1999). In addition, while several studies failed
to find a link between reading and growth in phonological skills (Lonigan et al.,
1996; Raz & Bryant, 1990; Sénéchal et al., 1998; Whitehurst & Lonigan,
2001), we recently found evidence that book reading had some impact on phonological awareness. Using a large sample ($n = 761$) drawn from Boston and

various North Carolina and Georgia communities, we found that parental reports of book reading helped account for significant variance in phonological awareness after we controlled for home demographics (Dickinson, Bryant, Peisner-Feinberg, Lambert, & Wolf, 1999). Our data, drawn from an entirely low-income sample, suggest that for some populations book reading may spur phonological awareness, as well as more general language growth.

While it is valuable to know that book reading in the home can have such an impact, it also is true that many families have difficulty providing children the book experiences they need. Most parents are busy; low-income parents commonly have limited access to appropriate books, and some have limited literacy skills themselves. Given these constraints, it is important that preschools do as much as possible to provide all children with varied and engaging opportunities to hear and discuss books.

Book Reading in Classrooms

Research also has been conducted on book reading in classrooms, with the bulk of this work focusing on the reading event itself. Detailed study of book reading conversations has demonstrated the complexity of the discourse that teachers can construct as they discuss books with children (Cochran-Smith, 1984, 1990). Studies of naturally occurring book reading in preschool classrooms have demonstrated that teachers spontaneously adopt different reading styles (Dickinson, 2001a; Dickinson, Hao, & He, 1995; Dickinson & Keebler, 1989; Dickinson & Smith, 1994; Martinez & Teale, 1993; Teale & Martinez, 1986). These analyses reveal that teachers differ on when and to what extent they engage children in conversations as they read, in the nature of questions they ask, and in the extent to which their reading includes dramatic qualities that help hold children's attention. All of these factors have an impact on children's engagement and many may affect their learning.

A growing body of evidence suggests that the quality of children's book experiences may have important effects. A correlational study of teacher–child interaction during book reading with 4-year-old low-income children found measurable effects on children's language learning a year later (Dickinson, 2001a; Dickinson & Smith, 1994). Research carried out using special interventions in preschool programs has shown that increased access to books and improved interactions as books are read can have at least short-term beneficial effects on children's language development (Arnold & Whitehurst, 1994; Duke, 2000; Karweit, 1989, 1994; Whitehurst & Lonigan, 1998, 2001).

While the actual book reading experience is clearly important, the benefits of books may extend beyond those times when teachers are reading them to children. Children may read and re-read books on their own, for example, and children's use of books throughout the day varies with the organization of the room and the manner in which books are made available. These differences in availability have their own impact on children's development (Neuman, 1999; Neuman & Roskos, 1997; Shimron, 1994). We also know that children can benefit from books as they re-enact the stories they have heard—both dramatic play and use of a story's language support children's developing capacities to understand books (Rowes, 1998).

A FRAMEWORK FOR EXAMINING BOOK READING IN CLASSROOMS

Given the demonstrated importance of book reading and its natural place in early childhood classrooms, it is important that we have an appropriate framework to guide us as we examine book reading. Such a framework can help researchers clearly distinguish the specific aspect of book reading that they are examining, relative to the full range of classroom practices. It can also help us develop a theoretical understanding of the organization and function of preschool classrooms. Equally important, a well-supported framework could guide practitioners as they consider the place of books in their classrooms. We propose that a full examination of the place of books and book reading in preschool classrooms should include the following elements:

1. *Book area.* Issues to consider include whether or not there is a book area, the quality of the area, and the quantity and quality of books provided. Other factors include the extent to which the area is discrete and appropriate in size (a space accommodating four to six children is optimal), comfortable, neat, and inviting. Books can be judged in terms of their numbers, as well as the variety of genres, difficulty levels, and languages represented (i.e., are there books in the languages spoken by the children in the room?).

2. *Time for adult–child book reading.* Time is a critical ingredient, and consideration should be given to the frequency and duration of adult-mediated reading experiences, including one-to-one, small group, and large group readings, as well as the number of books read during these sessions.

3. *Curricular integration.* Integration refers to the nature of connection between the ongoing curriculum and the use of books, both during full group times

and throughout the day. Important issues include whether books related to the current theme are read and made available for independent use, as well as whether varied kinds of books and other print (e.g., charts with words from songs and poems) are provided throughout the classroom. A complete examination of curriculum integration must also look at the amount of time provided for children to read books on their own, and the availability of a listening center.

4. *Nature of the book reading event.* When considering the nature of the book reading event, one should examine the teacher's reading and discussion styles and the nature of children's engagement. Other issues include the timing, amount, and kind of questions asked about the book, the teacher's approach to group management, and the children's attentiveness.

5. *Connections between the home and classroom.* The impact of a classroom's book program is not restricted to the time when the children are in the classroom; the most effective teachers and programs also strive to support reading at home through parent education, lending libraries, circulation of books made by the class, and efforts to encourage better use of community libraries.

Prior research has touched on all of these elements of book reading practice in one way or another, but comprehensive examinations of the place of books in the classroom have been rare. In our own work over the past 15 years we have addressed all five of these elements at one time or another. After briefly describing the sources for our data, we report descriptive results from past and ongoing studies in order to provide an overview of the nature of book reading practices in classrooms serving low-income children. We conclude by discussing issues that should be considered by those seeking to improve the use of books and book reading in classrooms.

Data Sources

The data we are using come from four distinct studies. The Home-School Study of Language and Literacy Development (HSLLD) was a longitudinal study that examined the home and classroom language environments of low-income children and related their experiences during the preschool years to later language and literacy growth. We visited the classrooms of 3- and 4-year-old children, videotaped large-group reading times, interviewed teachers, carried out observations of the curriculum, and audiotaped teacher–child conversations. These data provided a rich description of the language experiences of 85 children (Dickinson, 2001a) from when they were 3 years old (in 49 preschool classrooms) and 4 years old (in 79 classrooms).

We also have correlational data collected as part of the New England Quality Research Center (NEQRC).[1] This project was designed to examine the impact of various aspects of classroom quality on children's language and literacy development. During the fourth year of this project we used a set of research tools that provide information about book reading practices. Using these tools we collected data in 30 classrooms.

We also have data from our ongoing evaluation of the Literacy Environment Enrichment Program (LEEP), a professional development program that is designed to help preschool teachers become more skilled at supporting children's early literacy development. LEEP is provided to programs across New England by Head Start training and technical assistance personnel. Data on classroom quality and children were collected in the late fall of 1999 and 2000 prior to the course and in the spring of 2000 and 2001 after the course was over. In some cases, classrooms were visited for a day each fall and spring. We now have evaluation data from 2 years. Our sample includes classroom observational data from a no-treatment comparison group ($n = 40$) and from teachers participating in LEEP ($n = 30$).

DESCRIBING BOOK USE IN PRESCHOOL CLASSROOMS

We draw on all of these data sources in the following portrait of book reading practices, as found in New England early childhood classrooms in the 1990s. It should be noted that the bulk of our data (i.e., all but about 25 classrooms) come from Head Start classrooms. Based on Susan Neuman's work in community childcare settings (Neuman & Celano, 2001), we suspect that what we found reflects considerably stronger use of books than she found in community childcare classrooms. While we have no systematic data from classrooms serving higher income children, our informal observations and data from primary-grade public school classrooms (Duke, 2000) suggest that these practices are likely to be somewhat more common in such settings than what we report here.

Research Tools

We have employed several different tools for collecting data. Data that we report from HSLLD come from our coding of audiotaped book reading sessions (see Dickinson, 2001a; Dickinson et al., 1995; Dickinson & Smith, 1994).

---

[1]The NEQRC included researchers from the Education Development Center, Inc., Harvard Graduate School of Education, Boston College, and the Massachusetts Society for the Prevention of Cruelty to Children.

These reading sessions were videotaped and transcribed, and the transcripts were checked by a second viewer. Transcripts were then coded for the content and function of utterances. In addition, an automated analysis of patterns of vocabulary use was done using CHILDES software (MacWhinney, 1991). Analyses of book reading styles were conducted by viewing the videotapes and coding aspects of the mode of book presentation and child engagement. When we discuss details of teacher–child interaction here, the data that we are drawing on come from the HSLLD.

In addition to the audiotaped data, we interviewed teachers, asking questions about their book reading practices (e.g., length and frequency of book reading sessions, number of books read). Any teacher-reported data of book reading frequency also come from the HSLLD data.

The NEQRC and LEEP evaluation data were collected using three tools that comprise the Early Language and Literacy Classroom Observation (ELLCO) toolkit (Smith, Dickinson, Sangeorge, & Anastasopoulos, 2002). This kit included three tools that have been designed to be used together, to supply a broad portrait of support for literacy in classrooms:

1.   The classroom observation portion of the ELLCO focuses on two distinct aspects of instruction: the Language, Literacy, and Curriculum score, and the General Classroom Environment score. The tool is designed for use by both teachers and researchers, and consists of a 45-minute classroom visit during prime literacy instruction time and a brief followup interview with the teachers. Psychometric properties were assessed in 125 classrooms. The overall alpha is .90 for the entire tool. The General Classroom Environment subscale alpha is .83, while the Language, Literacy subscale alpha is .87.

2.   The Literacy Environment Checklist examines classroom equipment and organization. This tool is used to score classrooms for the presence or absence of literacy-related spaces and materials. The overall alpha is .77 ($n = 84$) for the entire tool. The alpha for the Books subtotal is .69 ($n = 90$) and for Writing is .66 ($n = 87$), showing acceptable internal consistency for both composites.

3.   The Literacy Activity Rating Scale measure asks observers to report information about literacy activities during each day spent observing the classroom, including the number of book reading sessions, the length of these sessions, and whether books were read with individual children or small groups. It also includes the number of books available and whether time is set aside during which children are asked to look at books alone or with a friend. Cronbach's alpha is .92 for the Full Group Book Reading subtotal, showing excellent internal consistency for this composite. Cronbach's alpha for the Writing subtotal is .70, showing acceptable internal consistency.

A QUANTITATIVE PORTRAIT OF REAL CLASSROOMS

Before we begin our focus on book reading, we must point out that classrooms which follow what is commonly viewed as "developmentally appropriate practice" may in fact be shortchanging language and literacy instruction (Dickinson, 2002). Traditionally, early childhood teachers have been encouraged to focus heavily on the emotional climate, management issues, and the organization of the environment; literacy instruction, the use of books, and support for literacy in the home have been of secondary importance. These differential emphases are borne out in results that we obtained using two subscales in the ELLCO. In 133 New England classrooms we found that scores for items assessing the traditionally valued features of classrooms were far stronger than the scores for items that assessed language, literacy, and curriculum strength (Smith et al., 2002). Indeed, 41% of the classrooms were rated as having a "strong" emotional and physical environment, while only 11% were rated as being of "low quality." We see a mirror image of those results when considering a composite score that includes language, literacy, and curriculum support in the classroom and teacher support of parental efforts at home: Only 13% of the classrooms were rated "strong," whereas 44% were rated as being of "low quality." These data can be viewed as cause for hope: many teachers have learned to create classrooms that provide the type of organization and emotional support that children need. Now they also need to learn how to provide children with more intentional instruction in language and literacy.

Book Area

To a moderate degree, current practice supports literacy acquisition in terms of the design of the classroom (see Table 5.1). Data collected as part of our NEQRC study and the LEEP evaluation reveal that roughly half (56%) of the classrooms had a separate book area, which also means that half did not. Seventy-one percent of the classrooms included soft materials in their book-reading areas. Almost all classrooms offered books with a range of difficulty. A mean score of 1.73 on the Literacy Checklist item regarding the number of factual books present means that the typical classroom included two or three factual books somewhere, which is far from the ideal of including many such books. The mean score of 2.45 on the Literacy Checklist indicates that most classrooms had about 25 books available for children, which is reasonably good and reflects the fact that Head Start provides funds for the purchase of educational materials.

TABLE 5.1
Mean Scores Assigned Preschool Classrooms for the Quality of Their Book Areas

	N	Mean	SD	Minimum	Maximum (meaning)
ELLCO					
Presence of books	92	3.63	1.26	1	5
Literacy Checklist					
Separate book area	97	.56	.50	0	1
Soft materials	97	.71	.46	0	1
Range of difficulty	97	.92	.28	0	1
Factual books	97	1.73	.87	0	3 (> 5)
Number of books available	95	2.45	.74	0	3 (> 26)
Listening center	97	.35	.48	0	1

Ambiguous evidence on the place of books in classrooms comes from the ELLCO scale that examines the presence of books in the classroom. Classrooms received an average rating of 3.63, meaning that there was some evidence that books were systematically used to support children's learning and development. This finding indicates that the settings and displays of books were approached in a thoughtful, organized manner, and that there may have been a separate book area. There were also sufficient numbers of books, in good condition, with some variety in genre and topic. The content and levels of available books were appropriate for the children in these classrooms.

This same rating signals that the classrooms were not ideal. The typical classroom did not necessarily include a distinct book area. Rather, the books were often stored in a multi-purpose meeting area, providing no distinct, cozy space in which children could read books alone or in a small group. Another important shortcoming was that the typical classroom's books did not necessarily represent varied racial and cultural groups, or non-stereotypical themes and characters.

Time for Adult–Child Book Reading

When we consider the extent to which classrooms provide adequate time for book reading, a sobering picture emerges (see Table 5.2). The Literacy Activity Rating Scale asks observers who spent at least one full day in a classroom to record the following: How many sessions of book reading did you observe during

TABLE 5.2
Time for Adult–Child Book Reading Observed in Preschool Classrooms

Literacy Activities Rating	N	Mean	SD	Minimum	Maximum
Number of book-reading sessions/day	98	1.16	.42	1	3
Number of books read	96	1.26	.51	1	3
Amount reading time	96	9.56	4.17	1	25 minutes
Individual/small group book read with adult	161	.36	.48	0	1
Kids look at books alone	166	.35	.48	0	1

Note. Discrepancy in N is due to the fact that the first three variables are based only on those occasions when book reading occurred, whereas the last two are relevant to all observations.

each day that you were in the classroom? How many books were read by an adult to the children each day? How much time did the class spend reading books as a group? Were there individual or small-group book readings with an adult? Was time set aside for children to look at books alone or with a friend?

We made a total of 166 observations in 99 classrooms (in 69 cases classrooms were visited twice). In one outstanding classroom, a teacher spent 45 minutes reading to students. In another, a teacher read eight books. These unusual cases distorted the average picture, and so were dropped from further analysis. No book reading was observed at all in 66 cases. Of the 100 observations where book reading did occur, an average of 1.26 books was read per day in 1.16 sessions, and the average amount of time spent reading books was 9.56 minutes ($SD = 4.17$). Adults only read to children individually or in small groups in 36% of the observations. Only 35% of the observations found time scheduled for children to look at books by themselves.

Data collected by the HSSLD provide further indication of the limited amount of time allocated to book reading in many classrooms. In this study we visited the classrooms of children whom we were studying when they were 3 and 4 years old. When the children in the study were 3 years old we obtained information from 61 teachers about their plans for book reading, and when the children were 4 years old we collected data from 70 teachers (Dickinson, 2001a). During both years we found that roughly 45% of the teachers planned to spend 1.5% or less of their weekly class time on book reading. When we visited these classrooms (3-year-olds $n = 54$; 4-year-olds $n = 74$) we audiotaped interactions throughout the morning, excluding the times when children were outside or leaving at the end of the day. These data provided us with a record of the amount of time children spent in different activities. Each year we found that 7%–8% of the day was spent reading books in any setting—a figure roughly 5% lower than the amount of time spent in transitions between activities.

In conclusion, data from separate studies throughout New England collected over the span of a decade clearly indicate that book reading is not a vital daily ingredient in many classrooms. Group book reading often occurs only on se- lected days of the week, and is often used as a transitional activity—a means to "hold" children while another activity is being prepared—with the content of the reading being determined by the vagaries of the moment. Book reading may even be dropped from the school day if the children are too energetic or the weather is too inviting.

INTEGRATION INTO THE CURRICULUM

Our evidence on the extent to which books were integrated into the curriculum came from NEQRC and LEEP evaluation data. These data suggest that there is considerable room for improvement (see Table 5.3). Important information about the allocation of time for book use comes from the ELLCO item assessing the approach to book reading. The average score of 3.19 indicates that there was some, but not strong, evidence of an intentional approach to book reading

TABLE 5.3
Curricular Integration

	N	Mean	SD	Minimum	Maximum (meaning)
ELLCO					
Approaches to book reading	91	3.19	1.37	1	5
Literacy Checklist					
3+ books related to theme	94	.19	.40	0	1
Books in science area	97	.37	.68	0	2 (4+)
Books in dramatic play area	97	.32	.65	0	2 (4+)
Books in block area	97	.31	.64	0	2 (4+)
Books in other areas	95	.42	.77	0	2 (4+)
Evidence of full group literacy	97	1.33	1.17	0	3 (> 5)

Note. Full group literacy referred to presence of print that could be read by groups of children (e.g., big books, charts): 1 = 1–2 examples; 2 = 3–5 examples.

that coordinated book choice and related classroom activities with explicit goals for children's language and literacy development. A typical shortcoming was that teachers did not coordinate book reading experiences with ongoing curriculum themes and learning goals. Such "average rooms" also showed no evidence that a variety of books was being used throughout the day for instruction and enjoyment. The displays of books were not coordinated with ongoing classroom activities and learning goals.

Further evidence of the limited extent to which book use was linked to a theme and current curriculum comes from Literacy Checklist data, which reveal that only 19% of the classrooms had three or more books related to a current curricular theme. Another indication of limitations in the linkages between classroom activities and books was the fact that books were rarely found in varied activity areas (e.g., science, dramatic play, blocks). In roughly two thirds of all classrooms, no books were to be found in such areas at all, despite the fact that ready access would be one easy means of encouraging children to pursue literacy in the context of developmentally appropriate practice. Another way that teachers could have linked curriculum to reading would have been to use print with large groups of children. For example, classrooms could have had charts with the words from songs, group discussions, or big books. An average of only one or two examples of such text were found in each classroom. Finally, only 35% of the classrooms had listening centers.

As a whole, these data suggest that books tend to be seen as objects to be kept neatly organized in the library area and used by children who are particularly interested in reading during choice time. Such teachers treat books as setting-specific options that children can use if they are interested.

Nature of the Book Reading Event

The Home School Study provides the strongest information about the nature of the book reading event itself. We examined stylistic issues related to the animation and energy of teachers' reading, including dimensions such as variability in pitch, volume, and pacing, and facial expressiveness. As is shown in Table 5.4, the typical teacher reads in a manner that we would rate as being of moderate quality. That is, while there is evidence of some effort to employ dramatic qualities, there is also room for improvement on all dimensions of dramatic quality, particularly facial expressiveness.

Teachers might be helped to realize the importance of increasing the dramatic quality of their readings if they were made aware of the linkage between behavior management and reading style. Teacher concern for management was

TABLE 5.4
Nature of Book Reading Event (HSLLS)

	3 years old (n = 49) Mean (SD) or %	4 years old (n = 79) Mean (SD) or %
Dramatic Quality (Style):		
Pitch/tone variation	2.18 (.74)	2.41 (.66)
Climax marked	1.91 (.64)	1.93 (.79)
Facial expression	1.66 (.70)	2.00 (.75)
Character voices used	2.13 (.71)	2.14 (.71)
Content of Talk During Book Reading[a]		
Limited Cognitive Demands:		
Task Organization	35%	27%
Chiming	2%	2%
Book Focus	2%	5%
Feedback	20%	23%
Naming	18%	12%
Immediate Recall	2%	3%
Higher Cognitive Demands		
Extended recall	1%	.6%
Text-reader connect	5%	9%
Text analysis	7%	12%
Text vocabulary	1%	3%
Text prediction	3%	2%
Teacher Management Style		
Explicit	2.21 (.70)	2.12 (.83)
Implicit	1.76 (.71)	1.74 (.93)
Awareness of child attentiveness	2.55 (.56)	2.55 (.60)
Child Involvement		
General interest	2.39 (.60)	2.47 (.60)
Appropriate responses	2.15 (.71)	2.40 (.68)
Excitement	2.18 (.63)	2.26 (.69)

Note. Means on a scale of 1 to 3.
[a]Percentages reflect the percentage of all comments that were coded as being of a given type.

eminently clear, as most teachers were rated as being aware of children's attentiveness. For some teachers management issues tended to dominate the event,
in what we have called an *explicit management* style. These teachers directly
called for children's attention, demanded that children raise hands to contribute to the conversation, talked about the rules of participation, and then continued to make explicit references to these rules. Given that these data were
collected in the spring, one would assume that the rules would already have
been internalized by that time. The continued explicit attention to rules suggests that some teachers continue to focus on them to the detriment of discussion quality.

In contrast, many other teachers adopted a more implicit management style.
These teachers used children's names, looked at the children, and asked questions about the story to control the group; *implicit* managers focused on the
story, as opposed to organization of the activity. The implicit style is one that
teachers would do well to practice more frequently, because implicit management techniques were found to be related to child attentiveness (Dickinson et
al., 1995). Such techniques not only accomplish crowd control, but also further
the goals of literacy instruction, because the more children actually attend to a
book reading, the more engaged they are, and the less they act out.

Of course the ultimate goal of effective management is to provide a setting in
which the story can be experienced without interruption, and during which
thoughtful discussion can occur. In our analyses we have found that thoughtful,
analytical conversations during book reading play an important role in supporting children's literacy development. We also found that the frequency of such
conversations among 4-year-olds was related to children's vocabulary development at the end of kindergarten, even after controlling for other aspects of
classroom quality (Dickinson & Smith, 1994; Dickinson, 2001a). Unfortunately, our evidence suggests that the types of conversation that foster language
growth is not common. The vast majority of teacher talk during book reading
(79% of such talk directed at 3-year-olds, 72% of that directed at 4-year-olds) is
devoted to issues that make few cognitive demands of the children. Teachers
mostly focus on organization of the task, simple feedback, and naming activities. Relatively little of the teachers' talk, then, makes higher cognitive demands of children (17% at age 3, 26.6% at age 4). Teachers need to be made
aware of the importance of engaging in discussions that link stories to children's
experiences, analyze the meanings of words, probe characters' motivations, and
examine the reasons why one event followed another. They also need to recognize that such conversations are most effective when they involve multiple,
connected conversational turns.

Connections Between the Home and Classroom

Teachers need to take responsibility for teaching their students; paradoxically, one of the most important ways they can accomplish this is by enlisting the help of parents. Numerous aspects of our prior research (see Dickinson & Tabors, 2001) point to parents' critical role in ensuring their children's successful acquisition of literacy. One ELLCO item measures this important aspect of book use: Of 91 classrooms assessed, the mean rating on a scale from 1 (minimal evidence of home support) to 5 (strong evidence) was 2.78 ($SD = 1.39$). This rating indicates that, in most of the classrooms observed, there was only moderate evidence that teachers considered home support integral to classroom-based programs and goals. That is, interactions between home and school included *some* information about ways to support children's language, literacy, and learning. Families were provided with materials and assignments that supported children's practice of literacy skills and could be understood and used by families. However, there was no evidence of regular interaction between home and school about children's first and second language learning or literacy acquisition. There was also no evidence that teachers were building on families' social/cultural experiences to develop meaningful assignments that supported children's practice and parent's facilitation of their children's learning. Nor was there any evidence that teachers encouraged families to seek out and use community resources in ways that contributed to their child's language and literacy learning.

TOWARD A DIMENSIONAL VIEW OF CLASSROOM QUALITY

The framework presented here may help advance the broader effort to develop a theoretically grounded understanding of how early childhood classrooms support children's literacy development. While there has been considerable research into the impact of early childhood programs on children's development (e.g., Barnett, 2001; Burchinal et al., 2000), relatively little attention has been focused on language and literacy; hence we have only a limited understanding of how to conceptualize those dimensions of classroom quality that affect children's literacy development, or how to situate literacy support with respect to other aspects of the classroom. At present, classroom dimensions tend to be broadly conceptualized (e.g., teacher–child interaction, classroom environment), but more fine-grained categories certainly exist. For example, with respect to literacy, it may be useful to look at the dimensions proposed earlier, in addition to conversational dimensions (e.g., teacher use of varied vocabulary, nature of child–child interactions) and the intellectual caliber of the curriculum. Such dimensions could then be juxtaposed with other, more generally acknowledged features of effective early childhood teaching, such as the extent of program individualization and the emotional warmth of the teacher. The identification of such discrete categories would help researchers better study the impact of distinct classroom features on children, and would enable teacher educators to guide prospective and practicing teachers to improve specific aspects of their practice.

We can provide two examples. First, HSSLD results were based on the analysis of data by classroom context (e.g., book reading, meal time, large group time, free play); this situation-specificity proved to be quite important. We found that the conversations that teachers have while reading books and their use of varied vocabulary at various times of the day have beneficial effects on children's language development (Dickinson, 2001a; Dickinson & Smith, 1994). But it appears that teachers do not consistently adopt effective practices throughout the day (Dickinson, 2001b). Teachers who engaged children in analytic conversations during book reading did not necessarily engage in high-level conversations at other times of the day; nor were teachers who used a broad variety of vocabulary during book reading inclined to do so at other times of the day. These findings suggest that teachers who adopt effective practices may not be consciously aware of what they are doing; rather, they may employ situation-specific strategies. Knowing this, teacher educators could strive to raise teachers' awareness of their own practices, extending their strengths into a variety of settings.

Our second example comes from the NEQRC and LEEP evaluation data, which revealed that there is no consistent relationship between our rating of the amount of time teachers spent reading books and the extent to which they integrated books into their curriculum. Here again we see an indication that literacy-related practices in many classrooms are governed more by standing patterns of classroom behavior than by a well-thought-out philosophy of literacy instruction.

The dimensional approach to language and literacy can also be employed to examine patterns of classroom change that result from program improvement efforts. Such research may shed light on the dynamics of program improvement. For example, in our intervention work we have seen that the ease with which teachers make improvements in their classrooms seems to vary by dimension: Teachers may quickly learn to distribute books around the classroom, but seem to have a harder time changing their allocation of time for books. Indeed, the adoption of new book reading and discussion methods may be the hardest change to implement, even though it is the one that may have the greatest impact on children.

In conclusion, we can now build on a half-century of data pointing to the importance of book reading for children's literacy development. Unfortunately, despite this well-established idea, both early childhood classroom practices related to books and researchers' efforts to study these practices leave considerable room for improvement. One way to improve research and practice is for researchers and practitioners to conceptualize the many dimensions of book use in classrooms. Ideally, such a dimensional approach to book reading can be linked with other, traditionally valued aspects of early childhood teaching, thereby creating a more comprehensive understanding of the multifaceted nature of early childhood teaching.

ACKNOWLEDGMENTS

Research reported in this chapter was supported by grants from the Agency for Children and Families (90YD0094), the Office of Educational Research and Improvement (R305T990312-00), the Interagency Educational Research Initiative (REC-9979948), and the Spencer Foundation.

REFERENCES

Arnold, D. S., & Whitehurst, G. J. (1994). Accelerating language development through picture book reading: A summary of dialogic reading and its effects. In D. K. Dickinson (Ed.), *Bridges to literacy: Approaches to supporting child and family literacy* (pp. 103–128). Cambridge, MA: Blackwell.

Barnett, S. (2001). Preschool education for economically disadvantaged children: Effects on reading achievement and related outcomes. In S. Neuman & D. K. Dickinson (Eds.), *Handbook of Early Literacy Development* (pp. 421–443). New York: Guilford Press.

Burchinal, M. R., Roberts, J. E., Riggins, Jr., R., Zeisel, S. A., Neebe, E., & Bryant, D. (2000). Relating quality of center-based child care to early cognitive and language development longitudinally. *Child Development, 71,* 339–357.

Bus, A. G., van IJzendoorn, M. H., & Pellegrini, A. D. (1995). Joint book reading makes for success in learning to read: A meta-analysis on intergenerational transmission of literacy. *Review of Educational Research, 65*(1), 1–21.

Chomsky, C. (1972). Stages in language development and reading exposure. *Harvard Educational Review, 42,* 1–33.

Clark, M. M. (1975). *Young fluent readers.* Portsmouth, NH: Heinemann.

Cochran-Smith, M. (1984). *The making of a reader.* Norwood, NJ: Ablex.

De Temple, J. (2001). Parents and children reading books together. In D. K. Dickinson & P. O. Tabors (Eds.), *Beginning literacy with language: Young children learning at home and in school* (pp. 31–51). Baltimore: Brookes.

Dickinson, D. K. (2001a). Book reading in preschool classrooms: Is recommended practice common? In D. K. Dickinson & P. O. Tabors (Eds.), *Beginning literacy with language: Young children learning at home and in school* (pp. 175–203). Baltimore: Brookes.

Dickinson, D. K. (2001b). Putting the pieces together: Impact of preschool on children's language and literacy development in kindergarten. In D. K. Dickinson & P. O. Tabors (Eds.), *Beginning literacy with language: Young children learning at home and in school* (pp. 257–287). Baltimore: Brookes.

Dickinson, D. K. (2002). Shifting images of developmentally appropriate practice as seen through different lenses. *Educational Researcher, 31*(1), 26–32.

Dickinson, D. K., Bryant, D., Peisner-Feinberg, E., Lambert, R. & Wolf, A. (1999, April). *Phonemic awareness in Head Start children: Relationship to language and literacy and parenting variables.* Paper presented at the annual meeting of the Society for Research in Child Development, Albuquerque, NM.

Dickinson, D. K., Hao, W., & He, Z. (1995). Pedagogical and classroom factors related to how teachers read to three- and four-year old children. In D. J. Leu (Ed.), *NRC Yearbook* (pp. 212–221). Chicago: National Research Council.

Dickinson, D. K., & Keebler, R. (1989). Variation in preschool teachers' styles of reading books. *Discourse Processes, 12,* 353–375.

Dickinson, D. K., & Smith, M. W. (1994). Long-term effects of preschool teachers' book readings on low-income children's vocabulary and story comprehension. *Reading Research Quarterly, 29*(2), 104–122.

Dickinson, D. K., & Tabors, P. O. (Eds.). (2001). *Beginning literacy with language: Young children learning at home and in school.* Baltimore: Brookes.

Duke, N. K. (2000). Print environments and experiences offered to first-grade students in very low- and very high-SES school districts. *Reading Research Quarterly, 35*(2), 202–224.

Durkin, D. (1966). *Children who read early.* New York: Teachers College Press.

Durkin, D. (1974–1975). A six-year study of children who learned to read in school at age of four. *Reading Research Quarterly, 10,* 9–61.

Goswami, U. (2001). Early phonological development and the acquisition of literacy. In S. B. Neuman & D. K. Dickinson (Eds.), *Handbook for research on early literacy* (pp. 111–125). New York: Guilford Press.

Karweit, N. (1989). The effects of a story-reading program on the vocabulary and story comprehension skills of disadvantaged prekindergarten and kindergarten students. *Early Education and Development, 1,* 105–114.

Karweit, N. (1994). The effect of story reading on the language development of disadvantaged prekindergarten and kindergarten students. In D. K. Dickinson (Ed.), *Bridges to literacy: Approaches to supporting child and family literacy* (pp. 43–65). Cambridge, MA: Blackwell.

Lonigan, C. J., Dyer, S. M., & Anthony, J. L. (1996, April). *The influence of the home literacy environment on the development of literacy skills in children from diverse racial and economic backgrounds.* Paper presented at the annual meeting of the American Educational Research Association, New York.

MacWhinney, B. (1991). *The CHILDES Project.* Mahwah, NJ: Lawrence Erlbaum Associates.

Martinez, M., & Teale, W. (1993). Teacher storybook reading style: A comparison of six teachers. *Research in the Teaching of English, 27,* 175–199.

Metsala, J. L. (1999). Young children's phonological awareness and nonword repetition as a function of vocabulary development. *Journal of Educational Psychology, 91*(1), 3–19.

Neuman, S. B. (1999). Books make a difference: A study of access to literacy. *Reading Research Quarterly, 34*(3), 286–311.

Neuman, S. B., & Celano, D. (2001). Access to print in low-income and middle-income communities: An ecological study of four neighborhoods. *Reading Research Quarterly, 36*(1), 8–26.

Neuman, S. B., & Roskos, K. (1997). Literacy knowledge in practice: Contexts of participation for young writers and readers. *Reading Research Quarterly, 32,* 10–32.

Raz, I. S., & Bryant, P. (1990). Social background, phonological awareness and children's reading. *British Journal of Developmental Psychology, 8,* 209–225.

Roach, K., & Snow, C. E. (2000, April). *What predicts 4th grade reading comprehension?* Paper presented at the annual meeting of the American Education Research Association, New Orleans, LA.

Rowes, D. W. (1998). The literate potentials of book-related dramatic play. *Reading Research Quarterly, 33*(1), 10–35.

Scarborough, H. S., & Dobrich, W. (1994). On the efficacy of reading to preschoolers. *Developmental Review, 14,* 245–302.

Sénéchal, M., LeFevre, J., Thomas, E. M., & Daley, K. E. (1998). Differential effects of home literacy experiences on the development of oral and written language. *Reading Research Quarterly, 13,* 96–116.

Shimron, J. (1994). The making of readers: The work of Professor Dina Feitelson. In D. K. Dickinson (Ed.). *Bridges to literacy: Approaches to supporting child and family literacy* (pp. 80–99). Cambridge, MA: Blackwell.

Smith, M. W., Dickinson, D. K., Sangeorge, A., & Anastasopoulos, L. (2002). *The Early Language and Literacy Classroom Observation.* Baltimore: Brookes.

Tabors, P. O., Snow, C. E., & Dickinson, D. K. (2001). Homes and schools together: Supporting language and literacy development. In D. K. Dickinson & P. O. Tabors (Eds.), *Beginning literacy with language: Young children learning at home and in school* (pp. 313–334). Baltimore: Brookes.

Teale, W. H., & Martinez, M. (1986). Teachers' storybook reading styles: Evidence and implications. *Reading Education in Texas, 2,* 7–16.

Wells, G. (1985). *Learning, language and education.* Philadelphia: NFER-Nelson.

Whitehurst, G. J., Falco, F. L., Lonigan, C. J., Fischel, J. E., DeBaryshe, B. D., Valdez-Menchaca, M. C., & Caulfield, M. (1987). Accelerating language development through picture book reading. *Developmental Psychology, 24,* 552–559.

Whitehurst, G. J., & Lonigan, C. J. (1998). Child development and emergent literacy. *Child Development, 69,* 848–872.

Whitehurst, G. J., & Lonigan, C. J. (2001). Emergent literacy: Development from pre-readers to readers. In S. B. Neuman & D. K. Dickinson (Eds.), *Handbook for research on early literacy* (pp. 11–29). New York: Guilford Press.

6

Reading Aloud to Young Children as a Classroom Instructional Activity: Insights From Research and Practice

William H. Teale
University of Illinois at Chicago

THE PROMISE AND PRACTICE OF READING ALOUD, HISTORICALLY CONSIDERED

Early childhood educators have long been interested in the role that reading aloud to young children in K–2 classrooms plays in children's early literacy development. Research indicating a positive correlation between being read to and eventual reading achievement has been published in journals for at least 50 years. In addition, statements about the importance of primary grade teachers' reading to children appear in virtually every reading "methods" book and early childhood literacy book published in the past 20 years.

Despite this long history of interest in and work on read-alouds, as late as 1982 I felt compelled to state the following: "The belief that … reading to young children is beneficial is accepted … (but) surprisingly little research has been conducted on the subject" (Teale, 1982). In other words, at that point in time the many conversations and recommendations had resulted in very few studies on the topic.

However, a decade later, when Elizabeth Sulzby and I completed our review of emergent literacy research for the second *Handbook of Reading Research,* we stated that: "… storybook reading as an aspect of young children's literacy experience has received more attention than any other" (Sulzby & Teale, 1991, p. 730).

In a relatively brief period of time, then, reading aloud evolved into a hot topic for research. It also became a virtual cause célèbre among early childhood teachers and advocates, emerging as a key facet of family literacy programs and the central focus of many public library outreach efforts (e.g., the Carnegie Library's *Beginning to Read* program, Project BEACON [see Segel & Freidberg, 1991, or http://www.beginningwithbooks.org], or the American Library Association's Born to Read initiative [www.ala.org/alsc/born.html]). This seems to be the result of several factors. First, a number of observational/ethnographic studies had examined parent–child reading aloud in home environments during the 1980s (see, e.g., Heath, 1982; Teale, 1986; or individual case studies like those conducted by Bissex, 1982, or Taylor, 1983), and emergent literacy instructional perspectives were being incorporated into kindergarten and first-grade classrooms. Second, early childhood policy makers were touting reading aloud as an excellent, developmentally appropriate instructional practice (Bredekamp, 1986). Finally, advocates like Jim Trelease (1984) and then-First Lady Barbara Bush were putting out messages about the importance of reading to children. All of these efforts meshed well with the rising whole language movement, resulting in a surge of interest and activity that swept reading aloud into position as a much-touted and much-used educational activity.

The oft-quoted line from *Becoming a Nation of Readers* (Anderson, Hiebert, Scott, & Wilkinson, 1985)—a major literacy policy document issued by the National Academy of Education's Commission on Reading, the National Institute of Education, and the Center for the Study of Reading—served as a rallying cry for the advocates of reading aloud. The report concluded that "the single most important activity for building the knowledge required for eventual success in reading is reading aloud to children" (p. 23).

Many of us in the research, teaching, and public arenas had worked hard for a number of years to establish reading aloud as a legitimate and significant instructional activity in early childhood classrooms. By the end of the 1980s, that legitimacy had been established on a number of fronts.

Since then, a great deal of research and development activity has focused on reading aloud for instructional purposes. An examination of the chapter on emergent literacy in the third volume of the *Handbook of Reading Research,* for example, shows that parent and teacher read-alouds remain one of the main foci for early literacy research (Yaden, Rowe, & MacGillivray, 2000). Furthermore, three recent, major policy documents on early education (Bowman, Donovan, & Burns, 2000; International Reading Association/National Association for the Education of Young Children, 1998; Snow, Griffin, & Burns, 1998) all strongly recommend reading aloud as a way for parents and teachers to promote children's early literacy development. Likewise, the numerous family literacy and Even Start projects that have sprung up over the past decade all stress the importance of reading aloud as a parent–child activity. Early childhood teacher educators also place considerable emphasis on reading aloud, both in school-based professional development programs and in preservice teacher preparation. For example, my review of five early childhood methods textbooks (e.g., Morrison, 1999; Schickedanz, 1996) and 10 reading methods textbooks copyrighted between 1991 and 2001 (e.g., Graves, Juel, & Graves, 2001; Leu & Kinzer, 1999; May, 1998) found that every one of these publications, except for one of the reading methods textbooks, specifically discussed (often at length) the importance of reading aloud as an instructional activity.

Perhaps most importantly, reading aloud rates highly as an instructional activity among the frontline early childhood personnel—classroom teachers. For one thing, teachers believe in the power of reading aloud as a classroom activity. For another, many teachers read aloud to their children on a regular basis. Data from a study conducted by Hoffman, Roser, and Battle (1993), for example, showed that approximately eight of every ten K–2 classrooms had a read-aloud on the day they were observed, and that when they did so, 95% of them spent between 5 and 20 minutes on this activity. A large-scale survey of U.S. elementary reading instruction practices conducted during the mid-1990s found that primary-grade teachers spent a moderate to considerable amount of time reading aloud to children (Baumann, Hoffman, Duffy-Hester, & Ro, 1998). And Morrow, Tracey, Woo, and Pressley (1998) listed reading aloud as a key type of reading experience provided in the cases of "exemplary" first-grade literacy instruction that they studied (p. 465).

Teachers seem to understand the various facets of literacy learning that can be developed from read-alouds. For example, when speaking to audiences of preschool and primary-grade teachers across the country, I often ask what aspects of early literacy are fostered by reading aloud. Typically, the teachers readily identify all of the facets on my overhead display: a joy of reading, background knowledge, vocabulary, familiarity with text structures, concepts about print, the distinctive character of written language (i.e., its "decontextualization" [Chafe, 1982; Olson, 1977] and prosodic features), and also, to a lesser degree, phonological awareness, letter knowledge, and letter-sound and sight word knowledge. Some of their beliefs in the importance of this practice seems to stem from the fact that reading aloud to a young child or a group of young children is a very pleasant way for an adult to spend time, because of the personal contact, the wide variety of excellent children's books available, and the breadth and depth of children's responses to those books. Small wonder, then, that reading aloud is such a valued and frequent activity in early childhood classrooms.

THE REALITY OF READING ALOUD: HOW MUCH DOES IT CONTRIBUTE TO LITERACY LEARNING?

Within the past few years, however, early childhood teachers and reading educators began to see reading aloud to children in a new light. In looking back, I believe advocates of reading aloud to children may have done their job too well. Hillary Clinton continued what Barbara Bush had started; Jim Trelease's message had become so popular that he was speaking everywhere and was featured in popular media outlets like *Smithsonian* magazine, which published a piece on his ideas entitled "Ready, Set, Read—20 Minutes Each Day Is All You'll Need" (Schwartz, 1995). Even the medical community began to focus on the importance of reading aloud with the initiation of the Reach Out and Read program (Needleman, Klass, & Zuckerman, 2002), which emphasizes reading to children as part of the general effort to meet their developmental needs. Early childhood educators and advocates almost everywhere had gotten the message from numerous sources, and story time was alive and well in the preschool and primary grade classrooms of America.

But then research findings from Scarborough and Dobrich (1994) and work by Meyer and colleagues (Meyer, Wardrop, Hastings, & Linn, 1993; Meyer, Wardrop, Stahl, & Linn, 1994) began to appear. The Scarborough and Dobrich meta-analysis of 31 empirical research samples from studies conducted between 1960 and 1993 had a major impact. After looking at how much variation in reading and oral language achievement could be accounted for by a child's having been read to as a preschooler, they concluded that read-alouds accounted for only approximately 8% of the variance in children's reading ability in the primary grades.

This figure knocked a lot of early childhood educators for a loop. Only 8%? How could that be? In fact, the Scarborough and Dobrich paper was so controversial that the editors of the *Developmental Review* published it together with a collection of responses. Lonigan (1994), for example, reanalyzed the same set of studies using different weighting criteria and assumptions about pathway influence, and concluded that the actual variance accounted for was more likely 12% or 13%.

To this day, I often hear audible gasps in response to the 8% figure when I discuss Scarborough and Dobrich's work with my early childhood educator audiences. Even Lonigan's higher figure seems inconceivably low to them. In their hearts and from their experience they know that reading aloud makes a great contribution to children's development—8% or 12% is just too little, they believe.

Certainly, Scarborough and Dobrich's conclusions about the efficacy of reading aloud are open to question. As a meta-analysis, it considered only quantitative studies, while ignoring findings from a considerable number of the descriptive studies available at the time. There are also questions about methodology: Are their effect sizes overly conservative because of analytic choices such as computing medians instead of means; because their relatively small sample contained too many poorly designed studies; because the studies they looked at used nonrepresentative samples; or because …?

Scarborough and Dobrich's work on the effects of parent–child read-aloud activity by no means reveals a full picture of the effects of reading aloud. But their findings are instructive, especially when considered in conjunction with the classroom read-aloud studies of Meyer et al. (1993, 1994). Meyer and colleagues (1993) conducted naturalistic observations in the classrooms of two cohorts of kindergarten teachers (14 teachers in all) and one cohort of first-grade teachers (15 teachers) over the course of a school year. They found low to moderate *negative* correlations between the amount of time teachers read aloud to their children and the children's reading achievement. A follow-up study (1994) recorded longitudinal observations of two cohorts of students in three school districts, beginning when the children entered kindergarten and ending in sixth grade. The districts differed demographically (urban, rural, suburban; varying ethnicities, income levels, etc.), as well as in how and how much they taught reading in kindergarten. The researchers found moderate to low negative correlations (ranging from $-.69$ to $-.14$) between teacher read-aloud activities and various measures of the children's literacy achievement. The only positive correlations for reading aloud were found on a measure of listening and on a test in which children responded orally to line drawings.

In Grade 1, Meyer et al. (1994) found no relation between achievement and the amount of reading aloud (correlations ranged from .02 to .07). The researchers did examine the possibility of a curvilinear relation between the two variables: that is to say, it may have been that there was a positive correlation between reading aloud and achievement up to a certain point, beyond which there was either no relation or a negative relation. However, they found no statistically significant relation of this type.

It is interesting that findings such as Scarborough and Dobrich's and those by Meyer and colleagues have been discussed rather infrequently in both early childhood and reading education journals. This is unfortunate, because without careful consideration of such results by the early childhood community it is difficult to develop sound theories or practices regarding reading aloud as an instructional activity.

What can be made of such studies, especially in light of the seemingly contradictory results from a series of experimental studies conducted by Feitelson and colleagues (Feitelson & Goldstein, 1986; Feitelson, Goldstein, Iraqi, & Share, 1993; Rosenhouse, Feitelson, Kita, & Goldstein, 1997), all of which indicated that a read-aloud program for kindergarten or first-grade children caused a significant rise in multiple aspects of reading achievement? The Feitelson et al. (1993) study might be set aside when examining how reading aloud in L1 (English, for example) functions as an instructional activity for children whose native language is English, because this study related to a specific condition in which children who spoke Arabic listened to stories in literary Arabic (a diglossic situation). The results of the study are convincing because of the strong experimental designs, but what they convince us *of* is that reading aloud contributes significantly to the language and literacy development of children who are learning to read in a school-based language that is different from their home language. It is debatable how much the same conclusions relate to children with English language backgrounds learning to read and write English, and it may ultimately be found that this research relates more directly to bilingual or multilingual situations.

But other work by Feitelson et al. (Feitelson, 1986; Rosenhouse et al., 1997) is more directly applicable. In the 1997 study, reading aloud was once again the intervention factor, but this time first-grade, Israeli-born Hebrew speakers were read to in Hebrew. Sixteen classes were randomly assigned to one of four treatment groups (*multiple-author,* in which children listened to stories by different writers; *single-author,* in which children listened to various stories by one author; *series group,* in which children listened to a series of stories written by an author; and a *control group* that engaged in regular learning activities but no systematic reading aloud). After 6 months of the intervention, children across the combined experimental groups scored significantly higher on posttest measures of decoding, reading comprehension, and picture storytelling than children in the control group. (There were also interesting variations among the experimental groups, with reading from a series of stories showing the greatest effect on reading achievement. These findings are discussed later, in the section "What to Read.") These results prompted Rosenhouse et al. to conclude that "[daily] exposure to any kind of reading [aloud] enhances literacy" (1997, p. 178).

Bus, van IJzendoorn, and Pellegrini (1995) also felt that the results of their quantitative meta-analysis of parent–child book reading challenged Scarborough and Dobrich's findings. Bus et al's. analysis of 29 studies with a combined effect size of .59 indicated that book reading had a medium to strong effect on language growth, emergent literacy, and reading achievement. The researchers concluded that these results provided "a clear and affirmative answer to the question of whether ... storybook reading is one of the most important activities for developing the knowledge required for eventual success in reading" (p. 19), and also noted that the findings indicated that reading to children was as strong a predictor of reading achievement as phonemic awareness. The authors were more forceful than Scarborough and Dobrich in their conclusions about the uniqueness and importance of reading aloud's contribution to young children's language and literacy development.

Finally, in attempting to sort out how we should think about reading aloud's contribution to children's literacy development, it is productive to consider the robust body of qualitative studies that have examined read-alouds in the contexts of individual homes and classrooms (cf. Yaden et al., 2000, and Sulzby & Teale, 1991, as well as the more recent work by Dickinson & Tabors, 2001). These studies are numerous and wide ranging, and a review of them is not possible here. But the details and examples that emerge from the methodologically strongest of these studies clearly show the impact that reading aloud can have on individual children or classrooms of children. Cochran-Smith's (1984) study was one of the earliest examples of this type, with its rich portrait of the emerging literacy development of a classroom of preschool children. Her close, theoretically informed descriptions of read-aloud activities provided great insight into children's construction of meaning during read-alouds, as well as their comprehension strategy learning. Martinez and Teale (1990) also provided detailed portraits of the relationship between kindergartners' story comprehension and their teachers' read-aloud styles. Over the past decade, Dickinson's work has delineated specific connections between children's learning and teacher read-aloud practices (see Dickinson, 2001, for an overview).

So where does this leave us overall? The Scarborough and Dobrich (1994) and Bus et al. (1995) meta-analyses, although different in their conclusions, are nonetheless similar in many respects. They both support the hypothesis that parent–preschooler read-aloud activity is related to language and literacy growth. And they both conclude that approximately 8% of the variance in outcome measures (language growth, emergent literacy, and reading achievement for Bus et al., and reading achievement for Scarborough and Dobrich) is accounted for by read-aloud activity.

The body of research on the effects of classroom read-alouds is perhaps not as robust as that on parent–child activity. However, work like that just discussed clearly indicates that a teacher's reading to his or her preschool or primary-age students can have positive effects on the children's language, emergent and conventional literacy, and attitudes toward reading. Certainly, Rosenhouse et al.'s (1997) research provides strong experimental evidence about the power of reading aloud in the classroom setting. But it also should be noted that their study was focused specifically on first-grade children "requiring reading enhancement" (p. 172). It is difficult to determine from their report which first graders in the United States or any other developed, English-speaking country might compare to such children, but they likely would be children currently described as "at risk."

Considering this wide range of studies and their various results, I see a pattern suggesting four especially important—and interrelated—conclusions. First, reading aloud can have significant, positive effects on children's literacy development. The strength of the effect has not been definitively established and certainly depends on a number of factors, but even if it accounts for only 8% of the unique variance in reading achievement at the end of Grade 1 and Grade 2, that is still a significant figure.

The second point, however, is that reading aloud is clearly no holy grail for solving the beginning reading instruction puzzle. We do not have unequivocal evidence that reading aloud in the classroom will significantly increase reading achievement during early childhood; and reading to children certainly does not teach them everything that they need to know in order to become literate.

Some readers may be tempted at this point to conclude that reading aloud is another one of those factors that should be considered as necessary but not sufficient. I suspect that is true for the vast majority of the children we see in classrooms—read-aloud experiences have contributed directly to the knowledge and skill that enable them to become literate. But, as I argued some two decades ago (Teale, 1982), and as a few studies have shown, some children become literate with virtually no experience in being read to (see Torrey, 1969, for example), while other children actually do not like to be read to (Bus, Belsky, van IJzendoorn, & Crnik, 1997; Gallas, 1997) but still achieve satisfactorily in reading. Thus, perhaps the most productive way to conceptualize the read-aloud experience is that, although it may not be necessary, it is certainly useful for most children.

Third, the work of Meyer et al. (1994) suggests that when reading aloud takes the place of other valuable instructional experiences (e.g., instruction on word recognition, phonics, or fluency) during the primary-grade years, it can actually *inhibit* literacy growth. Reading aloud does not directly contribute to all dimensions of literacy learning, and thus it is possible for teachers to read aloud too much, thereby giving up time needed for other early literacy experiences.

Finally, the body of research on relations between experience in being read to (by parents or teachers) and subsequent reading achievement exhibits considerable cross-study variability in the strength of the association shown between the two phenomena. This, taken in conjunction with the previous three points, leads me to the research and instructional issue that I believe is most deserving of our current attention: that it is not merely the presence or frequency of reading aloud that is important, but the "what" and "how" of that practice. In other words, what counts is what *actually happens* during the activity—the kinds of books that are being read and the nature of the children's experiences with those books. We know reading aloud can be an important activity, but we need greater insight into how to get the most out of it. The remainder of this chapter is devoted to examining the issue of how preschool and primary-grade (especially K and Grade 1) classroom teachers might optimize the benefits of this significant instructional activity.

MAXIMIZING THE INSTRUCTIONAL POWER OF READ-ALOUDS

Based on listening comprehension and vocabulary development research (e.g., Dickinson & Tabors, 2001; Hart & Risley, 1995), my own classroom observations over the past decade, and insightful studies of classroom read-alouds (such as the ones detailed in this section), the following four features seem especially worth considering as we seek to understand how reading aloud can contribute most significantly to young children's literacy development:

- *How much to read aloud*. Early childhood teachers universally report not having enough time for all the instructional activities that they want to use. How much time should be devoted to reading aloud? How many books should be covered? What is one adding—and sacrificing—when choosing to read aloud?
- *What to read*. The issue of what to read to young children involves us in very important discussions of content, quality, and text type, which pervade recent work on children's literature, early reading achievement, and the social-emotional dimensions of education.
- *How to read to children*. All read-alouds are not created equal—even when the same book is being read. The ways in which teachers read aloud vary;

that variability, in turn, can influence the effect of the activity on the children listening to the book.

• *The "place" of what is read aloud in the curriculum.* It helps to view reading aloud not merely as a specific instructional activity, but as part of the larger curriculum. How does the content of read-alouds fit into the overall curriculum design? What literacy skills or strategies are being developed through read-alouds?

One overarching question that should be kept in mind is: "What is the teacher trying to accomplish?" Of the many things that reading aloud can do for children, what effect does the teacher really expect to achieve in her or his particular classroom, given the children's other learning experiences and activities? The purposes and effects of reading aloud will be different, for example, for kindergartners who come to school having been read to a great deal at home than they will be for those who haven't had this experience. Furthermore, in some schools the librarian reads aloud to children on a regular basis. What will classroom read-alouds provide that library readings don't? These and other relevant questions help clarify the goals of reading aloud. Consideration of these goals is necessary before a teacher can decide how much to read, what to read, how to read, and where reading aloud fits in a particular teaching situation. Moreover, goals like these should be taken into account as researchers attempt to understand the practice and effects of reading aloud in classroom settings. That said, let us nevertheless attempt to illuminate the four issues just posed.

How Much to Read?

There is no simple answer to the question of how much time should be devoted to reading aloud in the course of an instructional day. It would be misguided to specify a certain number of minutes as optimal, or excessive, or insufficient. Perhaps a good way to think about this issue is to consider what reading aloud adds instructionally to the day and what, if anything, one gives up as a consequence of this choice. Even so, the decision of "how much" reading aloud is appropriate is not a simple zero-sum calculation. For example, reading the book *Houses and Homes* (Morris, 1995) to a group of kindergartners could be a way of teaching a central social studies curriculum, while also working on basic concepts about print and fostering children's familiarity with informational text structures. Similarly, a read-aloud of *Jiggle, Wiggle, Prance* (Noll, 1987) to first graders could be a means of enhancing their phonemic awareness as well as focusing on the development of vocabulary related to movement.

In answering the "how much" question, it is perhaps best to start by considering all the different aspects of literacy instruction that one believes are worth time in the primary grades. Although there is no universally accepted framework for how to use time in reading/language arts instruction, teachers have found proposals such as Cunningham's Four Blocks (Cunningham & Allington, 1999), Book Club Plus (Raphael, Florio-Ruane, & George, 2001), and Shanahan's Literacy Framework (Shanahan, 2001; Tatum, 2000) useful. Once general time allocations (for word study, comprehension, and so forth) have been determined, it is possible to examine how reading aloud can be used to meet the instructional needs of the children in the classroom. If, for example, five kindergartners in a particular class need the benefits of the small group read-aloud described by Morrow and Smith (1990), but aren't getting this support in the current pattern of activities, or if too much reading aloud is crowding out second graders' work on fluency, then these are problems that need to be addressed. Careful reflection on the actual role of reading aloud in the classroom can lead to a better understanding of how much children need to be read to.

I suspect that no research study will ever yield a definitive answer to this question. Rather, the answer is dependent on factors like the children's prior literacy knowledge and experience (as well as the teacher's choice of readings, and their decision on how to fit reading aloud into the curriculum—both factors discussed in the next two subsections). But research can help us explore the effects of reading aloud in a variety of conditions.

For now, the determination of how much to read aloud will need to be based on conversations among school staff. In my work with teachers, we have found it most helpful to examine this issue in grade-level or district-wide teams. This approach allows individual teachers to benefit from collegial discussions about the amount of reading aloud that seems appropriate to the needs of their particular school's or district's children. Follow-up monitoring and teacher reflection help guarantee that the "how much" question guides classroom decision making, and that reading aloud is neither the tail that wags the reading instruction dog, nor the neglected element in the language arts curriculum.

What to Read

An in-depth understanding of the effects of classroom read-alouds on children's literacy development can only come from careful consideration of content. Surprisingly, this topic has been examined in relatively few studies to date, and has received virtually no attention as a potential variable in quantitative analyses of the relation between reading aloud and emergent literacy/reading achievement (cf. the research examined in the Scarborough & Dobrich [1994] or Bus et al. [1997] reviews). Such a situation is unfortunate because it means that the policy decisions and future research agendas that result from these analyses inevitably overlook the possibility that content should be considered in classroom instruction choices, which, in turn, directly relate to student achievement.

Studies examining teachers' choices of reading materials most typically emanate from qualitative research on reader response and similar topics. For example, studies such as Sipe (2000), which examined first- and second-grade children's construction of literary understanding of books read aloud, and Lehr (1990), which studied how young children constructed their understanding of themes in books—as well as parent diaries of children's book selections and reactions (e.g., Butler, 1975; White, 1954/1984); and longitudinal parent observational studies such as Maduram's (2000) analysis of her daughter's responses to informational books during her preschool years—all provide portraits of children's responses to the genre, style, author, and topic of a book. Occasionally, even experiments such as Rosenhouse et al.'s (1997)—which examined content by creating three conditions for different types of texts to be read aloud (stories written by different writers; various stories by one author; and a series of stories written by one author)—provide evidence that what is read aloud matters. Such work indicates that the choice of readings can have a profound influence on children's literacy learning, but, overall, this dimension of reading aloud is greatly under-researched and in need of deeper insights.

From research on children's literature and reader response, as well as my work with classroom teachers on this subject, I have found it especially useful to focus on the quality and type of readings when looking at the classroom implications of reading choice.

Book Quality. Quality is an elusive characteristic, and critics continue to argue about the quality of individual books in publications like *Book List, Horn Book,* or *School Library Journal,* and over listservs devoted to the subject (e.g., CHILD_LIT). As is wont to happen whenever critics converse, some of these debates seem to focus more on the issue of Quality with an uppercase *Q*, but years of observation do suggest that the caliber of the books that teachers choose to read aloud can affect children's learning to a considerable degree.

There are a number of ways to address this question, but the following comments of folklorist and author Julius Lester (2001), offered in response to a question about what "makes a book literature, especially a children's book," are quite insightful:

There are many answers, but two have come to mind immediately. One is the quality of language. Literature cares about language, cares about enabling the reader to experience the possibilities in language, that how something is expressed enables one to experience anew that which he or she thought they knew.... Literature is the genre that enables us to experience that words matter....

Second, implicit in literature is a vision of what it is to be human. The literature that has endured—the Greek tragedies, Shakespeare, the great Russian novelists [sic], etc.—has done so because of the moral vision those works give us of the human condition.

Lester's comments remind us of the care and craft that go into good children's books, both fiction and nonfiction. It is useful to remember that most of the books that are read to young children are picture books: In the best of these the illustrations and the text complement each other to create a work which offers far more than either the pictures or words, no matter how good, could provide by themselves.

Finally, it is useful to think of quality not strictly as an inherent characteristic of a book, but as something that is defined through interaction with readers (or in this case, listeners). That is to say, one can only know how good a book is for a group of children by observing the children's responses to it. Thus, it may appear that quality is a somewhat vaporous concept—and perhaps even a questionable feature insofar as research is concerned. But as Robert Pirsig has tried to help us understand in his writings (e.g., Pirsig, 1974, 1991), scientific research should not ignore quality just because it is hard to define in empirical terms. The quality of teachers' reading selections probably does matter; the challenge for us as researchers is to try to get a handle on the *ways* in which it matters.

Types of Books.   The other dimension of content that warrants attention in this endeavor is the type of book that is read aloud. Research on this dimension has provided important insights, but has not gone far enough. The ability to read and comprehend a variety of types of text is central to the process of becoming a proficient reader, and the path to this goal can start in early childhood.

What do we know about the role that different types of text can play with respect to the effects of reading aloud? Some. Of course, the considerable body of literature on story grammar has convincingly demonstrated that exposing children to well-formed, interesting stories helps them internalize story grammar, which, as a psychological construct, promotes reading comprehension skills (Goldman & Rakestraw, 2000). And the work of researchers like Pappas (1991, 1993) and Duke (2000) has shown the importance of giving children experience with informational text during the preschool and primary-grade years.

Pappas, in particular, has shown that 5- and 6-year-olds attend to the distinctive linguistic and structural properties of different types of text. Finally, there is the large and diverse group of studies gathered under the heading of "reader response" (see Marshall, 2000, or Galda, Ash, & Cullinan, 2000, for a review of this literature). This work has examined readers' reactions to and interpretations of different kinds of texts, while often considering the social or instructional context within which the reading (or listening) takes place.

Research on the impact of different types of text on readers has largely focused on children's responses to various narrative genres, although some work has investigated their responses to poetic and informational texts. It should be mentioned that reader response studies have typically looked more closely at older students (middle grades through high school) than at the role of picture books in the early childhood years. Among the exceptions are the aforementioned Pappas and Duke studies of informational text, as well as work conducted by McGee (1992) and Galda (1990), who found that children responded to realistic fiction differently than they did to fantasy texts.

Thus, a handful of investigations has focused on the effects of young children's exposure to this or that genre, but virtually no one has examined the effects of various combinations of genres. For example, we know little about the effects of a read-aloud repertoire that consists almost exclusively of stories, as compared to one that blends stories and informational texts. Other combinations also remain to be examined. Because of this lack of data, I often suggest a "food approach"—providing the children with a balanced diet of different text types. Extrapolating from what research we do have and my own observations, I typically recommend (a) including stories, informational books (including both concept books and more extended forms of nonfiction), and word play books (among them, poetry); (b) using a range of multicultural texts on a regular basis; and (c) reading, from time to time, what I like to call "weighty books"—books that invoke substantive issues and provoke complex conversations among children about those issues.

The role of narrative and informational texts has already been discussed. The effects on young children of reading word play/poetry books aloud have actually been studied very little. But in relation to children's "skill" development in reading, for example, virtually every program designed to teach phonemic awareness contains a list of children's books recommended for reading aloud and incorporation into instructional activities. It is also possible that a focus on words and word play during early childhood can set the foundation for an interest in words that can enhance vocabulary development throughout school (Blachowicz & Fisher, 2002).

When it comes to multicultural literature, scores of articles and books have been published over the past two decades that present well-reasoned and often eloquent cases for making such texts central to school curricula or early childhood programs. Although many rich and even compelling anecdotes can be found in these publications, they have provided relatively little systematic data on the role of multicultural literature in young children's literacy learning, or even in their cultural or social-emotional development. My endorsement for including this literature in the read-aloud repertoire is based primarily on personal classroom observations and published anecdotes, all of which lead me to believe that such a recommendation is important, helpful to children, and just. One priority for future research is to examine (through rigorous ethnographic research, complemented by large-scale quantitative studies) how multicultural literature actually affects young children's emerging literacy, as well as various dimensions of their socio-emotional and cognitive development.

Weighty books? Virtually no one has examined their role in young children's literacy development. This category includes books like *Roses Sing on New Snow* (Yee, 1992), *The Empty Pot* (Demi, 1990), or any of a number of stories by William Steig—textually and graphically complex works that offer children lots of material to examine and think about. Steig's stories typically contain complex literary structures and uncommon, very "literary" vocabulary words (see, e.g., *Sylvester and the Magic Pebble* [1989] or *Shrek!* [1993]). Yee's book opens possibilities for primary-grade children to discuss the relationship between home and immigrant cultures, gender roles in culture and society, and the nature of artistic creations. *The Empty Pot* invites young children to consider issues related to honesty, trying one's best, and even how author/illustrator Demi designed her artwork to convey the central character's emotions and dilemmas. Weighty informational books may contain language or structures that are rather difficult for young children (e.g., Mitsumasa Anno's *All in a Day* [1986], which examines differences and similarities in people, places, and time zones around the world, or Steig's work, just described); or they may contain rather simple texts that nonetheless convey challenging content, provoking discussion, analysis, comparisons, connections to real-life activities, and so forth (e.g., Pat Hutchins' *Shrinking Mouse* [1997], a book about distance perspective written for young children).

It would be accurate to say that, outside of the story genre, relatively little study has been devoted to the role of book type in the effect of reading aloud on young children's development. Intuitively, it makes sense that what is read is significant to the impact of the activity. A scattering of studies and a large collection of anecdotes support this idea. Our challenge for the future is to understand this crucial dimension of the activity much more fully.

How to Read

There is a substantial body of research on how teachers read to children. A number of studies in this area have described typical read-aloud practices, thus providing a "status snapshot" of the activity. Dickinson (2001), for example, characterizes typical read-aloud practices observed among preschool teachers. Hoffman et al. (1993) gathered observational and self-reported data from primary grade teachers on various dimensions of read-alouds, such as frequency/duration, title selection, and use of response opportunities. Beck (2000) described typical interactions in kindergarten and first-grade classrooms as part of her collection of baseline data for an intervention study. All of these studies converge to indicate that the typical read-aloud leaves much to be desired. Beck questioned the ways in which background information was drawn upon and found that most of the questions posed by teachers provoked one-word answers, which clearly did not draw children into an in-depth consideration of the text. Because of their findings, Hoffman et al. recommend the need to move from what they characterized as typical classroom read-aloud practice (the modal) to a type of interaction closer to what research has shown to be effective (the model). Dickinson's extensive observations showed that, in preschool settings,

> rather few teachers seemed to approach book use in a carefully thought out, intentional manner. In some cases, teachers adopted effective reading styles but set aside relatively little time for books; in other cases, teachers allocated considerable time for books but failed to engage children fully in the book-reading experience. (pp. 200–201)

These studies, based on the premise that the ways in which teachers read to children make a difference, clearly indicate that reading aloud does not necessarily come naturally to educators, and that early childhood teachers can benefit from guidance in how to read aloud. The need for professional development in this area has recently been recognized. Over the past decade, a considerable number of initiatives mounted across the United States (and more recently still, over the Internet) by libraries, nonprofit organizations, community colleges, and other groups have been aimed at getting child-care professionals and preschool teachers to incorporate more and higher quality book readings into their daily activities.

By the same token, most of these initiatives have not yielded data showing that their training has significantly changed provider behaviors. Even fewer have been able to demonstrate any effect on children's knowledge, behavior, or achievement. Several reasons may help explain this lack of evidence. One is that many of these projects are funded at a level that enables them to deliver services, but not to collect evaluation data. Another is that the personnel running such programs typically have considerable content knowledge, but little strength in evaluation methodology. Finally, the vast majority of these projects seem to provide what might be described as "thin" interventions, because of their limited budgets. That is to say, they provide only a few hours of training, and limited or no followup. Such efforts typically are not powerful enough to demonstrate significant effects on either teachers or children. One of the most interesting things I have noticed about these initiatives is that virtually all of the data from unsuccessful efforts go unreported in the research literature. Again, there are a number of reasons for this, but the important result is that researchers, educators, and policy makers are currently operating with quite limited data on the topic.

I have observed two types of efforts that do work: (a) in the first, the training is substantive (15 hours and up) and ongoing (sessions are spaced across a reasonable interval, allowing teachers to implement strategies and return for followup [preferably site-based] with the trainer); (b) in the second, the model strategy is formulaic, and thus more easily learned (e.g., Whitehurst et al.'s [1994] dialogic reading).

Each of these approaches has its strengths and weaknesses. The former method is labor-intensive and costly (especially with the considerable turnover in preschool early childhood education) but helps teachers develop a deep understanding of the power and practices involved in reading aloud; the latter often results in measurable changes in teacher behaviors and certain aspects of children's emerging literacy, but is restrictive in that most teachers end up conducting read-alouds in a scripted fashion, rather than developing the underlying knowledge that can enrich their overall approach.

Finally, when thinking professional development in this area, it is useful to consider the nature of teacher growth. Teale, Martinez, and Dazey (1994) describe the changes in one kindergarten teacher's book reading style that were observed across a period of 3 years. They found that the positive changes that she exhibited had developed over this extended period of time, and resulted from complex interactions between additional study activities, mentoring, deliberate reflection, and a general move toward increased professionalism.

A complementary group of studies has provided detailed descriptions of the interactions between teachers and students during read-alouds. These studies have characterized teachers' read-aloud styles; many of them examined the effects of different styles on children's learning and achievement (e.g., Dickinson & Smith, 1994; Dickinson & Keebler, 1989; Martinez & Teale, 1993;

Whitehurst et al., 1994). This body of work has been very useful for indicating strategies and modes of interaction that teachers can profitably employ when reading to children. The following four conclusions are especially pertinent:

- Discussion about the book being read aloud is important. Children's language and literacy development is affected in part by the text and the illustrations in a book, but probably even more so by discussions intertwined with the reading. What teachers and children talk about before, during, and after reading has a significant impact on any content learning that does take place, and also affects children's absorption of literacy concepts and strategies from the reading.
- Teachers read in different ways. Their reading styles vary even when reading the same books. By the same token, a particular teacher's read-aloud style is usually quite consistent across different books.
- Read-aloud style relates to student learning and development. Children's comprehension strategies, dispositions to books and reading, and "ways of taking from text" (Cochran-Smith, 1984) are developed or reinforced by the way in which a teacher reads aloud.
- No one particular read-aloud style has proven superior to others; but some strategies seem to have greater payoffs for children (Dickinson, 2001), and cognizance of the range of available styles can make teachers more reflective about the ways in which they choose to conduct a reading.

These conclusions certainly offer some guidance on how to maximize the effectiveness of reading aloud as an instructional activity. It should also be clear, however, that they do not provide research-based answers to all educators' and researchers' questions about how to read aloud. Drawing on the body of research, on work with children in classrooms, and on the collective wisdom of librarians and early childhood teachers (who have discussed this topic for decades), I typically suggest the following strategies for using read-alouds to improve engagement and more fully benefit children:

- Scaffold the book as much as necessary in order to create a beneficial listening experience for the children.
- Encourage the children to use their background knowledge in meaningful ways when approaching the book. (The term "meaningful" is of the utmost importance here. Although it has almost become cliché to suggest that teachers should have their children apply background knowledge, Beck's (2000) recent work indicates that children are frequently invited

to do so without much attention toward integrating that knowledge with book content in a way that promotes comprehension.)

- Ask questions and invite reactions that keep children engaged in the book—especially generative questions/reactions that promote a variety of responses and encourage the children to reach beyond literal comprehension.
- Read in a lively, engaging way. Creating character voices and reading expressively help maintain children's engagement.
- Encourage children to predict during the reading. With narratives, children can speculate on what may happen next or what a character will choose to do. With informational books, they can focus on what kinds of information they expect to encounter in the next section.
- Focus on important text ideas. There are a great many aspects of most books which can be discussed. But young children tend to get distracted or uninterested when read-alouds go on for a long time or seem to drift. When reading concentrates on the most important parts of a story, or the main ideas and details of informational books, children typically recall more complete versions of what was read to them. (Of course, in certain instances it may be extremely productive for children to discuss particular details that they've latched onto, even if those ideas are a bit off the wall; it is just that such an approach should not be characteristic of one's overall read-aloud style.)
- Talk about a few of the words or phrases in the book in ways that build children's vocabulary knowledge.

Our overall goal should be to create readings that are at once thought-provoking and enjoyable. It is the bringing together of the cognitive and the affective that fully involves children and leads to the greatest learning and most positive disposition to literacy—and, I suspect, to significantly enhanced reading achievement. The preceding recommendations take into account the four broad conclusions that have emerged from the body of research on how to read aloud, as well as certain details from the research on classroom interaction during read-alouds. However, it is important to keep in mind that some of these recommendations are clearly based on more complete research data than others. Some ideas still await clarification through future research. We by no means have enough insight into how to read aloud to make definitive statements. But there is a rich and ever-increasing body of work that has produced results on which policy and practice can confidently be based.

Moreover, new opportunities for investigation are constantly developing. For instance, the recent dramatic increase in the availability of audio books has opened new opportunities for children to experience read-alouds. And although audio books do not provide the surrounding discussion that is so crucial to maximize the benefit of reading aloud, they do offer some advantages. For example, a teacher may not feel comfortable reading books containing dialect. Or a preschool provider who has a low literacy level may not be able to read certain books fluently. In such cases an audio book supplemented by discussion may prove more effective than a read-aloud by the teacher.

Then, too, there are "living books" available in CD-ROM or DVD format. These materials present oral readings and opportunities for interaction with the books. Research on the effects of these products has yielded many interesting insights (see, e.g., Labbo & Kuhn, 2000) but is only in its infancy. Thus, both new technologies and new applications of existing technologies are providing fresh opportunities for introducing read-alouds into early childhood classrooms, and are inviting innovative research efforts that will help us understand how these practices affect young children and their teachers.

The "Place" of What Is Read

The question of the "place" of what is read is essentially a content issue relating to the specific books that are read aloud. It may be helpful to think about the following three dimensions of place:

- How a book fits into the unit being studied.
- Connections among the books that are being read aloud.
- Opportunities for response to or extensions of the book beyond the actual reading.

Thoughtfully relating the content of the read-aloud to the unit being studied and helping children to make connections among multiple books both enable children to enrich their understanding of the books being read and the curriculum in general. Follow-up or extension activities—artistic, dramatic, musical, or writing projects related to the book—provide opportunities to develop a deeper understanding of the work itself. I have found that in classrooms where attention is paid to encouraging these connections and enrichments, a stronger sense of a literacy community results. Children and teachers recommend books, authors, and illustrators to each other; references to books spill over into conversations on the playground, at lunch, or during dramatic play; and even home–school associations related to books increase, perhaps because the members of the community now have a common body of knowledge to discuss.

In my discussions of what to read and how to read aloud, I mentioned that the research base was not particularly robust for certain issues. Research on the place of reading aloud is perhaps even less robust. Reading to children is usually examined as an instructional activity independent of its context. Some studies, such as the one conducted by Martinez, Cheyney, and Teale (1991) have shown interesting connections among the teachers' read-alouds, their scaffolding of dramatic reenactments of books, and children's subsequent independent dramatizations of stories. Hoffman, Roser, Farest, and Labbo (1992) investigated the effects of teaching units of study in which related books (on a common theme or topic, or books by a particular author or illustrator) are read aloud and then linked by class discussions based on a "language chart," which leads children to draw connections between the books. Studies like these suggest that the scaffolding of opportunities for children to see the bigger picture and respond to a read-aloud book through art, drama or other play, or music can deepen and enrich their experiences with the book. Such opportunities can promote comprehension, help with recall, and build additional affective connections to the book, thereby promoting a positive attitude toward reading. Greater research efforts to understand the place of read-alouds within the larger scheme of the curriculum and the classroom promise to yield important insights for the day-to-day interactions between teachers and students that form the fabric of the school literacy community.

RESEARCH AND READING ALOUD

It should be clear that the research of the past decade and a half has provided tremendous insight into the practice and effects of reading aloud to young children in a classroom setting. We have learned that reading aloud can be a powerful instructional activity. We have seen that for young children, the words and illustrations of a book, combined with the conversations between children and teachers, contribute to literacy development. We have gained considerable insight into how book reading influences children's learning and affective reactions. With respect to dimensions such as what to read, or the "place" of read-alouds, however, many gaps in our understanding remain.

One thing that becomes clear in an examination of the research literature on this topic is the relative paucity of studies which carefully investigate the relationship between diversity issues and reading aloud. Some intervention studies have been conducted on children who are considered "at risk" because of socioeconomic factors or low literacy achievement. Socioeconomic status has typically been considered in reviews or meta-analyses, but this variable seems to have been employed in a rather perfunctory manner, rather than as a way to look thoughtfully at economic, cultural, or linguistic factors.

Providers and teachers come face-to-face with diversity every day, as they interact with children with various backgrounds and abilities. But the research tends to look at the effects of reading aloud on children as a generic category, rather than on children with particular individual or group characteristics. As a result, we know relatively little about how this instructional activity affects children of diverse cultural backgrounds, children of different abilities, children with significantly different amounts or types of home literacy experience, children from different linguistic backgrounds, and so forth. As indicated herein, there are many potentially fruitful areas for further research on reading aloud. An examination of factors related to diversity should be a high priority, especially because findings about the instructional practice of reading aloud have such important implications for early childhood policy and curriculum choice.

CONCLUSION

About 15 years ago, a kindergarten teacher I was working with told the following story. She was ushering her children back into the classroom after lunch. The principal came by to let the teacher know she was there to do a classroom observation as part of the annual evaluation process. "Great," said the teacher, "Please come in; I'm just getting ready to read the children a story."

"Oh," said the principal, "that's okay. I'll come back some time when you're teaching."

I winced when I first heard that story, and I still do. Reading aloud *is* a significant instructional activity in early childhood education. But we should not merely think that a read-aloud is a read-aloud is a read-aloud. The choice of how much, what, why, and how to read are all enormously important factors influencing the effect of reading aloud on children's literacy learning and their attitude toward reading.

We should never believe that the children in our early childhood classrooms will learn to read merely by being read to—no matter how high the quality of the books or how engaging the reading. There is much more to teaching children to read than simply reading to them. But reading to children *does* help them develop the knowledge, strategies, and dispositions that are fundamental aspects of becoming literate. Read-alouds can easily become filler activities, which are done automatically and to not much effect. Like anything we do in our efforts to teach children, it is not the procedures of an instructional activity that make a difference; it is the principled way in which that activity is woven into the fabric of the classroom and addressed to the learning needs of the children that makes it significant. Reading aloud is a valued, and even special, instructional activity for most teachers of young children. It deserves that status so long as we continue to be thoughtful about the whats, whys, and hows of it.

REFERENCES

Anderson, R., Hiebert, E., Scott, J., & Wilkinson, I. A. G. (1985). *Becoming a nation of readers: The report of the Commission on Reading.* Washington, DC: The National Institute of Education.

Baumann, J. F., Hoffman, J. V., Duffy-Hester, A. M., & Ro, J. M. (1998). The first r yesterday and today: U.S. elementary reading instruction practices reported by teachers and administrators. *Reading Research Quarterly, 35,* 338–377.

Beck, I. (2000, April). *Text talk: Reading aloud to young children.* Paper presented at Illinois State Board of Education Reading Days Conference, Chicago, IL.

Bissex, G. (1982). *GNYS AT WRK: A young child learns to read and write.* Cambridge, MA: Harvard University Press.

Blachowicz, C., & Fisher, P. (2002). *Teaching vocabulary in all classrooms* (2nd ed.). Upper Saddle River, NJ: Prentice-Hall.

Bowman, B., Donovan, M. S., & Burns, M. S. (2000). *Eager to learn: Educating our preschoolers.* Washington, DC: National Academy Press.

Bredekamp, S. (1986). *Developmentally appropriate practice.* Washington, DC: National Association for the Education of Young Children.

Bus, A. G., Belsky, J., van IJzendoorn, M. H., & Crnik, K. (1997). Attachment and book reading patterns: A study of mothers, fathers, and their toddlers. *Early Childhood Research Quarterly, 12,* 81–98.

Bus, A., van IJzendoorn, M., & Pellegrini, A. (1995). Joint book reading makes for success in learning to read: A meta-analysis on intergenerational transmission of literacy. *Review of Educational Research, 65,* 1–21.

Butler, D. (1975). *Cushla and her books.* Boston: Horn Book.

Chafe, W. (1982). Integration and involvement in speaking, writing, and oral literature. In D. Tannen (Ed.), *Spoken and written language: Exploring orality and literacy* (pp. 35–54). Norwood, NJ: Ablex.

Cochran-Smith, M. (1984). *The making of a reader.* Norwood, NJ: Ablex.

Cunningham, P. M., & Allington, R. L. (1999). *Classrooms that work: They can all read and write* (2nd ed.). Reading, MA: Addison Wesley Longman.

Dickinson, D. K. (2001). Book reading in preschool classrooms: Is "recommended practice" common? In D. K. Dickinson & P. O. Tabors (Eds.), *Beginning literacy with language* (pp. 175–204). Baltimore: Brookes.

Dickinson, D. K., & Keebler, R. (1989). Variations in preschool teachers' storybook reading styles. *Discourse Processes, 12,* 353–376.

Dickinson, D. K., & Smith, M. W. (1994). Long-term effects of preschool teachers' book readings on low-income children's vocabulary, story comprehension, and print skills. *Reading Research Quarterly, 29,* 105–121.

Dickinson, D. K., & Tabors, P. O. (2001). *Beginning literacy with language.* Baltimore: Brookes.

Duke, N. K. (2000). 3.6 minutes per day: The scarcity of informational texts in first grade. *Reading Research Quarterly, 35,* 202–224.

Feitelson, D., & Goldstein, Z. (1986). Effects of listening to series stories on first graders' comprehension and use of language. *Research in the Teaching of English, 20,* 339–356.

Feitelson, D., Goldstein, Z., Iraqi, J., & Share, D. (1993). Effects of listening to story reading on aspects of literacy acquisition in a diglossic situation. *Reading Research Quarterly, 28,* 70–79.

Galda, L. (1990). Evaluation as a spectator: Changes across time and genre. In J. E. Many & C. Cox (Eds.), *Reader stance and literary understanding: Exploring theories, research and literature* (pp. 237–243). Norwood, NJ: Ablex.

Galda, L., Ash, G. E., & Cullinan, B. (2000). Children's literature. In M. L. Kamil, P. B. Mosenthal, P. D. Pearson, & R. Barr (Eds.), *Handbook of reading research* (Vol. 3, pp. 361–379). Mahwah, NJ: Lawrence Erlbaum Associates.

Gallas, K. (1997). Story time as a magical act open only to the initiated: What some children don't know about power and may not find out. *Language Arts, 74,* 248–254.

Goldman, S. R., & Rakestraw, J. A., Jr. (2000). Structural aspects of constructing meaning from text. In M. L. Kamil, P. B. Mosenthal, P. D. Pearson, & R. Barr (Eds.), *Handbook of reading research* (Vol. 3, pp. 311–336). Mahwah, NJ: Lawrence Erlbaum Associates.

Graves, M. F., Juel, C., & Graves, B. B. (2001). *Teaching reading in the 21st century* (2nd ed.). Boston: Allyn & Bacon.

Hart, B., & Risley, T. R. (1995). *Meaningful differences in the everyday experience of young American children.* Baltimore: Brookes.

Heath, S. B. (1982). What no bedtime story means: Narrative skills at home and school. *Language in Society, 11,* 49–76.

Hoffman, J. V., Roser, N. L., Farest, C., & Labbo, L. D. (1992). Language charts: A record of story time talk. *Language Arts, 69,* 44–52.

Hoffman, J. V., Roser, N. L., & Battle, J. (1993). Reading aloud in classrooms: From the modal to a "model." *The Reading Teacher, 46,* 496–503.

International Reading Association and National Association for the Education of Young Children. (1998). Learning to read and write: Developmentally appropriate practices for young children (A joint position statement of the International Reading Association and National Association for the Education of Young Children). *Young Children, 53*(4), 524–546.

Labbo, L. D., & Kuhn, M. (2000). Weaving chains of affect and cognition: A young child's understanding of considerate and inconsiderate CD storybooks. *Journal of Literacy Research, 32,* 187–210.

Lehr, S. (1990). The child's developing sense of theme as a response to literature. *Reading Research Quarterly, 23,* 337–357.

Lester, J. (2001, February). Writing for children & adults & other matters. [E-mail posting on child_lit: theory and crit website; CHILD_LIT@EMAIL.RUTGERS.EDU].

Leu, D. J., & Kinzer, C. K. (1999). *Effective literacy instruction* (4th ed.). Upper Saddle River, NJ: Prentice-Hall.

Lonigan, C. J. (1994). Reading to preschoolers exposed: Is the emperor really naked? *Developmental Review, 14,* 303–323.

Maduram, I. (2000). *Living with literature: A case study of a preschooler's response to the information book genre.* Unpublished doctoral dissertation, University of Illinois at Chicago, Chicago, IL.

Marshall, J. (2000). Research on response to literature. In M. L. Kamil, P. B. Mosenthal, P. D. Pearson, & R. Barr (Eds.), *Handbook of reading research* (Vol. 3, pp. 381–402). Mahwah, NJ: Lawrence Erlbaum Associates.

Martinez, M., Cheyney, M., & Teale, W. H. (1991). Classroom context and kindergartners' dramatic story reenactments. In J. F. Christie (Ed.), *Play and early literacy development* (pp. 119–140). Albany, NY: State University of New York Press.

Martinez, M., & Teale, W. H. (1990, December). *The impact of teacher storybook reading style on kindergartners' story comprehension*. Paper presented at the 40th annual meeting of the National Reading Conference, Miami, FL.

Martinez, M., & Teale, W. H. (1993). Teacher storybook reading style: A comparison of six teachers. *Research in the Teaching of English, 27,* 175–199.

May, F. B. (1998). *Reading as communication* (5th ed.). Upper Saddle River, NJ: Prentice-Hall.

McGee, L. (1992). An exploration of meaning construction in first graders' grand conversations. In C. K. Kinzer & D. J. Leu (Eds.), *Literacy research, theory, and practice: Views from many perspectives* (Forty-first yearbook of the National Reading Conference) (pp. 177–186). Chicago: National Reading Conference.

Meyer, L. A., Wardrop, J. L., Hastings, C. N., & Linn, R. L. (1993). How entering ability and instructional settings influence kindergartners' reading performance. *Journal of Educational Research, 86,* 142–160.

Meyer, L. A., Wardrop, J. L., Stahl, S. A., & Linn, R. L. (1994). Effects of reading storybooks aloud to children. *Journal of Educational Research, 88,* 69–85.

Morrison, G. S. (1999). *Fundamentals of early childhood education* (2nd ed.). Upper Saddle River, NJ: Prentice-Hall.

Morrow, L. M., & Smith, J. K. (1990). The effects of group size on interactive storybook reading. *Reading Research Quarterly, 25,* 213–231.

Morrow, L. M., Tracey, D. H., Woo, D. G., & Pressley, M. (1998). Characteristics of exemplary first-grade literacy instruction. *The Reading Teacher, 52,* 462–479.

Olson, D. (1977). From utterance to text: The bias of language in speech and writing. *Harvard Educational Review, 47,* 251–281.

Needleman, R., Klass, P., & Zuckerman, B. (2002, January). Reach out and get your patients to read. *Contemporary Pediatrics, 19*(1), 51–58, 65, 69.

Pappas, C. C. (1991). Young children's strategies in learning the "book language" of information books. *Discourse Processes, 14,* 203–225.

Pappas, C. C. (1993). Is narrative "primary"? Some insights from kindergartners' pretend readings of stories and information books. *Journal of Reading Behavior, 25,* 97–129.

Pirsig, R. (1974). *Zen and the art of motorcycle maintenance: An inquiry into values.* New York: William Morrow.

Pirsig, R. (1991). *Lila: An inquiry into morals.* London: Corgi.

Raphael, T. E., Florio-Ruane, S., & George, M. (2001). Book Club Plus: A conceptual framework to organize literacy instruction. *Language Arts, 79,* 159–168.

Rosenhouse, J., Feitelson, D., Kita, B., & Goldstein, Z. (1997). Interactive reading aloud to Israeli first graders: Its contribution to literacy development. *Reading Research Quarterly, 32,* 168–183.

Scarborough, H. S., & Dobrich, W. (1994). On the efficacy of reading to preschoolers. *Developmental Review, 14,* 245–302.

Schickedanz, J. (1996). *Curriculum in early childhood: A resource guide for preschool and kindergarten teachers.* Boston: Allyn & Bacon.

Schwartz, D. M. (1995). Ready, set, read—20 minutes each day is all you'll need. *Smithsonian, 25,* 82–86.

Segel, E., & Friedberg, J. B. (1991). "Is today liberry day?": Community support for family literacy. *Language Arts, 68,* 654–657.

Shanahan, T. (2001). *Literacy framework for higher achievement.* Manuscript in preparation.

Sipe, L. R. (2000). The construction of literary understanding by first and second graders in oral response to picture storybook read-alouds. *Reading Research Quarterly, 35,* 252–275.

Snow, C. E., Griffin, P., & Burns, M. S. (Eds.). (1998). *Preventing reading difficulties in young children*. Washington, DC: National Academy Press.

Sulzby, E., & Teale, W. H. (1991). Emergent literacy. In R. Barr, M. L. Kamil, P. B. Mosenthal, & P. D. Pearson (Eds.), *Handbook of reading research* (Vol. 2, pp. 727–757). White Plains, NY: Longman.

Tatum, A. W. (2000). Against marginalization and criminal reading curriculum standards for African American adolescents in low-level tracks: A retrospective of Baldwin's essay. *Journal of Adolescent and Adult Literacy, 43,* 570–572.

Taylor, D. (1983). Family literacy: *Young children learning to read and write*. Portsmouth, NH: Heinemann.

Teale, W. H. (1982, October). *Reading to young children: Its significance in the process of literacy development*. Paper presented at the University of Victoria Symposium on Children's Response to a Literate Environment: Literacy Before Schooling, Victoria, British Columbia, Canada.

Teale, W. H. (1986). Home background and young children's literacy development. In W. H. Teale & E. Sulzby (Eds.), *Emergent literacy: Writing and reading* (pp. 173–206). Norwood, NJ: Ablex.

Teale, W. H., Martinez, M. J., & Dazey, J. (1994). *Teacher storybook reading style: A case study in change*. Paper presented at the 44th annual meeting of the National Reading Conference, San Diego, CA.

Torrey, J. W. (1969). Learning to read without a teacher: A case study. *Elementary English, 46,* 550–556, 658.

Trelease, J. (1984). *The read-aloud handbook*. New York: Penguin Books.

White, D. (1954/1984). *Books before five*. New York: Oxford University Press; Portsmouth, NH: Heinemann.

Whitehurst, G. L., Arnold, D. S., Epstein, J. N., Angell, A. L., Smith, M., & Fischel, J. E. (1994). A picture book reading intervention in day care and home for children from low-income families. *Developmental Psychology, 30,* 679–689.

Yaden, D. B., Rowe, D. W., & MacGillivray, L. (2000). Emergent literacy: A matter (polyphony) of perspectives. In M. L. Kamil, P. B. Mosenthal, P. D. Pearson, & R. Barr (Eds.), *Handbook of reading research* (Vol. 3, pp. 425–454). Mahwah, NJ: Lawrence Erlbaum Associates.

CHILDREN'S BOOKS

Anno, M. (1986). *All in a day*. Illus. by R. Briggs, R. Brooks, E. Carle, G. Calvi, Z. Chengliang, L. & D. Dillon, A. Hayashi, & N. Popov. New York: Philomel.

Demi. (1990). *The empty pot*. New York: Holt.

Hutchins, P. (1997). *Shrinking mouse*. New York: Greenwillow.

Morris, A. (1995). *Houses and homes*. Photos by K. Heyman. New York: Mulberry Books.

Noll, S. (1987). *Jiggle wiggle prance*. New York: Greenwillow.

Steig, W. (1989). *Sylvester and the magic pebble*. New York: Simon & Schuster.

Steig, W. (1993). *Shrek!* New York: Simon & Schuster

Yee, P. (1992). *Roses sing on new snow: A delicious tale*. Illus. by H. Chan. New York: Macmillan.

7

The Nature of Storybook Reading in the Elementary School: Current Practices

Lesley Mandel Morrow
Rebecca Brittain
Rutgers University

Barbara, the reading specialist in a fifth-grade classroom, held the book *Terrible Things* (Bunting, 1989) up high, sometimes standing, other times walking through the room. Her voice sounded out clear, but instead of cutting through the silence of the classroom, it mingled with it, so that the silence and her voice were enveloped in the world of the story. There was a busy working chatter outside in another classroom, but no one noticed, for the dark, shadowy Terrible Things were taking away birds, squirrels, frogs, and fish for absolutely no reason at all. The other animals watched worriedly but passively, thinking that they would be safe. But they were not.

Carrie, wide-eyed, looked up, as most students did, at the book's penciled illustrations. A quick smile broke into her lips and out through her eyes; it was a knowing smile, as if she had made some connection with what was going on in the story. A moment later she resumed a concerned seriousness. Eric left his mouth hanging open and looked at the book with staring, vacant eyes. Mark twiddled his fingers and looked through the desk as if the story were unfolding on a screen way past its surface. There was one story being read, but how many worlds were created in the minds of the students—worlds, which although different, were held together by the common threads of the words of the story and the illustrations of the book.

Storybook reading stretches the imagination, offers information, and exposes students to perspectives that they might not otherwise encounter. It enables them to reflect on events and ideas, both from their own lives and the lives of others. Through listening and discussion, students become familiar with story language and structure. They hear fluent, expressive reading, and they can learn strategies to apply to their independent reading.

Although storybook reading received a great deal of attention in the 1980s, it was not a subject of focus during the late 1990s. It is important to revisit classroom storybook reading and its role in literacy development. The purpose of this chapter is to review current practices for classroom storybook reading. We begin the chapter with a review of the research literature; follow with a discussion of the results of a survey on storybook reading and a closer look at the implementation of storybook reading in first-, second-, and fifth-grade classrooms; and close with a brief discussion.

RESEARCH ON CLASSROOM STORYBOOK READING

Storybook reading not only opens up new worlds to students, but it also influences children's achievement in various aspects of literacy development. Investigations have shown that children in experimental classrooms who were read to daily over long periods of time scored significantly better on measures of vocabulary, comprehension, and decoding ability than children in the control groups who were not read to by an adult (Bus, van IJzendoorn, & Pellegrini, 1995; Cohen, 1968; Dickinson & Smith, 1994; Elley, 1989; Feitelson, Goldstein, Iraqi, & Share, 1993; Feitelson, Kita, & Goldstein, 1986; Robbins & Ehri, 1994; Sénéchal & Cornell, 1993; Sénéchal, Thomas, & Monker, 1995).

The Effects of Storybook Reading on Comprehension

Storybook reading, especially in conjunction with discussion and other activities, can have positive effects on students' comprehension. In experimental studies carried out in school settings where children participated with their teachers in some part of the storybook reading experience, the children's comprehension and sense of story structure improved in comparison to those of children in the control groups. The treatments involved activities implemented prior to, during story reading, and after story reading. Activities implemented *prior to* the reading included previewing the story through discussion, predicting, and setting a purpose for listening. Activities implemented *during* the reading focused on ideas related to the story, which were spontaneously discussed at appropriate times. Activities implemented *after* the reading included discussing predictions and purposes, role-playing and retelling stories, and reconstructing stories through pictures. Apparently, these activities enabled children to relate various parts of a story to each other and to integrate information across the entire story (Brown, 1975; Morrow, 1985; Pellegrini & Galda, 1982).

Styles of Interaction. The kind of interaction that takes place during storybook reading also influences students' comprehension. Studies focusing on teachers' interactive behaviors when reading to whole classes of children have documented the impact of the teachers' reading style on children's comprehension of stories (Dunning & Mason, 1984; Green & Harker, 1982; Peterman, Dunning, & Mason, 1985). Dickinson and Smith (1994) described three styles of teachers' storybook reading: (a) the *co-constructive* approach, consisting of large amounts of analytic talk during the reading; (b) the *didactic-interactional* approach, in which students either chimed in with the rhyming text or answered simple recall and comprehension questions; and (c) the *performance-oriented* approach, in which the text, read with little interruption, was preceded and followed by questions that required students to reconstruct the story or make connections to life experiences. Overall, the performance-oriented classrooms showed greater gains on measures of vocabulary and story understanding, whereas the didactic-interactional classrooms did significantly worse than the classrooms in which the other approaches were taken. Dickinson and Smith suggested that the lower outcomes associated with the didactic-interactional approach could partly have been the result of an almost exclusive use of books that contained limited vocabulary and minimal plot.

Sipe (1998) described different types of scaffolding utilized by the teacher during storybook readings: reading of the text; facilitation of discussion; clarification and exploration of links between children's comments; speculation and interpretation with the students; and utilization of teachable moments. He observed as students analyzed the text and accompanying illustrations, made connections with other texts and their own lives, entered the story world, and molded the stories for their own purposes.

Group Size. A series of investigations was carried out in classrooms to determine children's story comprehension in whole-class, small-group, and one-to-one settings (Morrow, 1987, 1988; Morrow & Smith, 1990). The interactions that occurred within these different settings were also studied. On a test of comprehension, children who heard stories in small-group settings performed significantly better than children who heard stories read one-to-one, who in turn performed significantly better than children who heard stories read to the whole class. In addition, children who heard stories read in a small-group or one-to-one setting generated significantly more comments and questions than children in the whole-class setting. Thus, reading to children in small groups offers as much interaction as one-to-one readings, and appears to lead to greater comprehension than whole-class or even one-to-one readings.

Repeated Readings. Children often request that favorite stories be read aloud. This common practice of rereading favorite stories has attracted the attention of many scholars. Researchers have questioned whether lasting cognitive and affective benefits result from repeated readings of a story. Investigators have sought to answer this question by studying the responses of children who have had the opportunity to hear such repeated readings. Roser and Martinez (1985) and Yaden (1985) suggested that children's comments and questions increase and become more interpretive and evaluative when they have listened to repeated readings. Case study investigations (Snow, 1983; Snow & Goldfield, 1983) of repeated storybook readings found that children discussed more aspects of the text, and in greater depth, in their comments and responses to these readings. Children also elaborated more often and interpreted issues in the story following repeated readings.

Effects of Storybook Reading on Vocabulary Various studies have shown that repeated storybook readings result in increased vocabulary acquisition (Leung & Pikulski, 1990; Elley, 1989; Eller, Pappas, & Brown, 1988). Robbins and Ehri (1994), for example, found that hearing a word four times in the context of storybook reading greatly increased, but did not guarantee, kindergartners' learning of the new word.

Discussion of words found in the stories read can also lead to greater vocabulary learning. In studies in which second-, third-, and fourth-graders were given explanations of targeted vocabulary words, the children learned more words than did students who simply listened to the stories (Elley, 1989; Brett, Rothlein, & Hurley, 1996). In addition, Dickinson and Smith (1994) showed that an increase in vocabulary acquisition took place in preschool classrooms where high levels of analytical talk, including vocabulary discussion, accompanied storybook reading. In a study conducted by Sénéchal (1997), 3- and 4-year-olds who listened to repeated readings *and* who used new vocabulary to answer simple questions posed by the teacher learned more words than children who only listened to the repeated readings.

MULTICULTURAL AWARENESS

Wham, Barnhart, and Cook (1996) showed that storybook reading of books from other cultures can positively affect student attitudes toward single-parent families, the elderly, the unemployed, families from different cultural and ethnic groups, and children with physical and mental disorders. One control group and one storybook reading group each from kindergarten, second-grade, and fourth-grade classrooms (six classrooms total) completed surveys regarding their attitudes toward diversity, both before and after the 7-month experimental period. Students who were exposed to multicultural books showed positive gains in their openness toward diverse populations, while the control group demonstrated negative change. This study suggests that the reading of multicultural books can be an effective tool for helping students embrace diversity.

Negative Effects

Meyer, Wardrop, Stahl, and Linn (1994) described negative effects on literacy development as a result of storybook reading. These authors suggested that reading stories does not exert a magical effect on literacy development; rather, it is the *quality* of the interaction that occurs during reading that results in positive effects. They reported that storybook reading sessions in classrooms are often not of sufficient quality to fully engage students and maximize literacy growth. Reading stories does not in itself necessarily promote literacy; however, the research suggests that certain methods, environmental influences, attitudes, and interactive behaviors apparently enhance the potential of the read-aloud event for promoting literacy development.

A THEORETICAL GROUNDING

A number of literacy theories share a consistent view of the nature of the learning that occurs as a result of adults reading storybooks with children. Wittrock's (1974, 1981) model of generative learning supports the notion that the reader or listener understands prose by actively engaging in the construction of meaning and making connections with the textual information he or she hears or reads (Linden & Wittrock, 1981; Wittrock, 1974, 1981). According to Vygotsky's (1978) cultural-historical theory, literacy appears to develop from children's social interactions with others in specific environments, of which reading, writing, and oral language are a part. The literacy activities and interactions that are mediated by the adults determine children's ideas about and skills acquired toward literacy development (Teale & Sulzby, 1987). Holdaway's (1979) model of developmental teaching, derived from observations of middle-class homes, asserted that children benefit most when their earliest experiences with storybooks are mediated by an adult who interacts with the child in a problem-solving situation. The child is asked to respond, and the adult offers information as needed to sustain the activity. In such situations, children and adults interact to integrate, construct, and develop understandings of the printed text.

The primary goal of storybook reading, then, is the construction of meaning from the interactive process between adult and child (Vygotsky, 1978). During story reading, the adult helps the child understand and make sense of text by interpreting the written language based on their own experiences, background, and beliefs (Altwerger, Diehl-Faxon, & Dockstader-Anderson, 1985). Teale (1984) described the interaction as being interpsychological first—that is, negotiated between adult and child together—and intrapsychological next, when the child internalizes the interactions and can function independently.

A SURVEY OF CURRENT STORYBOOK READING PRACTICES

The literature shows that storybook reading has the potential for positively affecting literacy development, especially when accompanied by interactive activities. Are these interactions taking place in classrooms? How often do teachers read to students, and what reasons do they give for doing so? We distributed 500 surveys to teachers from pre-kindergarten to Grade 8 to give us an idea about the answer to these and other questions regarding classroom storybook reading.

The teachers' responses indicated that the practice of reading aloud was thriving in preschool and elementary classrooms. The tables include data from the more than 300 of these surveys that were completed by teachers of pre-K to fifth grade, including reading specialists, basic skills teachers, and special education teachers. Except for 8% of the fourth- and fifth-grade teachers, all of the regular classroom teachers reported reading to their students, and a majority of the pre-K through third-grade teachers said that they read to their students at least five times each week. As might be predicted, the survey showed that as children got older, they were not read to as often. Basic skills and special education teachers did not read to students as frequently as regular classroom teachers, but this could have been the result of differing schedules and responsibilities (see Table 7.1).

TABLE 7.1
Number of Times Teachers Read to Their Students Each Week

Type of teacher	5 times		4 times		3 times		2 times		1 time	
	n	%	n	%	n	%	n	%	n	%
Pre-K and kindergarten	22	96	0	0	1	4	0	0	0	0
First	67	75	11	12	6	7	3	3	1	1
Second	32	73	7	16	3	7	2	5	0	0
Third	24	59	8	20	6	15	2	5	1	2
Fourth and fifth	21	42	8	16	9	18	6	12	3	6
Basic skills	15	34	2	5	9	20	3	7		
Reading specialist	13	54	3	13	3	13	2	8	0	0
Special education	4	36	2	18	4	36	0	0	1	9

Pre-K to Second Grade

Teachers of younger grades reported that they read to their students in order to instill in them a joy of reading, to motivate them to read, and to connect literacy to content areas. First- and second-grade teachers were even more likely to connect literacy to content areas than were the pre-K teachers (see Table 7.2). Picture books emerged as the reading material of choice.

The pre-K to second grade teachers stated that they often set purposes for reading, asked questions before and after reading, and facilitated interactive discussions. The second-grade teachers especially reported the use of interactive discussions.

According to the survey, teachers of the younger grades (especially pre-K and kindergarten teachers) were more likely to sit as they read to their students, either in a literacy center or on a rug. At times, however, some of the first-grade teachers (one-third of those surveyed) read to students who were seated at their desks. First- and second-grade teachers were more likely to stand up while reading to students than were pre-K and kindergarten teachers, but still would not do so as often as they sat (see Table 7.3).

Third to Fifth Grade

Although not as many third- to fifth-grade teachers read daily to their students as do teachers in the younger grades, almost 80% of third-grade teachers and almost

TABLE 7.2
Reasons for Reading to Sudents

Type of teacher	Joy of Reading		Motivation for Reading		To Connect Literacy to Content Areas	
	n	%	n	%	n	%
Pre-K an kindergarten	21	91	20	87	17	74
First	83	93	77	87	72	81
Second	41	93	34	77	34	77
Third	40	98	35	85	29	71
Fourth and fifth	46	92	39	78	33	66
Basic skills	27	61	33	75	22	50
Reading specialist	23	96	24	100	14	58
Special education	10	91	10	91	6	55

60% of fourth- and fifth-grade teachers read to their students four to five times a week (see Table 7.1). As in the younger grades, these teachers were motivated to read to students in order to impart both the joy of reading and encouragement to further reading. By the fourth grade, however, teachers were a little less likely to use read-alouds to connect literacy to content areas (see Table 7.2).

Although picture storybooks continued to be the reading material of choice, chapter novels also took on a prominent place in read-aloud sessions. In con-

TABLE 7.3
Places Where Teachers Read to Students

Type of teacher	In a Literacy Center		On a Rug		Students at Their Desks	
	n	%	n	%	n	%
Pre-K and kindergarten	9	39	20	87	3	13
First	29	33	80	90	29	33
Second	16	36	37	84	14	32
Third	5	12	36	88	13	32
Fourth and fifth	2	4	8	16	20	40
Basic skills	13	30	16	36	21	48
Reading specialist	7	30	11	46	11	46
Special education	1	9	2	18	8	73

trast to teachers of the younger grades, the third- to fifth-grade teachers were not as likely to engage students in interactive discussions during read-alouds, and in particular, the fourth- and fifth-grade teachers were less likely to set a purpose for reading or ask post-questions (see Table 7.4). Some reading would take place on a rug (especially in third grade), but by fourth grade more teachers indicated that they read books aloud while students were at their desks.

Regular classroom teachers, basic skills teachers, reading specialists, and special education teachers reported that they read to students in order to model fluent reading, build knowledge of story structure, integrate strategy instruction, build students' vocabulary, and enhance student writing. Teachers also sought to expose students to different topics and experiences, as well as to literature that was beyond the students' own reading level. Some of the pre-K and kindergarten teachers decribed reading aloud as being important for the development of emergent literacy and phonemic awareness.

Overall, then, the teachers who were surveyed integrated storybook reading as part of their regular teaching practice, and used read-alouds to broaden students' content knowledge, to model reading strategies, and to share the enjoyment of reading with children. Picture storybooks emerged as the most common reading material. Many teachers, especially those teaching younger grades, included questioning, discussion, and other activities before, during, and after the read-aloud, thereby seeking to maximize the positive effects of the storybook reading experience on their students' literacy development.

Table 7.4
Format of Read-Aloud

Type of teacher	Pre-Questions		Set a Purpose for Reading		Post-Questions		Interactive Student Discussions	
	n	%	n	%	n	%	n	%
Pre-K and kindergarten	18	78	16	70	19	83	18	78
First	75	84	81	91	73	82	65	73
Second	24	55	32	73	25	57	39	89
Third	22	54	31	76	31	76	25	61
Fourth and fifth	24	57	26	52	23	46	29	58
Basic skills	25	57	27	61	29	66	32	73
Reading specialist	10	42	17	71	9	38	16	67
Special education	8	73	8	73	8	73	7	64

CLASSROOM STORYBOOK READINGS

Now we shall see how some teachers are implementing storybook reading. We start by going back to where we left off, in Barbara's fifth-grade classroom. Barbara was finishing the reading of a picture book, *Terrible Things* (Bunting, 1989):

> The animals, taken by the Terrible Things, had gone. The book closed, Barbara's voice stopped, and even the accompanying silence disappeared with it, dissipating into the sound of shifting bodies and creaking chairs.
>
> "I'll give you about five minutes to draw a sketch of something you saw in your mind." Barbara's voice no longer drifted in the far away land of the Terrible Things, but resonated among the chairs and desks of the classroom. The students were now in the classroom with her.
>
> She continued. "Draw whatever the story triggered in your mind—what you saw in that newsreel in your head. I only showed you pictures for part of it. There are no right or wrong answers to this. What did you see?"
>
> Pencil lead and paper merged to shade the air with muted swishing sounds and a rapid fire of pencil-point. Emerging from the papers were some terrible things indeed—a face that looked like an angry Eskimo mask, a person cloaked in a whirling tornado, and a shadowy mass equipped with arms, nets, and animal cages. There were pictures of animals scurrying in fear, hiding behind rocks. There were especially rabbits.
>
> "Let's take a few minutes and see what you've got," broke in Barbara after 5 minutes. "Who's willing to share and explain their picture?"
>
> A few students showed their pictures. Then Erin raised her hand.
>
> "Go ahead, Erin, " urged Barbara.
>
> "I thought that the rabbit was gonna, like, go and tell other people to beware. He was going to tell them to get together and stop him." She held up a picture of a rabbit surrounded by animals.
>
> "So you drew the same animal as Anne but you were looking at a different aspect of it," Barbara commented. Anne had drawn a rabbit looking at its reflection in the water, thinking back about how he could have helped. Barbara peered at Erin's picture to see if she could read what she had written on her paper. "What is he saying?" she finally asked her.
>
> "To beware. And so then he can tell other people and stuff."
>
> "Your rabbit actually has a speech bubble coming out of his mouth, saying things," Barbara observed. "Does anybody else have speech bubbles?"
>
> Tory raised his hand and, staying in his seat, showed the class his picture. He hadn't drawn animals at all. Instead, he had drawn people caught in a giant net. An accompanying speech bubble declared, "Everyone who is a Jew shall be taken away."

A discussion ensued. The students pointed out that just as the animals looked the other way when terrible things happened, so did many people at the time of the Holocaust. They talked about how it was not always easy to stand up to someone that was stronger, but that if it had been done, things might have been different.

This fifth-grade class was studying the Holocaust. Some of the students were reading *Number the Stars* (Lowry, 1989) and others *The Devil's Arithmetic* (Yolen, 1988). Barbara supplemented their study of novels with read-aloud books. She read Mochizuki's *Passage to Freedom: The Sugihara Story* (1997) to help the students see the Holocaust from the perspective of a Japanese diplomat in Lithuania, who risked his life by writing exit visas for Polish Jews. She read Maruki's *Hiroshima No Pika* (1980) to provide background about what was going on during World War II in a different part of the world. The books served as a springboard for discussion of various issues surrounding the Holocaust.

Barbara also used the read-alouds to model strategies that the students could apply when they read their assigned novels independently. Before reading *Terrible Things* (Bunting, 1989), Barbara explained how visualization could help them understand texts. After discussing mood, she read *A Promise of a New Spring* (Klein, 1981), stopping at various times in the story to have the class identify the mood that the author was creating. She then had the students describe the mood of the novels that they were reading independently. At other times, Barbara asked students to make connections to their own lives, to other texts, and between events and themes within the story. Storybook reading not only provided additional perspectives and background information that supplemented study of the novels, but also served as a scaffold that enabled the students to independently analyze and apply strategies to the reading of their own novels.

Barbara is one of the 67% of reading specialists surveyed who reported engaging students in interactive discussions when reading to the class, and of the 71% who stated that they set a purpose for reading. Taking an approach that Dickinson and Smith (1994) labeled as "performance-oriented," Barbara encouraged talk before and after the reading. Before reading, she asked students to make predictions, set a purpose, and review vocabulary. After reading the story she had students explain their pictures and discuss their interpretations. Practices such as these can enhance students' comprehension and vocabulary development.

A First-Grade Classroom

Wriggling but attentive first-graders sat in the rug area in the corner of Laurie's classroom. Occasionally, a child's hand would shoot up, bullet-like, to answer one of Laurie's questions. At other times, the children responded chorally.

This week, Laurie's class was studying whales. They were reading *Ibis: A True Whale Story* (Himmelman, 1990) throughout the week; each day Laurie would read another story to them as well. *Swimmy* (Lionni, 1963), in big book form, stood on the table behind the children. A diagram of a whale hung on the bulletin board, with its parts labeled and accompanying descriptions converted into fill-in-the-blank sentences. A poster entitled "Meet the Ocean Animals" displayed photos of starfish, clams, and sharks. A pocket chart held whale vocabulary.

At one moment, the students were singing the words of the book *Baby Beluga* (Wolff, 1990), elongating the "u" of "Beluuuuuga" and bouncing their shoulders in rhythm. At the next moment, they were debating where the word "predator" belonged on a Venn diagram of whales and fish. In order to decide on an answer, they reminded themselves of what they had learned in the stories that Laurie had read to them, the poems that they had read together, and the songs that they had sung.

It is hard to separate storybook reading from the varied kinds of reading that take place in Laurie's classroom. The storybook reading of a big book like *Swimmy* (Lionni, 1963), first introduced through a picture walk and then read to the students, might evolve into a choral reading. A read-aloud of a whale poem could turn into echo reading, then into choral reading, and finally into individual reading. A read-aloud of a book like *Baby Beluga* (Wolff, 1990) might become a sing-aloud. Every day Laurie brought in a new book to further develop the theme, but the storybook reading was so intertwined with other activities that it was hard to make a distinction between a read-aloud and other types of reading that took place in this classroom.

Like many of the first-grade teachers who responded to the survey, Laurie connected literacy to content areas and intentionally integrated storybook reading into her thematic units. She made sure that she included a new read-aloud each day, and chose it so that it contributed to her theme for the week. In addition, she used a core book that was read each day throughout the week. At the end of the week, the students chose their read-aloud favorite and the book joined past favorites in a book basket for future independent reading.

The activities that accompanied Laurie's storybook reading were varied. Sometimes students discussed story elements, such as the characters, or the story's problem and solution. They made connections between the current text and texts that they had read previously. They identified vocabulary words and attempted to use context to determine their meaning. A "dictionary person" reminded students of meanings already learned, and vocabulary words were placed in the pocket chart for sorting and other activities.

Laurie sometimes read stories to the children to support independent reading. She began each week by reading a core book, which was often a big book. As the week progressed, the students became increasingly familiar with the text and became more independent in their reading. The large text of a big book or a charted poem that sometimes accompanied the read-aloud enabled Laurie to model the left–right sweep, and to point out the correspondence between print and the spoken word. Laurie used the text to teach concepts such as rhyming words, plurals, contractions, and letter combinations. Thus, Laurie not only used storybook reading to help children develop content knowledge, vocabulary, and comprehension strategies, but also to support children as they developed print skills and learned to read independently.

In various ways, Laurie is representative of many of the first-grade teachers that were surveyed. She read to the students daily, and usually more than once a day. The students sat around her on a rug, and she sat with them. She connected literacy to content areas, making the read-alouds an integral part of thematic units. She freely asked pre- and post-questions, set purposes for readings, and sometimes facilitated interactive discussions.

A Second-Grade Classroom

"We have a few more minutes of read-aloud time, so I thought we could start our new book," announced Trisha, pulling out a book and showing its cover. "Since you are all going to third grade, I thought it would be a good idea to read *The Terrible Truth of Third Grade* [McGuire, 1992]. How many of you think that third grade will be terrible?"

A few students raised their hands in response.

"It depends on what teacher you have," asserted Tiffany.

"We'll have to go *square dancing*," Kyle moaned. "Yuck." The two boys next to him wrinkled their noses and joined him in his groaning.

"Let's hear your predictions," Trisha urged.

"I know!" exclaimed Brad. "A girl is having a terrible time and she, like, tells everyone, uh, that third grade is terrible."

"That could be. Mark, what do you think?" asked Trisha.

"I think it's a girl who moves and has to go to a new school. It looks good on the outside and she kind of likes it, but then when she goes to her class she is like, scared and it's dark, and then the teacher walks in and says 'Hello, class.' The teacher is mean because she makes you study one word 20 times, but then she is nice like a person."

"So you are saying that she makes the students work hard but she is a nice person."

"Yeah, she is nice like a person."

"Carlie?"

"Mine is like Kyle's, but they have to do lots of homework and they have to clean the room after every subject," said Carlie.

"Well, that's not too bad," interjected Trisha.

"Yes, it *is*." Carlie groaned as if the teacher had, in fact, asked her to mop the floors and wash the desks right at that very moment.

"Emily?"

"Maybe she's like my sister's homeroom teacher—they had to take detention even if they didn't do anything."

Trisha's third graders were making predictions about the book that Trisha was going to read to them. Every afternoon, Trisha set aside time to read to her students so that they could relax and enjoy a story. She found that reading fun books was a great way to motivate reluctant readers. A few of her students who were not particularly interested in reading aloud would often take these books home to read them for themselves.

Trisha also read to the children during their studies of novels. These studies differed from the daily read-aloud time in a number of ways. When studying novels, each student had a copy of the book and followed along as Trisha read to them. Just as Laurie, the first-grade teacher, read books and other materials as scaffolding for more independent reading, Trisha would also read books aloud to familiarize the students with the text. Later, the students would read the book with a partner. Trisha believed that reading aloud while students followed along enabled the children to focus on the meaning of the text. They had other opportunities during the day (such as during guided reading) to read books individually.

Another difference between Trisha's read-aloud time and the study of novels was the type of discussion that took place. During the read-aloud time Trisha might have a student summarize the events from the previous reading, make a prediction, or react to the story after the reading was completed, but the reading itself took place with very little interruption. When studying the novels, however, Trisha sometimes stopped to ask students to modify their predictions, or to ask them to share what they would have done in a particular situation. Sometimes they guessed the meaning of vocabulary words by looking for context clues, and then checked their guesses with a dictionary.

During the read-aloud time, Trisha did not require the students to do any assignments related to the book, but she did give assignments when they were reading a novel. At the beginning of the year, when the second-graders' writing ability was more limited, they wrote a class book or an entry in their journal. By the end of the year they were writing and discussing answers to Trisha's questions. Trisha read to her students when teaching the content areas as well. When she read a non-fiction big book about rain forests, the students' interactions became even more spontaneous than when reading their novel. They told about trips to Puerto Rico and Mexico and described the exotic birds and butterflies they had seen there. They asked if the boa ate people and if an anteater could be taken home as a pet. They pondered the fate of the rainforest. They wondered why lions, though taken out of their habitat, didn't die in a zoo. The children took the initiative to ask questions, to share related experiences, and to make connections to things they had seen or information that they already had. They felt free to ask and answer questions, and the teacher was not the only one who supplied the answers.

Trisha read to her students in a variety of contexts, at different times in the day. Like many of the teachers who responded to the survey, she read to students for multiple purposes: to support independent reading, to teach skills, to inform, and to enjoy a book with the students. Like 89% of the second-grade teachers who responded to the survey, Trisha encouraged interaction, especially around the non-fiction selections.

DISCUSSION

Some common characteristics emerged from the storybook reading practices employed by these three teachers. First, they used read-alouds as scaffolding for the independent use of reading strategies. Second, they employed different styles of interaction in accordance with variations in the purpose of the storybook reading. Third, they read for a variety of overlapping purposes.

Barbara, Laurie, and Trisha all used read-alouds to help students learn how to use reading strategies independently. In the context of read-alouds, Barbara, the reading specialist in the fifth-grade classroom, introduced students to strategies such as making connections to texts, identifying mood, and visualizing, and then asked them to apply these newly learned strategies to the assigned novels. Laurie, the first-grade teacher, read big books, poems, and charts repeatedly so that her students could learn print-related skills, become familiar with the text, and then achieve increasing independence in their own reading of the text. By reading to her students during their studies of novels, Trisha enabled her students to focus on meaning, read more confidently with their partners, and learn reading strategies. Many of the teachers surveyed stated that they, too, used read-alouds to teach skills and strategies.

Some respondents indicated that they used multiple formats when reading to students. Likewise, Barbara, Laurie, and Trisha did not restrict themselves to one style of interaction. Trisha, for example, sometimes read with very little interruption, as in her daily read-aloud time, and at other times encouraged constant interaction, as when reading the big book about the rainforest. Barbara, who one day might stop a couple of times in the middle of a story for extended discussion about the mood of a story, reserved most discussion for the beginning and end, when teaching about visualization. Laurie sometimes asked a few short-answer questions about the letters and words in a poem, while at other times she asked students to speculate about what might happen in the story. All three teachers used a combination of pre- and post-questions, purpose setting, and interactive discussions. The style of interaction they employed depended on the type and purpose of the read-aloud.

Barbara, Trisha, and Laurie, like many other teachers from the survey, read for different purposes, but their primary purpose was never carried out to the exclusion of all others. Even when Trisha read a book for her students' enjoyment every day, the students still summarized the story events from the previous day, made predictions, and then talked about their predictions and personal reactions. A big book about animals in the rainforest kept students interested and entertained, and also became the means of teaching them about the purpose of a table of contents. As Barbara read to her students, she sought to help them better understand the issues surrounding the Holocaust, while at the same time helping them develop a visualization strategy. Laurie's various readings in her thematic unit on whales integrated enjoyment, the learning of print skills, and the learning of content. Although the teachers each had a primary purpose in mind for their chosen read-aloud, they incorporated secondary goals as well.

Research suggests that the kinds of interactions that accompanied storybook reading in Barbara, Laurie, and Trisha's classrooms can foster literacy development. These three teachers had children make predictions and connect the text to life experiences. They set purposes for reading, encouraged analytic talk, and discussed unknown words. Sometimes they gave repeated readings of a story. All of these activities potentially promote literacy growth, especially in the areas of comprehension and vocabulary development. Thus, at the same time that storybook reading creates and satisfies curiosity, opens up new worlds, and nourishes the imagination, it can also be a vehicle for learning, enjoyed by students and teachers alike.

REFERENCES

Altwerger, A., Diehl-Faxon, J., & Dockstader-Anderson, K. (1985). Read-aloud events as meaning construction. *Language Arts, 60,* 168–175.

Brett, A., Rothlein, L., & Hurley, M. (1996). Vocabulary acquisition from listening to stories and explanation of target words. *Elementary School Journal, 96,* 415–422.

Brown, A. (1975). Recognition, reconstruction and recall of narrative sequences of preoperational children. *Child Development, 46,* 155–166.

Bunting, E. (1989). *Terrible things: An allegory of the Holocaust.* Philadelphia: The Jewish Publication Society.

Bus, A. G., van IJzendoorn, M. H., & Pellegrini, A. D. (1995). Joint book reading makes for success in learning to read: A meta-analysis on intergenerational transmission of literacy. *Review of Educational Research, 65,* 1–21.

Cohen, D. (1968). The effect of literature on vocabulary and reading achievement. *Elementary English, 45,* 209–213, 217.

Dickinson, D. K., & Smith, M. W. (1994). Long-term effects of preschool teachers' book readings on low-income children's vocabulary and story comprehension. *Reading Research Quarterly, 29,* 105–122.

Dunning, D., & Mason, J. (1984, November). *An investigation of kindergarten children's expressions of story characters' intentions.* Paper presented at the 34th annual meeting of the National Reading Conference, St. Petersburg, FL.

Eller, R. G., Pappas, C. C., & Brown, E. (1988). The lexical development of kindergartners: Learning from written context. *Journal of Reading Behavior, 20,* 5–24.

Elley, W. B. (1989). Vocabulary acquisition from listening to stories. *Reading Research Quarterly, 24,* 174–187.

Feitelson, D., Goldstein, Z., Iraqi, U., & Share, D. (1993). Effects of listening to story reading on aspects of literacy acquisition in a diglossic situation. *Reading Research Quarterly, 28,* 70–79.

Feitelson, D., Kita, B., & Goldstein, Z. (1986). Effects of listening to series stories on first graders' comprehension and use of language. *Research in the Teaching of English, 20,* 339–356.

Green, J. L., & Harker, J. O. (1982). Reading to children: A communicative process. In J. A. Langer & M. T. Smith-Burke (Eds.), *Reader meets author/Bridging the gap: A psycholinguistic and sociolinguistic perspective* (pp. 196–221). Newark, DE: International Reading Association.

Himmelman, J. (1990). *Ibis: A true whale story.* New York: Scholastic.

Holdaway, D. (1979). *The foundations of literacy.* Sydney: Ashton Scholastic.

Klein, G. W. (1981). *Promise of a new spring.* Scottsdale, AZ: Phoenix Folios.

Leung, C., & Pikulski, J. (1990). Incidental learning of word meanings by kindergarten and first-grade children through repeated read aloud events. In J. Zutell & S. McCormick (Eds.), *Literacy theory and research: Analyses from multiple paradigms* (Thirty-ninth yearbook of the National Reading Conference, pp. 231–239). Chicago: National Reading Conference.

Linden, M., & Wittrock, M. C. (1981). The teaching of reading comprehension according to the model of generative learning. *Reading Research Quarterly, 17,* 44–57.

Lionni, L. (1963). *Swimmy.* New York: Scholastic.

Lowry, L. (1989). *Number the stars.* Boston: Houghton Mifflin.

Maruki, T. (1980). *Hiroshima no pika.* New York: Lothrop, Lee, and Shepard Books.

McGuire, L. (1992). *The terrible truth about third grade.* Mahwah, NJ: Troll Associates.

Meyer, L., Wardrop, J., Stahl, S., & Linn, R. (1994). Effects of reading storybooks aloud to children. *Journal of Educational Research, 88,* 69–85.

Mochizuki, K. (1997). *Passage to freedom: The Sugihara story.* New York: Lee and Low Books.

Morrow, L. M. (1985). Retelling stories: A strategy for improving children's comprehension, concept of story structure and oral language complexity. *Elementary School Journal, 85,* 647–661.

Morrow, L. M. (1987). The effect of small group story reading on children's questions and comments. In S. McCormick & J. Zutell (Eds.), *Cognitive and social perspectives for literacy research and instruction* (Thirty-seventh yearbook of the National Reading Conference, pp. 77–86). Chicago: National Reading Conference.

Morrow, L. M. (1988). Young children's responses to one-to-one story readings in school settings. *Reading Research Quarterly, 23,* 89–107.

Morrow, L. M., & Smith, J. K. (1990). The effects of group size on interactive storybook reading. *Reading Research Quarterly, 25,* 214–231.

Pellegrini, A., & Galda, L. (1982). The effects of thematic-fantasy play training on the development of children's story comprehension. *American Educational Research Journal, 19,* 443–452.

Peterman, C. L., Dunning, D., & Mason, J. (1985, December). *A storybook reading event: How a teacher's presentation affects kindergarten children's subsequent attempts to read from the text.* Paper presented at the 35th annual meeting of the National Reading Conference, San Diego, CA.

Robbins, C., & Ehri, L. C. (1994). Reading storybooks to kindergartners helps them learn new vocabulary words. *Journal of Educational Psychology, 86,* 54–64.

Roser, N., & Martinez, M. (1985). Roles adults play in preschoolers' response to literature. *Language Arts, 62,* 485–490.

Sénéchal, M. (1997). The differential effect of storybook reading on preschoolers' acquisition of expressive and receptive vocabulary. *Journal of Child Language, 24,* 123–138.

Sénéchal, M., & Cornell, E. H. (1993). Vocabulary acquisition through shared reading experiences. *Reading Research Quarterly, 28,* 360–374.

Sénéchal, M., Thomas, E., & Monker, J. (1995). Individual differences in 4-year-old children's acquisition of vocabulary during storybook reading. *Journal of Educational Psychology, 87,* 218–229.

Sipe, L. R. (1998). The construction of literary understanding by first and second graders in response to picture storybook read-alouds. *Reading Research Quarterly, 33,* 376–378.

Snow, C. E. (1983). Literacy and language: Relationships during the preschool years. *Harvard Educational Review, 53,* 165–189.

Snow, C. E., & Goldfield, B. A. (1983). Turn the page, please: Situation specific language acquisition. *Journal of Child Language, 10,* 535–549.

Teale, W. H. (1984). Reading to young children: Its significance for literacy development. In H. Goelman, A. A. Oberg, & F. Smith (Eds.), *Awakening to literacy* (pp. 110–121). London: Heinemann.

Teale, W. H., & Sulzby, E. (1987). Literacy acquisition in early childhood: The roles of access and mediation in storybook reading. In D. A. Wagner (Ed.), *The future of literacy in a changing world* (pp. 111–130). New York: Pergamon Press.

Vygotsky, L. S. (1978). *Mind in society: The development of psychological processes.* Cambridge, MA: Harvard University Press.

Wham, M., Barnhart, J., & Cook, G. (1996). Enhancing multicultural awareness through the storybook reading experience. *Journal of Research and Development in Education, 30,* 1–9.

Wittrock, M. C. (1974). Learning as a generative process. *Educational Psychologist, 11,* 87–95.

Wittrock, M. C. (1981). Reading comprehension. In F. J. Pirozzolo & M. C. Wittrock (Eds.), *Neuropsychological and cognitive processes in reading* (pp. 229–259). New York: Academic Press.

Wolff, A. (1990). *Baby beluga.* New York: Crown Publishers.

Yaden, D. (1985, December). *Preschoolers' spontaneous inquiries about print and books.* Paper presented at the annual meeting of the National Reading Conference, San Diego, CA.

Yolen, J. (1988). *Devil's arithmetic.* New York: Viking.

8

Taking Advantage of Read-Alouds to Help Children Make Sense of Decontextualized Language

Margaret G. McKeown
Isabel L. Beck
University of Pittsburgh

Reading aloud to children has been a commonplace activity in homes and schools for centuries, and there are indications that its effects are significant for children's literacy growth (Durkin, 1974–1975; Feitelson, Goldstein, Iraqi, & Share, 1993; Mason & Allen, 1986). Recently, researchers have suggested that the most important benefit read-alouds give to children is experience with decontextualized language, making sense of ideas that are about something beyond the here and now (Cochran-Smith, 1984; Heath, 1983; Snow, 1993; Snow & Dickinson, 1991; Snow et al., 1995). By the time children enter school, they are quite capable of talking about the world around them, a world they can see and point to. However, such contextualized experiences are quite different from ideas built only through words read from a book. But building ideas from words alone—decontextualized language—is essential to comprehending and learning from text.

WHAT'S THE KEY TO READING ALOUD?

The value of experience with decontextualized language to future literacy seems to derive not from merely listening to literary language, but from talking about the ideas. Cochran-Smith, Heath, and Snow and her colleagues all highlight the talk that surrounds book reading as a key contributor to becoming literate. Participation in decontextualized language, the formation of ideas about what was in a book, and their expression in ways that make sense to others are all ingredients of communication competence. Snow (1993) points out that quality talk around books can promote "[familiarity with] relatively rare vocabulary, understanding the lexical and grammatical strategies for adjusting to a nonpresent audience, identifying the perspective of the listener so as to provide sufficient background information, and knowing the genre-specific rules for various forms of talk such as narrative and explanation" (p. 15).

Snow et al. (1995) and Dickinson and Tabors (1991) have found evidence that preschool children's participation in talk around book reading enhances the growth of their literacy skills. Further evidence supporting this claim comes from studies by Morrow (1992) and Freppon (1991), in which the researchers concluded that "talk surrounding the text" (Morrow, p. 253), or "getting children to think about what was going on in the story" (Freppon, p. 144) was key to literacy growth.

FINDINGS ON READING ALOUD IN CLASSROOMS

Researchers who have explored teachers' read-aloud interactions in classrooms have noted a variety of styles, each of which has different effects on children's understanding. Dickinson and Smith's (1994) fine-grained examination of reading aloud in preschool classrooms revealed that certain features were particularly effective. Specifically, they found that the interactions that occurred as the story was read; that involved both children and teachers; and that were analytic in nature led to positive effects on kindergartners' vocabulary and story comprehension. Talk that was "analytic in nature" required children to reflect on the story content or language.

Teale and Martinez (1996) described the read-aloud styles of six teachers, each of whom had a distinct approach to the text content and the kind of interactions she encouraged. One teacher's style led to better story retelling by the children. This teacher's read-aloud style was characterized by attention to important story information before, during, and after the reading, and by her efforts to elicit responses from the children about the story episodes.

Teale and Martinez went on to point out stylistic features that may interfere with comprehension. Chiefly, these include less effective ways of dealing with children's responses, such as allowing children to stray well beyond the story line, or circumscribing the situation to allow only brief, literal responses, with the teacher quickly supplying answers when the children hesitate. Teale and Martinez suggest that the most effective way to encourage children's responses is to focus on important story ideas and allow the children to reflect, rather than expecting a quickly retrieved answer. Thus Teale and Martinez's ideas about the most effective read-aloud strategies seem quite consistent with Dickinson and Smith's. Yet it is clear from these investigations that the most effective read-aloud strategies are far from the most common ones, and that read-aloud experiences are not being effectively used to build children's language abilities.

MOTIVATION FOR TEXT TALK

In developing our own perspective on reading aloud as a means to promote young children's language abilities, we began by observing teachers reading to their kindergarten and first-grade children. We conducted observations of four teachers—two kindergarten and two first grade—in two different schools. We observed the teachers between two and four times each. Our observations confirmed the literature's finding that the most effective strategies are not being used as widely as they should be. In particular, we noted few instances in which children were encouraged to make sense of decontextualized language. That is, children were not prompted to think through ideas, connect them, and express their developing understanding of the story. Instead, interactions tended to focus on the most concrete and obvious story information. Questions typically asked for descriptive information: "Where did he go?" "What did she have on her head?" "What did he find on the sidewalk?" All of these prompts could be answered in a word or two with information retrieved directly from the story.

Given the contrast between our knowledge of effective practices and the rarity of their use in classrooms, we initiated a project called Text Talk, in which we sought to develop an approach based on the most effective strategies and then implement this approach in classrooms. Key to this effort was the goal of increasing children's opportunities to respond to decontextualized language in meaningful ways.

TEXT TALK DEVELOPMENT

Text Talk was developed by selecting books for kindergarten and first grade, and then creating and piloting a format for interactions during story read-alouds. We selected books that we judged would provide challenging content and meaningful experiences with decontextualized language.

The types of interactions we developed for the books were adopted from our earlier work on Questioning the Author, an approach to text-based instruction that we had developed around the principle of "teaching for understanding" (Beck, McKeown, Hamilton, & Kucan, 1997; Beck, McKeown, Worthy, Sandora, & Kucan, 1996; McKeown & Beck, 1998). Questioning the Author has been used with students from third grade through high school. Although Questioning the Author served as a starting point, it was originally developed for older students reading school texts, while Text Talk was aimed at younger children in a read-aloud situation.

The Text Talk format included an introduction to the story, interspersed open questions, follow-up questions, a story wrap-up, and vocabulary activities. We discuss each of these components in turn.

Introducing the Story

In Text Talk, the story is introduced briefly. This brief introduction is dramatically different from what we saw in our storytime classroom observations. Indeed, we were struck by how much time teachers spent on establishing background knowledge before reading a story, and on encouraging children to relate their experiences, no matter how tangential, to the story. It appeared that research showing the importance of background knowledge to comprehension had been elaborated in practice to a point at which the development of background knowledge had taken on a life of its own.

In analyzing how stories were introduced we observed several problematic tendencies. The most common of these was the discussion of ideas with limited relevance to the story. As an example, consider our observations of a teacher introducing the story Brave Irene (Steig, 1986) to a first-grade class. Brave Irene is about a little girl who plods through a blizzard to deliver a ball gown that her mother, a dressmaker, has made for the duchess. In addition to discussing the concept of bravery, the teacher introduced the term dressmaker, and offered a long explanation of how clothing used to be made, and how it is made today. Among the topics discussed was the idea that most of our clothing today is made by machines, in factories. Yet the only information that children needed to know about dressmakers in order to understand the story was that a dressmaker is someone who makes dresses. Digressions like these can distract children's attention. In fact, there is evidence that children may have difficulty separating story ideas from up-front talk of this sort (Neuman, 1990; Nicholson & Imlach, 1981).

A second common feature that we observed was the early introduction of information that wouldn't be encountered until well into the story. The problem is that such information may not be remembered when it is finally needed. For instance, about a third of the way into *Make Way for Ducklings* (McCloskey, 1941), Mr. and Mrs. Mallard molt. Certainly, the word *molt* is likely to be unfamiliar to young children. An explanation is clearly required, because molting prevents the ducks from flying, and knowing that they can't fly is important to understanding their later actions. However, rather than explaining *molt* before beginning the story, it would seem most effective to provide a parenthetical explanation at the point in the story when it is actually needed.

A third frequently observed feature of introductions to read-alouds was teachers' disclosure of events in the story. Knowing the plot details beforehand precludes children's need to attend to the story as it is read, and seriously diminishes the number of opportunities for them to develop ideas from decontextualized language.

Interspersed Open Questions

Text Talk questions are intended to encourage children to talk about the important ideas in a story as they occur. Open-ended questions are interspersed with story reading in order to encourage children to express and connect story ideas. This is in contrast to the kinds of closed questions that we observed, which asked children to simply retrieve small bits of text language.

As an example, compare the two sets of questions and responses in Table 8.1. The top set was collected from classrooms before implementation of Text Talk, while the bottom set came from interactions during implementation. As the table suggests, Text Talk questions resulted in more connected and elaborated responses. Although the open questions did move children's responses in the right direction, something more than open questions is required in order to prompt children to respond thoughtfully to text. To be effective, teachers often need to follow up students' responses. (We will address the matter of follow-up responses in a later section.)

Wrapping Up

As is the case with any lesson, a read-aloud experience needs to have a wrap-up. It is not enough to simply finish the story; a coda is required. In Text Talk we wrap up by asking children to think about some aspect of the story—perhaps a character or an idea. For example, after readings of *The Giant Jam Sandwich*

TABLE 8.1
Comparison of Closed and Open Questions and Answers

Baseline Classroom

Questions	Responses
Is he a new toy or an old toy?	Old.
Who is Joe? He's the what?	The baby.
Think back in the story. They went to pick up his …	Big sister.
Do you think Nelle is going to be happy or mad?	Mad.
Somebody else had already what?	Found him.
Was she being nice to her little brother?	Yeah.

Text Talk Classroom

Questions	Responses
How did the other kids like Stephanie's ponytail?	First they liked it when she didn't have it to her ear, and then they kept calling her ugly, and now they're gonna be jealous, real jealous.
What's going on?	George got into trouble anyway.
What's the problem with having a fawn as a pet?	Cause he'll eat everything. He's like a goat.
Charlie looked at the girls and purred. What's that tell us?	The girls are happy that they might have found him.
Why would termites be a worry for the owl?	Because the termites might eat the owl's home cause it's made out of wood.
What happened?	The people saw the signmaker and chased him into the woods and they thought that the signmaker did it, but the boy did.

(Lord, 1972), in which townspeople create a giant jam sandwich to trap the wasps that are menacing their village, the wrap-up asks children to talk about what the people in the town had to do to make their plan work. In the case of *Beware of the Bears* (MacDonald, 1998)—a sequel to the Goldilocks story in which the bears take revenge on Goldilocks by making a mess of her house—the wrap-up asks students to say what they think about what the bears did, and to explain why they came to such conclusions.

Vocabulary

Given the importance of vocabulary to comprehension, and the enormous dis-crepancy that exists in vocabulary size between high- and low-achieving learn-ers (Graves, Brunetti, & Slater, 1982; Seashore & Eckerson, 1940), attention to vocabulary acquisition is essential. In Text Talk we take advantage of the in-teresting and sophisticated words that good writers use to tell their stories. In addition to explaining words needed for comprehension as they occur, we sys-tematically focus on several words from each story in activities that take place after the story is read. We chose words that we thought would be unfamiliar to children but useful for their vocabulary repertoires. This is the type of words previously labeled as "Tier Two": that is, words that are frequently used by ma-ture language users and that are of general utility, neither limited to a spe-cific domain (e.g., *sonata, nebula, ambergris*) nor found in a basic oral vocabulary (e.g., *mother, house, walk*) (Beck, McKeown, & Omanson, 1987). Examples of Tier Two words include *unique, convenient, retort, influence, ponder,* and *procrastinate*.

The typical Text Talk vocabulary activity begins with a description of how a particular word was used in the story. The word's meaning is explained and a typical use is presented. This is followed by an elicitation of children's responses to the word's meaning—for example, asking children to judge the word's uses or create their own. The following activity is provided for the word *absurd*, after a reading of *Burnt Toast on Davenport Street* (Egan, 1997):

> *absurd:* In the story, when the fly told Arthur he could have three wishes if he didn't kill him, Arthur said he thought that was absurd. That means Arthur thought it was silly to believe a fly could grant wishes. When something is absurd—it is ridiculous and hard to believe.
>
> If I told you that your teacher was going to stand on his/her head to teach you—that would be absurd. If someone told you that dogs could fly—that would be absurd.
>
> I'll say some things, and if you think they are absurd, say: "That's absurd!" If you think they are not absurd, say: "That makes sense."
>
> I have a singing cow for a pet. (absurd)
>
> I saw a tall building that was made of green cheese. (absurd)
>
> Last night I watched a movie on TV. (makes sense)
>
> This morning I saw some birds flying around the sky. (makes sense)
>
> If I said "let's fly to the moon this afternoon," that would be absurd. Who can think of an absurd idea? (When a child answers, ask another if they think that was absurd, and if so, to tell the first child: "That's absurd!")

To sum up, the Text Talk format takes students from story introduction through wrap-up and subsequent vocabulary activities. The approach also focuses on interspersing questions throughout the reading, in order to initiate discussion of important story ideas.

PROCESSES AND RESULTS OF TEXT TALK IMPLEMENTATION

Implementing Text Talk in Classrooms

After developing Text Talk, we implemented the approach in two kindergarten and two first-grade classrooms in an urban elementary school. The children are all African American, and the majority of them are eligible for free or reduced lunch. The school district within which the school is located is among a handful that have been designated for state takeover if achievement is not improved in the near future.

The teachers had taught at the school for at least 2 years, and three of the four had more than 8 years of teaching experience. Two of the teachers were African American and two were European American.

We introduced Text Talk through a workshop that explained the approach and the motivations for its development. We then provided the teachers with books, accompanied by questions to frame the text interactions, and vocabulary activities. We worked closely with all four teachers during the year to modify and augment their interactions as issues arose. This meant that we observed each teacher once a week and provided feedback, and met with the group of teachers every 2 weeks. The focus of these meetings was how to help children develop and express their ideas about the story. Children's responses to the initial questions asked during a story reading were very limited, especially at first. The teacher's task was to help the children focus and elaborate their ideas into a full response, without providing so much information that the teacher took over responsibility for answering.

Text Talk asks teachers to carry on an interactive and coherent discussion with 5- and 6-year-olds about decontextualized ideas. This is a difficult task. Even though the teachers were provided with questions to begin their discussions, they still had to work hard to instigate discussions that helped their students build meaning.

Follow-Up Questions

The most difficult aspect of a teacher's job is supporting the development of children's initial responses to open questions into coherent, complete, and connected expressions of ideas. Indeed, probably about 60% of our meetings with the teachers were devoted to working on how to effectively follow up children's initial responses. In the course of our work we identified several types of responses that called for follow-up.

In our early observations, we noted the teachers' tendency to follow up by asking generic questions such as "What else?" or "Who has something to add?" The problem with such generic questions is that they do not clearly connect to the ideas that have been activated. Thus, "What else?" tends to elicit a list of unconnected responses, and "Who has something to add?" can result in students bringing in unrelated information. Such generic follow-ups simply do not promote coherent representation of the text. And coherent representation is necessary if discussion is to scaffold the development of children's comprehension ability.

In an effort to stimulate more productive follow-ups, we encouraged the teachers to look at what the child was doing in his or her response, and use that as a starting point for a follow-up question. In the examples that follow we present children's initial responses and then discuss the effective follow-ups that were developed.

Incomplete Responses.   Perhaps the most common problem was incomplete initial responses. For example, in the story *Six-Dinner Sid* (Moore, 1991), a vet figures out that Sid, a cat, has been getting dinner at six houses, because each person believes they are Sid's owner. At the point in the story where the vet realizes this and begins to call the various owners, the teacher asked, "What's happening?" The question was meant to elicit children's descriptions of the vet's realization. However, the first response, "The vet is calling the owners," merely described the action of making phone calls. Notice the teacher's followup and the child's response to it:

T: He's calling the owners? What's that all about?
S: There were owners in his book and there were six and all one cat.

What makes this follow-up useful is that it calls on the students to reflect on the response and consider what calling the owners had to do with what was going on in the story. That is, the original response merely described an action that had no explicit connection to the development of the plot (i.e., that Sid's been found out).

Repeating the Text.   Another type of frequent response contained words directly from the text. *The Wolf's Chicken Stew* (Kasza, 1987) is a story in which a wolf anonymously sends food to a chicken and her family in order to fatten them up for his dinner. At the point in the story when the chicken discovers that the wolf has been sending the food, the teacher asked, "What just happened?" After the child responded with words from the text, the teacher followed up by asking what the words meant, as a way to prompt the child to go further:

S: The chicken opened up the door and she said, "Oh, it's you, Mr. Wolf."

T: What did the chicken mean when she said, "Oh, it was you, Mr. Wolf?"

S: Because the chicken knew he was sending the food.

Focusing on the Wrong Things.   A third common situation occurred when the children focused on unimportant information. The following exchange occurred during a reading of *Curious George Plays Baseball* (Rey & Rey, 1986), after the following lines of text: "George sneaked over to the dugout. The balls and bats used for practice were lying on the ground."

T: Why did he sneak over to the dugout?

S: So he could practice.

T: Why would he sneak? Why didn't he just walk over to the dugout? Why did he sneak?

S: So nobody would see him.

T: So that no one would see him?

S: So he wouldn't get into trouble.

The focus of the questioning was George's sneaking away to avoid getting into trouble by being somewhere that he shouldn't have been. After the child's initial response, which concentrated just on George's moving over to the dugout, the teacher followed up by explicitly focusing on the word *sneak*.

Table 8.2 lists the stems of follow-up questions that seemed to effectively encourage children to elaborate their responses, while keeping focused on the ideas being developed. The ellipses stand for wording from the student's initial response that the teacher would then draw into her follow-up question. Such follow-ups signal children to more fully explain the thinking behind their initial response.

Results of Text Talk Implementation

The goal of our research on Text Talk was to investigate three issues. The first of these was the extent to which Text Talk influenced classroom discourse dur-

TABLE 8.2
Ideas for Following Up Student Responses

What does that mean …

What's that tell you, if …

… what's that about?

Think about what we already know about …

Why does the story say …?

What does that tell us about …?

So we know …, but why does it say …?

ing read-alouds. The second was the extent to which teachers used Text Talk principles on their own when reading aloud to their classes. The third was the program's effect on student comprehension and vocabulary. In this chapter we have reported findings about the first issue (the influence of Text Talk on classroom discourse). We are still collecting data about the second and third. At this point we can only report anecdotally: Teachers have told us that they use the Text Talk orientation during other read-aloud opportunities. We turn now to reporting our findings on the issue of classroom discourse.

To obtain a baseline of the teachers' reading-aloud interactions, each of the four teachers was tape-recorded reading a story to her class before the implementation of Text Talk. Each teacher then conducted about 25 lessons over the course of the year. All of the Text Talk lessons were recorded and transcribed.

To gauge the effects of Text Talk on classroom discourse, we compared the teachers' baseline read-aloud discussions with four of their Text Talk lessons. We then examined the nature of their questions and the relationship of types of questions to children's responses.

The analysis of questions looked first at questions that initiated discussion, categorizing them as open or closed. Open questions invite students to produce a response: Although the question is asked in anticipation that the response will include certain ideas, both the form and the content of response are left up to the child. Examples of open questions are found in the bottom half of Table 8.1. Closed questions, on the other hand, circumscribe the response and are answerable in just one or two words that are directly retrievable from the text. Examples of closed questions are found in the top half of Table 8.1.

We also examined teachers' follow-up questions after a student's initial response. As illustrated in the preceding examples, follow-up questions were re-

TABLE 8.3
Examples of Open and Closed Follow-Up Questions

Open Follow-Up Questions

S: Because the owl can't do nothing to him.

T: Why can't he do anything to him?

S: Everybody's starting to think of ideas.

T: OK, they're starting to think of ideas. Just any ideas?

S: If somebody gets too close he's going to throw milk at them.

T: OK, he was going to throw milk. So what does that tell us about the people of Chestnut Cove?

Closed Follow-Up Questions

S: He was walking backwards and bumped into somebody.

T: He's walking backwards. Is that the normal way to walk?

S: He wasn't really in Alaska.

T: He wasn't really in Alaska, he was just doing what?

S: He wants a pet.

T: He wants a pet, because does he have any friends to play with?

S: They feed [the cat] too much food.

T: Are they feeding him because they like him or because they don't like him?

---

lated to the initial question, and typically aimed for completion, elaboration, or clarification of initial responses. These questions were also scored as open or closed. Table 8.3 provides examples of open and closed follow-up questions. The student response that preceded the follow-up question is included in order to more clearly demonstrate the question's intent.

Figure 8.1 represents the percentages of open initial and open follow-up questions in baseline and Text Talk classes. As the figure shows, there was a dramatic difference in the proportion of open questions, both initial and follow-up, used in baseline and Text Talk lessons. Specifically, in baseline lessons over 80% of the initial questions were closed, while in the Text Talk lessons the proportions were reversed: over 80% of the questions were open. There was also a less dramatic difference in the proportion of open and closed follow-up questions. This clearly shows that open questions typified Text

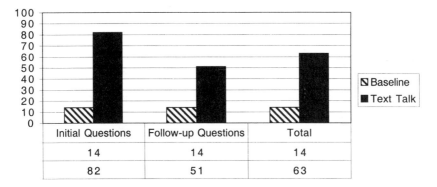

FIG. 8.1. Percentage of open initial and follow-up questions in baseline and Text Talk lessons.

Talk discourse, whereas closed questions had been more typical prior to Text Talk's implementation.

In addition to looking at types of teacher questions, we also examined the amount of student talk. Measuring how much children are saying helps to indicate the extent to which they are producing language and contributing ideas. To make this measurement, we calculated the number of words per student response in the baseline and Text Talk lessons. The result showed that the length of responses across all four classrooms increased from 2.1 words per response in the baseline lessons to 7.65 words per response in the Text Talk lessons.

To get a more fine-grained understanding of how the length of student responses was influenced by open questions (which are the central feature of the Text Talk discourse environment), we examined the length of student responses in each classroom in conjunction with the percentage of open questions in each classroom.

The top portion of Fig. 8.2 shows the number of words per response for each classroom during the baseline lesson, and the mean number of words per response across the four Text Talk lessons. The bottom portion shows the percent of open questions for baseline and Text Talk lessons in each classroom. As can be seen from the figure, the length of response varies with the proportion of open questions.

Finally, we explored how directly the open or closed nature of questions influenced the nature of students' responses. Specifically, we were interested in investigating the extent to which children treat open questions as invitations to produce ideas—as suggested in the bottom set of responses in Table 8.1. To do so, we analyzed the data for matches between question and response. Children's

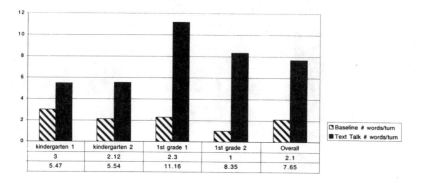

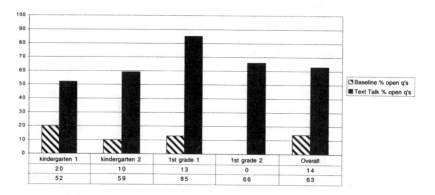

FIG. 8.2. Words per student turn (top panel) and percentage of open questions in baseline and Text Talk lessons in each classroom.

responses were coded as matching if the response to an open question was open, or if the response to a closed question was closed. Responses were scored as open if the children had constructed the responses themselves, rather than relying on the text or the question. Responses were scored as closed if they were directly retrieved from text or literally and simply followed the form of the question, such as responding to "How is George feeling?" with "He's feeling bad."

Responses were considered non-matching when students answered a closed question as if it had asked for a constructed response, or answered an open question as if it had asked for a retrieved or single-word response. One example would be a student answering the closed question "Is he a new toy or an old toy?" with the open response "That's his oldest toy cause he had that toy ever since he was a baby"; another example would entail answering the open question "How did the other kids like Stephanie's ponytail?" with the closed response "Ugly."

The match between the nature of the question and the nature of the response is shown in Fig. 8.3. The numbers in the figure are averaged across all four classrooms. As can be seen, the nature of the question strongly influences the nature of the response in both baseline and Text Talk lessons. In baseline lessons, virtually all of the responses matched the questions, and in Text Talk a large majority (83.5 %) matched.

It is of some interest to consider why non-matches occur in Text Talk lessons approximately 16% of the time, while being virtually absent from baseline lessons. First of all, open responses are more difficult for children to produce, so it seems understandable that the children might have been unable to do so at times, and instead responded to Text Talk's open questions in a closed manner. More interesting is the question of why children just as often make the opposite non-match—that is, providing open responses to closed questions. It seems that, in Text Talk, children become accustomed to constructing their responses openly, and sometimes do so even if the question does not explicitly require it.

Our results suggest, first, that teachers were able to change their read-aloud style to an approach based on interspersed open questions and follow-up scaffolding. Second, children responded to this read-aloud approach by producing language and expressing ideas about the stories they had heard (rather than simply parroting the text). Thus, our work with Text Talk supports the premise that increased interactions with decontextualized language benefit children's language and comprehension ability.

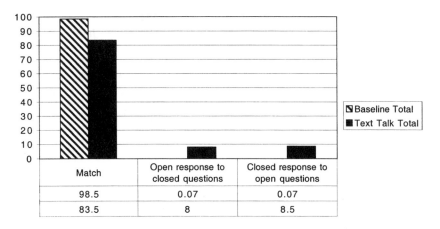

FIG. 8.3. Percentage of match between question and response for baseline and Text Talk lessons.

CONCLUSION

The results of Text Talk show that young children will pick up on the invitation to respond to text in a constructed fashion. Customarily, children are only invited to briefly add words to a teacher's response, or to echo language from the text. But children can also produce rich and complex responses to text when invited to do so.

These results bring to mind Gordon Wells' (1986) idea that most of the time we fail to exploit the full potential of language. Wells quotes Sapir to illustrate his point: "It is somewhat as though a dynamo capable of generating enough power to run an elevator were used almost exclusively to operate an electric doorbell" (Wells, 1986, p. 111). We need to activate children's potential to master decontextualized language, in order to meet the increasingly complex demands that they will encounter throughout their school years.

ACKNOWLEDGMENT

The authors are grateful to the Spencer Foundation for a grant that supported the work on which this article is based. The opinions expressed do not necessarily reflect the position or policy of the Spencer Foundation, and no official endorsement should be inferred.

REFERENCES

Beck, I. L., McKeown, M. G., Hamilton, R. L., & Kucan, L. (1997). *Questioning the author: An approach for enhancing student engagement with text.* Newark, DE: International Reading Association.

Beck, I. L., McKeown, M. G., & Omanson, R. C. (1987). The effects and uses of diverse vocabulary instruction. In M. G. McKeown & M. E. Curtis (Eds.), *The nature of vocabulary acquisition* (pp. 147–163). Mahwah, NJ: Lawrence Erlbaum Associates.

Beck, I. L., McKeown, M. G., Worthy, J., Sandora, C., & Kucan, L. (1996). Questioning the author: A year-long classroom implementation to engage students with text. *Elementary School Journal, 96*(4), 385–414.

Cochran-Smith, M. (1984). *The making of a reader.* Norwood, NJ: Ablex.

Dickinson, D. K., & Smith, M. W. (1994). Long-term effects of preschool teachers' book readings on low-income children's vocabulary and story comprehension. *Reading Research Quarterly, 29*(2), 104–122.

Dickinson, D. K., & Tabors, P. O. (1991). Early literacy: Linkages between home, school, and literacy achievement at age five. *Journal of Research in Childhood Education, 6,* 30–46.

Durkin, D. (1974–1975). A six-year study of children who learned to read in school at age of four. *Reading Research Quarterly, 10,* 9–61.

Feitelson, D., Goldstein, Z., Iraqi, J., & Share, D. (1993). Effects of listening to story reading on aspects of literacy acquisition in a diglossic situation. *Reading Research Quarterly, 28,* 70–79.

Freppon, P. A. (1991). Children's concepts of the nature and purpose of reading and writing in different instructional settings. *Journal of Reading Behavior: A Journal of Literacy, 23,* 139–163.

Graves, M. F., Brunetti, G. J., & Slater, W. H. (1982). The reading vocabularies of primary-grade children of varying geographic and social backgrounds. In J. A. Harris & L. A. Harris (Eds.), *New inquiries in reading research and instruction* (pp. 99–104). Rochester, NY: National Reading Conference.

Heath, S. B. (1983). *Ways with words.* Cambridge: Cambridge University Press.

Mason, J. M., & Allen, J. (1986). A review of emergent literacy with implications for research and practice in reading. In C. Z. Rothkopf (Ed.), *Review of Research in Education* (Vol. 13, pp. 3–48). Washington, DC: American Educational Research Association.

McKeown, M. G., & Beck, I. L., (1998). Talking to an author: Readers taking charge of the reading process. In R. Calfee & N. Nelson (Eds.), *The reading-writing connection* (Yearbook for the National Society for the Study of Education, pp. 112–130). Chicago: National Society for the Study of Education.

Morrow, L. M. (1992). The impact of a literature-based program on literacy achievement, use of literature, and attitudes of children from minority backgrounds. *Reading Research Quarterly, 27*(3), 250–275.

Neuman, S. B. (1990). Assessing inferencing strategies. In J. Zutell & S. McCormick, (Eds.), *Literacy theory and research* (National Reading Conference Yearbook, pp. 267–274). Chicago: National Reading Conference.

Nicholson, T., & Imlach, K. (1981). Where do their answers come from? A study of the inferences which children make when answering questions about narrative stories. *Journal of Reading Behavior, 13,* 111–129.

Seashore, R. H., & Eckerson, L. D. (1940). The measurement of individual differences in general English vocabularies. *Journal of Educational Psychology, 31,* 14–38.

Snow, C. E. (1993). Families as social contexts for literacy development. In C. Daiute (Ed.), *The development of literacy through social interaction* (No. 61, pp. 11–24). San Francisco: Jossey-Bass.

Snow, C. E., & Dickinson, D. K. (1991). Some skills that aren't basic in a new conception of literacy. In A. Purves & T. Jennings (Eds.), *Literate systems and individual lives: Perspectives on literacy and schooling* (pp. 175–213). Albany, NY: SUNY Press.

Snow, C. E., Tabors, P. O., Nicholson, P. A., & Kurland, B. F. (1995). SHELL: Oral language and early literacy skills in kindergarten and first-grade children. *Journal of Research in Childhood Education, 10,* 37–47.

Teale, W. H., & Martinez, M. G. (1996). Reading aloud to young children: Teachers' reading styles and kindergartners' text comprehension. In C. Pontecorvo, M. Orsolini, B. Burge, & L. B. Resnick (Eds.), *Children's early text construction* (pp. 321–344). Mahwah, NJ: Lawrence Erlbaum Associates.

Wells, G. (1986). *The meaning makers: Children learning language and using language to learn.* Portsmouth, NH: Heineman.

CHILDREN'S BOOKS

Egan, T. (1997). *Burnt toast on Davenport Street.* New York: Houghton Mifflin.

Kasza, K. (1987). *The wolf's chicken stew.* New York: G. P. Putnam's Sons.

Lord, J. V. (1972). *The giant jam sandwich*. New York: Houghton Mifflin.
MacDonald, A. (1998). *Beware of the bears!* Waukesha, WI: Little Tiger Press.
McCloskey, R. (1941). *Make way for ducklings*. New York: Puffin Books.
Moore, I. (1991). *Six-dinner Sid*. New York: Aladdin.
Rey, M., & Rey, H. A. (1986). *Curious George plays baseball*. New York: Houghton Mifflin.
Steig, W. (1986). *Brave Irene*. New York: Farrar, Straus and Giroux.

9

Dialogic Reading: A Shared Picture Book Reading Intervention for Preschoolers

Andrea A. Zevenbergen
State University of New York College at Fredonia

Grover J. Whitehurst
State University of New York at Stony Brook

Over the past several decades, many studies have demonstrated that preschoolers' experience with shared reading is linked to their development of language. Correlational studies have revealed that the frequency of shared picture book reading in the home is related to preschoolers' language skills (e.g., Mason, 1980; Payne, Whitehurst, & Angell, 1994; Wells, 1985; Wells, Barnes, & Wells, 1984). Experimental work bolsters these findings: Several researchers have demonstrated that shared picture book reading experiences result in gains in preschoolers' vocabulary (e.g., Elley, 1989; Jenkins, Stein, & Wysocki, 1984; Sénéchal & Cornell, 1993; Sénéchal, Thomas, & Monker, 1995; Vivas, 1996), oral language complexity (McNeill & Fowler, 1999; Valdez-Menchaca & Whitehurst, 1992), and narrative skills (Harkins, Koch, & Michel, 1994; Zevenbergen & Wilson, 1996). Studies also suggest a link between early experiences with shared picture book reading and later language and literacy skills (cf. Dickinson & Smith, 1994; Stevenson & Fredman, 1990; Wells, 1985). For example, Wells (1985) showed that the amount of time that children spent listening to stories between 1 and 3 years of age was significantly correlated with their language skills at age 5 and their reading comprehension skills at age 7. Similarly, Stevenson and Fredman (1990) found a significant relationship between the frequency of parent–child shared reading when children were preschoolers and their reading, spelling, and IQ scores at age 13.

Research that we have conducted (Arnold, Lonigan, Whitehurst, & Epstein, 1994; Whitehurst et al., 1988) as well as the work of others (e.g., Crain-Thoreson & Dale, 1999; Dickinson & Smith, 1994; Haden, Reese, & Fivush, 1996; Reese & Cox, 1999) suggests that the particular way in which preschoolers are read to is related to the language gains they obtain from the picture book reading experience. When adults give children opportunities to become active participants in the reading experience by using evocative techniques during the reading (e.g., asking the child questions about the pictures or the story, encouraging the child to tell the story along with the adult), children show greater language gains than when adults simply read the book to the child (Arnold et al., 1994; Whitehurst et al., 1988).

DIALOGIC READING TECHNIQUES

The specific reading technique that we have developed is called *dialogic reading*. This technique, first described in Whitehurst et al. (1988), is based on the theory that practice in using language, feedback regarding language, and appropriately scaffolded adult–child interactions in the context of picture book reading all facilitate young children's language development. Two sets of specific techniques have been developed: one for reading with children 2 to 3 years of age, and the other for reading with children 4 to 5 years of age. Across both age groups, the child is encouraged to become the teller of the story over time; the adult's role is to prompt the child with questions, expand the child's verbalizations, and praise the child's efforts to tell the story and label objects within the book (Arnold & Whitehurst, 1994). The adult also increases the standards for the child's verbalizations over time, following the principle of the zone of proximal development (Vygotsky, 1978). That is, the adult continually encourages the child to say just a little more than he or she would naturally do; this scaffolding is thought to lead to more rapid development in the child's language skills than would occur spontaneously.

Dialogic reading for 2- to 3-year-olds is taught to adults in two assignments. The assignments are taught 2 to 3 weeks apart. Adults are taught seven points in the first assignment:

1. *Ask "what" questions.* Ask children to name objects pictured in the book; also ask children simple questions about the story (e.g., "What did the pigs do next?").

2. *Follow answers with questions.* Follow the child's answers to questions with further, related questions. For example, if the child is able to label an object in the book, ask questions about attributes of the object (e.g., "Yes, that's a dog. What color is the dog?").

3. *Repeat what the child says.* Repeating what the child says serves to reinforce the child's verbalization, letting the child know that he or she is correct (e.g., "Yes, that's a wagon").

4. *Help the child as needed.* Sometimes the questions asked of children are initially difficult for them to answer. A child's inability to answer a question provides a good teaching opportunity. Answer the question posed to the child and have him or her repeat your verbalization (e.g., "That's called an octopus. Can you say, 'octopus'?").

5. *Praise and encourage.* Praise the child's attempts to talk about the book. Both general (e.g., "Good job!") and specific praise (e.g., "Good talking!" "You did such a good job of naming the animals!") are encouraging to the child.

6. *Follow the child's interests.* It is not important to read all the words in the book or to talk about every picture. If the child begins to talk about a part of the story or a picture on the page, follow his or her interests and encourage the child to talk more. Children are more likely to enjoy reading with adults if the adults are sensitive and responsive to their interests.

7. *Have fun.* One important goal of dialogic reading is that children enjoy the shared reading experience. Children do appear to enjoy dialogic reading, particularly when adults take a game-like, turn-taking approach to using the techniques. For example, children seem to enjoy when the adult reads one page, and the child "reads" the next page. If the child appears to be getting tired of the reading, read a few pages without questions or put the book aside for a later time.

For the second assignment, adults are instructed on the following three points:

1. *Ask open-ended questions.* In part one, the child is asked specific questions about objects in the book, attributes of the objects, and elements of the story. After the child has had practice with these types of specific questions, begin to ask him or her more open-ended questions. Examples of open-ended prompts include, "What do you see on this page?" and "Tell me what's going on here." As with part one, encourage and praise any responses from the child and offer help as needed.

2.   *Expand what the child says.* When the child says something about the book, repeat what he or she says and add a few more words to that verbalization. Then, have the child imitate what you have said. For example if the child says, "Big dog," the adult might say, "Yes, the big dog is red. Can you say that?"

3.   *Have fun.* As mentioned in part one, it is important that the child enjoy the experience. Turn-taking in talking about the book helps keep children interested.

Dialogic reading for children aged 4 to 5 uses different techniques from those used with younger children, in that the types of questions asked of the older children are generally more challenging. Adults are taught how to use dialogic reading techniques with 4- to 5-year-olds through a single assignment that focuses on asking the child specific types of questions, evaluating his or her responses, expanding those responses, and having the child repeat the expanded utterances (Whitehurst, Epstein, et al., 1994). The acronyms CROWD and PEER were developed to help adults remember these techniques. CROWD refers to the five types of questions asked by adults when engaging in dialogic reading with 4- to 5-year-olds. These question types are as follows:

1.   *Completion prompts:* Fill-in-the-blank questions (e.g., "When we went into the car, we all put on our _____")
2.   *Recall prompts:* Questions that require the child to remember aspects of the book (e.g., "Can you remember some of the things that Sticky-beak did at school?")
3.   *Open-ended prompts:* Statements that encourage the child to respond to the book in his or her own words (e.g., "Now it's your turn to tell about this page").
4.   *Wh-prompts:* What, where, and why questions (e.g., "What is this called?" "Why did Peter stay home from school?")
5.   *Distancing prompts:* Questions that require the child to relate the content of the book to aspects of life outside of the book (e.g., "Did you ever go to a parade like Susie did?")

The PEER strategy reminds adults to *prompt* the child to label objects in the book and talk about the story, *evaluate* the child's responses, *expand* the child's verbalization by repeating what the child has said and adding information to it, and encourage the child to *repeat* the expanded utterances. Although the term "evaluate" may seem to have negative connotations, adults are actually expected to praise the child's correct responses and offer alternative labels or answers for clearly incorrect responses. Corrections should be given to children in a way that is constructive and sensitive to their efforts to talk about the book. Children may respond well to corrections phrased in the following ways: "Well, that looks like a horse, but we would call it a cow," or "Well, Joey might have wanted to go to the park, but remember that Joey went to the circus in the story?" One may also evaluate a child's vocabulary usage as relatively simple and take the opportunity to teach the child a more specific word. For example, if the child says, "That's a dog," the adult might say, "Yes, that's a dog. It's a kind of dog called a 'beagle.' Can you say 'beagle'?"

A transcript of one parent–child dialogic reading interaction is presented in Appendix A. Although any picture book can be used for dialogic reading, the books that work particularly well have clear illustrations, relatively little text, and an engaging story. A list of some such books is presented in Appendix B.

VIDEOTAPE TRAINING

We have developed a set of videotapes to teach adults the dialogic reading technique (Whitehurst, 1991, 1994a, 1994b). Two of these tapes, both of which are 15 to 20 minutes long, were developed to teach parents the techniques for reading with 2- to 3-year-old children. The third 15-minute videotape was developed to teach parents the techniques for reading with 4- to 5-year-olds. An additional 15-minute videotape instructs teachers of 4- to 5-year-old children in the techniques. Each videotape explains the dialogic reading techniques, presents models of adults and children reading together using the techniques, and then "quizzes" the viewer on these techniques. The quizzes present an incorrect use of the given technique and then ask the viewer, "What could he or she have done instead?" The videotapes were developed in order to increase the number of individuals who could use dialogic reading techniques with their children; it is usually less costly for individuals to be trained through a videotape than by a trainer. Interestingly, Arnold et al. (1994) found greater gains in 2-year-olds' receptive and expressive vocabulary when their parents were taught the dialogic reading techniques by videotape than when the parents were taught the same techniques individually by a trainer. The authors suggest that the relative advantage of the videotape training may derive from the videotape's modeling of parent–child reading interactions. Studies demonstrating the importance of model similarity in skill acquisition (e.g., Bandura, 1977) suggest that parents or teachers studying dialogic reading techniques may best learn these skills by seeing other parents or teachers modeling them in practice.

EVALUATION OF THE EFFECTIVENESS
OF DIALOGIC READING

We have conducted a series of studies evaluating the effectiveness of dialogic reading for children from upper-, middle-, and lower-socioeconomic status (SES) groups, and also evaluating the relative effectiveness of dialogic reading interventions conducted in the home versus those occurring in a preschool environment. Overall, we have found that dialogic reading has a positive effect on the language and emergent literacy skills of children.

The Impact of Dialogic Reading on the Language Skills of Children From High-SES Families

The first study evaluated the effects of dialogic reading on the language skills of 2-year-olds from upper- and middle-SES families (Whitehurst et al., 1988). In this study, all participating parents were European American mothers. Half of the mother–child dyads were randomly assigned to the experimental condition, where they participated in a dialogic reading program for 4 weeks. The other half of the dyads were assigned to the control condition. The mothers in the experimental condition were taught the dialogic reading techniques in two half-hour training sessions (i.e., parts one and two described earlier). Mothers received individual, didactic instruction in the techniques; modeling of the techniques by the trainer and a research assistant who played the role of a child; and direct feedback, in which the trainer played the role of a child and gave the mother feedback about her performance. Mothers in the control group were not taught dialogic reading techniques but were told to read to their child over the 4-week period as usual. All mothers were asked to audiotape their reading sessions during the study period and to record information regarding the frequency of their reading over the 4 weeks.

Examination of reading frequency data revealed no difference between the experimental group and control group in frequency of mother–child reading. Analyses of the audiotapes revealed a significant increase in mean length utterance (MLU) among the children in the experimental group over the course of the 4 weeks. These children also showed significant gains in their expressive language skills during the same period. Specifically, children in the experimental group showed a 6-month gain in expressive vocabulary, as assessed by the Expressive One-Word Picture Vocabulary Test (EOWPVT; Gardner, 1981), and an 8.5-month gain in expressive language fluency, as assessed by the Expressive Language subtest of the Illinois Test of Psycholinguistic Abilities

(ITPA-VE; Kirk, McCarthy, & Kirk, 1968). No significant gain was seen in children's receptive vocabulary skills, as assessed by the Peabody Picture Vocabulary Test–Revised (PPVT-R; Dunn & Dunn, 1981) as a result of the intervention. Gains in children's expressive language skills were maintained at a 9-month follow-up assessment.

In a replication and extension of the work by Whitehurst et al. (1988), Arnold et al. (1994) taught mothers to read dialogically with their 2-year-old children through either videotape or direct training. Arnold et al. contrasted the effects of the two training conditions with a control condition, in which mothers were told to read to their children as usual. As in Whitehurst et al. (1988), the children in this study were from upper- and middle-SES European American families, and the intervention lasted for 4 weeks.

Both training conditions were found to have a significant effect on children's language skills. Specifically, children from the videotape training group scored significantly higher than those in the control group on the EOWPVT and the ITPA–VE. Children from the direct training group also scored significantly higher than those in the control group on the ITPA–VE. Additionally, children from the videotape training group scored significantly higher on the EOWPVT and PPVT–R than the children from the direct training group. Taken together, these results further suggest the positive influence of dialogic reading on the language skills of high- and middle-SES children. The results of Whitehurst et al. (1988) and Arnold et al. (1994) indicate that language development in high- and middle-SES children can be significantly enhanced with a relatively short (i.e., 4-week) intervention.

The Influence of Dialogic Reading on the Language Skills of Children From Low-Income Families Enrolled in Day Care

Several studies have shown that a substantial proportion of children from socioeconomically disadvantaged families enter kindergarten with language skills that lag behind those of their peers from higher-income families (e.g., Carnegie Foundation for the Advancement of Teaching, 1991; Walker, Greenwood, Hart, & Carta, 1994; Whitehurst, Epstein, et al., 1994). Although there is considerable variability across families (Payne et al., 1994), many children from low-income families have been found to have less access to home literacy (e.g., Feitelson & Goldstein, 1986; Harris & Smith, 1987; McCormick & Mason, 1986; Raz & Bryant, 1990), and fewer verbal interactions with their caregivers (Heath, 1982; Robinson & Rackstraw, 1967; Snow, Dubber, & deBlauw, 1982) than children from higher-income families. These home disadvantages may translate to lower levels of language skill at school entry for some children from low-SES families.

Valdez-Menchaca and Whitehurst (1992) assessed the effectiveness of a 7-week dialogic reading program in accelerating the language skills of 2-year-old children from low-income families attending day care in Mexico. Children in the intervention condition were read to by a graduate student using the dialogic reading techniques. Children in the control condition were given instruction in arts and crafts by the same graduate student. The dialogic reading intervention yielded significant gains in children's expressive and receptive language skills, as assessed by the EOWPVT, ITPA–VE, and PPVT–R. Specifically, at posttest, the children in the intervention condition were on average 7.3 months ahead of the control children in terms of language age on the EOWPVT; 8.2 months ahead on the ITPA–VE; and 3.3 months ahead on the PPVT–R. Moreover, children in the intervention condition also obtained higher scores on measures of linguistic complexity (e.g., MLU, sentence complexity, variety of use of nouns and verbs) than did children in the control condition. Thus, Valdez-Menchaca and Whitehurst demonstrated that dialogic reading can significantly affect the language skills of children from low-income families.

Whitehurst, Arnold, et al. (1994) showed that a 6-week dialogic reading program could positively influence the language skills of 3-year-olds from low-income families in the United States. In this study, children were enrolled in daycare centers that served low-income families. Approximately half of the children were African American, another quarter were European American, and the remaining quarter were Latino. Children within classrooms were randomly assigned to participate in one of three conditions: dialogic reading at home and in their classroom (school plus home condition); dialogic reading only in their classroom (school condition); or play activities in the classroom (control condition). Parents of children in the school plus home condition and all classroom teachers and aides were trained in the dialogic reading techniques through videotape and supervised role play. Parents received books to read to their children at home. Children in the school plus home condition and the school condition read dialogically with their classroom teachers or aides in groups of no more than five. Each reading group was scheduled to read together for approximately 10 minutes per day. The teacher or aide typically read with a small group of children while the other adult monitored the remaining children, who were engaged in another activity.

The dialogic reading intervention showed significant gains in children's expressive language skills, as assessed by the EOWPVT. Children who participated in the two dialogic reading conditions scored significantly higher on the EOWPVT at posttest than children in the control condition. Moreover, children in the school plus home condition scored significantly higher on the EOWPVT than those in the school condition alone. A 6-month follow-up revealed that the children in the two reading conditions were still scoring ahead of their peers in the control group on the EOWPVT. Children who participated in the dialogic reading conditions also showed posttest vocabulary gains on a test that we developed to assess children's knowledge of specific and relatively uncommon vocabulary words pictured in the books used in the intervention conditions. This test was not administered at the 6-month follow-up.

The positive results were tempered by findings of substantial variability in the fidelity with which teachers followed the intervention program. Of the five daycare centers that participated in the program, one center only minimally complied with the intervention program. This experience of minimal compliance led us to consider the possible barriers to conducting a dialogic reading program within a daycare or preschool classroom environment. Discussions with teachers and classroom observations revealed that teachers may find it difficult to engage in shared reading with small groups of children unless there are more than two adults in the classroom. Although theoretically one adult should be able to read with a small group of students while the other adult monitors the remaining children, this is challenging in practice, since individual children often need adult attention. In a classroom staffed by only two adults, if one adult is reading with a small group of children, and the other adult is attending to an individual child, there is no adult remaining to monitor closely the rest of the children. This does not mean, however, that dialogic reading is not possible within a daycare or preschool classroom environment. Clearly the results of Whitehurst, Arnold, et al. (1994) show that teachers in such classrooms can effectively manage reading dialogically to small groups. To increase the chances of consistent teacher–child shared reading interactions within a daycare or preschool classroom environment, teachers may use classroom volunteers either to conduct the shared reading interactions or to assist other children while the teacher reads with the group. Possible volunteers include parents, older elementary- and secondary-school students, college students, and elderly individuals.

Another potential barrier may be the philosophy held by some daycare centers and preschools that direct instruction interactions of this type are developmentally inappropriate for preschool-aged children. However, dialogic reading interactions can be quite child-directed. One might expect that as the child gradually becomes the teller of the story, he or she will naturally follow his or her own interests while discussing the story and pictures in a book. Thus, individual teachers may make their dialogic reading interactions as teacher-directed or child-directed as they choose.

Lonigan and Whitehurst's (1998) study of the effect of a dialogic reading program on the language skills of children from low-income families enrolled in daycare contrasted the effects of a no-treatment control group, a school-only reading condition, a home-only reading condition, and a school plus home reading condition. The children in this study were 3- and 4-year-olds, approximately 90% of whom were African American. The purpose of the study was to contrast the effect of school-only dialogic reading with that of home-only dialogic reading—a contrast that was not examined in the Whitehurst, Arnold, et al. (1994) study. The training of teachers and parents in the dialogic reading techniques and the details of the intervention program (e.g., length of program, procedures for classroom reading interactions) were all similar to those seen in Whitehurst, Arnold, et al.

Results of the study revealed that the dialogic reading intervention had a significant impact on children's expressive language abilities; however, as in Whitehurst, Arnold, et al., these gains varied as a function of daycare center compliance with the intervention program. In the high-compliance centers, children in the intervention conditions scored significantly higher on the posttest EOWPVT than children in the control condition. There was no significant difference between the three intervention conditions on the EOWPVT in these high-compliance centers; however, the effect size for the school plus home reading group was almost double that of the two other reading conditions. An intervention effect was also observed on the ITPA–VE. Children in the three intervention conditions scored significantly higher on this measure at posttest than children in the control condition. Moreover, children in the home-only condition scored significantly higher on the ITPA–VE than children in each of the other three conditions.

Intervention effects were also found on measures of spontaneous verbalization (e.g., MLU, semantic complexity) when reading an unfamiliar book with a researcher. On these measures of spontaneous verbalizations, minimal differences were found between the three intervention groups. Overall, the results of Lonigan and Whitehurst (1998) indicate that both parent-led and teacher-led dialogic reading can have a positive effect on preschoolers' language skills. Based on their data, Lonigan and Whitehurst surmised that parent–child dialogic reading may affect children's use of descriptive language more than teacher–child dialogic reading, and teacher–child dialogic reading may affect children's vocabulary acquisition more than parent–child dialogic reading.

The Influence of Dialogic Reading on the Language and Emergent Literacy Skills of Children Enrolled in Head Start

Given the relatively high academic risk of children from low-income families (Carnegie Foundation for the Advancement of Teaching, 1991), it is also important to assess how shared reading interventions affect the emergent literacy skills of children from low-income families. Emergent literacy comprises the skills, knowledge, and attitudes that are presumed to be developmental precursors to conventional forms of reading and writing (Sulzby, 1989; Sulzby & Teale, 1991; Teale & Sulzby, 1986). It thus includes skills such as letter knowledge, phonemic awareness, print awareness, and oral language skills (Lonigan & Whitehurst, 1998).

Whitehurst, Epstein, et al. (1994) and Whitehurst et al. (1999) demonstrated the positive impact of dialogic reading on the emergent literacy skills of children enrolled in Head Start. Head Start classrooms of 4-year-olds were randomly assigned to either an intervention condition, involving an add-on dialogic reading program conducted both at home and in the classroom, or a control condition, in which the children experienced only the regular Head Start curriculum. Children in the intervention condition also used an adaptation of a classroom-based sound and letter awareness program called *Sound Foundations* (Byrne & Fielding-Barnsley, 1992). This program introduces children to letters and the relationships between specific letters and phonemes (e.g., the letter *s* and the /s/ sound). Parents and teachers in the intervention condition were trained in the dialogic reading techniques through videotape and role play with a trainer. The dialogic reading portion of the intervention was conducted for 30 weeks; the letter and sound awareness portion took place over 16 weeks.

The Head Start intervention differed from the dialogic reading programs we had conducted in daycare settings (Whitehurst, Arnold, et al., 1994) or with parents only (Whitehurst et al., 1988), in that hints for "wh-" prompts were added to each page of the books, and hints for recall questions were added to the inside back covers of the books. Teacher and parent book guides developed for each text provided hints on how to read the book with children (Whitehurst, 1994c). These guides were modeled on materials developed by Karweit (1989). A lending library system was used so that books could be rotated from one intervention classroom to another on a weekly basis, and all children in the intervention condition could be exposed to 30 different picture books in the classroom and at home over the course of the program. Each week, children in the intervention condition were given a book to take home on Monday; the books were returned on the following Friday so that they could be used in another intervention classroom the next Monday. Parents were encouraged to read books dialogically with their children at least three times per week.

Whitehurst, Epstein, et al. (1994) describe the results of the initial intervention. Children were assessed on 21 language and literacy measures at the beginning and end of the Head Start year. These measures included the EOWPVT, the PPVT–R, the ITPA–VE, and 18 subscales from the Developing Skills Checklist (DSC) (CBT, 1990), a measure of children's emergent literacy skills. The DSC specifically assesses children's skills in the areas of narration, letter naming, phonemic awareness, print concepts, and emergent writing. Because of the relatively large number of measures administered to each child, a data reduction procedure was used to decrease the number of statistical tests conducted to assess the effect of the intervention. Using principal components analysis, the data were reduced to four factors: Language, Writing, Linguistic Awareness, and Print Concepts. The highest factor loadings on the Language factor were the three language tests (i.e., EOWPVT, PPVT–R, ITPA–VE) and the narrative subscale of the DSC. The highest factor loadings on the Writing factor were the child's ability to print from left to right, the child's ability to write his or her own name, and writing mechanics (e.g., using uppercase and lowercase letters correctly). The highest factor loadings on the Linguistic Awareness factor were the child's identification of sounds and letters, identification of words as same or different, and segmentation of sentences into words and words into syllables. The variables that loaded most highly on the Print Concepts factor were typical measures of concepts of print (e.g., identifying people reading, distinguishing between words, pictures, and numbers, identifying components of writing).

The intervention program was found to have a significant effect on the Writing and Print Concepts factors. As shown in Fig. 9.1, these intervention effects were substantial, corresponding to effect sizes of .516 and .624 for the Writing and Print Concepts factors, respectively. These fall into the category of medium effect sizes (Cohen, 1988); similar effect sizes have been interpreted in other studies of Head Start children as educationally meaningful (e.g., Lee, Brooks-Gunn, Schnur, & Liaw, 1990).

Another important finding in this study was that the extent to which parents complied with the reading program at home was related to children's scores on the Language factor. This relationship is shown vividly in Fig. 9.2, and bolsters the hypothesis that parent–child dialogic reading is related to children's language development in the preschool years.

Overall, Whitehurst, Epstein, et al. demonstrate that an emergent literacy intervention composed of dialogic reading and a sound and letter awareness

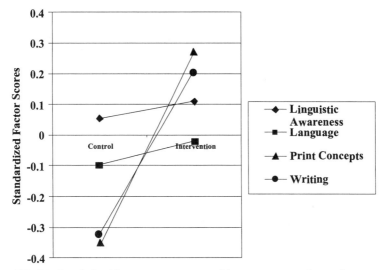

FIG. 9.1. Standardized factor scores at posttest of the intervention and control groups.

program can significantly influence the writing skills and print concepts knowledge of children enrolled in Head Start. The failure to find a significant intervention effect on the Language factor suggests that 4- and 5-year-olds from low-income families may need one-on-one reading interactions in order to make substantial gains in their language skills through dialogic reading. When teachers are reading dialogically with groups of 4 to 5 children, any one child in the group simply may not have very many opportunities to practice language use. Moreover, although open-ended questions to children (i.e., allowing the child to tell the story as much as possible) may offer the best opportunity for children to practice language use in the context of dialogic reading interactions, the intervention teachers in our study did not tend to ask open-ended questions. It may be that asking open-ended questions to individual preschool-aged children in the context of small-group dialogic reading permits the other children to go off-task. Although some children may benefit from reading dialogically in small groups (i.e., Whitehurst, Arnold, et al., 1994; Lonigan & Whitehurst, 1998) young children's language skills are likely to be more enhanced by one-on-one dialogic reading interactions than small-group dialogic readings. Thus, it is recommended that classroom teachers and volunteers engage in dialogic reading with individual children as much as possible. Additionally, it is recommended that Head Start and other similar programs focus on encouraging parents to engage in shared reading with their children. Whitehurst et al. (1999) showed that the gains which Head Start children

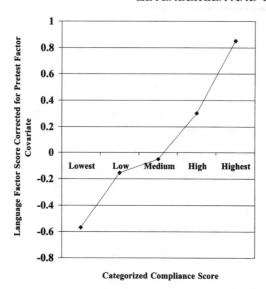

FIG. 9.2. Standardized language factor outcome scores as a function of parental compliance with the home dialogic reading program.

made during the emergent literacy program were maintained through the kindergarten year. Specifically, children who participated in the intervention obtained higher scores on tests of language abilities, knowledge of letters and sounds, and writing at the end of the kindergarten year than children who had participated in the control condition.

The gains were modest, and did not translate into differences in reading scores for these same children at the end of first and second grade. It may be that dialogic reading and other similar shared reading interventions conducted in the preschool years will yield more advantages for children during the later elementary school years, when they are reading to learn, than in the early elementary school years, when they are learning to read. The task for children in the early stages of learning to read is to break the alphabetic code by which letters in English are translated into sounds. Reading comprehension of connected text, which depends on vocabulary and world knowledge as well as decoding skills, will only come into play after a child has developed enough decoding fluency to move beyond individual words. The influence of shared reading and other experiences that enhance the knowledge needed for reading comprehension is likely to be increasingly important once children have mastered the decoding task. Of course, the knowledge that supports text comprehension needs to be continuously supported and enhanced over the preschool and elementary school years. Thus, we posit that dialogic reading during the preschool period needs to be linked with related experiences that promote vocabulary and conceptual growth during elementary school, if large effects on reading are eventually to be obtained.

DISCUSSION

The studies on dialogic reading intervention strongly suggest that this shared reading intervention can positively influence the language and emergent literacy skills of preschool-aged children. Dialogic reading facilitates the language development of children from families at all SES levels. Moreover, the effects of dialogic reading interventions are manifest whether it is parents or teachers who read with children.

Crain-Thoreson, Dale, and colleagues have also found that dialogic reading has a positive effect (Crain-Thoreson & Dale, 1999; Dale, Crain-Thoreson, Notari-Syverson, & Cole, 1996). Dale et al. (1996) found dialogic reading to be superior to a play-based language facilitation intervention for enhancing the language skills of preschoolers with language delays. Similarly, Crain-Thoreson and Dale (1999) showed that children with language delays spoke more, increased their MLU, and increased their vocabulary diversity during shared readings with an adult trained in dialogic reading techniques. Importantly, these two researchers added an instruction to parents to pause after asking questions of their child; the authors had observed in their earlier study that many parents of the children with language delays tended not to allow their children sufficient time to answer questions before verbalizing again (e.g., by asking another question, or answering the posed question). It is likely that nearly all children can benefit from having adults pause after asking the child a question—this allows the child ample time to respond.

Although the results of the dialogic reading studies have been encouraging, there are some challenges to implementation. First, it is often difficult for teachers to integrate small-group dialogic reading sessions into their curriculum. Dialogic reading with a small group of preschoolers requires the full attention of one teacher; another teacher must be available to monitor and assist children who are not involved in the reading interaction. Small group reading may be more manageable in preschool classrooms, to the extent that additional adults (generally volunteers) are more readily available to manage the classroom while the teacher reads with the group (or vice versa).

Second, it appears that many teachers may find it difficult to ask children open-ended questions in the context of classroom small-group dialogic readings. On the other hand, if children do not receive many such opportunities they are not likely to show many gains in their language abilities, although they may still make gains in other emergent literacy areas (e.g., knowledge of print concepts). One recommendation is that children be given as many opportunities as possible for individual shared reading with adults. The challenge facing Head Start, as well as other preschool settings and daycare centers, is how to recruit volunteers and maximize their use over the course of the day so that as many individual children as possible can engage in shared reading with adults.

A third challenge comes from parents' relative ability to adhere to home dialogic reading interventions. Whitehurst, Epstein, et al. (1994) revealed that the more that Head Start parents read dialogically to their children, the more gains the children made in their language abilities. However, Payne et al. (1994) showed that Head Start parents vary substantially in the extent to which they engage in home literacy behaviors with their children. The first author is currently conducting a study to identify the variables that predict the frequency of reading interactions in such families; the factors that are hypothesized to predict home reading frequency include daily stress, the experience of major life stressors, parental psychological difficulties, low social support, and family size (Whitehurst & Lonigan, 1998). That is, some low-income parents may believe that reading with their children is important, but are too overwhelmed with stress and daily tasks to allow time for this activity. Relatively low adherence to dialogic reading principles may also occur when parents are unsure how to implement dialogic reading techniques. McNeill and Fowler's (1999) study, which taught mothers how to use praise, expansions, open-ended questions, and pauses to encourage their preschool children's initiation into shared-reading interactions, found that some mothers needed many weeks to meet a criterion of four uses of a strategy per story (i.e., approximately one use of the strategy per minute). This suggests that some adults may need more extensive training in order to master shared-reading techniques.

FUTURE DIRECTIONS

Although dialogic reading affects children's development of print concepts and writing skills (Whitehurst, Epstein, et al., 1994), the most consistent gains have been found in the domain of expressive language. While well-developed expressive language skills are likely to facilitate literacy development, literacy acquisition requires more than just expressive language skills. Phonemic awareness, letter knowledge, familiarity with print concepts, vocabulary, and decontextualized language skills all appear to be important components of successful reading (e.g., Bryant, MacLean, Bradley, & Crossland, 1990; Dickinson, 1991; Paul & Smith, 1993; Reese, 1995; Stevenson & Newman, 1986; Tunmer, Herriman, & Nesdale, 1988; Wagner, Torgesen, & Rashotte, 1994; Whitehurst & Lonigan, 1998). Thus, programs that effectively facilitate the development of these skills among at-risk preschoolers are also needed. An emerging literature is detailing the effectiveness of some such programs. For example, Peterson, Jesso, and McCabe (1999) showed that teaching low-income mothers to encourage their preschoolers to tell narratives resulted in significant gains in the children's vocabulary and decontextualized language skills. The effects of their year-long intervention were maintained 1 year after the end of the program. In the domain of phonemic awareness, the work of Byrne and Fielding-Barnsley (1991, 1995) has revealed that preschoolers exposed to their *Sound Foundations* program, which teaches children phonemes in the initial and final positions of words, demonstrated greater phonemic awareness than children in a control condition who were exposed to storybook reading and a semantic categorization program. These gains were partially maintained through the second grade (Byrne & Fielding-Barnsley, 1995).

In looking toward future research in the domain of shared-reading interventions, we advance the following questions:

1.   What specific components of shared reading contribute the most to positive outcomes in children's language and emergent literacy skills? Does the role of specific components vary as a function of the child's age? A nascent literature is linking specific adult reading behaviors (e.g., describing pictures, using decontextualized speech, asking questions after the reading is completed) to specific gains in children's language, story comprehension, and print concepts skills (e.g., Dickinson & Smith, 1994; Haden et al., 1996; Reese & Cox, 1999). In a naturalistic observation study, Dickinson and Smith (1994) found that a performance-oriented style among preschool teachers was associated with greater gains in children's receptive vocabulary skills than a more interruptive style that posed questions to children throughout the reading. Reese and Cox (1999; Reese, Cox, Harte, & McAnally, this volume) found that a parental "describer" reading style, focused on describing and labeling pictures, was superior to a "comprehender" reading style, focused on story meaning and making inferences, for increasing children's receptive vocabulary and print concepts knowledge over the course of a 6-week study. On the other hand, Haden et al. (1996) showed a significant relationship between mothers' use of the comprehender reading style with their preschoolers and the children's story comprehension skills 2½ years later. The results of these studies suggest that there may be spe-

cific relationships between particular shared reading strategies and the language and literacy domains in which children make gains (Reese & Cox, 1999). Moreover, the impact of dialogic reading and similar shared-reading programs may be immediately clear in some areas of emergent literacy (e.g., vocabulary), while the effect on other areas may not be evidenced until children are significantly older (Whitehurst & Lonigan, 1998; Whitehurst et al., 1999).

2.   How might the type or genre of text relate to what children learn from shared reading experiences? Several researchers have identified variability in parent–child verbal interactions depending on the type of book. For example, Pellegrini, Perlmutter, Galda, and Brody (1990) found that low-income mothers interacted more with their children when reading expository texts than when reading narrative texts. Neuman (1996) showed that text type (highly predictable, episodic predictable, and narrative) influenced the types of verbalizations demonstrated by low-income parents and their preschoolers during shared book reading. Specifically, Neuman found that the use of predictable text frequently led to the child reading along with the text and the parent providing feedback (e.g., corrections and confirmations), while the use of narrative text was related to distancing types of statements or questions and recall questions. Interestingly, Neuman also found that type of text interacted with the reading proficiency of the parent to predict the amount of talking by the parent and the child during the reading: low-proficiency parents and their children talked more while reading the predictable texts; high-proficiency parents and their children talked more while reading the narrative texts.

3.   What accounts for the variability in results across shared-reading studies? A close examination reveals cross-study variability in the specific language and emergent literacy skills (e.g., receptive language, expressive language, knowledge of print concepts) that are positively influenced by dialogic reading intervention. Recent studies suggest that the emergent literacy skills which children bring to the shared reading intervention are related to their gains over the course of the intervention. For example, in their study of children with language delays, Dale et al. (1996) found that preschoolers with more advanced language skills responded to a dialogic reading intervention with improvements in their grammatical competence, whereas their peers with less advanced language skills responded to the intervention with growth in their expressive vocabulary. In a similar vein, Reese and Cox (1999) found that adults' reading styles interacted with children's initial receptive vocabulary and story comprehension skills to predict how much the children's receptive vocabulary and print concepts knowledge were enhanced by a reading intervention. It may be that the cross-study variability in results is related to cross-study variability in children's initial language skills.

4. What are the long-term effects of dialogic reading and other shared-reading interventions for children at various SES levels? Relevant outcome variables may include children's reading comprehension skills in late elementary school and secondary school, rate of referral to special education services, and level of educational attainment. We plan to follow up with the Head Start children from our studies to learn more about the long-term effects of our intervention.

Studies are needed that identify the best ways to encourage teachers and parents to read with children, that help adults integrate shared reading into the preschool classroom and the home, and that demonstrate the effectiveness of shared-reading interventions. Given the obstacles faced by children who begin school with below-average language and emergent literacy skills, research in the area of shared reading must continue.

ACKNOWLEDGMENT

Preparation of this work was supported in part by grants to Grover J. Whitehurst from the Administration for Children and Families (90-CD-0957 and 90-YD-0026). The views expressed herein are the authors' and have not been cleared by the grantors.

APPENDIX A: EXAMPLE TRANSCRIPT OF A PARENT–CHILD DIALOGIC READING INTERACTION

Parent and child are reading *The Snowy Day* by Ezra Jack Keats (1962).

Parent: "The Snowy Day." What's he doing here?

Child: Sliding.

Parent: Yeah. He's sliding down a hill. Can you say that?

Child: He's sliding down a hill.

Parent: Good. "One winter morning Peter woke up and looked out the window. Snow had fallen during the night. It covered everything as far as he could see." What does he see outside his window?

Child: Snow!

Parent: That's right. There's lots of snow outside.

Child: Yeah.

Parent: "After breakfast he put on his snowsuit and ran outside. The snow was piled up very high along the street to make a path for walking." Your turn. What's happening on this page?

Child: He's making steps in the snow.

Parent: That's right. He's making footprints.

Child: Footprints.

Parent: Do you remember when we played outside in the snow?

Child: Yeah. And we made snowballs.

Parent: You remember. We made lots of snowballs. I remember that you made footprints all around the yard too.

Child: Yeah.

Parent: "Then he dragged his feet s-l-o-w-l-y to make tracks. And he found something sticking out of the snow that made a new track." What do you think it was that made the new track?

Child: A dog?

Parent: Well, it looks like it might be something else that makes the track. Let's see what it is next. "It was a _____"

Child: Stick!

Parent: Yes. "It was a stick—a stick that was right for smacking a snow-covered _____"

Child: Tree.

Parent: Okay. What happens next?

Child: He got snow on his head.

Parent: That's right. And now it looks like he's going somewhere else. "He thought it would be fun to join the big boys in their snowball fight, but he wasn't old enough—not yet. So he made a smiling snowman, and he made angels." You tell the story now. What is he doing on these pages?

Child: He's going up and going down.

Parent: Yes. Here it says that he is pretending to be a mountain climber. Can you say that? Mountain climber.

Child: Mountain climber.

Parent: Good. And remember? We saw this picture before. What is he doing here?

Child: Sliding down a hill.

Parent: Very good.

APPENDIX B: RECOMMENDED BOOKS
FOR DIALOGIC READING

Bond, M. (1996). *Paddington's ABC*. New York: Puffin.

Bridwell, N. (1985). *Clifford takes a trip*. New York: Scholastic.

Caines, J. (1993). *I need a lunch box*. New York: Harper Trophy.

Dubanevich, A. (1983). *Pigs in hiding*. New York: Four Winds Press.

Duke, K. (1984). *Guinea pigs far and near*. New York: E. P. Dutton.

Duke, K. (1988). *What would a guinea pig do?* New York: E. P. Dutton.

Edwards, H. (1988). *Stickybeak*. Milwaukee: Gareth Stevens.

Freeman, D. (1972). *A pocket for Corduroy*. New York: Viking.

Gackenbach, D. (1983). *A bag full of pups*. New York: Houghton Mifflin.

Grossman, B. (1991). *Donna O'Neeshuck was chased by some cows*. New York: Harper & Row.

Hill, E. (1989). *Spot's baby sister*. New York: G. P. Putnam and Sons.

Johnson, A. (1990). *Do like Kyla*. New York: Orchard.

Keats, E. J. (1962). *The snowy day*. New York: Viking Penguin.

Kimmel, E. (1990). *I took my frog to the library*. New York: Viking Penguin.

Numeroff, L. J. (1985). *If you give a mouse a cookie*. New York: HarperCollins.

Rosen, M. (1997). *We're going on a bear hunt*. New York: Little Simon.

Saunders, D., & Saunders, J. (1990). *Dibble and Dabble*. New York: Bradbury Press.

Sendak, M. (1991). *Chicken soup with rice*. New York: Harper Trophy.

Shaw, N. (1991). *Sheep in a shop*. Boston: Houghton Mifflin.

Slobodkina, E. (1987). *Caps for sale*. New York: HarperCollins.

Yee, W. H. (1996). *Eek! There's a mouse in the house*. Boston: Houghton Mifflin.

Zion, G. (1976). *No roses for Harry*. New York: Harper Trophy.

REFERENCES

Arnold, D. H., Lonigan, C. J., Whitehurst, G. J., & Epstein, J. N. (1994). Accelerating language development through picture book reading: Replication and extension to a videotape training format. *Journal of Educational Psychology, 86,* 235–243.

Arnold, D. S., & Whitehurst, G. J. (1994). Accelerating language development through picture book reading. In D. Dickinson (Ed.), *Bridges to literacy: Approaches to supporting child and family literacy*. Cambridge, MA: Basil Blackwell.

Bandura, A. (1977). *Social learning theory*. Englewood Cliffs, NJ: Prentice Hall.

Bryant, P. E., MacLean, M., Bradley, L. L., & Crossland, J. (1990). Rhyme and alliteration, phoneme detection, and learning to read. *Developmental Psychology, 26,* 429–438.

Byrne, B., & Fielding-Barnsley, R. F. (1991). Evaluation of a program to teach phonemic awareness to young children. *Journal of Educational Psychology, 82,* 805–812.

Byrne, B., & Fielding-Barnsley, R. F. (1992). *Sound foundations: A scientifically researched method of introducing pre-reading skills*. Artarmon, Australia: Leyden.

Byrne, B., & Fielding-Barnsley, R. F. (1995). Evaluation of a program to teach phonemic awareness to young children: A 2- and 3-year follow-up and a new preschool trial. *Journal of Educational Psychology, 87,* 488–503.

Carnegie Foundation for the Advancement of Teaching. (1991). *Ready to learn: A mandate for the nation*. New York: Author.

CBT. (1990). *Developing skills checklist*. Monterey, CA: Author/McGraw-Hill.

Cohen, J. (1988). *Statistical power analysis for the behavioral sciences* (2nd ed.). New York: Academic Press.

Crain-Thoreson, C., & Dale, P. S. (1999). Enhancing linguistic performance: Parents and teachers as book reading partners for children with language delays. *Topics in Early Childhood Special Education, 19,* 28–39.

Dale, P. S., Crain-Thoreson, C., Notari-Syverson, A., & Cole, K. (1996). Parent–child book reading as an intervention for young children with language delays. *Topics in Early Childhood Special Education, 16,* 213–235.

Dickinson, D. K. (1991). Teacher agenda and setting: Constraints on conversation in preschools. In A. McCabe & C. Peterson (Eds.), *Developing narrative structure* (pp. 255–301). Mahwah, NJ: Lawrence Erlbaum Associates.

Dickinson, D., & Smith, M. (1994). Long-term effects of preschool teachers' book readings on low-income children's vocabulary and story comprehension. *Reading Research Quarterly, 29*, 104–122.

Dunn, L. M., & Dunn, L. M. (1981). *Peabody Picture Vocabulary Test–Revised*. Circle Pines, MN: American Guidance Services.

Elley, W. B. (1989). Vocabulary acquisition from listening to stories. *Reading Research Quarterly, 24*, 175–187.

Feitelson, D., & Goldstein, Z. (1986). Patterns of book ownership and reading to young children in Israeli school-oriented and nonschool-oriented families. *Reading Teacher, 39*, 924–930.

Gardner, M. F. (1981). *Expressive One-Word Picture Vocabulary Test*. Novato, CA: Academic Therapy.

Haden, C. A., Reese, E., & Fivush, R. (1996). Mothers' extratextual comments during storybook reading: Stylistic differences over time and across texts. *Discourse Processes, 21*, 135–169.

Harkins, D. A., Koch, P. E., & Michel, G. F. (1994). Listening to maternal story telling affects narrative skill of 5-year-old children. *The Journal of Genetic Psychology, 155*, 247–257.

Harris, M. M., & Smith, N. J. (1987). Literacy assessment of Chapter 1 and non-Chapter 1 homes. *Reading Improvement, 24*, 137–142.

Heath, S. B. (1982). What no bedtime story means: Narrative skills at home and at school. *Language in Society, 11*, 49–76.

Jenkins, J. R., Stein, M. L., & Wysocki, K. (1984). Learning vocabulary through reading. *American Educational Research Journal, 21*, 767–787.

Karweit, N. (1989). The effects of a story-reading program on the vocabulary and story comprehension skills of disadvantaged prekindergarten and kindergarten students. *Early Education and Development, 1*, 105–114.

Keats, E. J. (1962). *The snowy day*. New York: Viking.

Kirk, S. A., McCarthy, J. J., & Kirk, W. D. (1968). *Illinois Test of Psycholinguistic Abilities*. Urbana: University of Illinois Press.

Lee, V. E., Brooks-Gunn, J., Schnur, E., & Liaw, F. (1990). Are Head Start effects sustained? A longitudinal follow-up comparison of disadvantaged children attending Head Start, no preschool, and other preschool programs. *Child Development, 61*, 495–507.

Lonigan, C. J., & Whitehurst, G. J. (1998). Relative efficacy of parent and teacher involvement in a shared-reading intervention for preschool children from low-income backgrounds. *Early Childhood Research Quarterly, 13*, 263–290.

Mason, J. M. (1980). When children do begin to read: An exploration of four-year-old children's letter and word reading competencies. *Reading Research Quarterly, 15*, 203–227.

McCormick, C. E., & Mason, J. M. (1986). Intervention procedures for increasing preschool children's interest and knowledge about reading. In W. H. Teale & E. Sulzby (Eds.), *Emergent literacy: Writing and reading* (pp. 90–115). Norwood, NJ: Ablex.

McNeill, J. H., & Fowler, S. A. (1999). Let's talk: Encouraging mother–child conversations during story reading. *Journal of Early Intervention, 22*, 51–69.

Neuman, S. B. (1996). Children engaging in storybook reading: The influence of access to print resources, opportunity, and parental interaction. *Early Childhood Research Quarterly, 11*, 495–513.

Paul, R., & Smith, R. L. (1993). Narrative skills in 4-year-olds with normal, impaired, and late developing language. *Journal of Speech and Hearing Research, 36*, 592–598.

Payne, A. C., Whitehurst, G. J., & Angell, A. L. (1994). The role of home literacy environment in the development of language ability in preschool children from low-income families. *Early Childhood Research Quarterly, 9,* 427–440.

Pellegrini, A. D., Perlmutter, J., Galda, L., & Brody, G. (1990). Joint reading between Black Head Start children and their mothers. *Child Development, 61,* 443–453.

Peterson, C., Jesso, B., & McCabe, A. (1999). Encouraging narratives in preschoolers: An intervention study. *Journal of Child Language, 26,* 49–67.

Raz, I. S., & Bryant, P. (1990). Social background, phonological awareness, and children's reading. *British Journal of Developmental Psychology, 8,* 209–225.

Reese, E. (1995). Predicting children's literacy from mother–child conversations. *Cognitive Development, 10,* 381–405.

Reese, E., & Cox, A. (1999). Quality of adult book reading affects children's emergent literacy. *Developmental Psychology, 35,* 20–28.

Robinson, W. P., & Rackstraw, S. J. (1967). Variations in mothers' answers to children's questions as a function of social class, verbal intelligence test scores, and sex. *Sociology, 1,* 259–276.

Sénéchal, M., & Cornell, E. H. (1993). Vocabulary acquisition through shared reading experiences. *Reading Research Quarterly, 28,* 360–375.

Sénéchal, M., Thomas, E. H., & Monker, J. A. (1995). Individual differences in 4-year-old children's acquisition of vocabulary during storybook reading. *Journal of Educational Psychology, 87,* 218–229.

Snow, C. E., Dubber, D., & deBlauw, A. (1982). Routines in mother–child interactions. In L. Feagans & D. C. Farran (Eds.), *The language of children reared in poverty* (pp. 53–72). New York: Academic Press.

Stevenson, H. W., & Newman, R. S. (1986). Long-term prediction of achievement and attitudes in mathematics and reading. *Child Development, 57,* 646–659.

Stevenson, J., & Fredman, G. (1990). The social environmental correlates of reading ability. *Journal of Child Psychology and Psychiatry, 5,* 681–698.

Sulzby, E. (1989). Assessment of writing and of children's language while writing. In L. Morrow & J. Smith (Eds.), *The role of assessment and measurement in early literacy instruction* (pp. 83–109). Englewood Cliffs, NJ: Prentice Hall.

Sulzby, E., & Teale, W. (1991). Emergent literacy. In R. Barr, M. Kamil, P. Mosenthal, & P. D. Pearson (Eds.), *Handbook of reading research* (Vol. 2, pp. 727–758). New York: Longman.

Teale, W. H., & Sulzby, E. (1986). *Emergent literacy: Writing and reading.* Norwood, NJ: Ablex.

Tunmer, W. E., Herriman, M. L., & Nesdale, A. R. (1988). Metalinguistic abilities and beginning reading. *Reading Research Quarterly, 23,* 134–158.

Valdez-Menchaca, M. C., & Whitehurst, G. J. (1992). Accelerating language development through picture-book reading: A systematic extension to Mexican day care. *Developmental Psychology, 28,* 1106–1114.

Vivas, E. (1996). Effects of story reading on language. *Language Learning, 46,* 189–216.

Vygotsky, L. S. (1978). *Mind in society.* Cambridge, MA: Harvard University Press.

Wagner, R. K., Torgesen, J. K., & Rashotte, C. A. (1994). Development of reading-related phonological processing abilities: New evidence of bidirectional causality from a latent variable longitudinal study. *Developmental Psychology, 30,* 73–87.

Walker, D., Greenwood, C., Hart, B., & Carta, J. (1994). Prediction of school outcomes based on early language production and socioeconomic factors. *Child Development, 65,* 606–621.

Wells, G. (1985). *Language development in the preschool years*. New York: Cambridge University Press.

Wells, G., Barnes, S., & Wells, J. (1984). *Linguistic influences on educational attainment*. Final report to the Social Science Research Council, University of Bristol.

Whitehurst, G. J. (1991). *Dialogic reading: The hear–say method—A video workshop*. [Video]. (Available from G. J. Whitehurst, State University of New York at Stony Brook, Stony Brook, NY, 11794-2500).

Whitehurst, G. J. (1994a). *Dialogic reading for parents: Head Start, K and pre-K*. [Video]. (Available from G. J. Whitehurst, State University of New York at Stony Brook, Stony Brook, NY, 11794-2500).

Whitehurst, G. J. (1994b). *Dialogic reading: Head Start, K and pre-K*. [Video]. (Available from G. J. Whitehurst, State University of New York at Stony Brook, Stony Brook, NY, 11794-2500).

Whitehurst, G. J. (1994c). *The Stony Brook emergent literacy curriculum*. [Video]. (Available from G. J. Whitehurst, State University of New York at Stony Brook, Stony Brook, NY, 11794-2500).

Whitehurst, G. J., Arnold, D. S., Epstein, J. N., Angell, A. L., Smith, M., & Fischel, J. (1994). A picture book reading intervention in day care and home for children from low-income families. *Developmental Psychology, 30*, 679–689.

Whitehurst, G. J., Epstein, J. N., Angell, A. L., Payne, A. C., Crone, D. A., & Fischel, J. E. (1994). Outcomes of an emergent literacy intervention in Head Start. *Journal of Educational Psychology, 86*, 542–555.

Whitehurst, G. J., Falco, F., Lonigan, C. J., Fischel, J. E., DeBaryshe, B. D., Valdez-Menchaca, M. C., & Caulfield, M. (1988). Accelerating language development through picture-book reading. *Developmental Psychology, 24*, 552–558.

Whitehurst, G. J., & Lonigan, C. J. (1998). Child development and emergent literacy. *Child Development, 69*, 848–872.

Whitehurst, G. J., Zevenbergen, A. A., Crone, D. A., Schultz, M. D., Velting, O. N., & Fischel, J. E. (1999). Outcomes of an emergent literacy intervention from Head Start through second grade. *Journal of Educational Psychology, 91*, 261–272.

Zevenbergen, A., & Wilson, G. (1996). *Effects of an interactive reading program on the narrative skills of children in Head Start*. Paper presented at the Head Start's Third National Research Conference, Washington, DC.

III
Storybook Sharing as Cultural Practice

10

Storybook Reading in a Multicultural Society: Critical Perspectives

Jim Anderson
Ann Anderson
Jacqueline Lynch
Jon Shapiro
University of British Columbia

It is a late spring morning and we are in the family resource room in Pleasant Vale School in Vancouver, British Columbia. On a large piece of butcher paper, a young woman named Susan is using diagrams, charts, key words, and other visuals to help parents understand what they will be doing when they visit their children's classrooms later this morning to work with them in different literacy activities. Susan is the facilitator for PALS (Anderson & Morrison, 2000), a culturally responsive family literacy program developed in British Columbia to help parents support their children's early development. At one table, Trinh, the group's Vietnamese cultural worker, is busily translating for three parents. Five more parents listen attentively at another table as Ming, the other cultural worker, busily translates into Cantonese. Linda Tam, one of the kindergarten teachers, pitches in, conversing in Mandarin with a father and a grandmother. In another group, a mother originally from the Philippines, who speaks Tagalog, English, and some Spanish, is helping a group of newly arrived Spanish-speaking parents from Central America understand Susan's explanations.

The polyphony of languages that permeates the room reminds us that ours is an increasingly global and diverse society. In Vancouver, more than 50% of school children speak a language other than English at home. In some class-rooms, more than a dozen linguistic and cultural groups are represented. Ac-cording to Laframboise and Wynn (1994), 23 of the 25 largest school districts in the United States have a majority of students with limited proficiency in Eng-lish. But despite this diversity, North American educators tend to subscribe to a mainstream, Eurocentric view of education in general, and literacy in particular (Gunderson & Anderson, in press). Perhaps nowhere is this more apparent than in the centrality of storybook reading in North American literacy instruc-tion (Pellegrini, 1991), notwithstanding the fact that storybook reading to chil-dren is not practiced in many cultures (e.g., Heath, 1982; Mason, 1992). In this chapter, we examine storybook reading from a multicultural perspective. First, we contextualize storybook reading within current theories of literacy as social practice. We then trace the evolution of the phenomenon, especially in terms of literacy learning and teaching as defined by schools. Then we examine research on storybook reading in multicultural contexts. We conclude with a discussion of several pervasive issues.

LITERACY AS SITUATED SOCIAL PRACTICE

Until recently, research in literacy has been largely the domain of linguistics and psychology. Street (1984) posited that this research contributed to the "auton-omous" model of literacy that has dominated our conceptions of, and discourse about, literacy for most of the last century. Blackledge (1999) argued that "[t]his model of literacy assumes that the social consequences of literacy are given, and schools need only address the question of how literacy is taught" (p. 181)—and, we would add, how it is learned. However, emerging ethnographic and sociolinguistic work has caused a shift in thinking toward the view that reading and writing are not just a set of cognitive/linguistic skills, but complex social practices (Barton, Hamilton, & Ivanic, 2000). That is, as Clay (1993) and Blackledge (1999) indicate, there is considerable variation in literacy practices, in the meanings ascribed to literacy, and in the ways in which literacy is medi-ated across and within cultural groups.

Blackledge (1999) articulated this position thus:

> … the development of an individual's literacy is shaped by the structure and organiza-tion of the social situation in which literacy is practiced. Literacy development, ac-cording to this theoretical position, is driven by qualities of the individual's engagement in particular literacy practices. By emphasizing the patterns of individu-als' access to, and participation in, various roles within specific literacy practices, en-

gagement theory seeks to account for the rich variety and patterning of literacy within and across cultural groups. (p. 180)

Theorists within the "literacy as social practice" paradigm also argue that schools privilege certain literacy practices and dismiss or ignore others. Janes and Kermani (2001) pointed out that "as many theorists have demonstrated, schools have traditionally privileged an elite group by emphasizing language, content and interactional behaviour that is familiar to this group" (p. 458). Heath (1982) posited that it is generally accepted that "whatever it is that mainstream school oriented homes have, these other homes do not have it; thus these children are not from the literate tradition and are not likely to succeed in school" (p. 50). Referring to how storybook reading in middle-class homes embodies this privileging of particular literacy events, Heath elaborated, "the mother points and asks, 'What is X' and the child vocalizes and/or gives a non-verbal signal of attention. The mother then provides verbal feedback and a label. Before the age of two, the child is socialized into the 'initiation-reply-evaluation' sequences repeatedly described as the central structure of classroom lessons …" (p. 51).

A Brief Overview of Storybook Reading

While the emphasis on storybook reading to young children is a relatively new phenomenon, reading aloud—not silently—was historically much more prominent. For as Keller-Cohen (1993) pointed out, "literacy practice [in colonial America] was often interactive as well as collaborative. Families read aloud and discussed the Bible. When someone did not know how to read, neighbors and friends—indeed, whoever was available—assisted" (p. 291). Book reading to children, however, was given great impetus when Huey (1908), in his influential book, *The Psychology and Pedagogy of Reading*, commented, "The secret of it all lies in the parents reading aloud to and with the child" (p. 332). Research by Durkin (1966) in the United States and Clark (1976) in Scotland found that one factor common to precocious readers who had learned to read prior to formal instruction in school was that a parent or significant other had read to them regularly. This research reinforced the notion of the centrality of storybook reading in learning to read.

During the 1970s and 1980s, a flurry of research (e.g., Chomsky, 1972; Ferreiro & Teberosky, 1982; Heibert, 1981; Lomax & McGee, 1987; Sulzby, 1985; Taylor, 1983; Teale, 1986) began to show that children developed knowledge of literacy before receiving formal instruction in school. From this research it was hypothesized (e.g., Teale, 1986) that this emerging literacy knowledge developed as children interacted with significant others and participated in literacy events with them.

Despite the fact that storybook reading to children is not practiced in some cultures that produce a literate citizenry (e.g., Mason, 1992), it has still come to be perceived as the literacy event "par excellence" (Pellegrini, 1991). We believe that there are several reasons for this prominence. First, research revealed that storybook reading was a feature in the homes of many young children who had acquired considerable literacy knowledge before schooling. Even though ethnographic research documented a myriad of literacy activities and events in these homes (e.g., Taylor, 1983), it seems, as we have argued previously (Shapiro, Anderson, & Anderson, 1997), that researchers developed a theoretical blind spot, focusing on storybook reading as *the* factor accounting for early literacy development, while minimizing the role of other forms of literacy activity.

Second, there was evidence that middle-class parents used storybook reading to engage their children in the use of decontextualized language (Heath, 1982), a skill that Snow (1991) argued is essential for success as children move into the reading-to-learn stage in elementary school. Third, Wells' (1985) longitudinal study in Britain has been interpreted as establishing a strong relationship between storybook reading and early reading achievement, even though Wells concluded that it was the act of listening to stories that contributed to later achievement in literacy.

More recently, researchers have begun to examine the empirical evidence for the relationship between storybook reading and literacy development. As a result of their analysis of 31 studies, Scarborough and Dobrich (1994a) concluded that storybook reading accounted for only 8% of the variance in later reading achievement.

In another meta-analysis, Bus, van IJzendoorn, and Pellegrini (1995) also found that storybook reading accounted for only 8% of the variance in later achievement, though surprisingly they concluded that it is "a necessary preparation for beginning reading instruction in school" (p. 17). Interestingly, Bus seems to have tempered that position in later years, questioning the notion of the appropriateness of storybook reading for all cultural groups (Bus, Leseman, & Keultjes, 2000; Bus & Sulzby, 2000).

There are several implicit and explicit assumptions in the literature about storybook reading and its connections to literacy learning and teaching:

1. Reading books with young children is an important literacy activity contributing to their literacy development (De Temple & Tabors, 1994, p. 3).

2. Storybook reading is an important activity for language development (De Temple & Snow, this volume).
3. Bedtime story reading is a "natural" activity for parents to use to interact with their children (Heath, 1982, p. 51).
4. There are deficits in the quality and quantity of storybook reading in low-SES and non-mainstream homes (De Temple & Tabors, 1994).
5. Children's literacy development follows a predictable path, supported in particular ways by parents or significant others (McNaughton, 2001, p. 51).

We now examine these assumptions as they relate to research on storybook reading in multicultural contexts.

RESEARCH IN STORYBOOK READING IN MULTICULTURAL CONTEXTS

Because we had already conducted research in storybook reading and were familiar with the literature (e.g., Shapiro et al., 1997; Anderson & Matthews, 1999), we were able to use our past work to inform the review for this chapter. We also identified various descriptors and subject headings from studies familiar to us and used these to search the major databases (e.g., Education Resources Information Center [ERIC], Education Index, Psychological Abstracts). Our online searches of these databases identified thousands of articles; for example, 1,587 articles were identified through a search of the ERIC database using the "reading aloud" descriptor. We selected the abstracts of those identified sources that seemed relevant, and read and summarized these primary sources. Sources that seemed to be only peripherally related to our search were eliminated. Based on this exhaustive process and our knowledge of the field, we are confident that we present the majority of the research in this area.

As we review this literature in the following section, we attempt to locate each study within the context of the five assumptions extrapolated in the preceding section. We recognize that this is a rather arbitrary process, in that a study focused on "storybook reading and literacy development" might also have findings that pertain to "storybook reading and language development." What we attempt to do here is place the studies according to the assumptions to which their major findings speak.

Storybook Reading and Literacy Development

As we indicated previously, meta-analyses of the effect of storybook reading on children's literacy development have already been conducted by Bus et al.

(1995), and Scarborough and Dobrich (1994a). Thus, here, we examine only those studies with non-mainstream populations.

In a study that has become somewhat of a classic in the literacy field, Tizzard, Schofield, and Hewison (1982) investigated the effects on children when their parents listened to them read. The sample for this study was composed of children from different cultural groups attending six economically disadvantaged schools in the greater London area of England. Schools were randomly assigned to three groups: parent involvement, in which children read to their parents at home; no parent involvement, but extra help in reading provided at school by a reading specialist; and a control group. Parents in the parent involvement group were seen individually and apprised of the program. Those children receiving extra help from their teacher received instruction in all aspects of reading and also had opportunities to read to the teacher once or twice a week on average. Children in the control group received no intervention except the same pretesting and posttesting received by the other groups. Children receiving extra reading practice at home made significant gains compared to the control group. However, children receiving extra help at school did not make significant gains in reading when compared to the control group. This study is frequently cited as evidence of the effectiveness of storybook reading; however, Macleod (1996) has questioned that interpretation. Based on her re-analysis of the data, she asserted that "the persuasive evidence was found wanting. Not only did the researchers' design fall somewhat short of that which was originally intended and so threaten its internal validity, but their presentation and interpretation of the available evidence was found to be misleading" (p. 197).

Working with elementary school children, Walters and Gunderson (1985) compared the effects of reading in Cantonese and English. Students were randomly assigned to one of three conditions: hearing stories read aloud in Cantonese from Chinese books; hearing stories read aloud in English; and having time to do catch-up work but without any formal teaching. Care was taken to ensure that only high-quality books were read and that the four parent readers (two Cantonese and two English) were selected for their ability to read aloud in an engaging manner. All three groups made significant gains on a standardized reading test, but there were no significant differences between groups. In a study conducted in New Zealand, Glynn and Glynn (1986) examined the effects of a shared reading program with new Cambodian immigrants in the primary grades and their mothers attending ESL classes. During home visits the ESL teacher observed children reading a book to their mothers that they had also read in school that day. The mother then read the same material, with the child monitoring the reading. These sessions were recorded and errors in reading were counted. The authors concluded that the children made gains in reading development and that these gains were a result of the shared reading. This practice, they concluded, brought benefits above those gained in the children's classroom and ESL instruction.

In a study similar to that of Tizzard et al. (1982) but with older children, Giffin (1987) examined the effects of parental involvement through a program that involved parents in listening to their children read basal readers and self-selected materials, and attending monthly parent meetings where they heard and discussed presentations about literacy. Subjects were children attending Grades 2–7 in one rural Canadian elementary school, and variations in instruction were controlled by within-class groupings. After the 5-month intervention, children who had read to their parents on a daily basis showed greater gains on a standardized measure of reading achievement than those who had not. Post-hoc analyses indicated that gains in vocabulary were more dramatic than gains in comprehension.

These studies with different cultural groups, then, revealed mixed results. The children in the Glynn and Glynn (1986) study appeared to benefit from the shared reading, at least in terms of error reduction in their oral reading. Interestingly, children in the Giffin (1987) study showed greater gains in vocabulary than in reading comprehension, suggesting that storybook reading might contribute to language development more than to literacy development. Overall, these studies tend to show that storybook reading has a much more modest effect on literacy development of non-mainstream children than is commonly believed. For example, in the Walters and Gunderson (1985) study, there were no significant differences between the groups who were read to and the group who was not. Likewise, Macleod's (1996) re-analysis of the Tizzard et al. (1982) study questions their interpretation that storybook reading had a significant impact on children's reading development. Somewhat ironically, both of the latter studies are often cited as examples of the power of storybook reading for children who are learning English as a second language. Indeed, as Pellegrini (1991) pointed out, and as we argue elsewhere in this chapter, storybook reading is often prescribed as "the way" for children from non-mainstream families to learn to read, not withstanding the lack of empirical evidence that storybook reading plays such a central role in children's literacy development.

Storybook Reading and Language Development

While storybook reading is often viewed as central to children's literacy development, many educators see it as playing an important role in language development as well. We now turn to studies that have examined the contribution of storybook reading to the language development of children from different cultural and linguistic groups.

Feitelson and Iraqi (1990) investigated the effects of storybook reading on kindergarten children in Israel who spoke a local Arab dialect at home but who were instructed in literary Arabic. Experimental and control conditions were randomly assigned to 12 kindergarten classrooms. In the experimental classes, the teachers read to the children during the last 15 minutes or so of each day; in the control classrooms, teachers used the last 15 minutes or so to teach a structured language program. Feitelson and Iraqi reported that "[i]ndividual tests of listening comprehension and a picture-story telling task showed that [the] children who had been read to outperformed their peers ... on listening comprehension and several indices of active language use" (p. 264). It is noteworthy that the mimeographed stories read to each class of 35 children did not have illustrations. In this regard, the authors quote one of the teachers in the experimental group, who said, "We thought that without illustrations children would not be interested.... Now children don't even ask for illustrations" (p. 265).

Another study that investigated the relationship between storybook reading and children's achievement on standardized language and literacy tests was conducted by DeBaryshe (1992). She examined a treatment program that taught a group of parents to interact in specific ways with their children, and investigated the frequency versus the interactive quality of parent–child storybook reading. Fifty-five low-income children and their primary caregivers took part. The majority of the children were enrolled in Head Start, most were African American, and most of the mothers had a high school education. The training group was taught techniques to increase children's participation and enhance their oral language skills. The control group, reading frequency group, and treatment group looked the same at baseline but began to diverge during the intervention phase. The training group decreased their straight book reading by 25%, doubled their use of target questions, and increased their responsiveness by 65%. Children in the target group were seen to become more verbally active, but no effects were noted on the test battery, which consisted of the *Peabody Picture Vocabulary Test* and the *Test of Early Reading Achievement*. Thus, while the standardized instruments revealed no treatment effects, there was qualitative evidence of changes in language use.

Working with a group of multilingual children, Garcia and Godina (1994) examined the extent to which these preschoolers participated in classroom literacy activities. Fifteen bilingual children (5 Chinese, 3 Russian, 4 Urdu, and 3 African) were observed at least once a week for 2.5 hours. In addition, weekly videos were made of classroom literacy activities. Although the teacher spoke only English, children were encouraged to maintain their native language through the presence of native language tapes, books, and activities. At least once a week a family coordinator worked with the children in their native languages. Findings showed that the children were not generally attentive during the English-language book reading at whole group time. The researchers concluded that many of the children were not fluent enough in English to understand the texts. Furthermore, the teachers tended to choose informational texts. On the other hand, the Russian and Chinese children were more attentive when books were read in their respective native languages.

In a study conducted in Cacaras, Venezuela, with primary grade children (6- to 9-year-olds), Vivas (1996) studied the effects of storybook reading on language development. Approximately 83% of the children came from low-SES families, the remainder from middle-class homes. Very little storybook reading typically occurred in these homes, or at school, due to a dearth of books. The children were assigned to one of three conditions: home-based storybook reading, school-based storybook reading intervention, and a control group. Teachers and parents of the children in the two treatment groups were trained in the necessary procedures. Parents and teachers were provided with five books to be read, one each day for 12 weeks. Pretests, posttests, and follow-up tests (i.e., 9 months after the program had ended) were conducted using various language measures. Results showed significant gains in language comprehension and expressive language from hearing stories read either at home or at school. However, Vivas concluded that there was a washout effect and the gains were not maintained. That is, storybook reading appeared to have initial benefits for children's language development, but these benefits were not maintained as children progressed through school.

As was the case with the studies that examined the relationship between storybook reading and literacy development, the results here are inconsistent. For example, the children in the Feitelson and Iraqi study showed gains in language development even in a very difficult instructional situation. While the children studied by DeBaryshe (1992) did not exhibit these same gains on measures of language development, their storybook reading became more interactive. And while the Spanish-speaking children in the Vivas (1996) study initially exhibited language gains, these were not maintained. Garcia and Godina's (1994) study is also instructive, in that it suggests that young children for whom English is a second language might not benefit from hearing stories read in English, simply because they appear not to listen. Reference should also be made to the Giffin (1987) study reported in the previous section, which found greater increases in vocabulary than in reading comprehension, suggesting that children' language development is enhanced as a result of having someone read to them.

We interpret the results of these studies, which tended to be short-term interventions, as suggesting modest support for the theory that storybook reading enhances children's language development. However, we speculate that greater benefits will accrue if such reading is engaging, regular, and sustained.

The Bedtime Story Is a "Natural Activity"

One sometimes gets the impression from the literature that bedtime storybook reading is a natural event in families' lives. Furthermore, the implication seems to be that families who don't "naturally" read with their children can be taught to do so with relative ease. This position is often implicit in family literacy programs, and we believe it is widely accepted in the education community. Let us now examine this idea in the context of the following studies of non-mainstream families.

Over the last two decades, Pat Edwards has been a leading proponent of the need to teach non-mainstream parents to read to their children. In 1992, Edwards reported on a family literacy program involving African American mothers from low-income backgrounds in rural Louisiana (Edwards, 1992). The mothers and the researcher met in a school library for 23 two-hour sessions. During these meetings the researcher modeled effective book reading behaviors, had parents practice these behaviors in peer modeling situations, and then supported the parents as they read to their children. Edwards concluded that the project helped make parents more aware of how they could support their children's literacy development, more confident of their own reading ability, and more attuned to their children's emerging literacy knowledge.

As part of an ethnographic research project on narrative development, Bloome, Katz, Wilson-Keenan, and Solsken (2000) invited African American parents of children from a community center preschool in an urban area of the southern United States to share stories with their children. The researchers observed that many parents brought books from home to share. In follow-up interviews, the parents reported that as a result of their participation in the study they had changed their reading practices to meet what they believed were the teachers' and researchers' expectations. For example, parents tried to discourage children from reading to them, something that they had reported was a regular part of shared reading prior to the study. The parents also took on a "teacher" stance during the study, for example by asking questions to check comprehension. Whereas other researchers (e.g., Twymon, 1990; Janes &

Kermani, 2001) found that book reading became a tension-filled experience when parents tried to import an unfamiliar, "parent-as-teacher style" into their shared reading, this did not occur in the study by Bloome and his colleagues. And despite the common assumption that bedtime is *the* best time to read with children, these parents fit shared reading into their daily routines, with some parents, for example, reading to the children between 7:00 and 8:00 A.M. as they got ready for the day.

As indicated earlier, Edwards (1992) found that the African American parents with whom she worked were able to accommodate the school-like reading style she taught them. This is in stark contrast to the results of a study by Janes and Kermani (2001), in which they looked at a 3-year family literacy project serving low-income, immigrant caregivers from Central America and Mexico. Fifty bilingual undergraduate students were trained to work with these families. Drawing on the extant literature in emergent literacy, the program worked to help parents ask higher order questions as a part of storybook reading. Video-tape analyses of caregiver–child shared reading sessions revealed that most of the caregivers experienced great difficulty asking higher order questions and instead tended to "elicit evidence from the child that he or she had correctly understood the information" in the text (p. 460). Furthermore, unlike the non-mainstream parents in the Edwards (1992) study, who became more comfortable with reading as the result of training, the parents in Janes and Kermani's study saw storybook reading as a stilted, tension-filled chore. Probing still further, the researchers found that many of the caregivers reported that shared reading had been an unpleasant experience in their own childhoods, which they had regarded as punishment. Recognizing the situated nature of literacy, the researchers decided that instead of providing commercial texts for the caregivers, they would have the parents compose their own texts to share with children. Janes and Kermani reported that "the caregivers' stories were generally fact based; they related directly and with much affection to the children and families; and they had a high moralizing purpose" (p. 462). Analysis of the shared reading that occurred around these texts revealed that the experience was more pleasurable than the reading of commercial texts. Nevertheless, these researchers concluded, "It may be that storybook reading may not be the best route to literacy development; there has always, throughout the history of literacy, been [sic] multiple routes [to its acquisition]" (p. 465).

Edwards' work is interesting in that she seems to be able to train African American parents to assume school-like stances in storybook reading in an unproblematic way. The other studies, however, suggest that storybook reading is not a natural phenomenon in some communities. Especially troubling is Janes and Kermani's (2001) demonstration that storybook reading can be problematic when families feel pressured to share books in highly prescribed ways. We have made similar observations in our own work with family literacy programs (e.g., Anderson & Morrison, 2000) and now spend considerable time talking to parents about alternatives to storybook reading, as well as multiple ways of sharing texts with children. Furthermore, the work of Bloome et al. (2000) suggests that some parents will modify what they "naturally do," in order to meet what they believe are the researchers' (or teachers') expectations.

Deficits in Storybook Reading With Low-SES and Mainstream Parents

As we indicated earlier, there is a pervasive assumption among literacy researchers that non-mainstream families do not read to their children, or that they do so in inappropriate ways. Somewhat surprisingly, this assumption has been very well researched. We next examine a series of studies conducted with parents from a number of cultural groups (African American, Native American, Caucasian, East Indian, Surinamese, Turkish, Dutch, Mexican American, Japanese, Bangladeshi, and Hispanic) and socioeconomic strata, and conducted in different areas of the world.

Although there is a widespread assumption that non-mainstream parents differ significantly from middle-class parents in the ways in which they read with their children, researchers for some time have been presenting evidence to the contrary. For example, Pellegrini, Perlmutter, Galda, and Brody (1990) documented interactions in low-SES, African American mother–child dyads while sharing books that differed in genre (expository and narrative) and format (familiar and unfamiliar). The results indicated that genre, not format, determined the mother's interactions; that expository texts elicited more interaction from mothers and children than did narrative texts; and that mothers were able to adjust their level of interaction to the child's ability. The researchers proposed that expository texts may be more useful tools for mothers who are trying to teach vocabulary than are narrative texts. Pellegrini et al. concluded that the teaching strategies these mothers used in the shared-reading episodes were similar to those employed by middle-class mothers.

In a two-part study, DeBaryshe (1992) examined a program that trained parents to read to their children. Part 1 of the project studied low-income children and their parents. Most of the children attended Head Start, most were African American, and most of the mothers had a high school education. Parents were administered surveys of home reading practices and reading beliefs and were audiotaped reading a storybook. The author concluded that the stimulation-deficit model did not hold for this group. A majority of mothers provided regular joint reading experiences and positive models of adult literate behavior, such as reading for pleasure. Three fourths rated themselves as liking or loving to read. Most of the children had regular exposure to books: mothers started to read to their children at a mean age of 13.8 months and read aloud to them an average of 4.2 times per week. Children owned an average of 21.4 books each, and about one third of the children went to the public library at least once per month. The author found that mothers' education and literacy were predictive of reading beliefs. That is, the more education, the stronger the literacy orientation; the more facilitative belief systems, the broader and more frequent the reading experiences. Reading exposure was associated with children's reading interest, which in turn correlated with oral language. However, the author could only conclude that a modest portion of the individual differences in oral language were a function of home reading practices. That conclusion is consistent with the results of the aforementioned DeBaryshe (1992) and Vivas (1996) investigations of the relationship between storybook reading and language development.

DeBaryshe also found considerable variation within her sample of lower-SES parents, with only 10% reporting low to nonexistent joint reading and negative maternal and child skills and attitudes. Yet the author, in comparing this group to earlier work with middle-class and professional parents, found that the lower-SES parents read less often, owned fewer materials, and started reading at a later age. The higher-income parents asked more questions and provided more feedback to their children. She concluded that "individual differences in maternal and child skills are likely to interact with intervention effectiveness. In particular, the strong role of maternal belief systems suggests that intervention efforts must be designed to address parents' values and goals" (p. 18).

In a study with Native American kindergarten children and their parents, Abramson (1987) investigated the relationship between early literacy behaviors (assessed using Clay's Diagnostic Survey) and the children's home literacy environment, including parental practices. The economic status of the families ranged from low- to middle-class. While significant moderate to high correlations were found between the Index of Parental Provision for Literacy Activities and performance on most aspects of the Clay battery in both kindergarten and Grade 1, a wide range of scores were found for the measure of home environment, indicating that no "typical" profile of home literacy support could be found within this homogeneous population. Interestingly, Shapiro et al. (1997) reached the same conclusion with a sample of middle-class parents, who, in the popular literature at least, are assumed to have a homogeneous or "typical" approach to sharing books with their children.

In another study, involving families from different urban areas in the United States, De Temple and Tabors (1994) observed young mothers who were receiving welfare. The women ranged in age from 16 to 21, and were mainly of African American ancestry. The researchers asked these mothers to read and then discuss *The Very Hungry Caterpillar* (Carle, 1970) with their children, who were between 27 and 63 months old. Mothers demonstrated four reading styles: *straight reading,* in which the mother read the text with very few or no interactions; *standard interactive reading,* in which mothers paused to discuss the story; *non-reading,* which involved the mothers discussing the illustrations, rather than reading the text; and *recitation reading,* in which the mother asked the child to recite words or phrases after her. In results similar to those of other studies (e.g., Pellegrini et al., 1990), the researchers found that the vast majority of these mothers (79.7%) demonstrated the standard interactive reading style. Further analysis revealed that the majority of the interactions were classified as "immediate talk in which the information being sought or conveyed is immediately available from the text or illustration," while very little was "non-immediate talk in which the information being sought or conveyed extends beyond the information available from the book" (De Temple & Tabors, 1994, p. 5). Extrapolating from their earlier research, De Temple and Tabors contended that non-immediate talk plays a more important role in children's literacy development than does immediate talk. However, it is interesting to note that this group of mothers, often identified as being at risk of raising children with difficulties in their literacy development, read to their children in the interactive manner that was deemed the *correct* or *preferred* way by the popular literature (see also Dickinson & Tabors, 2001).

A comparative study by Haynes and Saunders (1998) documented the book reading strategies of middle-class, African American and Caucasian mothers with their toddlers, aged 18–30 months. Parents were videotaped reading a favorite book from home and a book titled *Where Is Clifford?* (Bridwell, 1989), the latter being read on two occasions to account for the effects of familiarity with the text. The results indicated no statistically significant differences in the questioning strategies used by the two groups.

While there are some questions about the generalizability of case studies, such research can offer insights into the complexity of a phenomenon such as storybook reading. In one case study, Manyak (1998) explored the diverse storybook reading experiences of one Mexican American immigrant family living in conditions of poverty. Little English was spoken by the parents; the three children (aged 5, 7, and 9) were all enrolled in a bilingual program at their elementary school. Storybook reading events were recorded during two 2-week periods. Six or seven stories in Spanish, both fiction and non-fiction, were taped during each session. Four categories of interactions emerged: children reading to their mother with little interaction except for the mother's correction of miscues; mother-directed exchanges that evaluated comprehension; collaborative interpretation that wove together prior knowledge and experience with the information in the text to produce socially constructed interpretations; and cultural transmissions, in which the mother highlighted or elaborated on events that evoked the family's traditions. Manyak concluded that the findings pointed to the significant impact of content on storybook reading interactions. When books related to the family's experience and knowledge, interactions were interpretive. Manyak (1998) asserted that

> storybook reading research undertaken with diverse populations must recognize the influence of unique cultural experiences and funds of knowledge on book reading interaction [and] ... programs should ... be sensitive to families' socio-cultural realities. While they may facilitate the use of mainstream practices such as storybook reading, programs should be permeable enough to allow families to adapt both the goals and forms of such activities. (p. 23)

Janes and Kermani (2001) reached a similar conclusion as a result of their study with parents from Central America and Mexico.

Hughes, Vaughn, and Schumm (1999) also investigated Hispanic parents' perceptions and practices with respect to home reading and writing. Half of their participants were parents of children with a learning disability (LD), and half were parents of average or above-average ability children in Grades 3 to 5. Interview and survey (Likert scale) questions addressed three issues: (a) types of activities children did at home; (b) types of activities parents perceived as feasible and desirable to do with children; and (c) barriers parents faced when implementing reading and writing activities. Open-ended interviews were conducted to ascertain a description of the use of home reading and writing activities. A Learning Activities Survey was designed to measure the frequency of home reading and writing activities, through a Likert-type scale. The Parents' Perceptions of Reading and Writing Activities Survey consisted of a list of 23 activities that parents ranked on a 4-point Likert-type scale with respect to desirability and feasibility. No significant differences were found between the two groups with respect to frequency of reading and writing activities. The most frequent activity reported by parents was storybook reading. Another frequently reported activity was taking the child to the library. Many parents provided magazines and books to encourage their child to read more at home. There was a statistically significant difference between the two groups on feasibility of providing reading materials for their child, with parents of average ability students expressing higher ratings. Parents suggested that schools and teachers needed to communicate with parents. In terms of barriers, the most common response was that parents had difficulty with English, which inhibited participation.

So far in this section, we have examined studies conducted in the United States. We now examine research from other parts of the world. For example, Hirst (1998) reported the findings of a survey conducted with 30 Asian families of preschoolers living in an inner-city area of England. Interviews were conducted in the homes of the participants, in their first language. Hirst indicated that half of the children were learning three languages at home and some were exposed to a fourth. The parents represented various SES strata: some of the breadwinners were out of work, others worked as taxi drivers or mechanics, some were white-collar workers and managers. Children ranged from 2 to 5 years of age. Results showed that 27 of the 30 children in the study participated in shared book reading, with more than half of the children owning their own books. Many of the children had favorite books, including traditional English-language texts (e.g., *Goldilocks, The Gingerbread Man*). Nearly all of the children looked at books on their own and pretended to read. In those families where the parents could not read, someone else read. Only in three families were children not read to at all.

In another comparative project, Leseman and de Jong (1998) studied immigrant Turkish, Surinamese, and native Dutch ($n = 47$) families living in the Netherlands. They found that in the Turkish group, relative to both of the other groups, mothers pointed far less to the pictures in the book and also uttered (slightly) fewer picture labels and picture descriptions. Turkish mothers made less use of pictures in the picture book to scaffold their young children's understanding of the story. In addition, percentages of utterances requiring literal repetition were very high in both the Surinamese and the Turkish groups, as compared to the Dutch group. Higher-level utterances (i.e., explanations, evaluations, and extensions) were more prevalent among the Dutch group. There were also differences in children's receptive knowledge of Dutch words, in that Turkish children's receptive knowledge of these words at ages 4 and 7 was two to three standard deviations below Dutch children's vocabulary. In a follow-up study, Bus et al. (2000) examined the interactions between parent–child dyads from the different cultural groups around an experimenter-selected storybook. They found different patterns of interaction for the three cultural groups, related to the literacy level of the parents. Less literate parents were more likely to center discussions around procedures, such as re-explaining to their children that they had to listen to the text. They also found that when literacy did not serve important personal needs for the parents, then those parents were less likely to engage children in meaning-related discussions, which might have made the text more understandable to the child. Bus et al. also found ethnic differences in the relations of parents to their children, with Surinamese-Dutch parents more discipline-oriented than the other groups. These differences in the way parents relate to children may underlie some of the differences in parent reading style found in this study and elsewhere.

Working with just one cultural/linguistic group, Minami (1999) examined Japanese-speaking mothers' book reading with their preschool children. Book reading interactions were recorded in the homes of middle-class mother–child pairs, where both mother and child were native Japanese speakers. Half of the children were 4 years old and half were 5. All mothers read the same book, the Japanese translation of Eric Carle's *The Very Hungry Caterpillar*. Only utterances other than reading were coded, using a modified version of the Coding System for Home Book Reading (De Temple & Tabors, 1994). The total number of maternal utterances was significantly higher than the number of child utterances. Book reading performance by the mothers and children varied considerably. Maternal and child utterances were positively correlated such that those mothers who asked a lot of questions and made many comments were likely to have children who frequently responded to those questions and comments. Furthermore, when mothers used immediate talk (see De Temple & Tabors, 1994), the children tended to use it, too; when mothers used non-immediate talk, the children tended to do the same. A fill-in-the-blank style of questioning was seen to be typical of Japanese mothers. Many of the fill-in-the-blank interactions fit the so-called three-part sequence (Cazden, 1988), in which mother initiates, child responds, and mother gives feedback. Minami points out that this recitation style is typical of the teacher-talk register that figures so prominently in North American classrooms.

Blackledge (1999) interviewed the mothers of 6-year-old Bangladeshi children about their own and their children's literacy development. Several days previously, each of the children had been recorded reading schoolbooks at home. The interviews were conducted in the first language of the participants through a bilingual interpreter—a member of the mothers' cultural group and community. The children's teachers were also interviewed. The mothers, who had been given advice about reading with their children, reported that the teachers assumed that they were illiterate and gave them suggestions on how to share the book (e.g., make up a story to accompany the illustrations; talk about the pictures) without actually reading. The researcher argued that all of the women were literate in Bengali and could have supported their children's literacy development by reading to them in that language. Furthermore, nearly all of the women indicated that they regularly told stories to their children at home. However, the value of this activity appeared to have been ignored by the school. Blackledge elaborated:

> [Their] responses make it clear that home language storytelling was thriving in the homes of these families. This oral activity was used to reinforce religious and cultural traditions. There was no evidence in the women's responses that their oral literacy skills were recognized or valued by the school. Teachers were aware of home-language storytelling opportunity, but its potential remains unfulfilled in the classroom. (p. 189)

So what can we conclude from this research on a range of different cultural and socioeconomic groups from a number of different geographical areas? As with studies discussed in other sections of this chapter, the results here were inconsistent and sometimes contradictory. For example, the studies involving mostly low-SES African American parents (DeBaryshe, 1992; De Temple & Tabors, 1994; Haynes & Saunders; 1998; Pellegrini et al., 1990) suggest that this group tends to read with their children in an interactive manner that many educators believe is the correct or effective way to share books with children. As we pointed out earlier, this group is often targeted by family literacy programs as needing training to read with children. The finding that low-SES parents read an interactive manner with their children appeared to hold across cultural groups, although DeTemple and Tabors (1994; see also Dickinson & Tabors, 2001), Leseman and de Jong (1998), and Bus et al. (2000) all concluded that non-mainstream parents tended to ask low-level, literal questions compared to middle-class parents. Interestingly, the middle-class Japanese parents in the Minami (1999) study also tended to ask literal questions. As is discussed in the following subsection, Ping's (1995) analysis of learning to read in China also found that Asian parents tend to place great emphasis on literal interpretation and memory of text.

From this research, it is evident that there is considerable variation within particular cultural groups, in both attitudes toward storybook reading and the manner in which young children's literacy is supported in general. Abramson (1987), for example, reported considerable variation in the home literacy environments provided by Native American parents; the Asian parents in the Hirst (1998) and Blackledge (1999) studies also varied in how they supported their children. This finding points to the need to avoid simplistic assumptions about how parents from a particular cultural, linguistic, or socioeconomic group support their children's literacy.

Some of these studies point to the fact that cultural groups impose their own style on literacy activities, as did the Mexican parents in the Manyak (1998) study, and the Mexican and Central American parents with whom Janes and Kermani (2001) worked. Furthermore, when parents deviate from what schools want, as the Asian parents in the Blackledge (1999) study did when they engaged in storytelling, then their storybook reading might not be recognized or valued. Taken together, the studies mentioned earlier seem to negate the notion that the storybook reading practices of low-SES or non-mainstream parents are universally deficient.

Literacy Development Follows a Predictable Path Supported in Particular Ways

According to McNaughton (2001), there is a dominant view in education that literacy development follows a single trajectory. He associates this view with constructivist notions of learning that are currently very much in vogue. This notion of a single pathway to literacy has been critiqued by a number of people along philosophical lines (e.g., Dyson, 1993; Reyes, 1992). Recently, scholars have begun to document the existence of different pathways to literacy development in different socio-cultural contexts.

For example, Fishman (1990) described the literacy development of 6-year-old "Eli Jr." as he made the transition from home to school in a rural Amish community in the United States. Literacy was very much a communal, family practice in this world, with the father playing a central role. Precise oral readings of the Bible and hymns written in journals were a regular event. The literal interpretation and memorization of texts was valued both at home and at school. There was a noticeable absence of fiction in this community, and originality in writing was not promoted. Fishman noted that because the literacy practices of the home and school were consistent, transition to school was smooth. Furthermore, despite their very traditional orientation to reading, the Amish supported children's early book reading in ways consistent with what contemporary proponents of emergent literacy would countenance. Fishman (1990) explained:

> Because oral reading as modeled by Eli, Sr., is often imitated by the others, Eli Jr. always shared his books by telling what he saw or knew about them. No one ever told him that telling isn't the same as reading, even though they may look alike, so Eli always seemed a reader to others and felt like a reader himself.... Eli never saw his own reading as anything other than real; he did not see it as make-believe or bogus and neither did anyone else. So despite the fact that before he went to school, Eli Jr. could not

read according to some definitions, he always could according to his family's and his own. (p. 332)

In a historical analysis of reading in China, Ping (1995) contrasted Chinese and Western views of storybook reading. She explained that the Chinese use what is called "the intensive approach," which she describes thus:

> Intensive reading focuses on careful word by word analysis ... With the intensive approach, for many students reading is a laborious process during which they analyze individual phrases and structures, look up new words in the dictionary, repeatedly read sentences and even memorize extended passages of text. (p. 35)

Ping argued that this method reflects a Confucian belief in the sanctity of text, which encourages Chinese people to see books as the "embodiment of knowledge, wisdom and truth" (1995, p. 39). Rather than conceiving of reading as a process wherein the reader constructs meaning using various forms of background knowledge, Ping claimed that Chinese readers see reading as the extraction of knowledge from text. Ping commented that in China, the number of books committed to memory is commonly considered a measure of one's knowledge. Furthermore, she explained, young children are not expected to understand what they have memorized, for one day when they are older they will understand the stories they have memorized.

One way of testing the generalizability of research findings across cultural lines is by replicating a study with different populations in different contexts. In our view, however, such studies are not sufficiently valued in the field of education. There are exceptions: in one such case, Anderson and Matthews (1999) replicated Sulzby's (1985) classic study, but with children from low-SES homes. Working with kindergarten children from middle-class homes, Sulzby had documented "developmental patterns of children's emergent reading from 'picture governed attempts' [i.e., oral-language-like labeling and commenting on pictures] to 'independent reading' or decoding print." (Anderson & Matthews, 1999, p. 294). On an 11-point scale that Sulzby developed out of her own classification scheme (Barnhardt, 1991), the mean score of the children in the original study increased from 4.3 to 5.7, from September to June. In their own study, Anderson and Matthews found that on the same scale the mean score of kindergarten children from working-class homes remained the same. Furthermore, the September and June scores in Sulzby's study were evenly distributed, while in the Anderson and Matthews study they were clustered toward the bottom of the scale. Anderson and Matthews' children were not moving into written-language-like categories, as the children in the original study had done. Elster's

(1994) study with Head Start preschoolers showed results consistent with the Anderson and Matthews study.

These findings, we believe, indicate that literacy learning is indeed a sociocultural process and will "look different" from one context to the next. Fishman's account of the Amish shows that this group does not value or support the "personal response, personal interpretation" view of literacy that is valued and promoted in school. Rather, it is more like the type of literacy that Ping found in China, where reading involves memorization and literal recall of texts—practices that we contend would currently be decried by many Western educators. And yet the Amish and the Chinese continue to become literate.

The Anderson and Matthews study, and that of Elster, call into question the notion of arbitrary sequences in literacy development, especially when tied to particular grade or age levels. Taken together, they suggest that there are different pathways to literacy. If we are to afford parents more than token roles in helping their children become literate, then we must acknowledge that they will do so in ways that we may find difficult to understand. Likewise, we must realize that the literacy development of many children will differ markedly from the type that has been reported in studies with children from middle-class homes. In our view, such studies have dominated the research literature and influenced our thinking about early literacy development. Much of the aforementioned research indicates that literacy development does not necessarily follow a predictable path supported in particular ways, but that diversity abounds.

Anyone who has witnessed the delight of a child and a caregiver engrossed and immersed in reading a classic like Margaret Wise Brown's *Goodnight Moon* or laughing their way through one of Jon Scieszka's postmodern tales has seen the potential power that storybook reading has *in some contexts*. As we have argued previously (Shapiro et al., 1997), storybook reading helps some children to develop a powerful and lifelong attachment to books and reading, by exposing them to enduring, classic literature.

We also believe that children's language development can be enhanced through storybook reading—for example by developing understanding of the "book language" (e.g., Wells, 1985) that is necessary for the essayist forms of literacy promoted in schools. That is, while we earlier problematized school literacy, we agree with Delpit (1995) that children need to learn this form of discourse if they are to participate fully in Western-style educational, financial, and political institutions, although like Delpit, we believe it is the responsibility of schools to make explicit and teach this knowledge. Furthermore, we believe that just as children acquire vocabulary knowledge by reading (Nagy, 1987), they also acquire knowledge by listening to texts. In that regard we wonder why

daily reading to students ceases in elementary school and—in our experience—is looked on as a waste of time in high school.

Finally, reading particular texts, such as nursery rhymes, riddles, and poems,
will help children develop phonemic awareness, an important skill in learning
symbol–sound correspondence (Stahl, this volume), although Yopp (1992) and
others have argued that phonemic awareness can also be developed through
oral language games and activities. All of these variables undoubtedly contribute to children's literacy development and are important. However, close examination of the evidence calls into question the prevailing view that storybook
reading plays a central role in literacy development in both mainstream and diverse populations.

This review of the literature also calls into question the notion that
non-mainstream parents do not read to their young children, or that they do so
in ways that differ significantly from those of mainstream parents. Overall, the
research reviewed here, from several continents and a number of different cultural and ethnic groups, does not support the stimulation-deficit hypothesis:
that is, the idea that mainstream parents provide the "right" kind of stimulation
in storybook reading, while non-mainstream parents do not. Furthermore,
while there appear to be some differences between groups, there are also differences within groups. However, there is little evidence that these differences
among or within sociocultural groups exert any influence on children's literacy
development.

Also of concern is the fact that many of the studies we reviewed were intervention studies of relatively short duration. Luke and Luke (2001) critique
many early literacy intervention programs as representing an "inoculation
model." Implicit in many programs, they contend, is the notion that children's
literacy learning can be enhanced (or more usually, that children's later literacy
difficulties can be prevented) through early "doses" of exposure to storybook
reading. There is a dearth of studies examining longitudinal programs, as well as
of studies looking at the long-term effects of early intervention programs. We
wonder if this is due to the fact that many of these programs are part of research
studies that by their nature tend to be focused on short-term goals, perhaps reflecting the publication-oriented culture of the academy, where most of the researchers are based.

There may also be justifiable concerns about how program outcomes and effectiveness are measured. Many of the studies discussed in this chapter reported
somewhat narrow measures of language or literacy achievement, such as vocabulary knowledge or letter name knowledge, obtained through standardized instruments like the Peabody Picture Vocabulary Test or the Test of Early

Reading Achievement. Program effectiveness is often determined by tests of statistical significance. As educators, we need to remind ourselves that what is of statistical significance may not necessarily be educationally significant, and that programs may have profound educational effects, even when results are not statistically significant. Similar concerns about outcome measures have also been expressed by Scarborough and Dobrich (1994b).

As was pointed out earlier, although there are some differences in storybook reading practices and values across cultural groups, there is also considerable similarity. To reiterate, there is little support for the stimulation-deficit hypothesis that is so pervasive. Especially problematic is the proliferation of family literacy programs targeted at low-income and non-mainstream families (Anderson, Smythe, & Lynch, in press). Auerbach (1995) contends that many of these programs reflect a deficit orientation based on the assumption that poor children need more exposure to books and that low-income parents need to be taught to read books to their children in the "correct" way. Tett and Crowther (1997) also question the ethics of such programs, arguing that they privilege a particular form of literacy at the expense of other, equally valid forms.

According to Janes and Kermani (2001), "in all cultures, caregivers find effective ways to teach children to make sense of their world and communicate with others" (p. 458). There is no reason why this principle should not hold for storybook reading. McNaughton (2001) posits a need for "textual dexterity" that would encourage "the addition of new text activities rather than the undermining of core cultural activities" (p. 43). And we believe there are models for how this might be achieved. Heath (1983) demonstrated that with support, schools are able to incorporate the literacy practices of the community into the curriculum. Bloome et al. (2000) described a "community centered" family literacy program that respects and incorporates literacy practices from the community. And finally, the PALS program (Anderson & Morrison, 2000) referred to at the beginning of this chapter is one more example of how a culturally responsive family literacy program might be developed in a multicultural context. Preliminary results suggest that parents and teachers value PALS highly, and that it is making a difference in children's literacy development (Shapiro, Anderson, Morrison, & Smythe, 2001).

In addition to the concerns just addressed, we see a real possibility that imposing storybook reading practices on parents and children might do more harm than good, and indeed might cause many children to disengage from reading. Scarborough and Dobrich (1994a) describe what they call the "broccoli" effect, maintaining that the practice of parents forcing storybook reading on their children is the same as forcing children to eat broccoli. As Janes and Kermani

(2001) cogently point out, prescriptive book reading practices imposed on parents and children for whom these practices are unfamiliar can turn storybook reading into a tense affair, to be avoided at all costs. As the adults in their study pointed out, the aversions to reading that develop can endure a lifetime.

As we proposed in the introduction of this chapter, current theories informed by ethnographic and sociolinguistic research define literacy as social practice, with considerable variation within and across sociocultural groups. McNaughton (2001) argues that prevailing constructivist ideas "tend to be associated with a view that in general children's literacy development follows a predictable and unitary sequence because endogenous processes direct acquisition" (p. 51). This seems strikingly true of storybook reading. In her historical overview of literacy in China, Ping depicts literacy practices that are strikingly different from their Western counterparts, valuing precision, memorization, and literal meaning over approximation, personal response, and interpretation. China has been a literate culture for thousands of years, even though pathways to literacy there run counter to many firmly held beliefs in the West. Anderson and Matthews (1999) and Elster (1994) also demonstrate that we need to question normative thinking about developmental trajectories of literacy development, especially in a society that is increasingly diverse.

Most educators have a strong sense of social justice and want to support all children's literacy development, especially those who come from homes that are underprivileged and marginalized. In our zeal to do that which is morally right, however, we need to constantly question our beliefs and assumptions. Nowhere is this need more important than in our view of the role of storybook reading within early literacy development. For as Scarborough and Dobrich (1994b) say:

> the question that we raised [about storybook reading] was whether by concentrating so much on just this one aspect of early experience, researchers have not paid sufficient attention to other manipulable aspects of young children's upbringing that may foster language and literacy development. (p. 345)

That question, we maintain, remains unanswered.

ACKNOWLEDGMENT

This research was supported by a grant from the Social Sciences and Humanities Research Council of Canada (410-99—0200).

REFERENCES

Abramson, S. (1987). *The relationship between parental support for literacy, school attendance and the reading behaviors of Musqueam children*. Unpublished master's thesis, University of British Columbia, Vancouver, British Columbia, Canada.

Anderson, J., & Matthews, R. (1999). Emergent storybook reading revisited. *Journal of Research in Reading, 22*, 293–298.

Anderson, J., & Morrison, F. (2000). *Parents As Literacy Supporters (PALS): A culturally responsive family literacy program*. Langley, British Columbia, Canada: Langley School District.

Anderson, J., Smythe, S., & Lynch, J. (in press). Family literacy. In J. Ponzetti (Ed.), *International encyclopedia of marriage and family relationships*. New York: Macmillan Reference USA.

Auerbach, E. (1995). Deconstructing the discourse of strengths in family literacy. *Journal of Reading Behaviour, 27*, 643–661.

Barnhardt, J. (1991). Criterion-related reliability of interpretations of children's performance on emergent literacy tasks. *Journal of Reading Behaviour, 23*, 425–444.

Barton, D., Hamilton, M., & Ivanic, R. (2000). *Situated literacies: Reading and writing in context*. London: Routledge.

Blackledge, A. (1999). Language, literacy and social justice: The experience of Bangladeshi women in Birmingham, UK. *Journal of Multilingual and Multicultural Development, 20*, 179–193.

Bloome, D., Katz, L, Wilson-Keenan, J.A., & Solsken, J. (2000). Interpellations of family/community and classroom literacy practices. *Journal of Educational Research, 93*, 155–164.

Bridwell, N. (1989). *Where is Clifford?* New York: Scholastic.

Brown, M. W. (1947). *Goodnight moon*. New York: HarperCollins.

Bus, A. G., Leseman, P. P. M., & Keultjes, P. (2000). Joint story book reading across cultures: A comparison of Surinamese-Dutch, Turkish-Dutch, and Dutch parent–child dyads. *Journal of Literacy Research, 32*, 53–76

Bus, A., & Sulzby, E. (2000, November). *Connections between characteristics of parent-child readings and characteristics of subsequent emergent readings*. Paper presented at the annual meeting of the National Reading Conference, Scottsdale, AZ.

Bus, A., van IJzendoorn, M. H., & Pellegrini, A. D. (1995). Joint book reading makes for success in learning to read: A meta-analysis on intergenerational transmission of literacy. *Review of Educational Research, 65*, 1–21.

Carle, E. (1970). *The very hungry caterpillar*. Cleveland: World Publishing Company.

Cazden, C. (1988). *Classroom discourse: The language of teaching and learning*. Portsmouth, NH: Heinemann.

Chomsky, C. (1972). Stages in language development and reading behavior. *Harvard Educational Review, 42*, 1–33.

Clark, M. (1976). *Young fluent readers: What can they teach us?* London: Heinemann.

Clay, M. (1993). Always a learner: A fable. *Reading Today, 3*, 10.

DeBaryshe, B. (1992). *Final report for the project early literacy and literacy activities in the home*. Washington, DC: U.S. Department of Education Field Initiated Studies Program (ERIC Document Reproduction Service No. ED 351 406).

Delpit, L. (1995). *"Other people's children": Cultural conflict in the classroom*. New York: New Press.

De Temple, J., & Tabors, P. (1994, December). *Styles of interaction during a book reading task: Implications for literacy intervention with low-income families*. Paper presented at the National Reading Conference Annual Meeting, San Diego, CA.

Dickinson, D. K., & Tabors, P. O. (2001). *Beginning literacy with language*. Baltimore: Pall Brookes.

Durkin, D. (1966). *Children who read early*. New York: Teachers College Press.

Dyson, A. (1993). From intervention to social action in early childhood literacy: A reconceptualization through dialogue difference. *Early Childhood Research Quarterly, 8,* 409–425.

Elster, C. (1994). Patterns within preschoolers emergent reading. *Reading Research Quarterly, 29,* 409–425.

Edwards, P. (1992). Involving parents in building reading instruction for African-American children. *Theory Into Practice, 31,* 350–359.

Feitelson, D., & Iraqi, J. (1990). Storybook reading: A bridge to literary language. *The Reading Teacher, 44,* 264–265.

Ferreiro, E., & Teberosky, A. (1982). *Literacy before schooling*. Portsmouth, NH: Heinemann.

Fishman, A. (1990). Becoming literate: A lesson from the Amish. In A. Lunsford, H. Moglen, & J. Slevin (Eds.), *The right to literacy* (pp. 29–38). New York: The Modern Language Association of America.

Garcia, G. E., & Godina, H. (1994, December). *Bilingual children's participation in classroom literacy activities: "Once upon a time" and its alternatives*. Paper presented at the annual meeting of the National Reading Conference, San Diego, CA.

Giffin, R. (1987). *Parental involvement in an experimental reading program, Grades 2–7*. Unpublished Master's thesis, University of British Columbia, Vancouver, British Columbia, Canada.

Glynn, T., & Glynn, V. (1986). Shared reading by Cambodian mothers and children learning English as a second language: Reciprocal gains. *The Exceptional Child, 33,* 159–172.

Gunderson, L., & Anderson, J. (in press). Multicultural views of teaching and learning. In A. Willis, G. Garcia, V. Harris, & R. Barrera, (Eds.), *Multicultural issues in literacy research and practice*. Mahwah, NJ: Lawrence Erlbaum Associates.

Haynes, W., & Saunders, D. (1998). Joint book reading strategies in middle-class African American and White mother–toddler dyads. *Journal of Children's Communication Development, 20,* 9–17.

Heath, S. B. (1982). What no bedtime story means: Narrative skills at home and school. *Language in Society, 11,* 49–76.

Heath, S.B. (1983). *Ways with words*. New York: Cambridge University Press.

Heibert, E. H. (1981). Developmental patterns and interrelationships of preschoolers print awareness. *Reading Research Quarterly, 16,* 230–260.

Hirst, K. (1998). Pre-school literacy experiences of children in Punjabi, Urdu and Gujerati speaking families in England. *British Educational Research Journal, 24,* 415–429.

Huey, E. B. (1908). *The psychology and pedagogy of reading*. New York: Macmillan.

Hughes, M., Vaughn, S., & Schumm, J. S. (1999). Home literacy activities: Perceptions and practices of Hispanic parents of children with learning disabilities. *Learning Disabilities Quarterly, 22,* 224–235.

Janes, H., & Kermani, H. (2001). Caregivers story reading to young children in family literacy programs: Pleasure or punishment? *Journal of Adolescent and Adult Literacy, 44,* 458–446.

Keller-Cohen, D. (1993). Rethinking literacy: Comparing colonial and contemporary America. *Anthropology and Education Quarterly, 24,* 288–307.

Laframboise, K., & Wynn, M. (1994). Oral participation in shared reading and writing by limited English proficient students in a multiethnic class setting. *Reading Horizons, 35,* 95–109.

Leseman, P., & de Jong, P. (1998). Home literacy: Opportunity, instruction, cooperation and social-emotional quality predicting early reading achievement. *Reading Research Quarterly, 33,* 294–318.

Lomax, R. G., & McGee, L. (1987). Interrelationships among young children's concepts about print and reading: Toward a model of word recognition. *Reading Research Quarterly, 22,* 177–196.

Luke, A., & Luke, C. (2001). Adolescence lost/childhood regained: On early intervention and the emergence of the techno-subject. *Journal of Early Childhood Literacy, 1,* 91–120.

Macleod, F. (1996). Does British research support claims about the benefits of parents hearing their children read regularly at home? A closer look at the evidence from three key studies. *Research Papers in Education, 11,* 173–190.

Manyak, P. (1998). *"Este Libro Es Mi Historia": Mother–child interactions during storybook reading in a Mexican-American household.* ERIC Document Reproduction Service No. ED 418 383.

Mason, J. (1992). Reading stories to preliterate children: A proposed connection to reading. In P. Gough, L. Ehri, & R. Treiman (Eds.), *Reading acquisition.* Mahwah, NJ: Lawrence Erlbaum Associates.

McNaughton, S. (2001). Co-constructing expertise: The development of parents' and teachers' ideas about literacy practices and the transition to school. *Journal of Early Childhood Literacy, 1,* 40–58.

Minami, M. (1999, August). *Styles of parent–child book-reading in Japanese families.* Paper presented at the annual conference of the Japanese Society for Language Sciences, Tokyo, Japan.

Nagy, W. (1987). Learning word meaning from context. *American Educational Research Journal, 24,* 237–270.

Pellegrini, A. (1991). A critique of the concept of at risk as applied to emergent literacy. *Language Arts, 68,* 380–385.

Pellegrini, A., Perlmutter, J. C., Galda, L., & Brody, G. (1990). Joint reading between Black Head Start children and their mothers. *Child Development, 61,* 443–453.

Ping, H. (1995). Chinese attitudes towards learning and reading. In M. Chapman & J. Anderson (Eds.), *Thinking globally about language education* (pp. 35–48). Vancouver, British Columbia, Canada: Research and Development in Global Studies, Centre for the Study of Curriculum and Instruction, University of British Columbia.

Reyes, M. (1992). Challenging venerable assumptions: Literacy instruction for linguistically different students. *Harvard Educational Review, 62,* 427–446.

Scarborough, H., & Dobrich, W. (1994a). On the efficacy of reading to preschoolers. *Developmental Review, 14,* 245–302.

Scarborough, H. S., & Dobrich, W. (1994b). Another look at parent–preschooler book reading: How naked is the emperor? *Developmental Review, 14,* 340–347.

Shapiro, J., Anderson, J., & Anderson, A. (1997). Diversity in parental storybook reading. *Early Child Development and Care, 127,* 47–59.

Shapiro, J., Anderson, J., Morrison, F., & Smythe, S. (2001, June). *Parents as literacy supporters: A family literacy program in inner city Canadian schools.* Paper presented at the European Reading Conference, Dublin, Ireland.

Snow, C. (1991). The theoretical basis for relationships between language and literacy in development. *Journal of Research in Childhood Education, 6,* 5–10.

Street, B. (1984). *Literacy in theory and practice.* Cambridge: Cambridge University Press.

Sulzby, E. (1985). Children's emergent reading of favourite storybooks: A developmental study. *Reading Research Quarterly, 20,* 458–481.

Taylor, D. (1983). *Family literacy: Young children learning to read and write*. Portsmouth, NH: Heinemann.

Teale, W. (1986). Home background and young children's early literacy development. In W. Teale & E. Sulzby (Eds.), *Emergent literacy: Writing and reading* (pp. 173–205). Norwood, NJ: Ablex.

Tett, L., & Crowther, J. (1997). Families at a disadvantage: Class, culture and literacies. *British Educational Research Journal, 24,* 449–460.

Tizzard, J., Schofield, W. N., & Hewison, J. (1982). Collaboration between teachers and parents in assisting children's reading. *British Journal of Educational Psychology, 52,* 1–15.

Twymon, S. (1990). *Early reading and writing instruction in the homes and school of three five-year-old children from Black working class families*. Unpublished doctoral dissertation, University of Michigan, Ann Arbor, MI.

Vivas, E. (1996). Effects of storybook reading on language. *Language Learning, 46,* 189–216.

Walters, K., & Gunderson, L. (1985). Effects of parent volunteers reading first language (L1) books to ESL students. *The Reading Teacher, 39,* 66–69.

Wells, G. (1985). Preschool literacy related activities and success in school. In D. Olson, N. Torrance, & A. Hillyard (Eds.), *Literacy, language and learning*. New York: Cambridge University Press.

Yopp, H. (1992). Developing phonemic awareness in young children. *Reading Teacher, 45,* 696–703.

11

Reading, Homes, and Families: From Postmodern to Modern?

Victoria Carrington
Allan Luke
University of Queensland

New economic, social, and cultural conditions have begun to alter the patterns of home–school transitions in two ways: first, by shifting the normative definitions of family in postindustrial communities and economies; and second, by shifting the basis of preschool linguistic and literate socialization from long-standing print culture to emergent, complex blendings of multiliteracies that engage digital and media texts. Our claim here is that for many children the normative site for storybook reading—the family—is changing, that the texts and discourses of home- and community-based literacy practices are changing, and therefore, that the background knowledge, expertise, and habitus that children bring from home to school are also in transition. The cases we describe model new patterns of identity and practice at work in the early childhood classroom—patterns for which a generation of print-trained and acculturated teachers have limited explanatory schemata other than those related to "deficit."

The chapters in this volume focus largely on the implications of storybook reading for the teaching and learning of literacy in schools. Since the prototypical case studies by Heath (1982) on "what no bedtime story means" for working- and middle-class American families, and the contemporaneous work by Wells (1986) and his colleagues in the Bristol Language Study, there has been a concerted focus on the significance of printed text in home–school transitions. Not surprisingly, the historical backdrop behind Wells' and Heath's work was the "class, codes, and control" premise developed by Bernstein (1976) and colleagues—including Hasan and Cook-Gumperz—in the 1970s. This premise was concerned with the constitutive effects of class-based early language socialization on later literacy development, overall educational achievement, and social and economic reproduction more generally. While the postwar U.K. and European debate pivoted on social class stratification, more recent U.K. research has documented the increased complexity and challenges for early childhood education raised by culturally heterogeneous societies and communities (Gregory, 1997; Gregory & Williams, 2000). Hence, much of the "new" research in family literacy has been an attempt, based on sociolinguistics and the ethnography of communication, to come to grips with the shift from normative "White" cultures (Frankenberg, 1993) to blended and resituated ethnic, migrant, indigenous, and non-English speaking cultures.

Particularly given the current policy enthusiasm for early intervention (Luke & Luke, 2001), it is not surprising that the home–school transition remains the Gordian knot of language education. Yet our understanding of how the complex interplay between family, early literacy experience in the home and community, and preschool language socialization mediates children's encounters with mainstream schooling remains modernist in its assumptions about both the family and the traditional print medium. The debates over language deficits and ameliorative activities and programs persist in our research and, perhaps more importantly, in the pedagogical imaginations of teachers who face increasingly diverse "at-risk" student populations in Australia, New Zealand, the U.K., Canada, and the U.S.

More specifically, researchers have focused on two related issues: differences in students' home–school transitions, and the practices of what has come to be called "family literacy." There is, of course, heated debate over the efficacy of various ways that families' textual practices help their children become "schooled before schooling," to cite Bourdieu and Passeron's (1990) term for the class-based inculcation of habitus among middle- and upper-class French children.

Regardless of where we stand on the desirability of parents reading to children, or on genre selection and the ideological content of such practices, dominant views of family literacy are premised on a particular normative view of the family—generally the Anglo-European nuclear family. Such a family stereotypically has one working parent, is heterosexual, relatively demographically stable, and possessed of sufficient surplus income, education, and leisure time to engage in print-rich socialization and English-as-a-first-language verbal play. The problem facing literacy researchers is thus as much sociological as it is psychological or cognitive. While reading to children appears to have effects that are transferable to early school-based literacy development, the underlying question, as raised by Heath almost two decades ago, is whether it is the normative interactive and disciplinary structures of middle-class child rearing that generate the schooling effects that have historically been masked as cognitive ability, or whether early reading per se actually has sustainable educational effects on student achievement. As Scribner and Cole's (1981) work has illustrated, disaggregation of the two factors is a difficult task.

In modern Western mythology, the form and function of the nuclear family are taken as moral and cultural ideals. A century and a half of family research, from Engels to the post-war structural-functionalist analyses of Talcott Parsons, to contemporary psychotherapeutic and psychoanalytic models have contributed to this construction (Carrington, 2002). The family in question is presumed to be a monocultural, heterosexual, White nuclear social unit. Such a theorization in turn affects the way we theorize community: less in terms of networks, synergies of "learning communities," the structuralist kinship relations of "tribal groups," and more in terms of the similar, loosely coupled though essentially isolated nuclear units that characterize postindustrial capitalist economies. This outdated model still guides schools' and principals' strategies on how to "manage" school–community relationships. It entails direct communication between schools and nuclear families through parents' and citizens' groups, newsletters, social and fundraising events, parent–teacher nights, and so forth—practices that can be problematic to communities with different cultural traditions around family structure, pedagogy, authority, governmentality, and learning (Gregory, 1997).

The effects of narrow normative models of the family are magnified by the rapid dissemination of mass media. The daily life of the nuclear family has been modeled on television, in children's books, in magazines and films, ranging from the Brady Bunch and the Cosbys to, of course, the new stereotypically postmodern anti-family, the Simpsons. In this way, the textual representations of "family" encountered by children normalize a set of family images and practices, which are supposed to mirror the family where the reading and viewing takes place (Baker & Freebody, 1987)—just as the images of Dick and Sally reading and "doing school" in basal readers represent, sanction, and reproduce the very pedagogical acts and literacy events of these books' uptake (Luke, 1988).

Taken together, these representations contribute to the pedagogic production of behavioral and role-based norms around the nuclear family—whether through the public pegadogy of mass media or the institutionalized instruction of readers and storybooks. Adult males are the primary wage earners and disciplinarians, while adult females, regardless of whether they are homemakers or employees, are assigned responsibility for early nurturing, socialization, and education of children—who themselves are represented and "imaged" in particular ways. The feminization of child care, early childhood education, nursing, and primary school teaching continues, post-feminism, with relatively unaltered employment patterns across the past 50 years.

The link between particular versions of family, literacy instruction in schools, and the emergence of particular family theories cannot be understood outside these broader political, ideological, and economic contexts. In the same way that monocultural social policy attempts to fit culturally and racially diverse individuals and groups into existing frameworks without attempting to reconceptualize nation, race, culture, ethnicity or identity, family literacy research blithely attempts to ignore issues of individual and family hybridity, fluidity of identity, and power and access. Given the shape of new economies and the rapid evolution of non-print textual forms, such an approach ultimately returns us, as sociologists, to the same old arguments about who gets literacy, knowledge, and power, not to mention how, in what forms, to what ends, and in whose interests.

This chapter outlines key aspects of the traditional home–literacy transition, showing how these are based on modernist presumptions about family and literacy. Second, we offer descriptive case studies of two young Australian school-age children making the transition from home to school. We take these children's paths as indicative of the need for a complete rethinking of family literacy literature and views on the home/school transition. We conclude with a consideration of the implications of these shifts for school literacy instruction.

New Economies and New Identities

The metaphor of globalization is, at best, a metaphor, rather than a powerful, fully articulated explanatory framework for explaining the changed social, cultural, and material conditions in which we, our students and communities, all find ourselves. We deliberately use the passive form here, for one of the emergent patterns in a sociology of globalization is the degree to which communities whose life pathways, livelihoods, and institutions have changed rapidly and in unprecedented ways have difficulty connecting these changes with their actions or, at times, even those of their governments (Castells, 1996). Given the prominent role of communications technologies in economic globalization, it is surprising that studies of literacy teaching and learning have in fact tended to become more national, focusing increasingly on the local and the parochial (Luke & Carrington, in press).

Whether in urban center or rural diaspora, among middle-class or migrants, patterns and practices of daily life are shifting in relation to economic and technological change, although not at regular and generalizable rates. In this new technological, social, and cultural environment, information, commodities, and people move with formerly unimaginable speed, effectively transforming the world. These processes encompass shifts in the economic system, in the ways in which we understand the world and our place in it and, as a result, they have an impact on identities and social practices. The consequences are changes in everyday uses and experiences of space and time, the emergence of new work practices and skills, patterns of leisure, habits of consumption of goods, images and discourses, and the emergence of hybridized and blended forms of identity and human expression. This shift is not a transient glitch in an otherwise modernist world. Mobility, diversity, and hybridity are markers of a new socioeconomic system: a post-Fordist world where the unstated rules of social and economic success have changed significantly in the space of a generation. These changes have been sustained by the emergence of new forms of information, and by communications technologies such as the computer, the Internet, e-mail, the VCR, the mobile phone, and cable television.

In response to changing times and changing economic requirements, an emergent literature is describing the training of a new citizen-worker—a worker who is mobile, flexible and multiskilled (Gee, Hull, & Lankshear, 1998). Those educational systems that have begun to implement curriculum reform based on the idea of "knowledge nations," "smart states," and "learning communities" (e.g., Singapore, Ireland, Queensland) are increasingly focusing not on basic skills and minimum competencies, but on critical and analytical skills, multimodal literacies, and new forms of intercultural and multilingual communication. In response to these needs and the prevalence of multimodal texts, new literacies are emerging, not just in multinational workplaces and advanced capitalist educational systems, but also in homes, shopping malls, and community centers.

The key issue now facing curriculum planners, teacher educators, and policy bureaucrats is how and to what extent print-based education systems—which are still tied up with the socialization and reproduction patterns of postwar industrial economics and national politics—can "cope" with these developments. Put simply, the response of most school systems has been to track and anticipate the needs of new workers through curriculum reform in middle school, high school, and vocational education. The early primary years have generally been seen as a domain not for future-oriented reform, but rather for the reinstallation, renewal, and reinforcement of traditional testing-based orientations to basic skills instruction (Gee, 2000). The discourses of "early intervention" have not attempted to deal with new economies, identities, or families through anything other than an ideological attempt at "restoration" of a print-based order on childhood, development, and schooling (Luke & Luke, 2001).

LITERACY AND THE HOME–SCHOOL CONNECTION

Underlying research into home–school literacy transitions and relationships is the desire to explain persistent disparities in school literacy achievement among various groups. Much of the research, whether based on developmental or cognitive views of literacy, has, over the last 30 years, identified some sort of deficit as a key factor. For instance, there is an extensive body of research arguing that lower-SES children are more at risk of school literacy failure than higher-SES children because their families do not read enough or lack book knowledge, that they do not value literacy or model it effectively (e.g., Cairney & Ruge, 1998; Mason & Allen, 1986; White, 1982). That is, families in low-SES circumstances do not foster "implicit knowledge of the intentionality of print, story structure, and the linguistic register of written language which is dependent upon extensive exposure to written language in many different forms during the pre-school years" (Purcell-Gates, 1986, p. 19). Families operating in poor and working-class contexts are therefore defined as deficient in their preparation of children for school literacies. More recently, the case has been made that single-parent families put their children at risk of school failure (Zill, 1996), and the ongoing debate over brain development has posited longitudinal neuropsychological effects of verbal neglect.

In contrast, working from a Hymsian, ethnographic approach to communication, Heath (1982) argued that working-class families clearly understand the importance of literacy to their children, undertaking home-based language socialization, often providing versions of what they thought might "count" as literacy education. What Heath's work made clear was that the literacy activities and oral language socialization taking place in such homes were mismatched to those of school, and therefore acted to disadvantage these children. Middle-class, educated, and professional parents, on the other hand, mobilized a powerful hidden curriculum of socialization into classroom-like interactional norms and sociolinguistic registers.

These twin strands of American research—cognitive/psychological and ethnographic/sociolinguistic—tend to place responsibility for emergent literacy failure on family literacy practices or the lack thereof, or on the inability of school literacy instruction—including storybook reading—to recognize and utilize culture- and community-specific background knowledge, sociolinguistic practice, and interactional competence. The latter position has spawned ambitious interventions that aim to engage both teachers and students in the analysis of community knowledges, and cultural and linguistic resources. This is exemplified in Moll (1992) and colleagues' efforts to assess the Arizona Hispanic community's "stocks of knowledge," both to inform and to adjust educational interventions in the school. The KEEP literacy program developed by Kathy Au was a deliberate attempt to alter the sociolinguistic norms of the mainstream classroom to accommodate the cultural practices of Hawai'ian children (Au, 1980; Au & Mason, 1983). And in the U.K. and Australia, "critical language awareness" approaches deliberately make community language use an object of classroom study, as part of a larger critical analysis of who uses language, where, and with what consequential power (e.g., Comber & Simpson, 2001; Fairclough, 1993).

The use of training programs to remediate early experiential deficits rested upon a view of literacy as emergent and developmental (Clay, 1972, 1991; Mason & Allen, 1986; Teale & Sulzby, 1986). Therefore, the problem was viewed principally in intrapsychological terms, with a focus on making the home more school-like. At-riskness is attributed to single-parent, working-class, and underclass families, NESB (non-English-speaking background) families, and so forth, who ostensibly lack the will or resources to provide school-like socialization. By this account, responsibility resides in the family's capacity to take on middle-class attitudes and practices in a nuclear-family model of interaction.

Implicit in this agenda has been a concern to make parents more "teacher-like." In Australia and elsewhere it has spawned school-based training programs to show parents how to read storybooks to their children (e.g., the Canberra-based Parental Involvement Program in the 1980s, and the 1997 public campaigns by Queensland curriculum authorities to encourage parents to read to children in bed and, quite literally, in the bath, with waterproofed materials). The aim here was to make home more like school by training parents to act and question around printed text in the same ways as classroom teachers. The programs range from parental training courses to the kind of popular "read-aloud" advocacy literature that abounds in retail bookstores and airport news agents (e.g., Fox, 2001; Trelease, 2001). The equation of "teacher-like" behavior with mainstream middle-class practices and values is based on differential valuations of various kinds of family and home settings. The fact that schools and early literacy programs might be failing students and their families quickly falls out of this equation.

In Australia, early childhood classroom literacy practices responded to these shifts with a "whole language" approach aimed at building "print-rich" environments and establishing child-centered and middle-class interactional patterns of home literacy events in the classroom (Butler & Turbill, 1984). The processes, skills, and knowledge involved in early literacy learning were to be encapsulated "naturally" within the social context, rather than through explicit, direct instruction models. It was assumed by many teachers, teacher educators, and researchers that this was the kind of enabling literate background that children needed in order to become literate. The focus was on shared reading and group discussion of printed texts (particularly picture books) on literary experience, on interpretation and comprehension, and on the modeling of "appropriate" literacy events and relationships.

By the 1990s, Australian research around literacy education was focusing much more strongly on sociocultural analyses of literacy practices, with a specific view that cultural and class differences were key factors in children's ability to translate home literacy practices into successful school literacies. This perspective argues that literacy is socially constructed (Cook-Gumperz, 1986), and can only be understood in context, within institutions, communities, workplaces and other social fields—all of which have differing and at times overtly conflicting interactional patterns, values, language ideologies, and rules of exchange. School-based literacy becomes, then, one of many literacies that individuals and/or groups may develop and use. In a significant move, sociocultural approaches argue against the notion of individual deficit, focusing instead on the difficult transitions of children from culture-, community-, and family-specific registers, discourses, and practices to the specialized and normative interactional "language game" of early literacy instruction.

In the largest Australian empirical study of home–school transitions, Freebody, Ludwig, and Gunn (1995) argued that Australian entry-level literacy instruction had become child-centered and progressivist in tenor and practice, but was ineffectual because of its class-based assumptions about preferred patterns of interaction and, indeed, childhood identity. In detailed discourse analyses of home and classroom events, the group concluded that the shape of Australian early literacy instruction systematically selects in favor of not only those middle- and upper-class children who know how to interact around books, but also in favor of intellectually and culturally vacuous childhood identities and practices that have little connection to the out-of-school worlds of children and teachers (cf. Baker & Freebody, 1987).

This kind of work is cognizant of the power of cultural and linguistic match or mismatch to decide an individual's ability to succeed in particular social fields

(Bourdieu & Passeron, 1990). Individual success, therefore, often pivots on the closeness of match between the cultural capital of each individual (and by extension, their family) and that of the school and its representatives. In their New South Wales study of family literacy, Cairney and Munsey (1992) noted: "The reality is that schools staffed by middle-class teachers reflect middle-class, culturally defined views of what literacy is and how it is best developed" (p. 4). This is a restatement of the mismatch hypothesis, albeit an augmentation of Heath's work with a stronger, Bourdieuian definition of capital.

Freebody et al. (1995) made a significant addition to this field with their finding that there is no compelling cognitive, linguistic, or educational rationale for many of the "school literacy" practices that cancel, ignore, and attempt to "uplift" the alleged home literacy "deficit." Simply put, many Australian school practices are not introductions into powerful mainstream "ways with words," but rather into specialized, highly selective, and irrelevant ways of interacting around texts—patterns of text handling that, as Baker and Freebody (1987) argued over a decade ago, have more to do with maintaining the social order of the school (and the social and cultural "comfort zone" of middle-class teachers) than with the teaching and learning of literacy per se.

While earlier views of schooling and literacy education were premised on the idea that student failure was due to some inherent individual flaw, the sociocultural perspective held that the cultural, economic, and social capital of individuals and groups mediated their relative success or failure. Individual ability is but one small aspect of these larger cultural wars. Influenced by this shift, Delgado-Geitan's (1990) study of Hispanic families in the Santa Barbara, California, area showed that part of the problem was the inaccessibility of necessary knowledge about the cultural practices and expectations of schooling, however mainstream and arbitrary these might be. Looking at the home–school transitions of indigenous Torres Strait Islander children in Australian schools, Luke and Kale (1997) noted the different cultural uses of language in non-White Australian homes and the inability of classroom teachers to accept non-mainstream discourses. The response of many Australian schools was to implement a genre-based approach to literacy, wherein students were explicitly and directly taught how mainstream academic and cultural texts worked, and how to reproduce school-like versions of them (Cope & Kalantzis, 1995). This was a significant departure from the implicit approach of the whole language approach; however, in many cases the choice of text types remained instructionally unlinked to local context or students' lives outside the classroom.

In the last decade, "family literacy" has emerged as a significant field of study. There has been recognition of the range of valuable literacies practiced at home

(Barton, 1994; Rivalland, 2000), and increasing pressure to connect children's early classroom literacy experiences to those of their home (Cairney & Ruge, 1998; Moll, 1992). As Solsken (1993) noted, interest in family literacy has remained focused on identifying the practices that are most like or unlike school practices. The child's ability to transition seamlessly into a pre-existing classroom context remains a core concern. Yet in most mainstream school systems, the normative patterns for "doing school" and "doing school literacy" remain constant—a kind of pedagogical default mode, in the face of what many teachers view as an increasingly diverse, difficult to understand, and "deficit" student body (Luke, Freebody, & Land, 2000).

When viewed as a whole, the home–school transition research makes a number of problematic assumptions. It assumes particular types of family and cultural categories and not others; it assumes deficit in relation to school literacy; and it is premised on the continuing canonicity of the printed text in early childhood. Up to this point there has been little scope for discussions of hybridity, new literacies, and new economies. What does this mean for children undertaking what can be a perilous transition from home through the initial years of school literacy instruction in new times? We now turn to sketch two cases from different social, class, and geographic backgrounds. Our aim here is to suggest that culture and language still matter, but perhaps not as discrete categories of "difference," independent of the economic reconfiguration of family and the emergence of multimediated, digitalized childhood.

EVE

Eve is about to turn 6 and has just lost her first front tooth. She is a middle-class child of Anglo-Australian descent.[1] Her parents are well educated and relatively well paid: Her father is a secondary school teacher and her mother a university lecturer. Eve lives in a pleasant suburban house, with a computer and a Playstation™ in the living room, cable TV, a small stereo system in her room, a bike, and roller blades. She is opinionated and articulate about her own needs. Her greatest aspiration at the moment is to have her own mobile phone one day soon.

But this is not a typical family. Her parents are divorced, reflecting Australia's estimated 40% divorce rate. Like a significant number of Australian children, she lives with her father rather than her mother.

---

[1]Eve is an actual case, with textual and ethnographic data compiled for this chapter.

Eve spends large chunks of her leisure time interacting with CD-ROMs and surfing the Web. She has her favorite web pages bookmarked (nick.com, barbie.com, disney.com). She writes emails to her mother on a daily basis and creates and prints her own illustrated stories using word-processing and clip-art programs. Given the hectic nature of life in a single-parent family, there is little "bedtime" reading or other conscious parental contact around printed texts. In fact, there is limited use or production of traditional printed text in the house. In some respects, Eve's father's busy schedule has created what several decades ago was construed as a "displacement" situation, in which she spends a great deal of time immersed in electronic media. The 1960s "displacement hypothesis" attributed failure with print to time spent watching television (Luke, 1989). But while the classical displacement model assumed that televiewing generated a print literacy deficit, it is clear that Eve's engagement with new technologies is generating complex authoring, composition, and reading skills.

Here are some examples of Eve's emails (complete with her own spelling and grammatical idiosyncracies):

To: < >
Subject: letter from EVE

Dear Mummy.

I love you. Hope you are OK in [place name]. Do you like work.HAVE YOU GOT ANY EMAIL FROM US. Hope you like my letter. Hope you get my letter soon.I love you very much. I hope you come home soon.

To: < >
Subject: EVE
Dear mummy

I didn't play on the monkey bars as Mrs Braceland said I was not to.

Mummy my hands are all blissted and sore. I hope you are having a good time at your school. And that you teach lots of good things. I like school . I love mummy when you will be coming home.I hope soon.

I love you mummy.

EVE

To: < >

Subject: letter from EVE

DEAR MUM.

I HOPE YOU ARE HAVING A GOOD TIME. WH EN ARE YOU
GOING TO GIVE US YOUR PHONE THING

HOPE YOU ARE HAVEING FUN.

I LOVE YOU MUMMY.

LOVE

EVE.XXXXXXXXXXXXXXXXXXXXXXXXXXXXXXXXXXXXXXXXXXXXX
XXXXXXXXXXX

XXXXX

XXXXXXXXXXXXXXXXXXXXXXXXXXXXXXXXXXXXXXXXXXXXXXX
XXXXXXXXXXXXXXXXXXXXXX

XXXXXXXXXXXXXXXXXXXXXXXXXXXXXXXXXXXXXXXXXXXXX
XXXXXXXXXXXXXX LOTS OF KISSES FOR MUMMY_

To: < >

Subject: letter from EVE

DEAR MUM

I HOPE YOU HAVE A GOOD TIME AT WORK . :- BYE FOR NOW
SIGNED BY EVE ...

MUM I MISSS YOU BECAUSE YOU ARE AWAY.

It is important to view these emails in the context of family relations. They are not one-off notes or letters, or even stories in the traditional sense described by family literacy research or by the genres listed in Eve's teachers' literacy teaching plans. They are their own genre, with their own purpose and style. Each email is part of an electronic turn-taking sequence, an exchange structure that constitutes in both field and tenor Eve's continuing affective relationship with her mother. That is, the emails lexically represent Eve's world (a world of "monkey bars," "emails," and "phone things") while also playing out the social relationships of a mother–daughter relationship (the recurrent use of affective verbs like "hope"; the pronominals "I" and "you"; the unmarked interrogative "Do you like work"; salutations, addresses and, of course, "XXXXX ...").

This is an evolving use and understanding of "writing" and "reading" unavailable to her in the classroom. In psychomotor terms, Eve shows a developing mastery of keyboarding skills. This in itself is significant. Not many years ago it was assumed that children came to school with many years of handwriting-friendly fine motor skills, acquired through play and a well-developed familiarity with some aspects of the manual technology of printing. However, new generations of children such as Eve spend large chunks of developmental time at keyboards and mouse pads, rather than with pencils. The fine motor skills of scrolling and clicking developed through the use of this technology are not necessarily the same as those required for handwriting in classrooms—but neither can they be construed simply as "deficit."

As we can clearly see by the style and layout, Eve is quite aware of the potential of the space bar for creating meaning. Her attempts at spelling out words are obvious, as is her ability to backspace in order to erase/correct as she goes. She uses both capitalization and spacing for emphasis and has incorporated the use of symbols. She clearly follows a standard email format—"Dear Mummy," "bye for now signed by Eve"—and has also personalized the format, using, for example, "lots of kisses for mummy" as an endnote to accompany her lines of "X"-kisses and a smiley face. In the first email, there also is evidence that she recognizes that letters and emails are distinct genres, in her inquiry about whether her "letter" has arrived. In other emails she creates faces and substitutes her own symbols for hugs. While she is reproducing and blending known genres, she is also creating and integrating new symbolic forms to construct and convey personal meaning.

Eve's production of each turn is based on a presumption of the interactive fidelity that typifies conversational exchange: the assumption that there will be rapid and felicitous response. In this regard, the email genre is far more interactive and exchange-based than the static print text that she will encounter in school—and certainly from the relatively static narratives about animals and community life that she is learning to read in shared book experience. She has mastered the use of the email medium to produce, edit, and immediately send her messages to places and people beyond her physical location. The texts she produces do not sit in an isolated classroom, nor do they disappear into a workbook to be read only by her teacher and returned with grades or comments a week or more later. Eve is independently creating electronic texts and sending them off into the real world to do work on her behalf. This power to communicate via writing—a digital and on-line multiliteracy—was inaccessible to earlier generations of children.

At school Eve is an average student. She attends a middle-class school in a large Australian provincial city, where she studies in an instructional program focused around shared book experience, with some direct instruction in phonemic awareness and print knowledge. In the classroom, she and other children learn how to participate in orchestrated IRE discussions ostensibly focused on textual meaning, but in reality also focused on the expression of particular middle-class forms of identity and expression (Freebody et al., 1995). Even though she is an articulate child, she is not confident of her ability to read school texts. She does not seem to be able to make a direct connection between her own production of text at home and the decoding of other, more foreign genres at school.

In school, Eve experiences moments of great sadness, particularly when class stories emphasize mother–daughter relationships (as they often do) and the "naturalness" of the nuclear family. Her ability to articulate her sadness about the end of her parents' marriage and her subsequent separation from her mother was viewed as distress and emotional turmoil by her teachers. She initially struggled with school and classroom participation, and is now a slightly below-average reader on state standardized tests. Her teachers attributed her difficulties to the recent divorce and the pressures placed on a father left to care for his young children by himself.

Her teachers have commented that they are worried about her concentration, her focus and, in turn, her long-term achievement. She has some difficulty decoding printed text and handwriting, and just as importantly, lacks the narrative knowledge that comes from bedtime stories and home literacy activities.

Eve's less-developed handwriting skills are the result of home-based keyboarding. Her apparent decoding deficits are attributed by teachers to the lack of a permanent mother in her life. Interestingly, however, Eve's teachers did not balance their concerns about her handwriting against her love of and talent for coloring, nor against her ability to negotiate web pages, load and play games, or create and send emails. This is important. There are, in fact, fundamental differences between the reading of linear texts and of the multimodal texts that Eve is mastering at home.

Many children's initial literacy knowledge and skills are now being shaped through Internet access and CD-ROMs. Children often learn to "read" these texts without direct parental mediation. As Eve's experiences suggest, these are not necessarily the same skills and knowledge that support the decoding of linear, print-based texts. Unlike print-based texts, multimodal practices involve the rapid and integrated coordination of aural, visual, and textual cues in an environment that requires interaction between reader and text, independent of the powerful mediating adult presence that has traditionally operated with linear textual forms. Yet at the same time Eve understands that her email messages to her mother are instant and interactive. These virtual textual exchanges are highly interactive, even though they lack the face-to-face scaffolding of bed-time storybook readings.

Once an assessment of risk was made, the usual print-text deficit programs were brought into play around Eve. Her teachers' response to her perceived classroom difficulty has been to increase the amount of "basic" decoding prac-tice. This intervention has taken a number of forms, reflecting ideas of what is "appropriate" within this early literacy instructional context. Efforts have in-cluded allocation of a "buddy" from Year 7 (7th grade) who meets with her once or twice a week to read with her from classroom texts, and small-group with-drawal sessions with an aide/parent, to practice and reinforce basic literacy skills. This second activity involves the completion of repetitive worksheets and purpose-made activities under direct adult supervision. Eve's father was called to the school to be informed of the teachers' concerns about Eve's emotional and academic well-being. Ostensibly, and by all conventional criteria, Eve is a privileged middle-class child, the least at risk of being caught in the state's Year Two Diagnostic Net or Year Three Benchmark Test, both of which assess early reading development. On the other hand, her life does not revolve around what are still considered to be the prerequisite skills for literacy success—bedtime stories, handwritten stories, home-based oral traditions of nursery rhymes and, crucially, the implicit assumption that she spends large amounts of time with her mother doing these things. It is assumed in the early literacy literature that mothers provide early nurturing and guide developmental activities. Early classroom literacy instruction continues this same presumption.

What do Eve's experiences tell us? How does a child living outside of the "normal" family structure, without the physically close mother–daughter rela-tionship assumed in early literacy research, deal with early literacy instruction and school? Eve does not fit into any of the traditional literacy "risk" categories: she is not male, she is not indigenous or from a marginalized socio-economic group, she is not the child of recent immigrants, nor is she is living in an isolated, rural area. However, she is still at risk. Her teachers have identified her as a child at risk of early literacy failure in terms of her capacity to use *school* literacies. Unfortunately, this assessment does not take into account her skills in other textual forms; consequently, there is no direct opportunity for conver-sion of these skills into the conventional literacy program, however child-cen-tered or progressive it might be. Unfortunately for Eve, and perhaps for many other children, the gap between her digital, virtualized family and the tradi-tional print, nuclear family is not as easily bridged as we have tended to assume. It may even be that being middle class is an insufficient condition to ensure success in school. The middle class on which school is based is not the middle class of many children's lives in new times.

JAMES

James is also 6 years old. He lives in a small, semi-rural community on the fringe of a large city.[2] In fact, the characteristics of this area can tell us much about the social and economic outcomes of structural change and the impact of globalization. James' neighborhood represents one of the many locations of "new" poverty, the emergence of which is linked to the changes in economic patterns and structures associated with globalization. In this particular location, the main sources of employment are manufacturing, construction, and transport. Unemployment, however, is high and growing: at the time of writing, female unemployment sits at around 11.8%, and male unemployment is as high as 12.3%. Unemployment rates are significantly higher in the 15- to 24-year-old category, reflecting the contemporary collapse of the full-time work market for the young—there are fewer and fewer jobs for young unqualified and underqualified workers, and fewer "positive" role models for youngsters like James. Low income, it is well documented, generally correlates with educational disadvantage and poor achievement.

Increasingly, location is also implicated. Edgar (1999) notes that "the life chances of Australians now depend even more heavily on regional location; inequality in incomes reflects a complex interaction between educational skill levels and geographic industry section concentration" (pp. 6–7). Reflecting these broader trends, there is an identifiable and growing division between a small number of high-income earners in James' community and a large population of families living at the other end of the wage spectrum. Even though both of his parents work, James' family sits at the lower end of that spectrum. This is not the only financially struggling family in this community—over 40% of the children attending his school live in families dependent on welfare.

Location and social class thus are not likely to work to James' advantage. Additionally, at home and out of school he spends limited time interacting with traditional texts. His parents work long hours and juggle childcare responsibilities, leaving limited time for, or interest in, middle-class "bedtime" storybook rituals: the family watches TV in its leisure time. Writing tasks are primarily lim-

----

[2]James, his schools, and his community are composites drawn from four Queensland and Tasmanian communities that we have studied in the past three years (see Luke & Carrington, in press).

ited to list-writing, and household interactions around text are often negative (concerning overdue accounts, new bills, bank and credit card statements).

Instead of practices and knowledge concentrating on printed text, James is developing multiliteracies through game-playing and web-surfing. While he does not have a computer in his home, his cousin has Internet access and a range of CD-ROMs of various genres. His best friend has a Playstation™, and James spends all of his spare time there. Even at his young age, James has developed the speed and coordination of aural and visual cueing systems necessary for dealing with non-linear texts. His keyboarding skills are not as well-developed as Eve's, but he has a functional grasp of the skill, which he uses mainly to surf the Internet. He is becoming confident at navigating around the Web using various search engines—his current favorite is "Google™," having recently moved on from "Dogpile™." Like James' engagement with game-playing, these searches and online activities are done in collaboration with others. In these home and community contexts, he is happy to take risks, to negotiate, to share information and knowledge. This is in contrast to his experiences at school.

When James goes to school each day, he is greeted by a middle-class teaching cohort with an average age of 45. Most of his teachers were trained before the advent of digital technology, and are not particularly interested in integrating it into their classroom practice. They commented to us that they felt "everybody had to learn how to deal with print before they could engage with computers." None of the teachers at his school live in the community. They commute from the two nearby cities, each of which are around 45 to 50 minutes away by highway. This is a school that struggles with high rates of transience, the need to accommodate some Aboriginal children, high numbers of children with diagnosed special education needs, and the perception that many of the students, like James, come from "difficult backgrounds."

James has not done well on classroom diagnostic tests, and shows little interest in the kinds of texts and activities that take place in his classroom—he is seemingly disconnected from the notion of story reading for its own sake, and has intractably untidy handwriting. He is reluctant to take part in oral reading or deskwork. He is not a particularly disruptive child; however, his teacher is concerned about his apparent disconnection from classroom literacies. In conversations with us, teachers stated their view that this was a typical "boys and literacy" problem that was due to poor role models, lack of motivation and interest in education at home, and the increasing physical, motor, and affective problems facing boys from lower socio-economic backgrounds.

Because James is experiencing "difficulty" with classroom texts, he has been assigned to a withdrawal group for additional basic decoding work—sound-letter relationships and sight words—done individually with a supervising adult. His classroom has two non-networked computers used for basic skill-and-drill activities such as "Math Blaster™." But while James is an enthusiastic techno-kid out of school, he seems disinterested in computers in the classroom environment. Nor does he have the opportunity to work collaboratively and interactively with his friends, as he does online or on the Playstation™.

Like Eve, James is a child at risk. He is increasingly at risk of the economic and social marginalization typical of children of his location and socioeconomic profile. In new times, James's family and community represent the new poor, characterized by lack of access to employment, intergenerational downward mobility, isolation in fringe zones, and tenacious financial insecurity. James' home literacy practices are disconnected from the print-based literacies of his classroom, and although his teachers have varying degrees of success with explicit phonics and word recognition approaches, it is clear to all that his problems are as much disinterest and lack of motivation to read and write within these frameworks as they are deficits per se. But it is becoming increasingly difficult for his teachers to disentangle the two.

Ironically, the multimodal literate practices that James is pursuing independently are the very ones that we would argue are necessary in new economies. Yet he is unable to convert them into valuable commodities in the print-oriented classroom, where his teachers perceive his interest in video games and popular culture as a distraction, rather than a strength.

NEW KIDS, NEW LITERACIESNEW WAYS
TO BE "AT RISK"

Literacy education is linked to the construction of knowledge and power. In no way is literacy education a neutral mastery of skill or an inevitable artifact of cognitive and linguistic development. From a critical sociological perspective, literacy education entails the reconstruction of habitus, and the recognition and conversion of cultural, economic, and social capital (Baker & Luke, 1991; Carrington & Luke, 1997). The mastery of particular literacies—as embodied in the habitus and certified by educational institutions—is linked to social mobility and economic payoffs in a broad range of social fields. New family formations, new literacies and technologies, then, are volatile and potentially disruptive of the longstanding "rules of the game" for literacy teaching and learning. These rules, stated and unstated, conscious and subliminal, have been built up for over a century to monitor, stream, and produce the print-literate subject, worker, and citizen. They are tenacious, embodied in the message systems of schooling, in our institutional structures, and indeed, in the bodies of teachers and students.

The family literacy movement has increasingly brought expectations of appropriate home-based literacy experiences and practices into line with the literacies of school. Family literacy is an attempt to reconfigure the social field of home and family to resemble that of the school. This repositioning has traditionally marked poor, migrant, non-English-speaking, and transient families as deficient. It is our contention that the changes to family and home literacy practices that have been invoked in the shift to new economies have the potential to disrupt expectations about the kinds of literacy knowledge and skills that children should bring from home to school, as well as expectations about what counts as "appropriate" home literacy.

One of our messages is that "being middle class," "being working class," and, indeed, "being underclass" are not what they used to be. Although they come from very different social and economic backgrounds, Eve and James share powerful out-of-school engagements with sophisticated information technologies. In these community and home sites they are developing literate practices and knowledge appropriate to new modalities, discourses, and texts (Carrington, 2001). In these community and home sites they are working within and across information environments, often without direct adult mediation or control.

The view of the teachers at James's local school that students are "disconnected" from school is telling. This is the mismatch hypothesis written with a difference, for the disconnection is not between the deficient working-class family and the school—it is a mismatch between the school's approach to literacy and the emergent information economies and knowledge environments where kids and adults increasingly live and work. Eve, too, has a new literate habitus that shines through her e-mails. She and James are not at risk because of the intrinsic strengths or weaknesses of these new multiliteracies, which no doubt are riddled with gaps and silences. Rather, they are at risk because the residual traditions of print-based pedagogy remain so absolute and powerful, rendering the children's competencies, knowledges, and backgrounds invisible. The one constant in this picture is the school.

Families and identities are undergoing reconstruction in the new economies. It would be exceedingly naïve to assume that if we just wait long enough, we will experience a return to traditional values and practices. The literacies and futures of children making the transition from home to school in this new century are increasingly those of the postmodern—multimodal, "glocalised" (Luke & Carrington, in press) and linked to shifting valuations of cultural capital in a new economy. The literacies of researchers, educators, and schools, on the other hand, remain strictly modern—fixated on mastery of specific types of textual practice and the inculcation of particular value systems.

Returning to the links between home and school literacies with which we began this chapter, it becomes apparent that the ways in which educators understand these connections must be rethought. The presumption that home can and should be made to resemble school is increasingly problematic. It is not just a question of the dubious ethical position that the state, the institution, and the corporation can tell people how to raise their children, or how to configure their families, or whose cultural version of childhood should count. This has always been the key moral and ideological dilemma faced by the family literacy movement in a pluralistic, democratic society. It is, moreover, a question of whether and how we can in good conscience reconfigure homes and communities in the image of an institution that is showing all the signs of becoming a creaky anachronism, in relation to new economies, cultures, and technologies.

ACKNOWLEDGMENTS

We wish to thank Eurydice Bauer for her invaluable editorial persistence and James Reische for his careful editorial engagement with the ideas and the typos. The authors are listed in alphabetical order.

REFERENCES

Au, K. H. (1980). Participation structures in a reading lesson with Hawaiian children: Analysis of a culturally appropriate instructional event. *Anthropology and Education Quarterly* 11(2), 91–115.

Au, K. H., & Mason, J. M. (1983). Cultural congruence in classroom participation structures: Achieving a balance of rights. *Discourse Processes* 6(2), 145–167.

Baker, C. D., & Freebody, P. (1987). *Children's first schoolbooks.* Oxford: Blackwell.

Baker, C. D., & Luke, A. (1991). *Towards a critical sociology of reading pedagogy.* Amsterdam: John Benajmins.

Barton, D. (1994). *Literacy: An introduction to the ecology of written language.* Oxford: Blackwell.

Bernstein, B. (1976). *Class, codes and control. Vol. 1.* London: Routledge.

Bourdieu, P., & Passeron, J. (1990). *Reproduction in education, society and culture.* (2nd ed.). London: Sage.

Butler, A., & Turbill, J. (1984). *Towards a reading-writing classroom.* Rozelle, New South Wales, Australia: Primary English Teaching Association.

Cairney, T., & Munsey, L. (1992). *Beyond tokenism: Parents as partners in literacy.* Carlton, Victoria, Australia: Australian Reading Association.

Cairney, T., & Ruge, J. (1998). *Community literacy practices and schooling: Towards effective support for students.* Canberra: Department of Employment, Education, Training and Youth Affairs.

Carrington, V. (2001). Emergent literacies: A challenge for educators. *Australian Journal of Language and Literacy 24*(2), 88–100.

Carrington, V. (2002). *New times: New families*. Amsterdam: Kluwer.

Carrington, V., & Luke, A. (1997). Literacy and Bourdieu's sociological theory: A reframing. *Language and Education, 11*(2), 96–112.

Castells, M. (1996). *Rise of the network society*. Oxford: Blackwell.

Clay, M. (1972). *Reading: The patterning of complex behaviour*. Auckland: Heinemann Educational Books.

Clay, M. (1991). *Becoming literate: The construction of inner control*. Auckland: Heinemann.

Comber, B., & Simpson, A. (Eds.). (2001). *Negotiating critical literacies in classrooms*. Mahwah, NJ: Lawrence Erlbaum Associates.

Cook-Gumperz, J. (Ed.). (1986). *The social construction of literacy*. Cambridge: Cambridge University Press.

Cope, B., & Kalantzis, M. (Eds.). (1995). *The powers of literacy*. London: Taylor & Francis.

Delgado-Geitan, C. (1990). *Literacy for empowerment: The role of parents in children's education*. London: Falmer Press.

Edgar, D. (1999). *Learning to live with complexity: Social trends and their impact on Queensland Education*. Brisbane: Education Queensland.

Fairclough, N. (Ed.). (1993). *Critical language awareness*. London: Longman.

Fox, M. (2001). *Reading magic*. Melbourne: Harvest Books.

Frankenberg, R. (1993). *The social construction of whiteness: White women, race matters*. New York: Routledge.

Freebody, P., Ludwig, C., & Gunn, S. (1995). *Everyday literacy practices in and out of schools in low socio-economic urban communities*. Canberra: Department of Employment, Education and Training.

Gee, J. P. (2000). The limits of reframing: A response to Professor Snow. *Journal of Literacy Research 32*(1), 121–128.

Gee, J. P., Hull, G., & Lankshear, C. (1998). *The new work order*. Sydney: Allen & Unwin.

Gregory, E. . (1997). *One child, many worlds: Early learning in multicultural communities*. New York: Teachers College Press.

Gregory, E., & Williams, A. (2000). *City literacies*. London: Routledge.

Heath, S. B. (1982). What no bedtime story means: Narrative skills at home and at school. *Language in Society, 11*(1), 49–76.

Luke, A. (1988). *Literacy, textbooks and ideology*. London: Falmer Press.

Luke, A., & Carrington, V. (in press). Globalisation, literacy, curriculum practice. In R. Fisher, M. Lewis, & G. Brooks (Eds.), *Language and literacy in action*. London: Routledge/Falmer.

Luke, A., Freebody, P., & Land, R. (2000). *Literate futures: The Queensland state literacy strategy*. Brisbane: Education Queensland.

Luke, A., & Kale, J. (1997). Learning through difference: Cultural practices in early childhood language socialisation. In E. Gregory (Ed.), *One child, many worlds: Early learning in multicultural communities* (pp. 11–29). New York: Teachers College Press.

Luke, A., & Luke, C. (2001). Adolescence lost, childhood regained: Early intervention and the emergence of the techno-subject. *Journal of Early Childhood Literacy 1*(1), 92–130.

Luke, C. (1989). *Constructing the child viewer*. New York: Praeger.

Mason, J., & Allen, J. (1986). A review of emergent literacy with implications for research and practice in reading. *A Review of Educational Research 1*, 3–47.

Moll, L. (1992). Literacy research in community and classrooms: A sociocultural approach. In R. Beach, J. Green, M. Kamil, & T. Shanahan (Eds.), *Multidisciplinary perspectives on literacy research* (pp. 211–244). Urbana, IL: NCTE.

Purcell-Gates, V. (1986). *Written language knowledge held by low SES inner city children entering kindergarten* (Research Report No. 143). Cincinnati, OH: University of Cincinnati.

Rivalland, J. (2000). Linking literacy across different contexts. In C. Barratt-Pugh & M. Rohl (Eds.), *Literacy learning in the early years* (pp. 27–56). Sydney: Allen & Unwin.

Scribner, S., & Cole, M. (1981). *The psychology of literacy.* Cambridge, MA: Harvard University Press.

Solsken, J. (1993). *Literacy, gender and work.* Norwood, NJ: Ablex.

Teale, W., & Sulzby, E. (Eds.). (1986). *Emergent literacy: Writing and reading.* Norwood, NJ: Ablex Publishing Corporation.

Trelease, J. (2001). *The read aloud handbook* (5th ed.). Harmondsworth, UK: Penguin.

Wells, G. (1986). *Language development in the preschool years.* London: Routledge.

White, K. R. (1982). The relation between socioeconomic status and academic achievement. *Psychological Bulletin, 91* (3), 461–481.

Zill, N. (1996). Family change and student achievement: What we have learned, what it means for schools. In A. Booth & J. Dunn (Eds.), *Family–school links* (pp. 139–174). Mahwah, NJ: Lawrence Erlbaum Associates.

12

Storybook Reading and Young Bilingual Children: A Review of the Literature

Rosalinda B. Barrera
Eurydice Bouchereau Bauer
University of Illinois at Urbana-Champaign

The number of students from bilingual homes continues to grow in classrooms throughout the United States, currently representing an unprecedented proportion of the total school enrollment nationwide. This national trend is not expected to abate anytime soon, paralleling demographic shift on a grander scale: the number of bilinguals worldwide is now claimed to outnumber the number of monolinguals, a rise expected to continue through the current century (Hamers & Blanc, 2000; Padilla, 1990). In marked contrast to the increased presence of bilingual students in U. S. schools (National Center for Educational Statistics, 2001) stands the continued relative absence of educational research on questions and phenomena of a bilingual nature, even in the crucial areas of language and literacy (Bialystok, 2001). This is particularly true in the field of early literacy (García, 2000; Jiménez, Moll, Rodriguez-Brown, & Barrera, 1999; Vernon-Feagans, Hammer, Miccio, & Manlove, 2001), an area presently receiving major attention at the national, state, and local levels.

When we set out to review for this volume the extant research on storybook reading with bilingual children, we suspected the research base would be limited. Therefore, we strove to identify the largest possible number of studies by considering research conducted not only in the U.S. but in other countries as well, acknowledging at the same time the global dimensions of bilingualism. We targeted studies conducted with children from preschool to Grade 3 (approximately ages 2–8 years) who were in the process of acquiring a second language or already had two or more languages. The search confirmed our suspicions: After screening out a number of published works that provided only indirect data on storybook reading with bilingual participants, we had a modest number to review, 11 set in the U.S. and three internationally.

In this chapter, we do the following: briefly examine the nature of this corpus of studies, with a focus on research contexts and participants; identify and discuss salient themes and patterns; and consider implications for future work in this area. We want to note that we brought to this review a strong interest in early childhood literacy among bilinguals, not to mention personal and professional experience in working with bilingual children and families, and considered this undertaking directly relevant to our own research with this population of learners.

THE CURRENT STATE OF KNOWLEDGE

Based on the studies examined, it appears that the published research on storybook reading and young bilingual children has focused predominantly on parent/caregiver–child interactions, or family storybook reading, rather than on storybook interactions between teachers and bilingual students. It is important to note that in the majority of these studies, set both in the U.S. and abroad, the participants have been first- and second-generation immigrant adults and their children, in the process of becoming bilingual by adding the dominant language of a new country to their linguistic repertoire. Basically, such individuals were learning to do storybook reading, often through explicit instruction, while acquiring a second language. In only two of the studies reviewed was storybook reading a naturally occurring activity in the homes of bilingual families. Thus, storybook reading has been studied largely as a new or unfamiliar activity for a rather circumscribed group of bilingual children and their families (relatively similar in terms of language, class, and acculturation status, for example). Storybook reading has not been explored among a range of bilingual children and parents/caregivers for whom it might be an established practice.

From a language standpoint, much of the existing research has focused on storybook reading in cases of successive, rather than simultaneous, bilingualism. According to Tabors (1997, pp. 10–11), simultaneous bilingualism "occurs when children are exposed to two languages from a very early age, while sequential bilingualism occurs when a child begins learning a second language after the first language is at least partially established." The focus of these studies clearly has been on the target, or second, language, rather than on storybook reading in the native language or a combination of the two languages. Most studies, particularly those set in the United States, have focused on Spanish-speaking participants from a host of countries. Most of the parent–child studies—especially those set within U.S. family literacy projects in which English language teaching and learning are prominent—have emphasized adults' language and literacy learning as much as, or more than, children's. Overall, two conditions—the incidence of storybook reading as a new social practice for specific bilingual families, and/or an educational intervention for both children and parents—provide the background for much of the research to be reviewed here.

SALIENT THEMES AND PATTERNS

Following are salient findings from our review of the extant research, organized into four categories that emerged during the analysis. The order of presentation roughly reflects the relative emphasis given these aspects in the corpus of focal studies.

Social-Interactive Aspects

Storybook reading is recognized as a socially created interactive activity, with the language and social interactions that surround the text being as much a part of the event as the book itself. The following sections describe some of the social-interactive behaviors and strategies documented between parents/caregivers and their bilingual children, and between teachers and their bilingual students, during storybook readings.

Parent–Child Reading. Two related themes appear to characterize studies of this ilk. Not surprisingly, these themes have to do with the adult participants: the first concerns change in parents' storyreading strategies over time; the second, variation in the storyreading behaviors of individual parents. Both themes appeared in Sulzby and Teale (1987) among a series of generalizations drawn by Teale for a longitudinal, naturalistic investigation of storybook reading that he conducted with eight families: four Mexican American and four Anglo (two families from each ethnic group were low-income, while the other two were middle-income). The children were preschoolers, ranging in age from 1:4 to 3:1. The results of the study showed that parent–child storybook reading interactions changed over time. In part, this was due to the fact that parents gradually released their control over the reading of the books as the children began to engage in emergent reading. Essentially, the interactions became less dialogic; readings of the same text also varied from one instance to the next. Furthermore, the ways in which the adults read the storybooks were found to reflect considerable linguistic and social variation, both within and between ethnic groups. Variation across income levels was difficult to determine due to scarcity of relevant data. It is important to note that the author did not feel that any one parental strategy affected a child's reading achievement more than any other.

Development and change in parents' read-aloud behaviors and strategies have also been documented by a group of studies in which storybook reading was a planned intervention. These investigations have been set within family literacy projects, many of long duration, serving English-language-learning (ELL) immigrant families in which parents had relatively low levels of schooling, and whose own language and literacy skills in English as a second language (ESL) were targets for enhancement. One of these projects' primary goals was to encourage parents to read to their children as a means for improving the children's school achievement—hence the attention on adult participants. The findings from these studies touch on various aspects of the social-interactive strategies of parents and bilingual offspring who are learning storybook reading as a new practice, and in a new language.

In studies by Eldridge-Hunter (1992) and Krol-Sinclair (1996), parents were explicitly taught new read-aloud strategies and how to refine previously acquired ones. These investigations, both of which were based on the same family literacy project, involved mainly Latino immigrant mothers from Central America. Eldridge-Hunter (1992) coded the mothers' storybook reading utterances into five different categories: interactions, responses, questions, functions, and focus, along with related subcategories. Four of the participants were audiotaped while reading at home over the course of several months. Results showed that the patterns of development in storybook reading were unique to each individual. The person's style prior to enrolling in the project appeared to influence her subsequent strategy acquisition. The behaviors most influenced by explicit instruction were maternal responsiveness to child-initiated utterances, semantic contingency of maternal responses, and focus of maternal responses on literacy. (It should be noted that one mother used both Spanish and English for reading; the rest, only Spanish.)

In the study by Krol-Sinclair (1996), parents were trained to implement a number of strategies for interacting with text, as part of an effort to have them lead classroom read-alouds. Again, parents were found to blend their personal read-aloud strategies with new ones recommended during the 12-week training program. The training had a positive impact on the seven parents' classroom reading performances, but had apparently greater impact on their choice of strategies at home. Although these two researchers provided parents with books to read in English or Spanish, both in the bilingual elementary classes (K–2) and at home, they reported little on which texts the parents read and in what language. The researchers also conveyed little about the impact of the readings on the children.

Parents in another family literacy project (Thornburg, 1993) also applied personal strategies to the new literacy, or storybook reading, context and added other strategies for supporting the text interactions of their children, whose ages ranged from 2 to 5 years. Specifically, these parents engaged children in storybook reading in ways that promoted questioning and personal connections by the young learners. Thornburg's study is unique among those we reviewed, in that the adult education model keeps storybook reading at its center by examining a triad of related activities: storybook reading, extension, and adult English instruction based on the storybook reading event.

Somewhat comparable findings resulted from a trio of case studies by Rodriguez-Brown and Mulhern (1993), which were embedded within a larger family literacy study investigating parents' home literacy activities with their 3- to 5-year-old children. In the overall study, the mostly Mexican immigrant mothers were encouraged to model literacy in their homes in either Spanish or English. The researchers found that the three case study parents used reading strategies similar to those taught in the program, including relating book content to their children's lives. During the reading interactions, parents and children asked each other questions, and all three focal children engaged in pretend reading.

In stark contrast to the preceding studies, Delgado-Gaitan (1996) found that questioning strategies explicitly taught to parents for use in storybook reading were counterproductive. Delgado-Gaitan coordinated a 2-year family literacy project in response to parental concerns about children's underachievement in reading, particularly in English. Parents were taught strategies for four types of questions—descriptive, personal interpretive, critical, and creative—aimed at increasing children's involvement during storyreading. Her research team found that with the passage of time, parents became increasingly comfortable reading with their children, and the complexity of their discussions grew. Parents were able to pose to their children the four different types of questions that had been taught to them.

However, the researcher noted that the particular questioning strategies limited the project's outcomes, primarily because parents were not used to working with school-type strategies, and the questions themselves excluded parents' cultural knowledge. In addition to learning the questioning categories, she concluded, parents could have incorporated their own process and framework for storybook interaction with the children. This might have allowed the parents to build on their family stories, thereby transforming storybook reading from a learned activity into a family activity.

Teacher–Student Storybook Reading.   If there is a general theme across the small but disparate group of studies in this category, it is that teachers have a role to play in mediating storybook reading in the second language for young bilingual students. One study (Battle, 1993) sought insight into the circumstances and conditions that promoted bilingual children's participation in L2 (second-language) storybook talk. During her 12-week study in a bilingual (Spanish-English) kindergarten, Battle focused on three dimensions of the children's whole-group discussions: characteristics of meaning making, participation structures, and uses of the two languages. As such, she was sensitive to the children's emergent bilingualism and its relationship to their collaborative interpretations of stories in L2, as well as to the bilingual techniques used by the teacher during the discussions. Battle found that both the text and the teacher played key roles in fostering children's joint meaning making during story discussions. Selected story text drew the children's interest and served as a springboard to joint meaning making, which the teacher furthered by capitalizing on particular aspects of the text or the children's story talk. Most importantly, however, the teacher facilitated this by demonstrating personal enthusiasm toward the stories, accepting the children's natural responses to stories, accepting their language and language patterns (English or Spanish or some combination of the two) without correction, and participating selectively in discussions.

Somewhat similar findings were reported in the previously mentioned study by Thornburg (1993), albeit for a different setting. In the family literacy project studied, a bilingual (English-Spanish) teacher read each storybook twice to participants, while a monolingual teacher modeled various ways to interact with the text to the participating parents and children, who had individual copies of the text. Qualitative data revealed that teacher–child interactions moved from abstract/cognitive to affective/interpersonal communications, and that teacher–parent interactions shifted from strictly differentiated roles (teacher vs. parent) which did not lead to much talk, to interactions that actively facilitated two-way talk. Although the overall goal of this program was to promote the acquisition of English, the bilingual teacher sometimes employed the families' home language (Spanish) for mediating instruction.

Another study in a bilingual education setting focused on storybook reading in English, but made little or no linkage to data on the teachers' or children's storybook behaviors in their native language. Hoffman, Roser, and Farest (1988) studied the literature-sharing strategies of teachers in bilingual kindergarten and first-grade classrooms over the course of several months. The majority of their students were classified as having "limited English proficiency," and the schools as low-performing. With the researchers' assistance, the teachers formulated a series of guidelines for literature sharing, based on what they considered to be effective practice. Their application and use of the guidelines were evaluated in February (pre-training) and October (post-training).

The guidelines addressed five components of literature sharing: physical space, management, preparation, book sharing, and book response. Strategies for book response included accepting/extending students' responses, linking books with students' lives, ensuring understanding of key vocabulary, using questions judiciously/purposefully, and providing for additional responses (e.g., art, writing, and drama). The researchers of this English-based study indicated that the teachers more effectively engaged students in before-, during-, and after-reading activities following the training (Hoffman et al., 1988); however, "[whether these strategies] enhanced learning on the part of students was not explored directly in this study" (p. 337).

Fayden (1997), in a 10-week treatment study, examined the influence of English-language storybook reading (in the form of shared reading) on the literacy development of one class of culturally diverse kindergartners. The children—the majority of whom were Native American and Hispanic, although we are not told if they were bilingual—engaged in shared readings of mostly predictable "big books" led by their teacher for a half-hour daily. The teacher utilized shared reading instructional strategies such as tracking words with a pointer, using oral cloze to help children identify unknown words, and eliciting predictions of story vocabulary and parts. Later in the day, the children also read from regular-sized versions of the big books. Analysis revealed that children's reading skills improved, with significant gains from pre- to post-treatment on Clay's Test of Reading Strategies and Sand Test.

Language Aspects

Language use is an important aspect of storybook reading events in general, but even more so when these involve bilingual individuals in particular. The range of language possibilities is broader for bilingual children, because the child, and, in many cases, the adult reader, have two languages from which to draw. Not surprisingly, our review found that the studies most concerned with language during storybook reading reflect this expanded and more complex orientation. They pursue serial research questions and factors ostensibly to capture the dynamic and complex nature of language during storybook reading events.

Parent–Child Storybook Reading.   The few studies that have examined aspects of language use during storybook reading interactions with bilinguals have shared a common view of code-switching as a *natural* aspect of these interactions, rather than as a *problem*. Two studies set in the Netherlands concerned themselves with code-switching by participating adults and children (Muysken, Kook, & Vedder, 1996; Vedder, Kook, & Muysken, 1996); another study, set in the U.S., focused mainly on code-switching among children (Bauer, 2000).

This line of inquiry is multi-layered and dynamic. For example, Muysken et al. (1996) and Vedder et al. (1996), although technically examining the language behavior of Papiamentu-Dutch bilingual immigrant parents and their children during joint storybook reading, also searched for factors that might determine code choice. (Papiamentu is a creole language spoken by the people of Curaçao, Bonaire, and Aruba.) Among the most important factors were intergenerational language shift, language of the book being read, and language proficiency of the parent and child. Three different texts were used: one written in Papiamentu, one in Dutch, and one wordless. It was hypothesized that storybook reading would be viewed as a school event by the immigrant parents and, therefore, that Dutch would dominate their interactions.

Interestingly, it was found that in general both mothers and children used more Papiamentu during storybook reading, although the mothers' use was relatively greater than that of the children, apparently reflecting intergenerational language shift. Code choice of the adult reader depended on both the children's language proficiency (e.g., active and passive vocabulary) and the language of the text. The study also generated other differential observations. Although the participants used more of their Papiamentu overall, they spoke more Dutch when interacting with the Dutch text then with the Papiamentu text. However, more Dutch was used when reading the wordless text on numbers than the other two texts. The authors postulated that the mothers viewed counting as a more school-like activity, and thus encouraged their children to use Dutch. When Papiamentu was used, it was for counting lower numbers.

In a related study of the same data set, Muysken et al. (1996) continued this multi-layered analysis by looking at language dominance, among other things. The researchers concluded that higher language skill in Papiamentu for parents and children resulted in more code-switching in that language, but the same was not true for families with a high level of Dutch language proficiency. A look at code-switching patterns for the families suggested that Papiamentu served as the "base" language in their utterances. Notably, the children in this study, who knew more Dutch than their parents, still favored Papiamentu.

A language-focused study by Bauer (2000) paid similar attention to the extended array of interconnecting factors and features that inhere in storybook reading with young bilinguals. Bauer investigated the impact of different types of storybooks on the literacy development of her daughter, from age 2:0 to 2:8. Unlike other U.S.-based studies, which dealt with Spanish-English bilingualism, this study involved the German-English bilingualism that characterized the focal child's upbringing. Her code-switching behavior during home storybook reading in the two languages was examined during repeated readings conducted with four picture books representing three genres: highly predictable, modern fantasy, and realistic fiction. Three of these books were in English, and one title was available to the child in both German and English.

Three observations were made about the readings that serve to underscore the kaleidoscopic nature of language use in storybook reading with young bilinguals. First, the child code-switched very little during shared reading of structurally predictable and rhythmic texts, concentrating instead on saying the exact words. Bauer believed that this behavior suggested that interest in the text's rhythm might have influenced the way that her daughter approached "reading" in the two languages. Second, the child code-switched most often when attempting to discuss books with more complex content. It was posited that talking about this text afforded the child more linguistic freedom. Third, the child's code-switching patterns during shared reading suggested that she interpreted this activity primarily as an English event. She appeared to be English-dominant during shared reading, although she had functioned as a German-dominant bilingual in play during the first 5 months of the study, until she began to show a preference for English in her talk.

When we look across this trio of investigations, it is possible to more fully entertain the idea of interplay between bilingualism and storybook reading with young children. However, these studies represent only a beginning step toward a better understanding of these types of interactions and, ultimately, of the bilingual mind itself.

Teacher–Student Storybook Reading. We came across only one study dealing with the linguistic dimension of storybook interactions between teachers and students (Feitelson, Goldstein, Iraqi, & Share, 1993). This study is provocative because it deals with a bidialectal situation that the researchers compared to bilingualism. Indeed, this study of Arabic immigrant children ac-quiring two varieties of Arabic in Israel—the literary standard and a local ver-nacular—reminded us of the experiences of some U.S. immigrant children who encounter in bilingual classrooms a distinction between their home dialect (e.g., Chicano Spanish) and the school-sanctioned dialect (Castilian Spanish).

In the Feitelson et al. (1993) study, kindergarten children from homes in which the Arabic vernacular (Aamiyya) was spoken were read stories written in the prestigious school dialect (Fusha) for a period of 5 months. The goal of this intervention was to facilitate the children's acquisition of Fusha in an effort to improve their academic performance. Ten of the 12 stories read aloud by the ex-perimental teachers during this period were prepared by the researchers, due to a lack of suitable storybooks in Fusha.

At the end of the intervention, the children's achievement was compared on a number of language and literacy measures. Listening to the stories read to them in Fusha enhanced children's general comprehension skills and led to in-creased use of that register. In addition, teachers' attitudes changed regarding the use of Fusha storybook reading as a bridge into the academic language. A by-product of this school intervention was parents' increased desire to read to their children in general, and to use the focal storybooks in particular.

This study raises several issues to which we want to call attention. For exam-ple, even though the texts were made especially for the focal children, the fact that the texts did not exist in the academic language suggests that this story-book reading intervention probably ran counter to the local cultural norm. An-other issue is that in light of the aforementioned limitations, the researchers apparently did not explore the possible links between the children's home dia-lect and the academic dialect. Above all, the study failed to explore possible cul-tural aspects of storybook reading.

Textual Aspects

The text is a key component of storybook reading. To not consider its role in storybook interactions with children is to overlook an important force shaping those interactions. In terms of attention to text, the studies we reviewed ranged from a belief that the text was of little significance in this context to the idea that the text mattered greatly. In this section, we examine the research for in-sights into particular textual aspects such as genre, language, and format.

One underlying view of text was that it is primarily an instructional tool for modeling early literacy skills and reading strategies. Such a view surfaced in a study by Fayden (1997), for example, in which reference is made primarily to text format (i.e., Big Books and corresponding little books), without consideration of other textual properties. Because this study so drastically limited its examination of the relevance of text, we cannot even begin to gauge its influence on the storybook event.

Yet another view and treatment of text was reflected in the study by Teale (reported in Sulzby & Teale, 1987), which investigated the availability and variety of books in the homes of participating families, of which half were bilingual Spanish-English. The primary concern here, however, was with *quantity* of books, either owned or borrowed by the families, and not necessarily *quality*. Of the 224 books counted and sorted by type, almost 65% were storybooks; the rest included expository books, concept books (labeling, counting, alphabet), books of rhymes, and religious books. Some of the books were in English, others were in Spanish, and still others contained parallel texts in both languages.

Teale's comparative analysis of texts was limited to one researcher-selected book that had been given to the families. The bilingual families' book choices were also analyzed for language preference. Teale was interested in finding out if the Latino parents would "read" by translating books from one language to the other. Three families showed a marked preference for selecting books written in English and reading them in English, while one family showed a marked preference for Spanish as the language for storybook reading by choosing to read both English and Spanish books in Spanish. This particular study expressed a general sensitivity to the role of text in storybook reading with bilinguals, but left many aspects of text underexplored.

Perhaps the most deliberate attention to textual aspects of storybook reading with young bilinguals was provided by Bauer (2000) and Delgado-Gaitan (1996). Bauer examined four books in three different genres and concluded that the structure of the text influenced language use. Meaningful text content also influenced language use during storybook reading, with text evoking a particular language from the child in connection with lived experiences reflected in the text. Delgado-Gaitan (1996) sought texts that would spark discussion by the participating families. Fifty books were used, with eight of these receiving greater attention in the researcher's analysis because of their non-sexist, non-racist, and non-classist stories. The books, whose titles are provided by the researcher, varied in length; participants proceeded from shorter to longer stories. Together, these two studies provide a wider outlook on the role of text in storybook reading events. Not only do we get a sense of text language, but also of text structure, content, and complexity. Without such a lens, we cannot fully explore the potential that storybook reading holds for bilinguals.

Cultural Aspects

Storybook reading is increasingly viewed as cultural practice, one of various "ways with words" (Heath, 1983) that is not universal across human communities. Given that language and culture are inextricably related, we might ask what the storybook research tells us about individuals who, by virtue of being or becoming bilingual, bring cultural differences to the storybook reading event. Not surprisingly, given the general inattention to language in these studies, we found that some studies ignored the cultural characteristics of readers, listeners, texts, and storybook events altogether. Other researchers, however, explicitly addressed cultural aspects of storybook reading with bilingual children.

Our review revealed a great deal about underlying conceptions of culture. This can be illustrated through two telling examples. The first comes from the study by Sulzby (reported in Sulzby & Teale, 1987) that explored language–culture connections in the emergent storybook readings of bilingual Latino children at the pre-kindergarten and kindergarten levels. Sulzby examined the children's text re-enactments in both Spanish and English for developmental characteristics and for the influence of a cultural practice—the oral monologue—on that performance. Specifically, three research questions were posed: Would the children's storybook reading behaviors parallel those of monolingual counterparts researched previously? Would their behaviors be comparable across languages? Would they reflect more oral monologues characteristic of the Spanish oral tradition?

Sulzby found that the emergent reading behaviors of bilingual children were like those of the monolingual children she had researched earlier, and were also comparable across the children's two languages. She concluded that the children's oral traditions led to a higher frequency of oral monologues in their text re-enactments, more so in Spanish than in English. While commendable for exploring a particular dimension of students' culture, this study did not go far enough in exploring the larger dimensions of culture. In short, the study superimposed a framework designed primarily for monolingual children on the storybook reading behaviors of young bilinguals.

Delgado-Gaitan (1996), on the other hand, viewed culture as permeating the whole of storybook reading, including participants, texts, and contexts. Significantly, she explicitly acknowledged the cultural limitations of her study, highlighting the difficulty encountered by Latino parents when they were asked to adopt specific school-type questioning strategies during storybook reading with their children. She candidly observed that: "overlooking the families' native literacy left the cultural part of the project wanting.... Criticism of the school curriculum [by parents] in COPLA [Comite de Padres Latinos] meetings cited the absence of home culture in the school curriculum and then the FLP [Family Literacy Project] neglected this critical aspect of the home culture" (p. 117). Delgado-Gaitan concluded that the sharing of family stories—a cultural strength of the home predating the Family Literacy Project—ought to have been incorporated into the project and school's curriculum along with commercial children's literature.

IMPLICATIONS FOR RESEARCHERS AND EDUCATORS

As mentioned earlier, our primary interest in reviewing the research was to try to arrive at a better understanding of the learning processes of bilinguals during storybook reading. In our estimation, the findings clearly point to the need to move beyond the accepted view that what we know about monolinguals is sufficient for understanding bilinguals (Grosjean, 1982). In effect, research conducted with bilingual individuals should utilize a bilingual "lens" in order to provide a better understanding of the bilingual mind (Cook, 1992, 1999). Such a lens would allow us to see more clearly the fluid and dynamic nature of the processes involved in bilingual development. Unfortunately, existing studies more often than not give us a static view of bilinguals, as seen through a monolingual lens. That is, the linguistic and cultural factors that influence the lives of these children are often underexplored, thereby limiting our understanding of these children on their own terms.

Children's bilingualism may have a great deal to do with the way they approach storybook interactions (Bauer, 2000). Research that has examined the oral interactions of young children with adults has shown that these children are very aware of the language(s) of their interlocutors and make use of that information (Genesee, 1989; Meisel, 1994). Such behavior reveals sensitivity to sociocultural norms and to the expectations implicit in the communicative context (Nicholadis & Genesee, 1996). What is less evident from the storybook studies we have examined is the question of how young bilinguals make use of their *awareness of their bilingualism* during storybook reading. Thus far, findings from just a few studies seem to suggest that children's responses to storybook events are affected by the languages of the adult and child (Bauer, 2000; Muysken et al., 1996), by the text being read (Bauer, 2000), and by the child's perception of the task's goal (Bauer, 2000).

One way that research can improve our understanding of what reader and child gain from these interactions is by exploring more fully what it is that bilinguals bring to storybook reading. For example, at present we do not know much about how these children define "storybook reading," nor about how they respond to this event when people from different language backgrounds do the reading. In order to explore matters such as these, researchers must adopt a sociocultural perspective on language and literacy. Such a perspective would take into consideration the whole of storybook reading, at minimum integrating the important dimensions that have been presented here—social-interactive, linguistic, textual, and cultural. A sociocultural stance also would question the research divide traditionally imposed between oral and written language, and would invite cross-cultural exploration of relationships among storytelling, story reading, and literacy.

In sum, we cannot state strongly enough that a great need exists to explore the intersection between bilingualism and storybook reading. At present we can only speculate on what young bilinguals do or do not gain from this activity, due to insufficient data. Understanding how bilinguals respond to the different texts read to them can provide the literacy field with a broader understanding of the full power of storybook reading.

REFERENCES

Battle, J. (1993). Mexican American bilingual kindergarteners' collaborations in mean-ing-making. In D. J. Leu & C. K. Kinzer (Eds.), *Examining central issues in literacy research, theory, and practice: Forty-second yearbook of the National Reading Conference* (pp. 163–170). Chicago: National Reading Conference.

Bauer, E. B. (2000). Code-switching during shared and independent reading: Lessons learned from a preschooler. *Research in the Teaching of English, 35*(1), 101–130.

Bialystok, E. (2001). *Bilingualism in development: Language, literacy, and cognition*. Cambridge: Cambridge University Press.

Cook, V. (1992). Evidence for multicompetence. *Language Learning, 42*(4), 557–591.

Cook, V. (1999). Going beyond the native speaker in language teaching. *TESOL Quarterly, 33*(2), 185–209.

Delgado-Gaitan, C. (1996). *Protean literacy: Extending the discourse on empowerment*. London: Falmer Press.

Eldridge-Hunter, D. (1992). Intergenerational literacy: Impact on the development of the storybook reading behavior of Hispanic mothers. In C. K. Kinzer & D. L. Leu (Eds.), *Literacy research, theory, and practice: Views from many perspectives. Forty-first yearbook of the National Reading Conference* (pp. 101–110). Chicago: National Reading Conference.

Fayden, T. (1997). What is the effect of shared reading on rural Native American and His-panic kindergarten children? *Reading Improvement, 34,* 22–30.

Feitelson, D., Goldstein, Z., Iraqi, J., & Share, D. L. (1993). Effects of listening to story read-ing on aspects of literacy acquisition in a diglossic situation. *Reading Research Quarterly, 28*(1), 71–79.

García, G. E. (2000). Bilingual children's reading. In M. Kamil, P. Rosenthal, P. D. Pearson, & R. Barr (Eds.), *Handbook of reading research* (Vol. 3, pp. 813–834). Mahwah, NJ: Law-rence Erlbaum Associates.

Genesee, F. (1989). Early bilingual development: One language or two? *Journal of Child Language, 16,* 161–179.

Grosjean, F. (1982). Neurolinguists, beware! The bilingual is not two monolinguals in one person. *Brain and Language, 36,* 3–15.

Hamers, J. F., & Blanc, M. H. A. (2000). *Bilinguality and bilingualism.* Cambridge: Cambridge University Press.

Heath, S. B. (1983). *Ways with words.* Cambridge: Cambridge University Press.

Hoffman, J. V., Roser, N. L., & Farest, C. (1988). Literature-sharing strategies in classrooms serving students from economically disadvantaged and language different home environments. In J. E. Readence & R. S. Baldwin (Eds.), *Dialogues in literacy research. Thirty-seventh yearbook of the National Reading Conference* (pp. 331–337). Chicago: National Reading Conference.

Jiménez, R. T., Moll, L., Rodriguez-Brown, F., & Barrera, R. B. (1999). Conversations: Latina and Latino researchers interact on issues related to literacy learning. *Reading Research Quarterly 34*(2), 217–230.

Krol-Sinclair, B. (1996). Connecting home and school literacies: Immigrant parents with limited formal education as classroom storybook readers. In D. L. Leu, C. K. Kinzer, & K. A. Hichman (Eds.), *Literacies for the 21st century: Research and practice. Forty-fifth yearbook of the National Reading Conference* (pp. 270–283). Chicago: National Reading Conference.

Meisel, J. M. (1994). Code-switching in young bilingual children: The acquisition of grammatical constraints. *Studies in Second Language Acquisition (SSLA), 16,* 413–439.

Muysken, P., Kook, H., & Vedder, P. (1996). Papiamento/Dutch code-switching in bilingual parent–child reading. *Applied Psycholinguistics 17*(4), 485–505.

National Center for Educational Statistics (2001). *Condition of education, 2001.* [On-line]. Available: http://nces.ed.gov/pubsearch/pubsinfo.asp?pubid=200172.

Nicholadis, E., & Genesee, F. (1996). A longitudinal study of pragmatic differentiation in young bilingual children. *Language Learning 46,* 439–464.

Padilla, A. M. (1990). Bilingual education: Issues and perspectives. In A. M. Padilla, H. H. Fairchild, & C. M. Valadez (Eds.), *Bilingual education: Issues and strategies* (pp. 15–26). Newbury Park, CA: Sage.

Rodriguez-Brown, F. V., & Mulhern, M. (1993). Fostering critical literacy through family literacy: A study of families in a Mexican-immigrant community. *Bilingual Research Journal, 17*(3–4), 1–16.

Sulzby, E., & Teale, W. H. (1987). *Young children's storybook reading: Longitudinal study of parent-child interaction and children's independent functioning.* Final report to the Spencer Foundation. Ann Arbor, MI: The University of Michigan.

Tabors, P. (1997). *One child, two languages: A guide for preschool educators of children learning English as a second language.* Baltimore: Brookes.

Thornburg, D. G. (1993). Intergenerational literacy learning with bilingual families: A context for the analysis of social mediation of thought. *Journal of Reading Behavior, 25*(3), 323–352.

Vedder, P., Kook, H., & Muysken, P. (1996). Language choice and functional differentiation of languages in bilingual parent–child reading. *Applied Psycholinguistics, 17*(4), 461–484.

Vernon-Feagans, L., Hammer, C. S., Miccio, A., & Manlove, E. (2001). Early language and literacy skills in low-income African American and Hispanic children. In S. B. Neuman & D. K. Dickinson (Eds.), *Handbook of early literacy research* (pp. 192–210). New York: Guilford Press.

IV
Where Do We Go
From Here?

13

Research on Book Sharing: Another Critical Look

Anne van Kleeck
University of Georgia

Which skills appear to provide preschoolers with important foundations for their later development of print literacy? How important is sharing books with preliterate children to their development of those skills? After nearly three decades of research, including a fair amount of controversy regarding the relative importance of book sharing to later literacy (Bus, van IJzendoorn, & Pellegrini, 1995; Dunning, Mason, & Stewart, 1994; Lonigan, 1994; Scarborough & Dobrich, 1994), research has made it increasingly clear that many of the different skills fostered during book sharing facilitate the later development of print literacy. Nonetheless, a number of conceptual and methodological problems have not been addressed to date. The goal of this chapter is to discuss persistent problems in this body of research, and to point to potential solutions for future research.

The conceptual and methodological wake-up call was first sounded by Scarborough and Dobrich in their 1994 review of empirical work on the impact of book sharing for preschoolers' language and literacy development. Scarborough and Dobrich concluded that this impact was not terribly significant, and certainly far more modest than seemed to be generally accepted. Direct responses to their review by Dunning et al. (1994) and Lonigan (1994) took the stance that the Scarborough and Dobrich conclusion was premature. They pointed out a few misinterpretations, but mostly discussed various methodological weaknesses in the studies which Scarborough and Dobrich had reviewed, suggesting that the findings from these studies should be inter-preted with caution.

While I interweave many of the points raised in all three of these articles, I fo-cus on concerns that I have not seen adequately addressed in previous critiques of book sharing research. This discussion covers three broad areas: (a) aspects of adult–child interaction during book sharing that have been ignored in previous research; (b) the need to consider various characteristics of the books that are shared during these interactions; and (c) aspects of the nature and timing of measurements used in book sharing research.

ASPECTS OF ADULT–CHILD BOOK SHARING INTERACTION IGNORED IN PREVIOUS RESEARCH

In this section, I discuss three dimensions of adult–child interaction during book sharing. They are: (a) a consideration of how much challenging input (i.e., either new information or information that requires children to stretch their cognitive or linguistic abilities) is effective in a learning situation; (b) the possi-bility that book sharing interactions in mainstream culture families are as much (or perhaps more) about socializing children to verbally display their knowledge for adults as they are about fostering the development of literacy skills; and (c) the need to consider both the children's and adults' levels of participation in the interaction.

What Amount of Challenging Input Is Best for Learning?

Van Kleeck, Gillam, Hamilton, and McGrath (1997) designed a study to look at the relationship between levels of concrete and abstract language in mothers' and fathers' book sharing discussions when their children were between ages 3;6 (years;months) and 4;1, and their children's gains on a formal measure of abstract language knowledge 1 year later. We found significant correlations be-tween the amount of book sharing discussion at three of four different levels of abstraction (Levels I, II, & IV, with IV being the highest level of abstraction; see Table 13.1) and children's subsequent gains at the highest level of abstraction (Level IV). While it made sense that the amount of parental discussion at the highest level of abstraction was related to the children's gains at that level, why was the amount of input at the two lowest levels of abstraction (Levels I & II) re-lated to gains at the highest level? We reasoned that one possibility may lie in the nature of a successful learning environment.

TABLE 13.1
Coding Categories for Levels of Abstraction

Level I: Matching Perception

Label	Name an object or person (even with "Who did X?" kind of questions or "Do you know what this is called?" or "What do you think that is?") including negative label ("It's not an X.").
Locate	Locate an object or character, including the use of prepositions (e.g., "under the table."); ask "where" question.
Notice	Direct attention to a pictured object and either name it or don't name it.
Rote counting	

Level II: Selective Analysis/Integration of Perception

Describe characteristics	Focus on perceptual properties (size, shape, color) or parts of objects or characters; say colors or numbers if there is a referent; specify type of object (e.g., "What kind of X?"); discuss possession (e.g., "Bear's apple") or quantity (e.g., "more," " several," "some").
Describe/notice scene	Describe or notice actions that are immediately perceptually present in text or pictures.
Sentence completion	Pause to allow child to complete sentence.

Level III: Reorder/Infer About Perception

Infer	Discuss something not explicitly stated in text (e.g., "It must be nighttime now.").
Recall information	Focus on prior information presented in book during current or previous reading; summarize (code pieces of information separately), synthesize information from a series of pictures.
Judgment/evaluation	Focus on non-perceptual qualities (e.g., "clever") and internal states (e.g., "sad," "hungry") of characters, objects, or ideas; sometimes introduced by epistemic verbs (e.g., "I think," "I'll bet"); judgments (e.g., "beautiful," "funny"); provide point of view (an interpretation of what character is thinking or feeling).
Identify similarities/differences	Compare and contrast things in book (e.g., "That looks like an X") or different stages of development of one thing (e.g., "Before it was a caterpillar, but now it's a butterfly!").

(Continued)

TABLE 13.1
(Continued)

Level IV: Reasoning About Perception

Predict	Predict what will happen next or outcome of story (used when child doesn't know, or doesn't seem to know, story—otherwise code as Level III "recall information").
Factual knowledge/definitions	Provide general information that is not directly provided in book (e.g., "Real bears sleep all through the winter. They hibernate."); define word meaning or name subordinates of a superordinate category (e.g., "Bees and flies are kinds of insects."); distinguish between fantasy and reality (e.g., "Can the bear really fly?").
Explain	Go beyond story or actions to provide an explanation, often indicated with words like "because," "so that," "since," or responses to "why" questions.

Coding Categories Not Tied to a Level of Abstraction

Relate life to text	Relate a concept in the book to the child's experiences, including past, present, and future experiences.(e.g., "You planted a flower at school, didn't you?)"; make a reference to another book that the child may be familiar with (e.g., "Remember? Peter Pan and Wendy flew just like the bear.").
Book/print conventions	Instruct the child in how to handle book (turning pages, etc.); teach other book conventions such as making references to the book's title, author, illustrator, and page numbers; evaluate entire book (e.g., "I like that book."); socialize in how to participate in book reading (e.g., "Let's read the book and find out." "Do you want me to read everything on the page or do you want to turn the pages faster than I can read?"); discuss aspects of print.
Interaction	Provide feedback (e.g., "That's right." "Uh-huh." "No."); imitate the child's utterances; comment on child's behavior; discipline the child; ask clarification questions; make references to the video camera equipment; try to keep child's attention on the book; attempt to prompt child for a correct answer.

We had adapted our levels of abstraction from work by Blank and her colleagues that focused on the discourse of preschool teachers (Blank, Rose, & Berlin, 1978a). These authors had suggested that preschool teachers should aim to raise about 30% of their discourse to a level that would challenge children, while keeping the other 70% at a level that the children had already mastered, and which would therefore allow them to respond successfully. Amazingly, as a group, the 70 parents (35 mothers and 35 fathers) in our study provided an average of 37% of their book discussion at the two higher levels of abstraction (Levels III & IV) and 63% at the lower levels (Levels I & II).

These percentages, along with the significant correlations we had observed between parents who provided more input at Levels I, II (lower), and IV (highest) and children who made the greatest gains at the highest level of abstraction, led us to conclude that perhaps abstract language skills in children are fostered simultaneously in two very different, and seemingly opposite, ways. The first method keeps most of the interaction at levels the child has already clearly mastered, in order to create a climate in which the child feels competent and successful. The second method involves raising about a third of the interaction to levels that the child has not yet mastered, thereby creating challenges and opportunities for growth.

A similar finding was reported by DeLoache and DeMendoza (1987), but with children who were substantially younger than those in the van Kleeck et al. study. DeLoache and DeMendoza noted two levels of complexity in the information provided by mothers during book sharing with children who were 12, 15, and 18 months old. They found that 74% of the information provided was simple (almost all labels), while the remainder was more complex (factual information, dramatizations, references to the child's experiences with related objects). They also noted, however, that the older children received significantly more complex input, with elaborations increasing from 12% to 23% to 42% across the three ages studied. Both the van Kleeck et al. (1997) and the DeLoache and DeMendoza (1987) studies suggest that the ratio of non-challenging to challenging input is an important factor for future book sharing research to consider.

Verbal Display of Knowledge

There may be other, partial explanations for the fact that the majority of linguistic input during book sharing takes place at lower levels of abstraction, which children have already mastered or almost mastered. Another "agenda" may be at work—teaching children to "tell what they already know" or "verbally display their knowledge." Scollon and Scollon (1981) noted that the practice of asking children to verbally display their knowledge is fostered by cultural beliefs, and is clearly not a universal phenomenon. In mainstream American culture, adults often ask a child to answer a question to which the adult already knows the answer. Such "known information" or "test" questions abound in parent–child book sharing routines, particularly with infants and toddlers.

This practice socializes young children into the cultural practices for displaying knowledge that they will later encounter in the classroom (Watson, 2001). Indeed, Reid (2000) noted that Mehan's (1979) IRE model (teacher Initiation, followed by a child Response, followed by teacher Evaluation) is still the most common classroom participation structure, and that the most common type of teacher initiation is the "known information" question. Teachers are likely to think that children who display their knowledge are the children who have the knowledge. They are unlikely to recognize that children who do not respond simply may have been differently socialized in this regard (see Vigil & van Kleeck, 1996, for a discussion of the many other reasons children may not respond). The impact of this assumption on teachers' perceptions of children's competence, on teacher–child interactions (or lack thereof), and subsequently on children's achievement is an empirically documented story with which we are all familiar.

The Scollons (1981) pointed out that the practice of having young children verbally display their knowledge is culturally determined. They noted that in American mainstream culture, the subordinate child is the "exhibitionist," who is expected to "show off his abilities," especially in school. For a child, such exhibition would include verbal displays of knowledge to adults. In other cultures, such as the Athabaskan societies studied by the Scollons (1981), the relationship is reversed: children are assigned the "spectator" role, while adults display their skills (p. 17). In such cultures, children are not socialized to verbally display their knowledge to adults.

Heath (1989) suggested that such variations in practice stem from different cultural beliefs about children's development. In the United States, where mainstream adults typically believe that children are "raised" or "trained," adults exhibit a more directive, pedagogical style of interaction. In other societies, where children are believed to "grow up" largely apart from parental intervention, adults "do not intervene with highly specific verbalizations of the 'here and now' or request recounts of shared events, except for societal ceremonial occasions" (p. 345). Such children might display their knowledge through actions, rather than verbalizations.

In subaltern cultural groups within the United States, verbal display may not be part of children's socialization. Heath (1983) found that African Americans in the community she studied rarely asked children known-information (or test) questions, and when they did, it was in order to chastise. Heath (1989) also observed that many Mexican American communities refrain from known-information questions, except when teasing children (see Valdés, 1996, for more on the children of Mexican immigrants).

Verbal display of knowledge is rarely addressed in book sharing research. I have seen two exceptions: one is a study of book sharing (DeLoache & DeMendoza, 1987); the other—Goodman, Larrivee, Roberts, Heller, and Fritz, 2000—is worth mentioning for its methodology, although it actually focused on mother–child interaction during spontaneous play. The DeLoache and DeMendoza study looked at mothers interacting with 12-, 15- and 18-month-old children. The authors examined the mothers' beliefs about their children's knowledge of words taken from the book that had just been shared, and asked the mothers to indicate whether the child could produce, comprehend only, or was unfamiliar with each word. The mothers were significantly more likely to skip over pictures when they thought their child did not know the label for that picture (they asked for such labels only 8% of the time). They were also much more likely to ask the child for labels they thought the child could produce (49% of label requests), than for those that they believed the child could only comprehend (18% of label requests).

Goodman and her colleagues (2000) had mothers complete the McAurther Communication Development Inventory (Fenson et al., 1993), a measurement tool that asks a parent to indicate all the specific vocabulary items that their child knows. In comparing these maternal reports to the questions the mothers asked their 30-month-old children during play, it was found that the children already knew 94% of the words that they were asked to supply in response to their mothers' questions. While Goodman et al. concluded that the mothers' agenda appeared to be the maintenance of discourse with their children, and not the teaching of new vocabulary, their data would also strongly support the idea that the mothers were socializing their children to verbally display their knowledge. Interestingly, in a series of studies by Sénéchal and her colleagues exploring the impact of book sharing on vocabulary development, the idea that children are being socialized to verbally display their knowledge is not discussed (e.g., Sénéchal, 1997; Sénéchal & Cornell, 1993; Sénéchal, Thomas, & Monker, 1995).

The verbal display theory suggests a variety of possible refinements for future research. First, the possibility that the best learning environment has ample opportunity for both success and challenge might shape how book sharing discussions are studied and interventions are designed. Research exploring the role of the environment in a child's learning should consider the possibility that success is bred by a combination of something like 70% guaranteed success (i.e., opportunities for the child to display what she or he already knows) and 30% challenge for growth. One way in which this possible distinction in input might be revealed would be a change in how book sharing discourse is typically analyzed. Researchers often collapse the illocutionary functions of adults' book sharing conversations. For example, several recent studies of the concrete-to-abstract dimension of adults' book sharing language have not distinguished between questions and comments (e.g., De Temple & Snow, 1996; Sigel & McGillicuddy-DeLisi, 1984; van Kleeck et al., 1997). And yet these different illocutions may foster different abilities: questions may primarily socialize the child into the verbal display of knowledge, while comments may serve either to teach what the parent believes to be new information, or to model higher levels of thinking about information presented in the book.

In designing child outcome measures, researchers might likewise consider that the child may be internalizing the broader cultural interest in verbal displays of knowledge, in addition to learning more specific skills. One possibility for how this distinction might be revealed comes from a re-interpretation of a consistent finding in intervention studies conducted by Lonigan and his colleagues. Lonigan (1994) discusses how, in many of these interventions, "consistently larger and more enduring effects of the intervention have generally been found on measures of expressive language skills than on receptive language skills" (p. 307; i.e., Arnold, Lonigan, Whitehurst, & Epstein, 1994; Lonigan, 1991, 1993; Valdez-Menchaca & Whitehurst, 1992; Whitehurst, Falco, Lonigan, Fischel, DeBaryshe, Vandez-Menchaca, & Caulfield, 1988). In one respect, these findings do not make sense. If language knowledge is improved, one would expect an equal or greater improvement in receptive language skills, as receptive skills are typically somewhat more advanced than expressive skills. However, it may be that these children are actually increasing both their basic language knowledge (reflected in receptive language gains) and their ability to verbally display their language knowledge (expressive language skill gains).

Improving children's ability to verbally display their knowledge through intervention may contribute to their later success in school. Early in their school careers, children are beginning to picture themselves as either competent or incompetent learners (Delpit, 1995; Ogbu, 1990). Because "test questions" still abound in classroom interactions, as noted earlier, comfort with the verbal display of knowledge may foster the child's self-concept as a competent learner, as well as the teacher's image of the child as a competent learner. We all know the benefits that will accrue from this.

Child's Level of Participation

In another chapter in this volume, van Kleeck and Vander Woude discuss the relative lack of participation in book sharing by children with language delays.

This issue looms large in a population for which interaction is considered fundamental to the fostering of language development. In a classic and still widely used text on working with preschoolers with language delays, for example, Fey (1986) devotes an entire chapter to facilitating the spontaneous talk of these children, and another chapter to encouraging their responsiveness to conversational partners. And indeed, book sharing intervention studies of children with language delays have often reported increases in participation as a positive outcome of the intervention (e.g., Crain-Thoreson & Dale, 1999; Dale, Crain-Thoreson, Notari-Syverson, & Cole, 1996; McNeill & Fowler, 1999). One such study by DeBaryshe (1992) also showed similar increases in the participation of children who were developing normally.

Recent work by Hart and Risley (1999) beautifully demonstrates that the amount that normally developing children talk between 11 and 36 months of age is positively related to their vocabulary at 36 months. Furthermore, children match their parents in their amount of talk—parents who talk to their children less have children who talk less, and hence get less practice talking, and vice versa. Children, it seems, are socialized regarding how much to talk, as well as how to talk.

The issue of participation in book sharing among normally developing children has rarely been addressed, except in a few studies looking at repeated readings of familiar versus unfamiliar books (e.g., De Temple & Snow, 1996; Goodsitt, Raitan, & Perlmutter, 1988; Robinson & Sulzby, 1984). And yet, following from the work of Hart and Risley, one should expect that adult conversation about the content of a book will only be effective if the child participates in the conversation. As such, instead of just measuring later child language and literacy outcomes as they are related to various styles of adult book sharing interaction, it may be illuminating to also measure the child's participation in those interactions, to determine if the level of participation is a factor in language and literacy development. Also, the relative proportion of adult (versus child) participation would be expected to change over time, as it does for other types of parent–child interaction (Hart & Risley, 1999). And indeed, book sharing research has revealed this to be true for at least one side of the conversation. As preschoolers get closer to school age, their mothers tend to read more and talk less about the books that they are sharing with their children (e.g., Goodsitt et al., 1988; van Kleeck & Beckley-McCall, 2002).

As Yaden states elsewhere in this volume, however, simply noting the amount of adult and child participation through traditional coding categories (such as questions, comments, and responses) reveals little about how the flow of conversation unfolds, and how this flow affects the child's ability to gain conventional knowledge from the book sharing context. Yaden suggests that dynamic systems theory may help us discern patterns, by viewing interactions as nonlinear, rather than as the sum of isolated categories of conversational participation.

In addition to the kind of refinements suggested by Yaden, future book sharing research needs to consider the nature of discourse in the more complex, but certainly not infrequent, context of a parent reading simultaneously to two preschool children of different ages and developmental levels. Van Kleeck and Beckley-McCall (2002) provide evidence from a study of five families, showing that such simultaneous reading differs substantially from reading to either child individually, along a wide array of discourse dimensions.

BOOK CHARACTERISTICS: THE IGNORED DIMENSION OF THE ADULT–CHILD–BOOK TRIAD

In 1985, Martinez and Roser began a research report by stating, "Reading to children involves three components—the child, the adult, and the story. Previous descriptions of the story time interactions have focused on two of these components—the child and the adult reader" (p. 168). In a 1985 study by Pellegrini, Brody, and Sigel, the authors suggested that the "absence of high and medium cognitive demand strategies was probably due to the relatively simple plots" (p. 337). And in 1989, Dickinson and Keebler noted that the type and amount of questioning by teachers varied, depending on how difficult they perceived the book to be for their children. In the ensuing years, surprisingly little attention has been paid to the book component of book sharing interactions. In 1998, Elster stated, "there has been little research on the influence of particular books on patterns of emergent reading" (p. 44). In this section I discuss three characteristics of the books shared with children that should be considered by book sharing research—genre, familiarity, and complexity.

Genre

Most studies of book sharing with preschoolers have focused on storybooks. And indeed, there is evidence from a number of studies that storybooks are chosen for reading time by families far more frequently than other genres of books (e.g., De Temple & Snow, 1996; Dickinson, De Temple, Hirschler, & Smith, 1992; Goodsitt et al., 1988; Phillips & McNaughton, 1990). Nonetheless, there is growing and compelling evidence that the genre of a book shared with a child can have a dramatic impact on the nature of the resulting adult–child interaction. Furthermore, different kinds of books may foster different kinds of learning among preschoolers of different ages. The most dramatic examples accrue from studies that have compared storybooks to alphabet books (see Stahl, this volume, for a detailed discussion).

A number of studies have shown that parents tend to focus overwhelmingly on meaning, rather than print, when they are sharing a storybook (e.g., Bus & van IJzendoorn, 1988; Morrow, 1988; Philips & McNaughton, 1990, Snow & Ninio, 1986; van Kleeck, 1998), as do their children (e.g., Yaden, Smolkin, & Conlon, 1989). With alphabet books, age is a complicating factor. When reading to younger children, parents typically treat alphabet books as if they were merely picture books. In other words, they frequently ignore the letters (DeLoache & DeMendoza, 1987; van Kleeck, 1998). Even when parents do try to focus their children on printed forms, the children tend to initially treat letters semantically. That is, they seem to think that letters refer to the animals and objects pictured, rather than standing for units of sound within the spoken language (Yaden, Smolkin, & MacGillivray, 1993; see Yaden, this volume, for further discussion). With older preschoolers, discussion about alphabet books increasingly focuses on the print itself (Bus & van IJzendoorn, 1988; Smolkin, Yaden, Brown, & Hofius, 1992; van Kleeck, 1998).

The case study analyses by Yaden and his colleagues (1993) demonstrated that children often treat individual letters as having semantic meaning (rather than being meaningless units that represent sounds within words), even when their parents are explicitly focused on "teaching" them about letters. This brings up an interesting issue that it might behoove researchers to consider—the possible gap between what an adult believes she or he is providing to the child, and what the child is actually gaining from or understanding about that input. All too often, we tend to assume a direct relationship between input and outcome. Even the parents themselves may be making this assumption, as witnessed by Yaden et al. (1993), who noted that "parents, interestingly enough, do not seem to be aware that they are being misunderstood" (p. 44).

However, it is possible that what we are seeing here is a reflection of the *gradual* social transmission of knowledge described by social-constructivist theories of child development, a point that is discussed in detail later in this chapter. Because knowledge is gained gradually, we might expect the child's initial understanding to be fuzzy at best, and totally off the mark at worst. And indeed, Yaden et al. (1993) discussed how "it is this drive to make meaningful connections with letters that perhaps keeps the process moving forward as the child increases in understanding of their actual referent to the phoneme level of language which may come some months or years later" (p. 60). They also suggested that "what is often overlooked in Piaget's biological analogy is his emphasis on the dynamic flow or trajectory over time of the development of cognition" (p. 46). Researchers need to keep in mind that development is gradual and nonlinear. Furthermore, both adult input and children's understanding of that input need to be taken into account to gain a better understanding of what is going on in book sharing interactions.

In light of the findings on the influence of age on parents' treatment of alphabet books, it may be interesting to future researchers to consider evidence suggesting that there are two general stages of emerging literacy development—the first stage being meaning-focused, and the second introducing a print focus in some contexts, and expanding the meaning focus in others (see van Kleeck, 1998). These stages are discussed later in this chapter.

Less dramatic examples of differences in interaction as a function of the genre are also found in the research comparing expository (informational) texts to stories. When sharing expository texts, children tend to participate more in the interaction (Pellegrini, Perlmutter, Galda, & Brody, 1990; Sulzby & Teale, 1987) and adults focus more on vocabulary, concept-building (by providing demonstrations and concrete examples), and discussion of questions posed in the texts themselves (Mason, Peterman, & Kerr, 1989). There are also qualitative differences in the kind of vocabulary found in these two genres. In a comparison of repeated pretend readings of narrative and expository texts by preliterate kindergarten children, Pappas (1993) found that expository books dealt more with classification and technical vocabulary (e.g., animals who make tunnels), whereas storybooks tended to provide vocabulary that focused on character development and mental states. In sharing stories, adults provide more book convention information (e.g., information on authors and illustrators), predictions, and interpretations of story actions and character motivations (Mason et al., 1989). Here again, as when comparing storybooks and alphabet books, it is clear that children may learn different emergent literacy skills from different kinds of books at different ages. Future studies should certainly take these factors into account.

Book Familiarity

Book familiarity has been shown to clearly affect the nature of book sharing interactions. With a familiar book parents engage in less "beyond the text" talk (De Temple & Snow, 1996; Goodsitt et al., 1988; Robinson & Sulzby, 1984; van Kleeck et al., 1997), while their children talk more about the book (De Temple & Snow, 1996; Goodsitt et al., 1988; Robinson & Sulzby, 1984). Although parents engage in less discussion in general when sharing familiar books, they focus more on the content of the story when they make excursions beyond the text (Goodsitt et al., 1988), and they use more abstract language to discuss the familiar book (Anderson-Yockel & Haynes, 1994; Beals, De Temple, & Dickinson, 1994; Fagan & Hayden, 1988; Heath, 1982). It should be noted, however, that the genre of a book may interact with differences in adult's book sharing styles. Haden, Reese, and Fivush (1996) found that some of the mothers in their study did not change their styles when reading a familiar (versus an unfamiliar) book.

The shifts that often occur as books become familiar appear to reflect the social transmission of knowledge on a micro- (rather than macro) level. That is, as the child internalizes more and more information about a particular book, the adult is able to relinquish more of the responsibility for mediating between child and text. When a new book is introduced, the responsibility temporarily shifts back to the adult. However, while the adults are doing less in general as a book becomes more familiar, they are also "upping the ante" by challenging the child at higher levels of abstraction or cognitive demand regarding the book content.

For these reasons, it is important for researchers to consider the potential impact of book familiarity on book sharing interactions. This dimension is frequently not mentioned at all in studies of book sharing. When it is mentioned, unfamiliarity often is not verified by asking parents, teachers, or the child being studied if the child has ever had the book read to them in the past (e.g., Goodsitt et al., 1988). Van Kleeck et al. (1997) did verify with the parents and children in their study that the children had not seen the book before, and offered similar but unfamiliar books to those parents or children who indicated previous exposure. Likewise, the *degree* of familiarity is often not assessed. Instead, researchers often just ask parents to bring a book from home "that the child liked" (Goodsitt et al., 1988), to bring a book "the child enjoys and a frequently read book" (Anderson-Yockel & Haynes, 1994), or "to select one of the child's favorite 'story' books rather than a counting book, alphabet book, or book about a routine event" (van Kleeck et al., 1997).

Future research might also tell us whether adults who do not differentiate their reading styles when sharing more-familiar books are also less likely to change their manner of book sharing as the child develops cognitively and linguistically. In other words, do the micro-level differences (or lack thereof) in adult book sharing interactions reflect macro-level differences (or lack thereof) in interaction as the child develops more broadly?

Book Complexity

Many studies of book sharing treat the critical variable of book complexity superficially, by describing the books used in the research only in limited terms: as containing simple, repetitive language and a high level of predictability (Anderson-Yockel & Haynes, 1994); as having short texts and colorful pictures (McNeill & Fowler, 1999); as being developmentally appropriate (Hockenberger, Goldstein & Haas, 1999); as being age-appropriate and not excessively long (Hargrave & Sénéchal, 2000); as having pictures and telling a story (Martin, 1998); as being representative of storybooks widely available (Reese & Cox, 1999); as having pictures with minimal text (Cornell, Sénéchal, & Broda, 1988); as having many vivid and easily described pictures (Whitehurst, Falco, et al., 1988); as being equated for length and theme (Pellegrini et al., 1985); or as being realistic (Leseman & De Jong, 1998). Numerous studies briefly describe the book's plot or theme, but they provide no further information (e.g., Bradshaw, Norris, & Hoffman, 1998; Bus & van IJzendoorn, 1988; Dickinson et al., 1992; Elley, 1989). Some studies are a bit more helpful, describing the books' complexity by noting the number of words and sentences in the book and the average number of words per sentence (Crowe, 2000; van Kleeck et al., 1997); the number of lines of text per page (Goodsitt et al., 1998); the number of words per page (Martin & Reutzel, 1999); or the number of illustrated pages and independent clauses (Haden et al., 1996).

The research community might turn to recent work by Elster (1998) and Purcell-Gates (1996), as well as an older study by Martinez and Roser (1985), for guidance in ways to more thoroughly address the issue of complexity. Elster (1998) included a wide variety of measures of the books in his study, including length in pages, number of words, number of T-units (one main clause, plus all subordinate clauses and non-clausal structures grammatically attached to it, from Hunt, 1970), mean length of utterance (sentence), the degree of fantasy in the story, the relative strength of the story structure, the relative number of repeated phrases, the relative amount of literate language (formal and complex as opposed to colloquial and dialogic), and the picture-dependence of the story. Purcell-Gates (1996) conducted analyses of a variety of print materials in low-income homes, including storybooks. She looked at the degree of distance between the writer and intended reader, the degree to which the text had to carry the message, the degree of syntactic complexity, the degree of literacy vocabulary, and the degree of exclusive use of exophoric reference. De Temple and Snow (this volume) suggest that we might pay attention to lexical inventories, as well.

Martinez and Roser (1985) approach book complexity by looking at stories' inference demands. They based their analysis on a system developed by Warren, Nicholas, and Trabasso (1979), in which each story is described as an "event chain," and each event within the chain is a type of proposition (e.g., event, action, goal). The logical links between propositions are determined, as is the question of whether those links are explicit or implicit. The distance between the propositions that must be inferentially linked is also determined.

Another important aspect of complexity not addressed in the research to date is how well it is matched with a child's cognitive and linguistic skills. This is not to say, of course, that the match should be perfect. We would expect, following Vygotskian theory, that the ideal book would fall in a child's "zone of proximal development" for his or her cognitive and/or linguistic skills. This zone is defined as "the distance between the actual developmental level as determined by independent problem solving and the level of potential development as determined through problem solving under adult guidance or in collaboration with more capable peers" (Vygotsky, 1978, p. 86).

ASPECTS OF THE NATURE AND TIMING OF MEASURES USED IN BOOK SHARING RESEARCH

A variety of measurement issues bear upon our understanding of book sharing. Of the four discussed here, the first two have not been addressed in the research to date: (a) the preponderance of concurrent correlational methodologies (studies in which the predictor and outcome variables being related are obtained at the same point in time) and the question of how this methodology violates the social-constructivist orientation prevalent in book sharing research; and (b) the use of one-time skill measures in prospective and retrospective correlational studies, instead of measures of children's gains on the skills of interest. The other two issues have only been touched upon briefly thus far, and are ignored by most of the research: (c) the too-global nature of much book sharing research, and (d) the need for this research to consider stages of emerging literacy development, in addition to stages of written language development.

A MISMATCH OF THEORY AND METHODOLOGY: CONCURRENT MEASUREMENT OF PREDICTOR AND OUTCOME VARIABLES

This category concerns those studies in which book sharing is related to preliterate children's language or emerging literacy skills only, and not studies relating book sharing with preschoolers to their later print literacy abilities, for the obvious reason that it is impossible to do a concurrent correlational study comparing book sharing with the preschooler (who is not yet reading) to the same child's later print literacy achievement. I first raised these concerns in a study (van Kleeck et al., 1997) designed to look at the relationship between abstract language in parents' book sharing discussions and children's gains on a formal measure of abstract language knowledge 1 year later. A previous study by Sigel and McGillicuddy-DeLisi (1984) had posed a similar question, but in obtaining concurrent correlations between parents' abstract language during book sharing (which they called "distancing strategies") and preschoolers' performance on a number of cognitive measures, Sigel and McGillicuddy-DeLisi found that the amount of abstract parental language was generally not associated with children's cognitive performance. If we look at this lack of relationship through the lens of Vygotksian theory, their findings make perfect sense.

In Vygotsky's work, knowledge is transmitted gradually in social-interactive contexts. Initially, the more competent member of the dyad takes a great deal of responsibility for the interaction (referred to as "other regulation"), but gradually relinquishes this control as the less-competent member's skill increases ("self regulation"). From this perspective, we would not expect adult behavior to immediately affect a child's behavior, especially a child's independent skill performance in contexts with little or no interactive support (such as the formal intelligence tests these researchers used). We would instead expect the child to only gradually internalize the adult's interactive behaviors, and to show this impact later in development. A model depicting this gradual transmission is shown in Fig. 13.1 (cf. van Kleeck, 1994, and Vigil & van Kleeck, 1996, for further discussion of the model). So we would not expect high levels of adult input to correspond positively to the child's *simultaneously* exhibiting high levels of the same skill. In fact, the movement from other-regulation to self-regulation predicts the opposite—that high levels of adult input might be negatively related to a child's simultaneous performance on the same skill.

Given this notion, we reasoned that Sigel and McGillicuddy-DeLisi's findings may have been due to the concurrent measurement of parental input and children's test performance. And indeed, these researchers did find seven significant negative correlations, one significant positive correlation, and many low and non-significant correlations between parental distancing strategies and the scores of the children on various tests of intelligence (this was true for the children who were typically developing; the results were somewhat different for the group of children with communication disorders).

For this reason, in our own study (van Kleeck et al., 1997), we measured children's performance on a four-level test of language abstraction, both concurrently with our measures of parental book reading input and again 1 year later, in order to calculate gain scores. We measured concurrent correlations between pa-

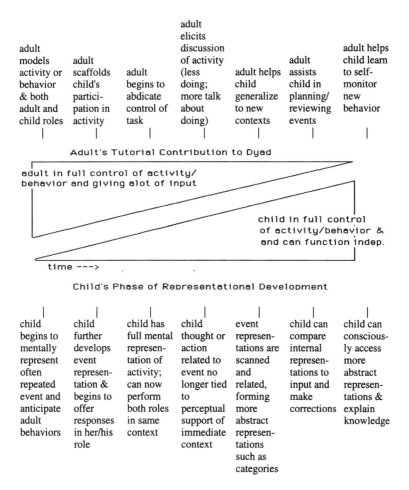

FIG. 13.1. Model from van Kleeck (1994), combining social constructivist and mental representational models of development, wherein the tutorial role of the adult decreases and changes over time as the child's mental representation improves and gradually guides her or his independent behavior.

rental book sharing input and children's abstract language scores to see if we would essentially replicate Sigel and McGillicuddy-DeLisi's (1984) findings of significant negative correlations, and many low and non-significant correlations. And indeed, our concurrent correlations were strikingly similar to theirs.

We would certainly have drawn a "no impact" conclusion from both of these studies if we had stopped at that juncture. But after looking at the relationship between parental abstract language input and children's gains in performance 1 year later on a test of abstract language abilities, a different picture emerged. Instead of having some significant negative and many low and non-significant correlations, we now had some significant positive correlations (ranging from .39 to .50). The significant correlations were between a composite measure of mothers' and fathers' book sharing discussions at three of the four different levels of abstraction, and the children's gains at the highest level of abstraction 1 year later. What is impressive here is not the size or number of significant correlations we obtained, which were modest, but how much the picture of the same group of parents and children seemed to change when we compared concurrent correlations against prospective correlations with gain scores.

If one looks at the tables in Scarborough and Dobrich's (1994) review, of the nine studies relating the *frequency* of adult–child book sharing to children's oral language skills, seven of these used concurrent measures of predictors and outcomes. One additional study reported a combination of concurrent and prospective data. Of the five studies that conducted single correlations, there were a total of three significant correlations and 13 non-significant correlations. Perhaps here, too, the general lack of significant correlations was due to the fact that the predictors and outcomes were measured at the same point in time.

Another table in the same review lists studies relating the *quality* of book sharing to children's emergent literacy and/or language skills. Three of these studies used concurrent correlations. The results of two of them are compelling for the discussion at hand: one had nine out of nine nonsignificant correlations, and the other had 11 out of 12 (the third study using concurrent correlations had confounded results). Do these overwhelmingly nonsignificant findings indicate a lack of relationship between the frequency or quality of parent book sharing and their children's language and emergent literacy outcomes? Or are they generated by a methodology that is contrary to the theoretical position claimed in much of this research—that book sharing is effective because it supports a gradual transmission of skills from the adult to the child?

Of course, there are other potential problems with the correlational methodologies used in book sharing research (including concurrent, retrospective, and prospective correlations). Some scholars have discussed the fact that correlations will be low if there is little range on the factors being correlated (Dunning et al., 1994; Scarborough & Dobrich, 1994). Parent report measures of frequency of reading are often discussed in this light. Researchers should report information on the ranges and distributions of variables to support the validity of their correlational analyses. There have also been problems with small sample sizes, often combined with the study of a large number of variables (Lonigan, 1994). While correlations indicate linear relationships, Scarborough notes that

the development of many components of language consists of peaks and pla-
teaus, rather than incremental, linear advances. Measurements taken during
plateau periods may miss relationships that do, in reality, exist (Scarborough,
2001; Scarborough & Dobrich, 1994).

There is also the important issue of correlations of variables being only as
good as the measures of the variables used. In book reading research, it may be
the case that many of the measures used have been insensitive because they
have been too global (Lonigan, 1994; Scarborough & Dobrich, 1994). I discuss
this last issue at length later in this chapter.

ONE-TIME MEASURES OF CHILDREN'S PERFORMANCE

Much research of emerging literacy skills and preschoolers' language skills is
also hampered by the fact that correlations are obtained with a one-time performance measure for the children. This concern is an offshoot of the concurrent
correlations issue. The simultaneous measurement of predictors and outcomes
naturally excludes any measure of the child's improvement on the outcome skill
over time. For this reason, gain scores would seem to be a better indicator of parents' impact on children's performance. This is only true when the outcome develops gradually over the child's preliterate years; otherwise, gain scores are not
calculable. But if gains can be determined, then they adjust for the possibility
that some children may have relatively high scores without much improvement
over time (e.g., a very bright child in a relatively unstimulating environment).
Other children may have lower scores but show a great deal of improvement
(e.g., a slow-developing child in a highly stimulating environment). Of the
studies reviewed by Scarborough and Dobrich (1994) and Bus et al. (1995),
none of those that used prospective or retrospective correlational methodology
used gain scores.

Measures That Are Too Global

Lonigan noted in 1994 that the more global the measures used in book sharing
research, the less likely it is that relationships will be discerned. In a related vein,
others have suggested that future research needs to focus on how aspects of
emergent literacy are related to aspects of home and school literacy experiences, and how different emergent literacy factors predict different aspects of
reading and writing (Purcell-Gates, 1996; Whitehurst & Lonigan, 1998).
Three recent publications have come up with convergent conceptualizations of
the component emergent literacy skills (Scarborough, 2001; van Kleeck, 1998;

Whitehurst & Lonigan, 1998). My own model of emergent literacy skills is pre-sented in the following paragraphs, and includes discussion of how it relates to the models of Scarborough and Whitehurst and Lonigan. My model serves as an organizing framework for future efforts to analyze the relationships that may ex-ist between literacy experiences, emergent literacy skills, and later reading achievement.

To understand the range of different skills that preschoolers are simulta-neously acquiring and applying during book sharing, I draw on a model of the later reading process developed by Seidenberg and McClelland (1989) and fur-ther elaborated by Adams (1990). A brief introduction to this model provides a helpful starting point for considering the domains of preliteracy development. The model has four components that are tightly integrated for the fluent reader: an orthographic processor, a phonological processor, a meaning processor, and a context processor (see Fig. 13.2).

Individual letters are the input for the *orthographic processor*, which contains individual letter recognition units and, over time, the associative linkages be-tween and among them that allow sequences of letters to be simultaneously pro-cessed. The *phonological processor* allows for the phonological translation of print, or the ability to turn letters on a page into sound sequences that comprise

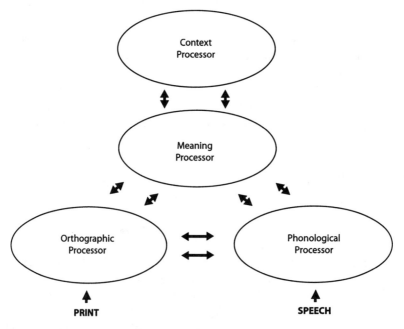

FIG. 13.2. Adams' (1990) model of the reading process (based on Seidenberg & McClelland, 1989).

spoken words. In an alphabetic language, this conversion requires conscious awareness of the phonemes that make up words. Phonological translation is accomplished by vocalizing or subvocalizing, and is essential for decoding unfamiliar words and comprehending complex syntax—according to Waters, Caplan, and Hildebrandt (1987), readers prevented from subvocalizing cannot remember or comprehend complex sentences. These two processors relate to the form component of print—the sounds within words, the letters of the alphabet, and the correspondences between them.

The *meaning processor* deals with the meaning of individual words, and consists of the reader's lexical knowledge. The *context processor* takes the reader beyond the word level, and is in charge of constructing a coherent, ongoing interpretation of the text. These latter two processors function to attach word-, sentence-, and text-level meaning to print form.

Adams (1990) repeatedly emphasized the coordinated nature of the various processors involved in reading. These processors work in concert and cannot replace, preempt, or overcome each other. As such, no one processor is any more important than another. The orthographic processor, although the anchor of the system, is useless by itself. It is only through its interactions with the other processors that it serves the reading process. Given this high degree of interactivity, which only increases as development proceeds, Adams' proposed model equally emphasizes the form and meaning components of print.

Although the processors are inseparable for fluent readers, for preliterate preschoolers the component skills are only very loosely integrated, with some more integrated than others. Figure 13.3 shows a model of emergent literacy. The relatively separate initial development of the skills related to each processor is indicated by not depicting the bidirectional arrows between the processors that are found in Adams' model. As the child becomes a more fluent reader, the component skills become more tightly integrated. Scarborough (2001) depicted this idea by the metaphor of a rope, in which the "strands" are preliteracy skills that are gradually being brought more tightly together.

As can be seen in Fig. 13.3, most of the skills related to the top two processors (context and meaning) are general skills that are also useful outside of reading and are certainly developed in other contexts as well. The exceptions are book conventions and perhaps word awareness. For example, children use their syntactic knowledge in many contexts, not just when someone is sharing a book with them, and develop syntactic knowledge in many other contexts as well.

All of the skills noted as part of the context and meaning processors are helpful to the child's eventual development of reading *comprehension*. As such, they are related to the meaning aspect of print. During emerging literacy, these skills help the child derive meaning from texts that are read aloud (although I cer-

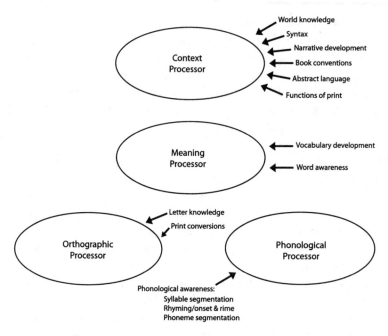

FIG. 13.3. Model of components of emerging literacy, adapted from van Kleeck (1998).

tainly acknowledge that deriving meaning from text is not exclusively the child's job, since the reader may often extend considerable effort to ensure the child's comprehension). Later, of course, these skills will help the child in comprehending what she or he reads independently.

The skills related to the orthographic and phonological processors are, for the most part, specific to reading an alphabetic writing system such as English, and are useful for developing the form aspect of print in beginning reading. Interestingly for the purposes of this book, there is building evidence that the sharing of storybooks is often *not* predictive of skills related to the orthographic and phonological processors (alphabet knowledge and phonological awareness). These skills appear to be fostered by experiences with different genres of books (alphabet or rhyming) or other kinds of activities (word play, phonological awareness training, and so forth).

Scarborough (2001) and Whitehurst and Lonigan (1998) also made distinctions between two broad types of emergent literacy skills. Scarborough sorted them into skills that eventually support language comprehension and those that eventually support word recognition. Whitehurst and Lonigan (1998) divided their list into what they called "outside-in" processes (understanding the context in which writing occurs) and "inside-out" processes (rules for translating writing into sounds).

Although named differently, the categories in these models are essentially the same as my own. The skills related to meaning aspects of print (van Kleeck, 1998) are those that will support print comprehension (Scarborough, 2001) and correspond to the outside-in processes (Whitehurst & Lonigan, 1998). Likewise, the skills related to print form are those that will eventually support word recognition (the inside-out processes). Although the three studies vary somewhat in the subsets of skills that they include under these two broad headings, there is a remarkable degree of overlap. Validity for this broad distinction can be seen in the fact that a similar distinction can be made for the reading process itself. Gough and Tunmer (1986), for example, "divided" reading (R) into decoding (D) and comprehension (C), and provided the formula $R = D \times C$. This division relates directly to two stages of preliteracy development—an earlier stage, focused on meaning, and a later stage that begins to incorporate a print form focus into literacy activities.

Following is a description of ways in which future research might endeavor to determine more direct correspondences between specific skills and outcomes. Consideration is also given to ideas about which genres of books, styles of interaction, and different kinds of experiences might best foster certain skills.

Context Processor Skills. Figure 13.3 shows several skills related to the context processor. These skills give children contextual frameworks for interpreting the printed information that is read to them as prereaders and that they themselves read later on. The child's extant *knowledge of the world* is clearly helpful in understanding similar objects and events that they encounter in books, just as information in books can also serve to further the child's knowledge of the world. Though I know of no specific research on the impact of book sharing on children's general world knowledge, this may be because the impact is so basic and obvious. Any time children share a book about an experience that they have not personally had, or about a place they have not been, they are undoubtedly learning something new about the world. As a basic example, many children who have never themselves seen a variety of farm or zoo animals may well recognize many of these animals from books. Of course, this is not to say that there are not other ways to gain world knowledge. For preschoolers, these other avenues would certainly include television, computers, and other audio-visual media.

The most obvious way in which future book sharing research might look at children's existing knowledge about the world is to consciously consider children's experience in choosing sharing books for descriptive or intervention studies. Many children's books seem fairly neutral in this respect, but it is still a worthwhile consideration. It might also be helpful to consider what the child might learn about the world from particular books, and to include rather specific pre- and posttest measures of this learning. It would seem logical that certain genres (such as expository texts) are more influential in expanding a child's general knowledge about the world than others (such as rhyming books or alphabet books). It may also be the case that pre-existing levels of knowledge interact with other kinds of learning fostered by sharing a particular book. So, for example, if a child already has fairly solid knowledge about the content of a book, this may allow a different kind of learning to take place, such as the kind needed to display that knowledge verbally. Extending this logic, we could speculate that different things are learned as the same book is repeatedly shared with a child.

Syntactic knowledge comes into play in the general comprehension of written text, as well as in word recognition. As Adams (1990) pointed out, for skillful readers "the process through which they interpret the text is regulated by the grammatical structures and interrelationships of its phrases and clauses. Furthermore, analyses indicate that as proficient readers proceed through connected text, they identify the grammatical function of each word as it is encountered" (p. 9). While the impact of syntactic knowledge on pre-readers' comprehension of shared text has not been studied in detail, it certainly plays a role in the comprehension process, as well as in the comprehension of texts that children later attempt to read by themselves.

A number of studies have shown that syntactic development predicts later literacy development. Walker and colleagues (Walker, Greenwood, Hart, & Carta, 1994), for example, found that preschoolers' mean length of utterance (MLU) predicted their later reading scores in Grades 1 through 3. From the opposite perspective, Scarborough (1991) found that children who were poor readers at the end of Grade 2 had poorer syntactic development (length and complexity of sentences) at ages 2½, 3, 3½, and 4.

Here again there is clearly a bi-directional influence, with book sharing also facilitating syntactic development. Purcell-Gates (1988) demonstrated how preschoolers who were read to extensively in their homes began their formal reading instruction with knowledge of the syntactic features typical of written discourse. Many other studies have found that book sharing fosters receptive or expressive language skills more generally by obtaining significant correlations (e.g., DeBaryshe, 1993; DeBaryshe et al., 1991; Donachy, 1976; Lonigan, 1993; Mason & Dunning, 1986; McNeill & Fowler, 1999; Valdez-Menchaca & Whitehurst, 1992), although other studies have not obtained significant correlations (e.g., Crain-Thoreson & Dale, 1992; Dunn, 1981). Possible reasons for these contradictory findings were explored earlier, in our discussion of the difficulties with concurrent correlations.

Future knowledge might consider children's syntactic knowledge in any number of ways, including looking at syntactic development or the syntactic complexity of the book being shared in order to determine their impact on the nature of the book sharing interaction, on the child's comprehension of the book, or both. For the last several years, professionals interested in fostering the syntactic development of preschoolers with language delays have suggested reading them books loaded with particular syntactic structures as a starting point (e.g., Gebers, 1990), although I have seen no intervention research documenting the efficacy of this approach. One might also consider, as did Purcell-Gates (1988), the impact of book sharing on children's learning of the literate syntactic structures characteristic of written, as opposed to oral, discourse. It may be that certain styles of reading or genres of books would better foster such development than others. The fostering of written discourse skills might be better reflected in outcomes measuring the oral narratives of younger children (elicited by pictureless storybooks, for example) and the written narratives of older children.

Narrative skills allow a child to connect and understand text (linguistic input involving more than one sentence at a time). To date, developmental research on narrative skills has most often focused on story grammar and cohesion analyses. Story grammar studies look at how universal elements of stories such as setting, initiating events, internal responses, attempts, consequences, and reactions are woven into episodes (e.g., Mandler & Johnson, 1977; Peterson & McCabe, 1983; Stein & Glenn, 1982). Cohesion analyses look at the word choices (e.g., beginning a sentence with "next" or "therefore") and sentence structures that tie together the sentences in a text (see the classic work of Halliday & Hasan, 1976, on cohesion in English). Children's budding knowledge of how stories are constructed from story elements (a generalized level of the meaning aspect of stories) and cohesive devices (forms used to tie together meaning) helps them derive meaning from the texts that are read to them as preschoolers, and those they later attempt to read or write themselves. And indeed, narrative skills have been related to later literacy development in several studies (Snow, 1981; Wells, 1985). From another perspective, studies have shown that deficits in narrative ability can negatively influence a child's reading achievement (Feagans & Short, 1984; Merritt & Liles, 1987; Roth & Spekman, 1986). And evidence is accruing that narrative skills are fostered by book sharing (Elster, 1998; Harkins, Koch, & Michel, 1994; Purcell-Gates, 1996; Zevenbergen & Wilson, 1996). It should be remembered, however, that narrative skills are cultural skills, and the form they take will vary accordingly (see Westby, 1994, for a review of this issue).

Future research might consider narrative skills as one aspect of literacy knowledge that is potentially fostered by storybook sharing, and consider using orally produced stories with younger children and written fictional narratives with older children as possible outcome measures for this aspect of development. It may also be that various dimensions of the story's complexity, familiarity, and style (the manner in which it is shared) are critical factors in determining the level or aspects of narrative skill that are fostered.

Book conventions refers to developing knowledge about how books are created and how they function. Snow and Ninio (1986), for example, list several rules for interacting with books that inform young prereaders about how books function, including: (a) books are for reading, not manipulating; (b) in book reading, the book controls the topic; (c) pictures are not things, but representations of things; (d) pictures are for naming (especially when the child is in the single- and two-word stage of language development); (e) pictures, though static, can represent events; (f) book events occur outside real time; and (g) books represent an autonomous fictional world. An older preschooler may learn more advanced ideas about books and how they are created, with adults explaining that books have authors, illustrators, dedications, copyright dates, and so forth. As with the other context processor skills, knowledge of these book conventions supports the preschool child's ability to interpret the information presented in books, and is fostered by repeated book sharing.

In my model, I have separated book conventions (a skill related to the context processor) from print conventions (a skill related to the orthographic processor) and alphabet knowledge (another skill related to the orthographic processor), because I see them as arising differently and having different kinds of impacts on the reading process. For example, knowledge of book conventions might help a child place a book in broader context by helping him or her understand that a particular person wrote that particular book at a particular point in time. At some point, this kind of knowledge leads to insights—such as recognition of the possibility of different viewpoints—which shape the information and meaning conveyed in books.

Print conventions, on the other hand, are not specific to books, and refer to the knowledge that in alphabetic languages, print proceeds from left to right, top to bottom, and (in books) from front to back. Punctuation is also considered a print convention. These skills are important for decoding print. But print conventions are different from alphabetic knowledge. The research to date rarely makes this distinction, which may be why studies attempting to discern the impact of book sharing on these skills show rather muddy results. These studies often report on a child's knowledge of "concepts of print," which tends to include some combination of information about the functions of print, print conventions, and book conventions. Nonetheless, in her review, Scarborough (1998) cites seven studies showing a predictive correlation between concepts of print and later reading achievement. These studies had a mean correlation of .46, and a median of .49.

One book sharing intervention study has shown a substantial effect (.624) on children's development of concepts about print (Whitehurst et al., 1994), whereas another intervention study showed no impact (Justice & Ezell, 2002). Each of these studies, however, had adults emphasize different skills during book sharing. Whitehurst and his colleagues asked adults to engage in dialogic techniques (including asking children specific types of questions, evaluating and expanding their responses, and having them repeat expanded utterances). Justice and Ezell, on the other hand, had adults use what they called "print referencing behaviors" (including prompts about print conventions, concept of word, and alphabet knowledge). It is interesting that Justice and Ezell's study of print concepts did not show a change in the children's subsequent print concept development, while the Whitehurst et al. study, which did not have such a specific focus, showed a measurable impact on these skills.

Perusing the research on book sharing, it is clear that print conventions are not very often measured, either as a pretest/posttest variable in intervention, or as an outcome variable in predictive correlational studies. It is hard to imagine, in spite of the lack of empirical verification, that these concepts could be developed in any context other than book sharing.

Abstract language is another skill related to the context processor. As children from print-rich homes develop from infancy through the preschool years, their parents often place increasing cognitive demands on them during book sharing routines by using more abstract language in their comments and questions about the book. As such, the child is exposed to and does participate in higher and higher levels of linguistically conveyed reasoning over time (e.g., van Kleeck & Beckley-McCall, 2002; van Kleeck, Vigil, & Beer, 1998). A number of different terms have been used in the research to refer to this important dimension of parent book sharing discussion, including "immediate" versus "non-immediate" language (Dickinson et al., 1992), "decontextualized" language (e.g., Denny, 1991; Heath, 1982, 1983; Snow & Ninio, 1986), "distancing" language (McGillicuddy-DeLisi, 1982; Sigel & McGillicuddy-DeLisi, 1984), "representational demand" of language (Blank, Rose, & Berlin, 1978a), "disembedded" language (e.g., Donaldson, 1978; Wells, 1985), and the "symbolic potential" of language (e.g., Wells, 1987).

DeLoache and DeMendoza (1987) found some subtle changes in input along this dimension while studying 12-, 15-, and 18-month-olds. With the younger children, picture labeling predominated. With the older children, pictures were elaborated on, features were pointed out, and more factual information was provided. Snow and Goldfield (1981) demonstrated such changes in one mother–child dyad beginning when the child was 2 years, 5 months old, and continuing over the next 11 months. Although item labels were very frequent at first, they decreased substantially over time. Eventually the cognitive demands of maternal input and child participant increased, and events, rather than objects, were most often discussed.

Other research looking at older preschoolers has found that the higher levels of cognitive demand placed on children during book sharing involve such skills as making inferences, reasoning about the information, giving factual information, providing clarifications, and anticipation of future events (e.g., De Temple & Snow, 1996; Goodsitt et al., 1988; Heath, 1982, 1983; Martin, 1998; Ninio & Bruner, 1978; Sigel & McGillicuddy-DeLisi, 1984; Snow & Ninio, 1986; Sorsby & Martlew, 1991; van Kleeck, 1998; van Kleeck & Beckley-McCall, 2002; van Kleeck et al., 1997; Wheeler, 1983). These differences in the group data for different ages may occur if all parents are not engaged in increasingly abstract language as their preschooler matures linguistically and cognitively. Indeed, Haden et al. (1996) found that the use of abstract language was related to a stable style reflective of only 5 of the 19 mothers they studied.

Engaging children in abstract reasoning about book content is believed to help them deal in sophisticated ways with the information presented in books. Inferencing and reasoning are particularly helpful later on when the school curriculum shifts from "learning to read" to "reading to learn," at around the third or fourth grade (e.g., Heath, 1982, 1983). Some scholars refer to this general kind of discussion as "literate language," and have argued that it is a robust predictor of early school-based literacy (Pellegrini, 2001; Pellegrini & Galda, 1998; Pellegrini, Galda, Bartini, & Charak, 1998).

Another body of research underscores the importance of apprenticing preschoolers in the use of abstract language and, in particular, modeling for them questions about the information presented in more abstract books. The more abstract questions asked by the parents (those requiring inference, explanation, and prediction) directly correspond to the questions that mature readers spontaneously ask to aid their comprehension of written texts (e.g., Collins & Stevens, 1982; Garner & Alexander, 1982). Furthermore, in a review of research on the effectiveness of inserting questions into reading passages to enhance comprehension, Hanmaker (1986) found that higher level cognitive questions were more effective than their lower level counterparts. Effective text comprehension interventions have also relied on strategies that include higher level cognitive or more abstract language. For example, Palinscar and Brown

(1984) used summarizing, questioning (oneself about the text content), clarifying, and predicting to improve children's comprehension.

It seems that nearly all current studies looking at the nature of parents' or preschool teachers' interactions during book sharing have some system for distinguishing the concrete and abstract dimensions of adult talk, thus acknowledging the critical importance of this distinction. And while many studies have shown that input during book sharing becomes increasingly demanding as preschoolers grow older, few have specifically related this kind of input to children's development of abstract language abilities (see van Kleeck et al., 1997, for one exception). As such, future researchers in this field might find it fruitful to measure children's abstract language abilities, in addition to coding adult book sharing discussion for this dimension (a new version of the Blank, Rose, & Berlin [1978b] formal test of these abilities is soon to be released by Pro-ed Publishers of Austin, Texas).

Given the correspondence between the kind of abstract language that adults use with preschoolers and children's later, independent self-questioning to enhance their written text comprehension, it seems that it might be useful to look at outcomes specifically related to reading comprehension. It also seems reasonable to expect that this aspect of emerging literacy would be fostered by certain genres (e.g., story and expository books), but that such learning may also be affected by the complexity of individual books, and the reading styles of the adults who are reading to them.

Meaning Processor Skills.   The skills associated with the meaning processor include *word awareness* and *vocabulary development*. Word awareness consists of two different skills: segmentation and consciousness. The ability to segment sentences into component words is based on the child's awareness that words are a unit of language. This ability is required in order to establish word boundaries, which undoubtedly aid story comprehension. The confusion that might abound without this skill is indirectly demonstrated in a study by Chaney (1989), in which she asked children to recite just one word at a time of the Pledge of Allegiance. Her subjects' word boundary errors included such things as "for witches stand" (for which it stands) and "night of steaks/stakes" (United States).

Word consciousness is the knowledge that words are separable from their referents. It is manifested in the ability to identify whether or not a particular sound sequence is a word, and to identify qualities of words (such as length or difficulty) based on their form (e.g., "caterpillar is a long word because it has lots of letters") as opposed to their meaning (e.g., "train is a long word because trains are very long"). In younger children, word consciousness may also be spontaneously manifested when children make up words or switch the names for things. A child may, for example, playfully call butter *sish* (making up a word) or *applesauce* (see van Kleeck & Schuele, 1987). Many researchers believe that word consciousness is learned in part through exposure to print (e.g., Ehri, 1976; Lomax & McGee, 1987; Spencer, 1986). Such knowledge helps the child understand that the same sound sequence can refer to two totally different things (e.g., bark on a tree and the bark of a dog), which understanding would facilitate comprehension of texts. It might also help children focus separately on the form of a word when they get to the stage of actually decoding print, rather than getting sidetracked (as by focusing on the meaning of "four" when trying to decode the word "fortune," for example). There is no solid body of research relating book sharing to children's development of word consciousness.

Vocabulary development can be thought of in terms of *general* vocabulary development, as well as the learning of *specific* metalinguistic terms unique to books and reading, such as *page, book, story,* and *letter* (see Goodman, 1986). Receptive vocabulary is a very robust predictor of later literacy development (see Scarborough, 1998, for a review of 20 studies that show such a relationship). Book sharing and vocabulary development are mutually promoting: children's vocabulary helps them to understand the books that are read to them, and the reading of books further develops children's vocabulary. Indeed, of all the meaning processor skills, vocabulary development is emerging from correlational studies (e.g., DeBaryshe et al., 1991) and experimental studies (e.g., Elley, 1989; Hargrave & Sénéchal, 2000; Jenkins, Stein, & Wysocki, 1984; Sénéchal, 1997; Sénéchal & Cornell, 1993; Sénéchal et al., 1995) as one of the most important outcomes of sharing books with young preschool children. Other studies, however, have not found any relationship between book sharing and vocabulary development (Crain-Thoreson & Dale, 1992; Dunn, 1981; Lonigan, 1993), or have found that these relationships do not persist at followup (Whitehurst et al., 1988).

A number of issues should be heeded in future book sharing research on vocabulary development. The genre of the book, the age of the child, and the adult's sharing style may all be interacting variables. For example, because alphabet books are initially treated primarily as picture books (De Loache & DeMendoza, 1987; van Kleeck, 1998), they may foster toddlers' vocabulary development, while later on fostering letter knowledge (van Kleeck, 1998). Reese and Cox (1999) found an interaction between the initial vocabulary levels of the children in their study and the style of reading that best supported their further vocabulary development. Children with higher initial vocabulary levels benefited most from a reading style that provided a dramatic reading with discussion at the end of the text, but very little interruption during the reading itself. Children with lower initial vocabulary levels, however, benefited most from a reading style with high levels of interaction during the book sharing. These studies point to just of few of the myriad interrelationships that influence vocabulary development during book sharing. And, as discussed earlier, future research must also distinguish between actually learning new vocabulary and learning to verbally display prior knowledge.

Orthographic Processor Skills. The skills related to the orthographic processor include print conventions and letter knowledge. At the most basic level, knowledge of print conventions would include knowing that one reads print and not pictures: the print conventions of English orthography include such phenomena as directionality. That is, English print goes from left to right and top to bottom of the page, and from the front of the book to the back. Preschoolers exposed to books generally pick up on these rudimentary conventions (see Goodman, 1986).

There are three aspects of alphabetic or letter knowledge: knowledge of the names, shapes, and sounds of letters. Because letter knowledge is the anchor for the entire reading "system," it behooves preschoolers to solidly learn or even overlearn letters (Adams, 1990). Preschoolers' knowledge of letters is a strong predictor of their speed in learning to read. Scarborough's (1998) review of 24 research samples since 1976 found a median correlation of .53 (and a mean of .52) between letter naming scores and subsequent reading achievement. Furthermore, not knowing letters leads, not at all surprisingly, to difficulty in learning letter sounds and recognizing words (Mason, 1980; Sulzby, 1983). But simply teaching children letter names has no notable impact on their learning to read (e.g., Gibson & Levin, 1975)—a fact that underscores the need to develop emerging literacy skills related to *all* of the processors.

Letter knowledge is clearly an important predictor of reading achievement, particularly in the early stages of learning to decode print. However, it is not a skill that appears to be fostered among preschoolers by storybook sharing (McCormick & Mason, 1986; Sénéchal, LeFevre, Thomas, & Daley, 1998), although one study did find a positive correlation (Crain-Thoreson & Dale, 1992). The general lack of relationship may be a result of the near or total absence of references to print in storybook reading interactions (Phillips & McNaughton, 1990; Snow & Ninio, 1986; van Kleeck, 1998; Yaden, Smolkin, & Conlon, 1989). Furthermore, letter activities and book sharing appear to be unrelated in the home (Evans, Shaw, & Bell, 2000; Sénéchal et al., 1998). For example, Sénéchal and her colleagues (1998) found no correlation between parents' exposing their children to storybooks and parent-reported efforts to teach their preschoolers to read or print words.

As noted earlier, parents overwhelmingly favor storybooks when sharing books with their preschoolers. This may account for the general lack of correlation between book sharing and letter knowledge, since parents focus almost exclusively on meaning, and not on print, when sharing storybooks. This does not mean that book sharing cannot foster letter knowledge. Storybooks with salient print do invite more of a print focus than those in which the print is not particularly salient (Mason et al., 1989; Yaden et al., 1989). Furthermore, in a study using a rhyming book, parents were effectively trained to focus on print, which led to an increase in their children's letter knowledge (Justice, Weber, Ezell, & Bakeman, 2002).

Alphabet books, of course, are a fine tool for fostering knowledge about letters. Research has shown that when reading alphabet books to preschoolers, the emphasis shifts from meaning to print as the children get older (Bus & van IJzendoorn, 1988; van Kleeck, 1998). The emphasis also shifts more to print as an alphabet book is read more times (Phillips & McNaughton, 1990; Smolkin et al., 1992). The impact of sharing alphabet books on preschoolers' letter knowledge has not been directly studied, however. Sénéchal and her colleagues (1998) did find that preschoolers' alphabet knowledge was correlated with their parents' teaching them to read and write words, as assessed by parent report.

It may also be the case that parental belief determines whether or not alphabet knowledge is taught to preschoolers in their homes. In one study, Neuman and her colleagues found a great deal of difference in African-American teenage mothers' beliefs about learning and literacy (Neuman, Hagedorn, Celano, & Daly, 1995). These authors broke the continuum of beliefs down into three general approaches to child development, only one of which emphasized the child's early acquisition of discrete skills such as knowledge of letters, numbers, and colors. This orientation was observed in only 10 of the 19 mothers studied.

Six other mothers in the Neuman et al. study held a more "maturational" belief that their children were not yet ready to be read to. This orientation seems to align with the findings of a study of low-income families by Purcell-Gates (1996), who found that a child's entrance into school initiated parent involvement in teaching them about print. Parents of schoolchildren engaged "in four times as many literacy events that focused on the teaching and learning of literacy as compared to the parents of preschoolers" (p. 424).

From the research to date on alphabet knowledge, we can conclude that this knowledge is an important emerging literacy skill, which is generally not learned by preschoolers in the book sharing contexts typical of many or most homes. What remains to be determined by future research is the role of alphabet books in developing alphabet knowledge, and whether parents who typically teach the alphabet tend to do so in other literacy contexts. It is also important to consider the kind of information provided in any given alphabet book. Finally, it is clearly important to ascertain the role of parents' beliefs about their children's learning and literacy development. The continuum of parental beliefs developed in the Neuman et al. (1995) study could provide the basis for a questionnaire designed to assess these beliefs. Parental beliefs may be a much more meaningful indicator than SES for understanding variability in the home literacy experiences of preschoolers.

Phonological Processor Skills.   The skills related to the phonological processor (*syllable segmentation, rhyming,* and *phoneme segmentation*) all rely on phonological awareness, or conscious awareness of the sound components of words. Some scholars prefer to call this "phonological sensitivity," arguing that children may be able to perform these skills without a high degree of consciousness (e.g., Stanovich, 1992). The skills correspond to the three types of sounds within words that preliterate children are capable of recognizing: syllables, subsyllabic units (onsets and rimes), and phonemes. Syllable awareness is the earliest to emerge (e.g., Fox & Routh, 1975; Sawyer, 1987), followed by the subsyllabic units of onset and rime (e.g., Treiman, 1992). Phonemic awareness, which allows a child to engage in phonemic segmentation, is the most difficult and hence latest-developing aspect of phonological awareness (e.g., Fox & Routh, 1975; Sawyer, 1987).

Rhyming is often discussed as involving segmentation at the level of onset and rime.[1] *Stop* is rhymed with *pop*, for example, by separating the onset *st* from the rime *op* and then replacing it with the onset *p*. While there is some controversy about whether onset and rime constitute a genuine linguistic level in children's phonological awareness (e.g., Carlisle, 1991) and whether phonological awareness is on a continuum with phoneme awareness (e.g., Goswami & Bryant, 1990; Morais, 1991), there is general agreement that rhyming activities sensitize children to the sound structure of words. Furthermore, a number of studies have shown that rhyming ability predicts subsequent early reading and spelling achievement (e.g., Bradley & Bryant, 1983; Ellis & Large, 1987;

---

[1]"Onset" refers to the initial optional consonant or consonant cluster of a syllable; the "rime" is the remainder of the syllable, containing a vowel nucleus and an optional final consonant or consonant cluster.

Lundberg, Olofsson, & Wall, 1980). Some studies (e.g., Bowey & Francis, 1991; Bryant, MacLean, & Bradley, 1990) have further shown that rhyming ability contributes to early reading and spelling ability, independent of its contribution to the awareness of individual phonemes in words (cf. van Kleeck, 1994, and Goswami & Bryant, 1990).

A large body of research has shown that phonological awareness and early reading ability are highly correlated and that the phonological awareness skills of prereaders predict early reading achievement (cf. reviews by Adams, 1990, Blachman, 1994, and Wagner & Torgesen, 1987). More important for the current discussion, preliterate children can be effectively trained in phonological awareness with a subsequent positive impact on early reading ability (Blachman, 1994; Lundberg, Frost, & Petersen, 1988). Furthermore, phonological awareness can be effectively taught to preschoolers with speech and language disorders (van Kleeck, Gillam, & McFadden, 1998).

One longitudinal study has shown that training programs in which the sound segments taught in phonological awareness training are connected to letters lead to even greater gains—both in beginning reading and in follow-ups 4 years later—than do programs that focus on phonological awareness training alone (Bradley & Bryant, 1983, 1985). Similar results were achieved by Byrne and Fielding-Barnsley (1991). Ball and Blachman (1988, 1991) also found superior reading achievement in children trained (during separate activities) in both phonological awareness and letter names and sounds, compared to a control group. Furthermore, they found that training in both these areas was needed, as children who were trained solely in letter names and sounds did not make greater reading gains than the control group. These studies all support the idea that the teaching of connections between the processors depicted in Fig. 13.3 helps children integrate the entire range of skills.

Phonological awareness may rely on the development and integrity of phonological representations in long-term memory. As discussed earlier, there is some discussion that the unit of representation may in fact go through reorganizations up until the age of 7 or so, progressing from whole-word shapes to syllables to subsyllabic units to phonemes (e.g., Fowler, 1991). Other researchers discuss the quality of phonological representations, suggesting that degraded ("weak," "fragile," or "underspecified") or inefficient representations may cause some children's problems with skills, such as phoneme awareness, that rely on the use of phonological representations (e.g., Brady, 1991; Fowler, 1991; Gathercole & Baddeley, 1990; Mann & Liberman, 1984; Rapala & Brady, 1990). This notion has been extended even further to suggest that initial perception of speech may be inadequate, leading to poor-quality representations (e.g., Jorm & Share, 1983). Children who have difficulty with phonological awareness in spite of specific and prolonged training may have such degraded phonological representations.

Like alphabet knowledge, phonological awareness does not appear to be fostered by book sharing (Lonigan, Anthony, Dyer, & Collins, 1995; Whitehurst et al., 1994), although one study did find a significant correlation of .30, with a correlation of .29 being significant at $p < .05$ for their sample size of 47 (Sénéchal et al., 1998). Here again, however, the genre of the book may be critical. Previous research showing that preschool rhyming ability predicts beginning reading ability (e.g., Bradley & Bryant, 1983; Ellis & Large, 1987; Lundberg et al., 1980) would certainly suggest a possible connection between the sharing of rhyming books and phonological awareness, or at least the rhyming aspect of phonological awareness. To date, there has been no authoritative study of the impact of sharing rhyming books in the home on children's emerging phonological awareness skills.

Other kinds of home experiences—such as rhyming and other word games played outside the context of sharing rhyming books—may also foster phonological awareness. However, some researchers believe that explicit training is necessary in order to achieve phoneme awareness (e.g., Lundberg et al., 1988). Even those who have found that storybook sharing can be effectively used to foster phoneme awareness have achieved these effects by careful training of the adult who is sharing the book, and by embedding very explicit phonological awareness training episodes in the storybooks (McFadden, 1998).

This raises two questions for future research: Can rhyming ability be enhanced by sharing rhyming books? And if so, does that enhanced ability lead to greater phonological awareness at the phoneme level? As with storybooks, it may be that the book sharing style is also important when reading rhyming books. On the one hand, to make the sound relationships between words salient it may be important to read the text without interruption. On the other hand, it may be important to stop and point out rhyming words in order for children to learn about rhyming in this context.

CONSIDERING TWO STAGES OF EMERGENT LITERACY

Convergent evidence from a number of studies suggests that the eventual integration of these processors in fluent reading takes place in two stages. The first is meaning-focused. In this stage, meaning is almost an exclusive focus when storybooks are shared (Phillips & McNaughton, 1990; Snow & Ninio, 1986; van Kleeck, 1998; Yaden et al., 1989), and even alphabet books are treated primarily as picture books (Bus & van IJzendoorn, 1988; van Kleeck, 1998; Yaden et al., 1993). In the second stage, older preschoolers are introduced to various aspects of the print form: The focus of alphabet book reading shifts to print (Bus & van IJzendoorn, 1988; van Kleeck, 1998), while a continued and more complex exploration of meaning occurs in other contexts and with other genres. Of course, print form and meaning cannot exist in total isolation from each other, and a child is undoubtedly learning at least the rudiments of both in nearly all literacy-related activities. As such, the first stage really delimits the time when the literacy activities constructed by adults seem to place a marked emphasis on print meaning, while in the second stage an emphasis on print form may emerge in some, but not all contexts.

Several scholars have described similar stages in early reading development, with a function/meaning foundation stage followed by a stage focused on teaching the formal aspects of print through techniques like decoding. A third stage that incorporates skills from these previous two phases facilitates reading comprehension (Chall, 1983; Downing, 1979; McCormick & Mason, 1986). In a review of empirical studies comparing whole-language/language experience approaches with basal reader approaches to beginning reading, Stahl and Miller (1989) provide support for emphasizing the meaning and functional aspect of print before the form aspect. This conclusion was upheld in an updated review conducted by Stahl, McKenna, and Pagnucco (1994). The authors of both reports concluded that whole language/language experience approaches might be most effective for teaching functional aspects of reading, whereas more direct approaches might be better for helping a student master the word recognition skills prerequisite to effective comprehension. They also found that whole-language/language experience approaches may be more effective if used when children are in kindergarten, while the more form-oriented approaches should be saved for first grade.

My own research on mothers' book sharing discussions with their preschoolers provides compelling evidence of an early meaning foundation and a later form introduction stage. In a longitudinal study, 14 mothers read three books (a storybook, a rhyming book, and an alphabet book) to their preschoolers when they were 2, 3, and 4 years of age (van Kleeck, Vigil, & Beer, 1998). Any utterances by the mothers that went beyond the text were coded as focusing on meaning, form, or other aspects of the mother–child interaction, such as getting the child's attention and controlling the child's behavior. The meaning, form, and interaction coding schemes each had several subcategories (see Tables 13.1 and 13.2 for the meaning and form codes). The study clearly demonstrated that meaning was emphasized when the children were 2

TABLE 13.2
Coding Scheme for the Form Component of Print
(Includes Maternal Comments and Questions)

Aspect of Form	Description
Spelling	Partially or completely spelling words.
Writing	Any comment or cue about writing letters/words ("You can write that").
Word awareness	"What does this say?" "This is a hard (long) word."
Alphabet range & sequence	Saying or singing all or part of the alphabet; general knowledge of alphabet sequence.
Letter name	Individual letter names; saying all or part of the alphabet.
Letter sound	Single sound; sound reiteration (e.g., /b/, /b/, /b/ ...); onomatopoetic sounds for letters.
Letter shape	
Identification	Of shape, with gesture or tracing with finger in the book.
Matching shape	Finding a letter that matches another letter's shape; discuss similar letter shapes.
Case identification	Upper and lower case.
Associations	
Letter–word/picture	"A is for apple," "That begins with A," or attempts to get a label for the association (e.g., "A is for ... what? ... what's that?").
Sound–letter	Identifying the sound that a letter stands for.
Sound–word	Identifying sounds in words; such as, "/k/ is for cat" or "/k/ is for ... what?"
Sound reiteration–word	Repeating a sound and identifying it with a word, "/k/-/k/-/k/-cat."
Sound reiteration–letter	Repeating a letter name and identifying it with a letter, "/d/-/d/-D-D."

years old (see Fig. 13.4). This was true even when the book being shared was an alphabet book designed to present children with early form–meaning (initial letter–word) correspondences. The mothers continued to focus exclusively on meaning when sharing storybooks or rhyming books, even when their children were 3 and 4 years old. When discussing the alphabet books, however, they began emphasizing the form component of print and early

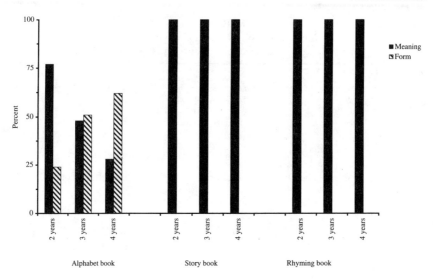

FIG. 13.4. Percentages of total maternal utterances focused on form and meaning while sharing alphabet, story, and rhyming books when children are 2, 3, and 4 years old ($n = 10$).

form–meaning correspondences in the majority of their utterances by the time their children were 3 years of age.

The findings for the 4-year-olds in the longitudinal study were replicated in a second study involving 24 children between 3 years, 6 months, and 4 years of age (van Kleeck, Gillam, & Breshears, 1998). Here again, the mothers read a storybook, a rhyming book, and an alphabet book (see Fig. 13.5). Neither form nor early form–meaning correspondences were ever mentioned by the mothers as they shared the story and rhyming books, but both were clearly emphasized when they read the alphabet book. Furthermore, the transcripts of the alphabet book interactions made it very clear that these mothers were making a conscious effort to teach their children about letter names, shapes, and sounds. For example, in reference to the letters in the alphabet book, the mothers said things like, "You know that one. We've been working on that one. Don't you remember? That's a 'B.' That makes the /b/ sound. /b/, /b/, /b/, like in ball."

Taken together, these two studies indicate that, at first, mothers attempt to help their preschoolers understand that print is meaningful. They often treated even alphabet books as if they were regular picture books without letters in them. However, by the time the children were 3 years old—and even more so when the children were 4—these mothers made it abundantly clear that they were very concerned with teaching their children about print form. Even so, the meaning component of print was certainly not abandoned: during storybook and rhyming book sharing the mothers continued to focus exclusively on print

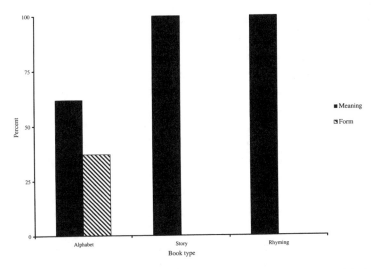

FIG. 13.5. Percentages of total maternal utterances focused on form and meaning while sharing alphabet, story, and rhyming books with preschool children (mean age = 3;6; n = 28).

meaning. It should be noted, however, that this may not have been due simply to the mothers' intentions. Children certainly influence the nature of their interactions with adults, including book sharing interactions. It is possible that children's growing interest in letters may in some cases be at least as much of a determinant on the process of alphabet book sharing as maternal intent.

By learning that print is useful, children are developing an attitudinal basis for later reading development. In the second stage of emerging literacy development, the meaning of print remains an important focus. However, children are also learning in separate activities about aspects of print form, which will be increasingly integrated with meaning as they begin actually decoding print. The second stage begins to introduce print form by fostering alphabet knowledge in some contexts.

Research on book sharing with preschoolers has rarely taken into account these two stages of preliteracy development, with the different kinds of interaction and learning that take place during each. The role of book sharing in the preliteracy development of young children could be more clearly ascertained if the domains of learning were related to more specific kinds of literacy experiences, and the child's age and developmental level were taken into account.

CONCLUSION

In this chapter, I have discussed a broad array of issues that would likely help future researchers clarify the role that book sharing with preschoolers plays in fostering various aspects of their language and preliteracy skills, as well as their subsequent literacy development. However, for the most part I have considered these issues in a relatively isolated fashion. As research in this area continues, it will be critical to consider even greater complexities than I have explored here. Undoubtedly, the areas of preliteracy development and aspects of book sharing interact in complex ways.

I offer as one example a line of research, recently discussed by Whitehurst and Lonigan (2001) and Goswami (2001), which has begun to find relationships between vocabulary and phonological awareness development. One possible reason for this relationship is "lexical restructuring" (Fowler, 1991; Metsala, 1999; Metsala & Walley, 1998; Walley, 1993), which hypothesizes that as children's vocabularies get larger, it becomes inefficient for them to store words as whole sound sequences, thus forcing them to rely on smaller and smaller units of phonological representation over time. As such, children's phonological representations of words become increasingly segmented, moving from syllables to onsets and rimes, and then individual phonemes. Since these smaller units of representation can be shared by many words, storage is more efficient and retrieval easier. Because words are composed of these smaller sound units, children can access the units and hence demonstrate phonological awareness or sensitivity.

Goswami (2001) discussed a far more specific relationship between vocabulary and phonological awareness. Words that share phonological similarities are referred to as "phonological neighbors"—English has a prevalence of rime neighbors, for example (De Cara & Goswami, 1999). Where there are many neighbors, the neighborhood is dense; where there are few, it is more sparsely populated. Reasoning that "restructuring theory proposes that implicit comparisons between similar-sounding words constitute the basis for the emergence of phonological awareness," De Cara and Goswami (1999) compared rhyming awareness in 4-, 5-, and 6-year-olds for word pairs from "dense" and "sparse" neighborhoods. They found, as expected, that children at all three age levels made significantly more accurate rhyming judgments about words from dense neighborhoods than they did for words from sparse neighborhoods. Metsala (1999) obtained similar findings for a phoneme blending task conducted with 3- and 4-year-olds.

These investigations suggest one way in which book sharing research might illuminate the relationship between vocabulary and phonological awareness. Very little work has been done with rhyming books to date. Specific rhyming books might make particular lexical neighborhoods more salient to children, and by enhancing their vocabulary and increasing the density of the lexical neighborhood, might simultaneously enhance children's phonological awareness of rhymes from within that same neighborhood.

This is only one example of the kinds of interactions that might be considered in future book sharing research. Undoubtedly, there are many other such relationships to examine between preliteracy skills and the contexts, materials, and interactional styles that foster them.

ACKNOWLEDGMENTS

I would like to thank Lisa Hammett and Judy Vander Woude for their helpful editorial suggestions and their insightful comments on ideas presented in this chapter, and T. J. Ragan for her help in putting together the references.

REFERENCES

Adams, M. (1990). *Beginning to read: Thinking and learning about print.* Cambridge, MA: MIT Press.

Anderson-Yockel, J., & Haynes, W. O. (1994). Joint book-reading strategies in working-class African American and White mother–toddler dyads. *Journal of Speech and Hearing Research, 37,* 583–593.

Arnold, D., Lonigan, C., Whitehurst, G., & Epstein, J. (1994). Accelerating language development through picture-book reading: Replication and extension to a videotape training format. *Journal of Educational Psychology, 86,* 235–243.

Ball, E., & Blachman, B. (1988). Phoneme segmentation training: Effect on reading readiness. *Annals of Dyslexia, 38,* 208–225.

Ball, E., & Blachman, B. (1991). Does phoneme awareness training in kindergarten make a difference in early word recognition and developmental spelling? *Reading Research Quarterly, 26*(1), 49–66.

Beals, D., De Temple, J., & Dickinson, D. K. (1994). Talking and listening that support early literacy development of children from low-income families. In D. Dickinson (Ed.), *Bridges to literacy: Children, families, and schools* (pp. 19–40). Cambridge, MA: Blackwell.

Blachman, B. (1994). Early literacy acquisition: The role of phonological awareness. In G. Wallach & K. Butler (Eds.), *Language learning disabilities in school-age children and adolescents: Some principles and applications* (pp. 251–274). New York: Macmillan.

Blank, M., Rose, S. A., & Berlin, L. J. (1978a). *The language of learning: The preschool years.* New York: Grune & Stratton.

Blank, M., Rose, S. A., & Berlin, L. J. (1978b). *Preschool language assessment instrument: The language of learning in practice.* New York: Grune & Stratton.

Bowey, J., & Francis, J. (1991). Phonological analysis as a function of age and exposure to reading instruction. *Applied Psycholinguistics, 12,* 91–121.

Bradley, L., & Bryant, P. (1983). Categorizing sounds and learning to read: A causal connection. *Nature, 30,* 419–421.

Bradley, L., & Bryant, P. (1985). *Rhyme and reason in reading and spelling.* Ann Arbor, MI: University of Michigan Press.

Bradshaw, M. L., Norris, J. A., & Hoffman, P. R. (1998). Efficacy of expansions and cloze procedures in the development of interpretations by preschool children exhibiting delayed language development. *Language, Speech, and Hearing Services in Schools, 29*, 85–95.

Brady, S. (1991). The role of working memory in reading disability. In S. Brady & D. Shankweiler (Eds.), *Phonological processes in literacy* (pp. 129–152). Mahwah, NJ: Lawrence Erlbaum Associates.

Bryant, P., MacLean, M., & Bradley, L. (1990). Rhyme, language, and children's reading. *Applied Psycholinguistics, 11*, 237–252.

Bus, A. G., & van IJzendoorn, M. H. (1988). Mother–child interactions, attachment, and emergent literacy: A cross-sectional study. *Child Development, 59*, 1262–1272.

Bus, A. G., van IJzendoorn, M. H., & Pellegrini, A. D. (1995). Joint book reading makes for success in learning to read: A meta-analysis on intergenerational transmission of literacy. *Review of Educational Research, 65*(1), 1–21.

Byrne, B., & Fielding-Barnsley, R. (1991). Evaluation of a program to teach phonemic awareness to young children. *Journal of Educational Psychology, 83*, 451–455.

Carlisle, J. F. (1991). Questioning the psychological reality of onset-rime as a level of phonological awareness. In S. A. Brady & D. P. Shankweiler (Eds.), *Phonological processes in literacy: A tribute to Isabelle Y. Liberman* (pp. 85–96). Mahwah, NJ: Lawrence Erlbaum Associates.

Chall, J. (1983). *Stages of reading development*. New York: McGraw Hill.

Chaney, C. (1989). I pledge a legiance to the flag: Three studies in word segmentation. *Applied Psycholinguistics, 10*(3), 261–281.

Collins, A., & Stevens, A. (1982). Goals and strategies of inquiring teachers. In R. Glaser (Ed.), *Advances in instructional psychology* (Vol. 2, pp. 65–119). Mahwah, NJ: Lawrence Erlbaum Associates.

Cornell, E. H., Sénéchal, M., & Broda, L. S. (1988). Recall of picture books by 3-year-old children: Testing and repetition effects in joint reading activities. *Journal of Educational Psychology, 80*(4), 537–542.

Crain-Thoreson, C., & Dale, P. S. (1992). Do early talkers become early readers? Linguistic precocity, preschool language, and early reading. *Developmental Psychology, 28*, 421–429.

Crain-Thoreson, C., & Dale, P. S. (1999). Enhancing linguistic performance: Parents and teachers as book reading partners for children with language delays. *Topics in Early Childhood Special Education, 19*(1), 28–39.

Crowe, L. K. (2000). Reading behaviors of mothers and their children with language impairment during repeated storybook reading. *Journal of Communication Disorders, 33*, 503–524.

Dale, P. S., Crain-Thoreson, C., Notari-Syverson, A., & Cole, K. (1996). Parent–child book reading as an intervention technique for young children with language delays. *Topics in Early Childhood Special Education, 16*(2), 213–235.

DeBaryshe, B. D. (1992). *Final report for the project Early Literacy and Literacy Activities in the Home*. Washington, DC: U.S. Department of Education Field Initiated Studies Program. (ERIC Document Reproduction Service No. ED 351 406).

DeBaryshe, B. D. (1993). Joint picture-book reading correlates of early oral language skill. *Journal of Child Language, 20*, 455–461.

DeBaryshe, B. D., Caulfield, M. B., Witty, J. P., Sidden, J., Holt, H. E., & Reich, C. E. (1991, April). *The ecology of young children's home reading environments*. Paper presented at the Meeting of the Society for Research in Child Development, Seattle, WA.

DeCara, B., & Goswami, V. (1999). *Phonological neighborhood density, sonority profile and the development of rime processing*. Manuscript submitted for publication.

DeLoache, J. S., & DeMendoza, A. P. (1987). Joint picturebook interactions of mothers and 1-year-old children. *British Journal of Developmental Psychology, 5,* 111–123.

Delpit, L. (1995). *Other people's children: Cultural conflict in the classroom.* New York: The New Press.

Denny, J. P. (1991). Rational thought in oral culture and literate decontextualization. In D. O. N. Torrance (Ed.), *Literacy and orality* (pp. 66–89). Cambridge: Cambridge University Press.

De Temple, J., & Snow, C. (1996). Styles of parent–child book-reading as related to mothers' views of literacy and children's literacy outcomes. In J. Shimron (Ed.), *Literacy and education: Essays in honor of Dina Feitelson.* Cresskill, NJ: Hampton Press.

Dickinson, D., De Temple, J., Hirschler, J., & Smith, M. (1992). Book reading with preschoolers: Coconstruction of text at home and at school. *Early Childhood Research Quarterly, 7,* 323–346.

Dickinson, D. K., & Keebler, R. (1989). Variation in preschool teacher's style of reading books. *Discourse Processes, 12*(3), 353–376.

Donachy, W. (1976). Parent participation in pre-school education. *British Journal of Educational Psychology, 46,* 31–39.

Donaldson, M. (1978). *Children's minds.* New York: Norton.

Downing, J. (1979). *Reading and reasoning.* New York: Springer-Verlag.

Dunn, N. E. (1981). Children's achievement at school-entry age as a function of mothers' and fathers' teaching sets. *Elementary School Journal, 81,* 245–253.

Dunning, D. B., Mason, J. M., & Stewart, J. P. (1994). Reading to preschoolers: A response to Scarborough and Dobrich (1994) and recommendations for future research. *Developmental Review, 14,* 324–339.

Ehri, L. (1976). Word learning in beginning readers and prereaders: Effects of form class and defining contexts. *Journal of Educational Psychology, 68,* 832–842.

Elley, W. B. (1989). Vocabulary acquisition from listening to stories. *Reading Research Quarterly, 24,* 174–187.

Ellis, N., & Large, B. (1987). The development of reading: As you seek so shall you find. *British Journal of Psychology, 78,* 1–28.

Elster, C. A. (1998). Influences of text and pictures on shared and emergent readings. *Research in the Teaching of English, 32*(1), 43–78.

Evans, M. A., Shaw, D., & Bell, M. (2000). Home literacy activities and their influence on early literacy skills. *Canadian Journal of Experimental Psychology, 54*(2), 65–75.

Fagan, W. T., & Hayden, H. R. (1988). Parent–child interaction in favorite and unfamiliar stories. *Reading Research and Instruction, 27*(2), 47–55.

Feagans, L., & Short, E. J. (1984). Developmental differences in the comprehension and production of narratives by reading-disabled and normally achieving children. *Child Development, 55,* 1727–1736.

Fenson, L., Reznick, H., Thal, D., Bates, E., Hartung, J., Pethnick, S., & Reilly, J. (1993). *MacArthur Communicative Development Inventories (CDI).* San Diego: Singular Publishing.

Fey, M. (1986). *Language intervention with young children.* San Diego: College-Hill.

Fowler, A. E. (1991). How early phonological development might set the stage for phoneme awareness. In B. Shankweiler (Ed.), *Phonological processes in literacy* (pp. 97–117). Hillsdale, NJ: Lawrence Erlbaum Associates.

Fox, B., & Routh, D. K. (1975). Analyzing spoken language into words, syllables, and phonemes: A developmental study. *Journal of Psycholinguistic Research, 4*(4), 331–342.

Garner, R., & Alexander, P. (1982). Strategic processing of text: An investigation of the effects on adults' question-answering performance. *Journal of Educational Research, 75,* 144–148.

Gathercole, S., & Baddeley, A. (1990). Phonological memory deficits in language disordered children: Is there a causal connection? *Journal of Memory and Language, 29,* 336–360.

Gebers, J. L. (1990). *Books are for talking too! A sourcebook for using children's literature in speech and language remediation.* Tucson: Communication Skill Builders.

Gibson, E., & Levin, H. S. (1975). *The psychology of reading.* Cambridge, MA: MIT Press.

Goodman, J., Larrivee, L., Roberts, J., Heller, A., & Fritz, D. (2000, November). *Parental prompts by syntactic category and prompt type.* Paper presented at The American Speech-Language-Hearing Association Annual Convention, Washington, DC.

Goodman, Y. (1986). Children coming to know literacy. In W. Teale & E. Sulzby (Eds.), *Emergent literacy.* Norwood, NJ: Ablex.

Goodsitt, J., Raitan, J. G., & Perlmutter, M. (1988). Interaction between mothers and preschool children when reading a novel and familiar book. *International Journal of Behavioral Development, 11*(4), 489–505.

Goswami, U. (2001). Early phonological development and the acquisition of literacy. In S. B. Neuman & D. K. Dickinson (Eds.), *Handbook of early literacy development.* New York: Guilford Press.

Goswami, U., & Bryant, P. (1990). *Phonological skills and learning to read.* Mahwah, NJ: Lawrence Erlbaum Associates.

Gough, P., & Tunmer, W. E. (1986). Decoding reading, and reading disability. *Remedial and Special Education, 1,* 6–10.

Haden, C. A., Reese, E., & Fivush, R. (1996). Mother's extratextual comments during storybook reading: Stylistic differences over time and across texts. *Discourse Processes, 21,* 135–169.

Halliday, M. A. K., & Hasan, R. (1976). *Cohesion in English.* London: Longman.

Hanmaker, C. (1986). The effects of adjunct questions on prose learning. *Review of Educational Research, 56,* 212–242.

Hargrave, A. C., & Sénéchal, M. (2000). A book reading intervention with preschool children who have limited vocabularies: The benefits of regular reading and dialogic reading. *Early Childhood Research Quarterly, 15*(1), 75–90.

Harkins, D. A., Koch, P. E., & Michel, G. F. (1994). Listening to maternal story telling affects narrative skill of 5-year-old children. *The Journal of Genetic Psychology, 155,* 246–257.

Hart, B., & Risley, T. R. (1999). *The social world of learning to talk.* Baltimore: Brookes.

Heath, S. B. (1982). What no bedtime story means: Narrative skills at home and school. *Language in Society, 11,* 49–76.

Heath, S. B. (1983). *Ways with words: Language, life, and work in communities and classrooms.* Cambridge: Cambridge University Press.

Heath, S. B. (1989). The learner as cultural member. In M. Rice & R. Scheifelbusch (Eds.), *The teachability of language.* Baltimore: Brookes.

Hockenberger, E. H., Goldstein, H., & Haas, L. S. (1999). Effects of commenting during joint book reading by mothers with low SES. *Topics in Early Childhood Special Education, 19*(1), 15–27.

Hunt, K. W. (1970). Syntactic maturity in school children and adults. *Society for Research in Child Development Mimeographs* (1), 134–135.

Jenkins, J. R., Stein, M. L., & Wysocki, K. (1984). Learning vocabulary through reading. *American Educational Research Journal, 21,* 767–787.

Jorm, A. F., & Share, D. L. (1983). Phonological recoding and reading acquisition. *Applied Psycholinguistics, 4,* 103–147.

Justice, L. M., & Ezell, H. K. (2002). Use of storybook reading to increase print awareness in at-risk children. *American Journal of Speech Language Pathology, 11,* 17–29.

Justice, L. M., Weber, S. E., Ezell, H. K., & Bakeman, R. (2002). A sequential analysis of children's responsiveness to parental print references during shared book reading interactions. *American Journal of Speech Language Pathology, 11,* 30–40.

Leseman, P. P. M., & de Jong, P. F. (1998). Home literacy: Opportunity, instruction, cooperation and social-emotional quality predicting early reading achievement. *Reading Research Quarterly, 33*(3), 294–318.

Lomax, R., & McGee, L. (1987). Young children's concepts about print and reading: Toward a model of word reading acquisition. *Reading Research Quarterly, 22,* 237–256.

Lonigan, C. J. (1991). *Environmental influences on language acquisition: An examination of the maternal-input hypothesis in the context of a picture book reading intervention.* Unpublished doctoral dissertation, State University of New York, Stony Brook, NY.

Lonigan, C. J. (1993). Somebody read me a story: Evaluation of a shared reading program in low-income daycare. *Society for Research in Child Development Abstracts, 9,* 219.

Lonigan, C. J. (1994). Reading to preschoolers exposed: Is the emperor really naked? *Developmental Review, 14,* 303–323.

Lonigan, C. J., Anthony, J. L., Dyer, S. M., & Collins, K. (1995). Evaluation of a language enrichment program for pre-school aged children from low-income backgrounds. *Association for the Advancement of Behavior Therapy Abstracts, 2,* 365.

Lundberg, I., Olofsson, A., & Wall, S. (1980). Reading and spelling skills in the first school years predicted from phonemic awareness skills in kindergarten. *Scandinavian Journal of Psychology, 21,* 159–173.

Lundberg, I., Frost, J., & Petersen, O. (1988). Effects of an extensive program for stimulating phonological awareness in preschool children. *Reading Research Quarterly, 23*(3), 268–284.

Mandler, J., & Johnson, N. (1977). Remembrance of things parsed: Story structure and recall. *Cognitive Psychology, 9,* 111–151.

Mann, V. A., & Liberman, I. Y. (1984). Phonological awareness and verbal short-term memory. *Journal of Learning Disabilities, 17*(10), 592–599.

Martin, L. (1998). Early book reading: How mothers deviate from printed text for young children. *Reading Research and Instruction, 37,* 137–160.

Martin, L. E., & Reutzel, D. R. (1999). Sharing books: Examining how and why mothers deviate from the print. *Reading Research and Instruction, 39*(1), 39–70.

Martinez, M., & Roser, N. (1985). A case study of the effects of selected text factors on parent–child story time interactions. In J. A. Niles & R. V. Lalik (Eds.), *Issues in literacy: A research perspective. Thirty-fourth yearbook of the National Reading Conference* (pp. 168–174). Chicago: National Reading Conference.

Mason, J. (1980). When do children begin to read: An exploration of four-year-old children's letter and word reading competencies. *Reading Research Quarterly, 15,* 203–227.

Mason, J., & Dunning, D. (1986, April). *Toward a model relating home literacy with beginning reading.* Paper presented at the annual meeting of the American Educational Research Association, San Francisco, CA.

Mason, J., Peterman, C., & Kerr, B. (1989). Reading to kindergarten children. In D. Strickland & L. Morrow (Eds.), *Emerging literacy: Young children learn to read and write* (pp. 52–62). Newark, DE: International Reading Association.

McCormick, C., & Mason, J. M. (1986). *Use of little books at home: A minimal intervention strategy that fosters early reading* (Tech. Rep. No. 388). Champaign, IL: University of Illinois at Urbana-Champaign.

McFadden, T. U. (1998). Sounds and stories: Teaching phonemic awareness in interactions around text. *American Journal of Speech Language Pathology, 7*(2), 5–13.

McGillicuddy-DeLisi, A. V. (1982). The relationship between parents' beliefs about development and family constellation, socioeconomic status, and parents' teaching strategies. In L. Laosa & I. Sigel (Eds.), *Families as learning environments for children* (pp. 261–299). New York: Plenum.

McNeill, J. H., & Fowler, S. A. (1999). Let's talk: Encouraging mother–child conversations during story reading. *Journal of Early Intervention, 22*(1), 51–69.

Mehan, H. (1979). *Learning lessons*. Cambridge, MA: Harvard University Press.

Merritt, D. D., & Liles, B. Z. (1987). Story grammar ability in children with and without language disorder: Story generation, story retelling, and story comprehension. *Journal of Speech and Hearing Research, 30,* 539–551.

Metsala, J. L. (1999). Young children's phonological awareness and nonword repetition as a function of vocabulary development. *Journal of Educational Psychology, 91,* 3–19.

Metsala, J. L., & Walley, A. C. (1998). Spoken vocabulary growth and the segmental restructuring of lexical representations: Precursors to phonemic awareness and early reading ability. In J. L. Metsala & L. C. Ehri (Eds.), *Word recognition in beginning literacy* (pp. 89–120). Mahwah, NJ: Lawrence Erlbaum Associates.

Morais, J. (1991). Constraints in the development of phonemic awareness. In S. B. D. Shankweiler (Ed.), *Phonological processes in literacy* (pp. 5–27). Mahwah, NJ: Lawrence Erlbaum Associates.

Morrow, L. M. (1988). Young children's responses to one-to-one story readings in school settings. *Reading Research Quarterly, 23*(1), 89–107.

Neuman, S. B., Hagedorn, T., Celano, D., & Daly, P. (1995). Toward a collaborative approach to parent involvement in early education: A study of teenage mothers in an African-American community. *American Educational Research Journal, 32*(4), 801–827.

Ninio, A., & Bruner, J. (1978). The achievement and antecedents of labeling. *Journal of Child Language, 5,* 1–15.

Ogbu, J. U. (1990). Minority status and literacy in comparative perspective. *Daedalus, 119,* 141–168.

Palincsar, A. S., & Brown. A. L. (1984). Reciprocal teaching of comprehension-fostering and comprehension-monitoring activities. *Cognition and Instruction, 1*(2), 117–175.

Pappas, C. (1993). Is "narrative" primary? Some insights from kindergartners' pretend reading of stories and information books. *Journal of Reading Behavior, 25,* 97–129.

Pellegrini, A. D. (2001). Some theoretical and methodological considerations in studying literacy in social context. In S. B. Neuman & D. K. Dickinson (Eds.), *Handbook of early literacy development*. New York: Guilford Press.

Pellegrini, A. D., Brody, G. H., & Sigel, I. E. (1985). Parents' book-reading habits with their children. *Journal of Educational Psychology, 77*(3), 332–340.

Pellegrini, A. D., & Galda, L. (1998). *The development of school-based literacy: A social ecological perspective*. London: Routledge.

Pellegrini, A. D., Galda, L., Bartini, M., & Charak, D. (1998). Oral language and literacy learning in context: The role of social relationships. *Merrill-Palmer Quarterly, 44,* 38–54.

Pellegrini, A. D., Perlmutter, J. C., Galda, L., & Brody, G. H. (1990). Joint reading between Black Head Start children and their mothers. *Child Development, 61,* 443–453.

Peterson, C., & McCabe, A. (1983). *Developmental psycholinguistics: Three ways of looking at a child's narrative*. New York: Plenum.

Phillips, G., & McNaughton, S. (1990). The practice of storybook reading to preschool children in mainstream New Zealand families. *Reading Research Quarterly, 25*(3), 196–212.

Purcell-Gates, V. (1988). Lexical and syntactic knowledge of written narrative held by well-read-to kindergartners and second graders. *Research in the Teaching of English, 22,* 128–160.

Purcell-Gates, V. (1996). Stories, coupons, and the TV Guide: Relationships between home literacy experiences and emergent literacy knowledge. *Reading Research Quarterly, 31*(4), 406–428.

Rapala, M., & Brady, S. (1990). Reading ability and short-term memory: The role of phonological processing. *Reading and Writing, 2,* 1–25.

Reese, E., & Cox, A. (1999). Quality of adult book reading affects children's emergent literacy. *Developmental Psychology, 35,* 20–28.

Reid, D. K. (2000). Discourse in classrooms, *Language development, differences, and disorders* (pp. 3–38). Austin, TX: Pro-ed.

Robinson, F., & Sulzby, E. (1984). Parents, children, and "favorite" books: An interview study. In J. Niles & L. Harris (Eds.), *Changing perspectives on research in reading/language: Thirty-third yearbook of the National Reading Conference* (pp. 54–59). Rochester, NY: National Reading Conference.

Roth, F. P., & Spekman, N. J. (1986). Narrative discourse: Spontaneously generated stories of learning-disabled and normally achieving students. *Journal of Speech and Hearing Disorders, 52,* 8–23.

Sawyer, D. (1987). *Test of awareness of language segments (TALS).* Rockville, MD: Aspen.

Scarborough, H. S. (1991). Early syntactic development of dyslexic children. *Annals of Dyslexia, 41,* 207–220.

Scarborough, H. S. (1998). Early identification of children at risk for reading disabilities: Phonological awareness and some other promising predictors. In B. K. Shapiro, P. J. Accardo, & A. J. Capute (Eds.), *Specific reading disability: A view of the spectrum* (pp. 75–119). Timonium, MD: York Press.

Scarborough, H. S. (2001). Connecting early language and literacy to later reading (dis)abilities: Evidence, theory, and practice. In S. B. Neuman & D. K. Dickinson (Eds.), *Handbook of early literacy development.* New York: Guilford Press.

Scarborough, H. S., & Dobrich, W. (1994). On the efficacy of reading to preschoolers. *Developmental Review, 14,* 245–302.

Scollon, R., & Scollon, S. (1981). *Narrative and face in inter-ethnic communication.* Norwood, NJ: Ablex.

Seidenberg, M. S., & McClelland, J. L. (1989). A distributed, developmental model of word recognition and naming. *Psychological Review, 96*(4), 523–568.

Sénéchal, M. (1997). The differential effect of storybook reading on preschoolers' acquisition of expressive and receptive vocabulary. *Journal of Child Language, 24,* 123–128.

Sénéchal, M., & Cornell, E. H. (1993). Vocabulary acquisition through shared reading experiences. *Reading Research Quarterly, 28*(4), 360–374.

Sénéchal, M., Thomas E., & Monker, J. (1995). Individual differences in 4-year-old children's acquisition of vocabulary during storybook reading. *Journal of Educational Psychology, 87*(2), 218–229.

Sénéchal, M., LeFevre, J. A., Thomas, E., & Daley, K. (1998). Differential effects of home literacy experiences on the development of oral and written language. *Reading Research Quarterly, 33*(1), 96–116.

Sigel, I. E., & McGillicuddy-DeLisi, A. V. (1984). Parents as teachers of their children: A distancing behavior model. In A. D. Pellegrini & T. D. Yawkey (Eds.), *The development of oral and written language in social contexts* (pp. 71–91). Norwood, NJ: Ablex.

Smolkin, L. B., Yaden, D. B., Brown, L., & Hofius, B. (1992). The effects of genre, visual design choices, and discourse structure on preschoolers' responses to picture books during parent–child read-alouds. In C. K. Kinzer & D. J. Leu (Eds.), *Literacy research, theory, and practice: Views from many perspectives. Forty-first yearbook of the National Reading Conference* (pp. 291–301). Chicago: National Reading Conference.

Snow, C. (1981). Literacy and language: Relationships during the preschool years. *Harvard Educational Review, 53,* 165–189.

Snow, C., & Goldfield, B. (1981). Building stories: The emergence of information structures from conversation. In D. Tannen (Ed.), *Analyzing discourse: Text and talk* (pp. 127–141). Washington, DC: Georgetown University Press.

Snow, C. E., & Ninio, A. (1986). The contracts of literacy: What children learn from learning to read books. In W. H. Teale & E. Sulzby (Eds.), *Emergent literacy: Writing and reading* (pp. 116–137). Norwood, NJ: Ablex.

Sorsby, A. J., & Martlew, M. (1991). Representational demands in mothers' talk to preschool children in two contexts: Picture book reading and a modeling task. *Journal of Child Language, 18,* 373–395.

Spencer, B. (1986). The concept of *word* in young children: Tacit and explicit awareness of children at different operational levels. In J. Niles & R. Lalik (Eds.), *Solving problems in literacy: Learners, teachers, and researchers* (pp. 271–280). Rochester, NY: National Reading Conference.

Stahl, S. A., & Miller, P. D. (1989). Whole language and language experience approaches for beginning reading: A quantitative research synthesis. *Review of Educational Research, 59*(1), 87–116.

Stahl, S. A., McKenna, M. C., & Pagnucco, J. R. (1994). The effects of whole language instruction: An update and a reappraisal. *Educational Psychologist, 29*(4), 175–185.

Stanovich, K. (1992). Speculation on the causes and consequences of individual differences in early reading acquisition. In P. Gough, L. Ehri, & R. Treiman (Eds.), *Reading acquisition* (pp. 307–342). Mahwah, NJ: Lawrence Erlbaum Associates.

Stein, N., & Glenn, C. (1982). Children's concept of time: The development of a story schema. In W. Friedman (Ed.), *The developmental psychology of time* (pp. 255–282). New York: Academic Press.

Sulzby, E. (1983). A commentary on Ehri's critique of five studies related to letter-name knowledge and learning to read: Broadening the question. In L. Gentile, M. Kamil, & J. Blanchard (Eds.), *Reading research revisited* (pp. 155–161). Columbus, OH: Merrill.

Sulzby, E., & Teale, W. H. (1987). *Young children's storybook reading: Longitudinal study of parent–child interaction and children's independent functioning* (Final Report to the Spencer Foundation). Ann Arbor, MI: University of Michigan.

Treiman, R. (1992). The role of intrasyllabic units in learning to read and spell. In P. B. Gough, L. C. Ehri, & R. Treiman (Eds.), *Reading acquisition* (pp. 65–106). Mahwah, NJ: Lawrence Erlbaum Associates.

Valdés, G. (1996). *Con respeto: Bridging the distances between culturally diverse families and schools.* New York: Teachers College Press.

Valdez-Menchaca, M. C., & Whitehurst, G. J. (1992). Accelerating language development through picture-book reading: A systematic extension to Mexican day care. *Developmental Psychology, 28,* 1106–1114.

van Kleeck, A. (1994). Metalinguistic development. In G. Wallach & K. Butler (Eds.), *Language learning disabilities in school-age children and adolescents: Some principles and applications* (pp. 53–98). New York: Merrill.

van Kleeck, A. (1998). Preliteracy domains and stages: Laying the foundations for beginning reading. *Journal of Children's Communication Development, 20*(1), 33–51.

van Kleeck, A., & Beckley-McCall, A. (2002). A comparison of mothers' individual and simultaneous book sharing with preschool siblings: An exploratory study of five families. *American Journal of Speech-Language Pathology, 11,* 175–189.

van Kleeck, A., Gillam, R., & Breshears, K. D. (1998, November). *Effects of book genre on mother's emphasis on print meaning and form during book sharing.* Paper presented at the annual convention of the American Speech-Language-Hearing Association, San Antonio, TX.

van Kleeck, A., Gillam, R., Hamilton, L., & McGrath, C. (1997). The relationship between middle-class parents' book-sharing discussion and their preschoolers' abstract language development. *Journal of Speech-Language-Hearing Research, 40,* 1261–1271.

van Kleeck, A., Gillam, R., & McFadden, T. (1998). A study of classroom-based phonological awareness training for preschoolers with speech and/or language disorders. *American Journal of Speech-Language Pathology, 7*(3), 65–76.

van Kleeck, A., & Schuele, M. (1987). Precursors to literacy: Normal development. *Topics in Language Disorders, 7*(2), 13–31.

van Kleeck, A., Vigil, A., & Beer, N. (1998, November). *A longitudinal study of maternal book-sharing emphasis on print from and print meaning with preschoolers.* Paper presented at the annual convention of the American Speech-Language-Hearing Association, San Antonio, TX.

Vigil, A., & van Kleeck, A. (1996). Clinical language teaching: Theories and principles to guide our responses when children miss our language targets. In M. Smith & J. Damico (Eds.), *Childhood language disorders* (pp. 64–96). New York: Thieme.

Vygotsky, L. S. (1978). *Mind in society: The development of higher psychological processes* (M. Cole, V. John-Steiner, S. Scribner, & E. Souberman, Eds. & Trans.). Cambridge, MA: Harvard University Press.

Wagner, R. K., & Torgesen, J. K. (1987). The nature of phonological processing and its causal role in the acquisition of reading skills. *Psychological Bulletin, 101*(2), 192–212.

Walker, D., Greenwood, C., Hart, B., & Carta, J. (1994). Prediction of school outcomes based on early language production and socioeconomic factors. *Child Development, 65,* 606–621.

Walley, A. (1993). The role of vocabulary development in children's spoken word recognition and segmentation ability. *Developmental Review, 13,* 286–350.

Warren, W. H., Nicholas, D. W., & Trabasso, T. (1979). Event chains and inferences in understanding narratives. In R. O. Freedle (Ed.), *New directions in discourse processing* (pp. 23–52). Norwood, NJ: Ablex.

Waters, G., Caplan, D., & Hildebrandt, N. (1987). Working memory and written sentence comprehension. In M. Coltheart (Ed.), *Attention and performance XII: The psychology of reading* (pp. 531–555). Mahwah, NJ: Lawrence Erlbaum Associates.

Watson, R. (2001). Literacy and oral language: Implications for early language acquisition. In S. B. Neuman & D. K. Dickinson (Eds.), *Handbook of early literacy development* (pp. 43–53). New York: Guilford Press.

Wells, G. (1985). Preschool literacy-related activities and success in school. In D. R. Olson, N. Torrance, & A. Hildyard (Eds.), *Literacy, language, and learning: The nature and consequences of reading and writing* (pp. 229–253). Cambridge: Cambridge University Press.

Wells, G. (1987). The negotiation of meaning: Talking and learning at home and at school. In B. Fillion, C. Hedley, & E. DiMartino (Eds.), *Home and school: Early language and reading* (pp. 3–25). Norwood, NJ: Ablex.

Westby, C. (1994). The effects of culture on genre, structure, and style of oral and written texts. In G. Wallach & K. Butler (Eds.), *Language and learning disabilities in school-age children and adolescents: Some principles and applications* (pp. 180–218). New York: Merrill.

Wheeler, M. P. (1983). Context-related age changes in mothers' speech: Joint book reading. *Journal of Child Language, 10,* 259–263.

Whitehurst, G. J., Falco, F. L., Lonigan, C. J., Fischel, J. E., DeBaryshe, B. D., Valdez-Menchaca, M. C., & Caulfield, M. (1988). Accelerating language development through picture book reading. *Developmental Psychology, 24*(4), 552–559.

Whitehurst, G. J., Epstein, J. N., Angell, A. L., Payne, A. C., Crone, D. A., & Fischel, J. E. (1994). Outcomes of an emergent literacy intervention in Head Start. *Journal of Educational Psychology, 86*(4), 542–555.

Whitehurst, G. J., & Lonigan, C. J. (1998). Child development and emergent literacy. *Child Development, 69*(3), 848–872.

Whitehurst, G. J., & Lonigan, C. J. (2001). Emergent literacy: Development from prereaders to readers. In S. B. Neuman & D. K. Dickinson (Eds.), *Handbook of early literacy development* (pp. 11–29). New York: Guilford Press.

Yaden, D. B., Smolkin, L. B., & MacGillivray, L. (1993). A psychogenetic perspective on children's understanding about letter associations during alphabet book readings. *Journal of Reading Behavior, 25*(1), 43–68.

Yaden, D. B., Smolkin, L. B., & Conlon, A. (1989). Preschoolers' questions about pictures, print conventions, and story text during reading aloud at home. *Reading Research Quarterly, 24*(2), 188–214.

Zevenbergen, A., & Wilson, G. (1996, June). *Effects of an interactive reading program on the narrative skills of children in Head Start.* Paper presented at the Head Start's Third National Research Conference, Washington, DC.

14

Joint Reading as a Context: Explicating the Ways Context Is Created by Participants

A. D. Pellegrini
Lee Galda
University of Minnesota

Images of mothers reading to young children and of teachers reading to primary-grade students are among the most powerful icons of early literacy. Joint reading is an instructional context with almost sacred appeal for parents and teachers alike.

The study of book reading has also been critically important to the research community. Such studies, beginning with the work of Ninio and Bruner (1978), have been in the vanguard of a more general movement to study the social context of cognitive and language development. Despite the widespread and implicit acceptance of the value of book reading to children's early language and literacy learning (though see Bus, van IJzendoorn, & Pellegrini, 1995, for evidence on its effectiveness) and the incredible number of "social contextual" studies on the subject, we still have only a limited understanding of the complex social "context" in which transactions among children, adults, and text occur. In this chapter we look at what children may learn during joint reading. We then discuss our model of social context and how it relates to joint reading interactions.

WHAT GETS LEARNED IN JOINT READING?

Although the answer to the question of what is learned in joint reading contexts may at first seem obvious, the question is actually open to a number of interpretations. Some scholars would simply answer that reading itself is what is learned. Indeed, most researchers implicitly assume that interactions around books teach children the specific conventions associated with early school-based literacy. Teale (1984), a pioneer in this tradition, stated the idea most clearly: Children learn the conventions of print, such as grapheme-phoneme relations, and the idea that oral language can be expressed in print. Heath (1983) pointed to similarities between parents reading traditional storybooks to their children and the literacy events of early schooling. Important design features of joint reading include the use of narrative trade books and specific styles of verbal interaction, such as the question–answer routine.

In this view, the similarity in design features of literacy and joint reading events in middle-class homes and those in school accounts for children's success in school-based literacy (Bernstein, 1971; Cook-Gumperz, 1977; Heath, 1983). Specifically, mother–child and teacher–child reading events have children and adults looking at a very similar sample of children's books and talking about those books in very specific and similar ways. This overlap has been illustrated in the ways in which children are expected to tell stories in school (Michaels, 1981), to talk about books (Scollon & Scollon, 1981), and to talk to teachers and students during school literacy events (Bernstein, 1971; Cook-Gumperz, 1977). In joint reading with a parent, children generally learn to talk about words, stories, and characters, and to answer specific types of questions about these features. These patterns are similar to those expected in the classroom.

In this case, the power of book reading lies in the process of cultural transmission: Joint reading exposes children to reading conventions and provides them with countless opportunities to practice these skills. It is also probably the case that the skills learned in this context have minimal transfer to other cognitive domains; for example, we would not expect school-based literacy per se to affect other aspects of cognitive processing, such as categorization and abstract thinking. The work of Scribner and Cole (1978) on different varieties of literacy is consistent with these assumptions.

There is another explanation for the importance of joint reading, which is more cognitive than the "design features" argument presented earlier. From this cognitive view, literacy is more a particular extension of general cognitive processing, and less a set of discrete skills to be learned by themselves (Olson,

1977). Thus, in book reading, as in other sorts of interactions, parents help their children learn to reflect upon the thought- and meaning-making processes by asking them questions about language, text, and ideas (Wertsch, 1979). Accordingly, children's metacognition is seen to have its origins in the social interchange between children and their tutors. These dialogic strategies are eventually internalized by children into their private speech and thought. For example, while reading together, parents often ask their children to reflect upon the language and conventions used in the text (Pellegrini, Perlmutter, Galda, & Brody, 1990). In the course of responding, children come to use "meta" terms (e.g., *read; talk about; think*) and strategies (e.g., "Start here"; "Take your time"), which are indicative of their more general metalinguistic and metacognitive awareness. They then begin to practice using the "meta" terms learned in their book reading during pretend play with their peers, and during more realistic discourse with peers and adults (Pellegrini & Galda, 1991), eventually applying these concepts on their own in cognitively demanding circumstances, such as when reading.

Yet a third point of view suggests that book reading may really be a specific manifestation of more general social relationships between participants, and their associated emotional and cognitive processes. For example, as we address in the following discussion, children may construct "working models" of social relationships with their primary caregivers and then generalize these working models to other relationships. A securely attached child with a trusting view of the world will consequently develop synchronous interactions with other adults and peers. This trust should enable the child to take chances and explore unfamiliar territory. The combination of these factors should certainly result in children being successful in school, to the extent that they should get along well with teachers and peers, and should be willing to take chances with and explore new curriculum content.

WHAT IS A SOCIAL CONTEXT?

In this section we briefly outline some of the larger issues associated with studying social interaction around book reading. Discussions of joint reading are often part of a larger discussion about the social context of instruction and development, yet our understanding of the social dynamics of joint reading is generally limited to the study of its interactions. Interactions are behaviors exchanged between individuals (Hinde, 1980). Most of the research on book readings, and, indeed, on social influences on literacy, has taken place at this level of abstraction. For example, there have been numerous studies of the interactions between mothers and children and teachers and children while reading books (e.g., Pellegrini, Moshovaki, & Meadows, in press). Teacher and child behaviors are described, interrelated, and typically used to predict children's subsequent literacy. The assumption here is that adults socialize children into literacy practices.

We consider a context to be something jointly constructed by participants around a specific task. From this view social contexts are transactional: Adults do not merely socialize children, but children and adults have dynamic effects on each other, and these interactions vary, in turn, depending on the demands of the specific task at hand.

CONTEXT AS TRANSACTIONAL

There is a transactive relation between individuals and their social and physical surroundings. Individuals take an active role in choosing and creating context; they do not merely respond to it. That is, individuals choose and "furnish" environments and these environments, in turn, affect individuals: By this we mean that individuals choose to inhabit specific niches—within certain ranges, of course. Their choices reflect individual differences and preferences. As they occupy these niches individuals shape them in ways that are consistent with their differences. These factors, in turn, affect interactions and relationship between individuals.

This model of context, influenced by Hinde (1980), begins with individuals, who each have unique properties, such as temperament and different levels of competence with various tasks. Individuals also interact with other social actors, with whom they have different relationships.

An example may help make this more concrete. A shy child may seek out interactions with a limited and familiar cadre of adults who share their behavioral propensities (e.g., quiet talk, close physical contact, and strong positive affect). When the adult and child interact with each other, they create an environment that supports and encourages these sorts of behaviors. They may choose to read a book rather than engage in rough-and-tumble play, or to play with replica toys. Each individual initiates behaviors and responds to the contingencies of others' interactions that are in some ways unique to that particular relationship. So, a child may interact with his father in one way and his mother in another.

Individuals' selection of a specific text around which to interact is an example of choosing a context, furnishing it with relevant interactions, and being influenced by it. Individuals choose a specific book or type of text around which to interact. The choice of text is based on experiential factors, such as the forms of text found in the home (Heath, 1983; Pellegrini et al., 1990) and temperament factors (active youngsters may prefer texts that elicit loud responses from participants). The format and content of the text, in turn, affect the behaviors of the participants. Thus, the specific texts chosen by participants represent an important dimension of context. Individuals have preferences for different types of text and for different literary genres. The choice of specific text, as we will see, is an active bit of "niche furnishing," which affects interactions around those texts.

This view is in contrast to the more common view of social context—the socialization model—which has adults transmitting knowledge to children in ways consistent with variants of learning theory, such as social learning theory (e.g., modeling, imitation) or operant conditioning (successive approximation of desired responses). In such cases interaction is viewed as a unidirectional process, proceeding from the adult "tutor" to the less-skilled child or novice. The extent to which individual children contribute to the interaction process in ways that are separate from this socialization process is typically not specified. The adult's job is to help the child "internalize" the appropriate cognitive strategies, using teaching techniques such as modeling and reinforcement, which result in children learning adult-provided strategies (Whitehurst et al.,1988).

A MODEL OF SOCIAL CONTEXT FOR JOINT INTERACTION AROUND TEXT

The model presented in Table 14.1 suggests that individual-level factors (such as kinship and temperament), social relationships (such as attachment relationships and friendships), and aspects of the texts being read all influence each other in a dialectical fashion and are realized in the social interactions between participants. We preview these components here, and discuss them in greater depth in subsequent sections.

Briefly, social interactions are shaped by individual-level, biologically mediated factors. These differences (which are often constitutional and stable), in turn, affect social interactions and relationships. On a distal level, kinship

TABLE 14.1
A Transactional Model of Joint Reading

Individual Factors	Relationships	Text	Social Interactions
Kinship	Attachment	Genre	Metalanguage
Temperament	Friendship	Format	Narrative competence

should affect interactions to the extent that closer relatedness (mothers with their offspring, compared to mothers with their nieces or nephews) should result in more cooperative interaction. However, it may be more difficult to sustain interaction with children who are temperamentally "active." These sorts of individual differences are often used to illustrate the ways in which individuals, especially children, affect interactions and relationships. In short, individual-level effects on interactions are important because they illustrate "child effects" on adults.

The next level of abstraction is the affective relationship. In general, affective relationships are usually dyadic, and are based on both the history of previous interactions and any anticipated future interactions between the individuals involved. Differences in the nature of these relationships (attachment relationships and friendships are two of the most common types) are generally understood to affect interactions.

Lastly, we also consider the ways in which specific task demands, genre, and format affect the interactions that go on around book reading.

INDIVIDUAL-LEVEL FACTORS IN SOCIAL CONTEXT

Recognition of individual-level factors in children and adults is crucial to a transactional view of social context. Individuals carry with them specific attributes or differences, which set them apart from others. These individual attributes can be placed on a continuum, ranging from stable differences with constitutional/biological origins, such as kin status, to those that are more labile and have environmental origins, such as expertise in a particular task. Considering individual differences along such a continuum assumes that biological and environmental factors influence each other. We begin with kinship.

Kin Status

This section is speculative, and based on the evidence generated by evolutionary developmental psychological and sociobiological theory (Bjorklund & Pellegrini, 2000). We speculate that the form and content of interactions is influenced by factors relating to evolutionary history. A basic premise of these theories (Wilson, 1975) is that individuals are motivated by concerns with "fitness," or maximizing their own opportunities to reproduce, and, once they reproduce, are concerned with ensuring the survival of their offspring, so that they, too, can reproduce. There is also evidence that adults interact with children differently, depending on the level of kin relatedness. Specifically, evolutionary theory holds that parents invest more effort in supporting their offspring because they want them, and their genes, to survive (Trivers, 1972). According to this argument, parents should be more supportive of kin than non-kin, and more supportive of their own offspring than of cousins (since a parent shares more genes with the former than with the latter).

By extension, the supportiveness of the child-rearing environment carries implications for the ways in which parents interact with their children. In stable and supportive situations, mothers adopt a "k selection strategy," in which they invest their resources (e.g., time, energy, and willingness to take risks) in a relatively small number of offspring, assuming that most of them will reach maturity and then reproduce (Wilson, 1975). This level of parental investment results in a secure parent–child attachment relationship (Belsky, Steinberg, & Draper, 1991). As we discuss later, interactions between mothers and securely attached children tend to be synchronous and supportive.

With an "r selection strategy," on the other hand, parents in unstable environments do not develop such relationships. Instead, such parents produce a greater number of offspring, and invest minimally in each (Wilson, 1975). These sorts of environments and the correspondingly low levels of maternal investment that result also predict insecure parent–child attachment relationships. Interactions in these relationships are typically fractious, and are often characterized by the child's noncompliance and sexually promiscuous behavior at maturity (Belsky et al., 1991).

Individual Differences in Children

Individual differences in children, such as variations in temperament, are often characterized as being biologically mediated, to the extent that they appear very early in life and are relatively stable across the life span. Although there is very little research, to our knowledge, addressing book reading with children of different temperaments, we do know that active children tend to have more problems in school than sedentary individuals, because schools tend to value quiet and reflective behavior (Pellegrini & Horvat, 1995).

In an earlier study of parent–child book reading, we examined differences in the ways that mothers and fathers read to preschool children who were communicatively disabled and the way they did so with typically developing children (Pellegrini, Brody, & Sigel, 1985). In our middle-class sample we found, first of all, that there were *no differences* between mothers and fathers in the ways that they interacted with their children around books. Both mothers and fathers modified their interactions around books according to the child's level of competence. They were more supportive (e.g., pointing to words, patting children on the shoulder) and less demanding (e.g., labeling pictures, asking yes–no questions) with disabled and younger children than they were with older and non-handicapped children. Parents allowed children from the latter group to take more initiative, and presented more demanding questions to them about the texts. In both cases parents used strategies that maximized children's participation in the book reading process. However, they varied their interactions to accommodate the children's individual differences.

These results are consistent with the assumption that individual differences in the child affect parents' interactive styles: parents are most concerned with having their children participate in the interactions around books, and gauge their interactions to maximize children's participation. Of course, this is a basis premise of Vygotsky's zone of proximal development (1978): Children learn through participation in a task. In order to maximize participation, children with low levels of competence require more support and direction from adults than do more competent children, who elicit more demanding but less supportive strategies (Pellegrini et al., 1985; Pellegrini et al., 1990). Thus, interaction around books is transactional. It involves adults gauging each child's competence on an utterance-by-utterance basis, and adjusting their interactive strategies to maximize the child's participation.

This process of fine-tuning is best illustrated by the actual sequences of utterances comprising these interactions. In another study of preschool children's interaction with their mothers—this time with Head Start children and their mothers—around different sorts of text, we examined the sequential probability of mothers' adjusting their interaction styles to the adequacy of children's responses (Pellegrini et al., 1990). We found that mothers were indeed sensitive to children's level of competence, but this sensitivity, as we will see, occurred only around specific types of texts. Specifically, mothers tended to begin an interaction with a cognitively demanding utterance. If the child responded inappropriately to this high-level mental demand, then the mother lowered the level of difficulty in her subsequent utterances. If the child responded appropriately to the cognitively demanding utterance, on the other hand, then the mother continued to generate high-level utterances. Again, these mothers were concerned with maximizing their children's participation and tailored their interactions to accomplish this goal.

To conclude, our suggestion that biology influences social interaction should not be interpreted as biological determinism. As specified earlier, individuals and their environments influence each other in a dynamic fashion. People are not mere vehicles governed by environmental reinforcements. Children are capable of negotiating "alternative routes" to competence under adverse circumstances, such as with a non-responsive caregiver. In such cases, children tend to avoid interaction with their mothers, and seek stimulation from others (Main & Weston, 1981). The classic cases presented by Anna Freud (Freud & Burlingham, 1944) and Suomi and Harlow (1972) illustrate how juveniles deprived of maternal stimulation can use their peers as substitutes for this purpose. Such varied and adaptive responses indicate that there are different routes to competence (i.e., children need not have a "secure" attachment relationship in order to flourish) and that the individual child has some discretion in shaping those routes.

ATTACHMENT AND FRIENDSHIP RELATIONSHIPS

We begin by describing caregiver–child attachment relationships and how these affect joint reading behaviors. Attachment relationships are formed as a result of repeated interactions between infants and their caregivers (frequently their mothers). Children then construct a "working model" of this social relationship, based on the history of interactions. This cognitive model of the child's social world, in turn, guides them in their interactions with other adults and peers. If children are securely attached, then their working models will most likely reflect a trusting and supportive view of the world. If they are insecure, then they may develop models that are hostile and distrustful.

A basic premise of attachment research is that infants become securely attached to their mothers as a result of a history of supportive and predictable interactions. For example, attachment status affects the way in which parents play with children (Slade, 1987). The pretend play between "securely attached" children—relative to insecurely attached children—and their mothers is more coordinated and sophisticated (Slade, 1987). Where the caregiver is also the child's biological mother, we would expect forces related to kinship to affect interaction, though attachment relationships can also be formed between children and non-kin caregivers (Schaffer & Emerson, 1964) or peers (Suomi & Harlow, 1972).

To our knowledge, Bus and van IJzendoorn are the only scholars who have examined the role of attachment on book reading (1988, 1995; see also Bus, this volume). Consistent with theory, they found differences in the book reading behaviors of securely and insecurely attached preschoolers. Most basically, securely attached children were read to more than their insecurely attached peers (Bus & van IJzendoorn, 1995). Further, securely attached children and their mothers were more responsive, cooperative, and synchronous. Mothers of securely attached children also pointed and their children responded more frequently, or children initiated and mothers responded more frequently. The insecure children, on the other hand, were more disruptive and less attentive to the text (Bus & van IJzendoorn, 1988). In short, securely attached children were cooperative and easier to teach than their less securely attached counterparts. The implication of these patterns should be clear: The interpersonal orientation of securely attached children should result in their learning more effectively, whatever it is that is being taught in joint reading contexts. Attachment theory predicts that children's subsequent *social relationships* are the important outcomes, whereas more social learning-related theories emphasize the importance of learning skills specific to literacy.

Of course, provision should also be made for those children whose attachment relationships are "avoidant." To our knowledge, there has been no systematic study of the social routes to early literacy taken by these children. Do they interact with more supportive siblings or peers? Or do they learn on their own, by interacting with text?

Friendship

In the section on kinship we speculated that the degree of genetic relatedness (kinship) influenced interactions between participants in joint reading sessions. Accordingly, kin should be more cooperative than non-kin, in that cooperation maximizes fitness. Cooperation between non-kin can be adaptive, however, when interactants know that they will meet repeatedly. The principle of reciprocal altruism (Axelrod & Hamilton, 1981) tells us that individuals will cooperate with each other and even make sacrifices for each other more often when the participants know they will be meeting each other repeatedly, than they will when they are unfamiliar with each other and unsure of the likelihood of subsequent meetings. The basic idea is that individuals from the former group will invest in each other because they assume that their investments will be reciprocated quid pro quo. So youngsters will cooperate with each other, accommodate to the needs of others, and even make sacrifices if they expect to remain in close proximity over time. They do this with the (often implicit) expectation that these good turns will be reciprocated.

Continued proximity between children, or "propinquity," often results in friendships (Hartup, 1996). Friendships are dyadic relationships that are formed after repeated interactions and are based on shared interests, values, and behavioral styles. It is probably the case that friends' long history with each other supports their reciprocity and mutuality.

Reciprocity is more typical of friends interacting in literacy events than it is of acquaintances in the same situation (Daiute, Hartup, Shool, & Zajac, 1993; Pellegrini, Galda, Bartini, & Charak, 1998). For example, we found that dyads of first-grade friends engaged in early literacy tasks, such as playing with narrative props and talking and writing about narrative texts, more readily resolved conflicts, talked about the conflicts, and talked about the task at hand than did pairs of acquaintances (Pellegrini et al., 1998). Additionally, friends generated more literate language in these events. The data support a process model wherein friends, because of their mutuality and emotional closeness, are more likely to resolve conceptual conflicts. Similar to Piaget's (1983) equilibration theory, these conflict–resolution cycles lead children to reflect on the social, linguistic, and cognitive dimensions of their interactions, as evidenced by their use of "metalanguage." This metalanguage, in turn, predicts standardized measures of early reading and writing (Pellegrini, Galda, Flor, Bartini, & Charak, 1997).

The practical implication of these findings is that children and adults should be paired in social groups for sustained periods, in order to maximize cooperative and synchronous interactions. In this regard, children should also be paired with friends in certain peer learning situations, in order to maximize learning. The emotional dimension of such relationships supports cognitive growth. This recommendation goes against folk practices, which have teachers separating friends.

Emotional support can be maximized in school by keeping children together as a cohort with one teacher, across a number of years. The emotional component of the close teacher–child relationship should be focused on improved student performance. Merely examining differences in achievement might disguise the important mechanism (emotional investment) responsible for the change.

THE NATURE OF THE TEXT

Lastly, we examine the nature of the text being read, as a dimension of context. Participants choose specific texts to furnish their interactional niches, embellish or ignore specific and predictable parts of the text, and are also influenced by those texts.

The texts that are read in adult–child joint reading contexts have only recently received attention. Indeed, in some of the early studies of mothers reading to children (e.g., Ninio, 1980a, 1980b), the types of books that the mothers read to their children were not even described. The obvious assumption here is that the type of book or text did not matter and was irrelevant to the context.

This was particularly surprising to us in light of the fact that this research was examining SES differences in book reading. By ignoring such important information as the nature and genre of the texts, these researchers assumed that SES and cultural differences resided in the participants themselves, not in the wider context as we have defined it here.

It is a well-known fact that middle-class families have more literacy props and books in their homes than low-SES families, and that the props in middle-class homes are similar to those employed in most school literacy events (Heath, 1983). Thus, the extent to which middle-class parents and children are familiar with and value a specific type of text will determine the difference between their behaviors and those of low-SES dyads. In other words, differences in book reading behavior may be due to differences in families' familiarity with the specific texts used, and these differences in familiarity may in part be class-based. Class differences are minimized when both groups are familiar with props, and maximized when middle-class familiar toys are used (McLoyd, 1982).

A decade ago we examined joint readings by Head Start children and their mothers. Like others before us (e.g., Heath, 1983), we found that low-SES families did not have many children's books in their homes (Pellegrini et al., 1990). Furthermore, when we observed mothers and their children reading traditional children's books, such as *The Tale of Peter Rabbit*, we found that the mothers often had difficulty reading these books, and that their interaction patterns with children were neither effective nor responsive to the children's needs. Not surprisingly, the children's level of participation around these types of texts was very low as well.

We did find, however, that these low-SES mothers and children often interacted around toy advertisements and comics from the local free newspaper. When we observed these interactions around indigenous texts, we formed a very different picture: Mothers were sensitive to children's levels of expertise and modified their strategies accordingly. By implication, children were more involved in the interactions around these texts than they had been around the more traditional texts.

At another level of text choice, the literacy genre of the book being read also affects interaction patterns. This point was made abundantly clear to us one evening following a symposium on young children's narratives and early literacy. One of our colleagues expressed great surprise at the fact that her child's responses to book readings were not narrative in style. One of us (LG) noted that this should not be surprising, given the fact that the book being read to the child was not narrative—it was a word list book! Again, genre was of such low concern that our colleague did not even consider it.

Of course, the genre of the books read with children has a basic effect on the interactions around those books (e.g., Cornell, Sénéchal, & Broda, 1988; Pellegrini et al., 1990; Sorsby & Martlew, 1991). Adults and children seem to choose narratives and expository texts for different reasons, possibly because of the sorts of demands these texts make on the participants. With narratives, the reader and the text interact with each other. With expository texts, which usually present a series of disjunct informational bits, there is no narrative thread holding the participants' interest. Consequently, this latter format is more supportive of interaction between reader and child, often in ways that resemble a tutorial. The adult asks questions about items in the book and the child responds. In this regard, expository texts are preferable for teaching vocabulary.

CONCLUSION

In this chapter we have sketched out a model of the social context of joint reading. Much of what we have presented is speculative, and merits further empirical study. Especially needed is research addressing the ways in which children with different temperaments interact with adults during joint reading events. It may be that children of certain dispositions will participate most effectively around certain types of text. For example, physically active children may be best matched with adventure narratives and texts that elicit active participation.

The role of peers in joint reading events also merits attention. It may be that close relationships like friendships support high levels of cognitive engagement around text. Such findings would, however, require some educators to rethink "folk" wisdom policies that typically keep friends separate during instruction.

ACKNOWLEDGMENT

We acknowledge the comments of anonymous reviewers on an earlier draft of this chapter. Writing of the chapter was partially supported by a grant from the Spencer Foundation to the first author.

REFERENCES

Axelrod, R., & Hamilton, W. (1981). The evolution of cooperation. *Science, 21*(1), 1390–1396.
Bernstein, B. (1971). *Class, codes, and control* (Vol. 1). London: Routledge & Kegan Paul.
Bjorklund, D. F., & Pellegrini, A. D. (2000). Child development and evolutionary psychology. *Child Development, 71*, 1687–1708.

Belsky, J., Steinberg, L., & Draper, P. (1991). Childhood experience, interpersonal development, and reproductive strategy: An evolutionary theory of socialization. *Child Development, 62,* 647–670.

Bus, A. G., & van IJzendoorn, M. H. (1988). Mother–child interaction, attachment, and emergent literacy. *Child Development, 59,* 1262–1272.

Bus, A. G., & van IJzendoorn, M. H. (1995). Mothers reading to their 3-year-olds: The role of mother–child attachment security in becoming literate. *Reading Research Quarterly, 30,* 998–1015.

Bus, A. G., van IJzendoorn, M. H., & Pellegrini, A. D. (1995). Joint book reading makes for success in learning to read: A meta-analysis on inter-generational transmission of literacy. *Review of Educational Research, 65,* 1–21.

Cook-Gumperz, J. (1977). Situated instructions: Language socialization of school age children. In S. Ervin-Tripp & K. Mitchell-Kernan (Eds.), *Child discourse* (pp. 103–124). New York: Academic Press.

Cornell, E., Sénéchal, M., & Broda, L. (1988). Recall of picture books by 3-year-old children: Testing and repetition effects in joint reading activities. *Journal of Educational Psychology, 80,* 537–542.

Daiute, C., Hartup, W., Shool, W., & Zajac, R. (1993, April). *Peer collaboration and written language development.* Paper presented at the biennial meetings of the Society for Research in Child Development, New Orleans, LA.

Freud, A., & Burlingham, D. T. (1944). *Infants without families.* New York: International Universities Press.

Hartup, W. W. (1996). The company they keep: Friendships and their developmental significance. *Child Development, 67,* 1–13.

Heath, S. (1983). *Ways with words.* New York: Cambridge University Press.

Hinde, R. (1980). *Ethology.* London: Fontana.

Main, M., & Weston, D. R. (1981). The quality of toddler's relationships to mother and to father: Related to conflict behavior and readiness to establish new relationships. *Child Development, 52,* 932–940.

McLoyd, V. (1982). Social class differences in sociodramatic play: A critical review. *Developmental Review, 2,* 1–30.

Michaels, S. (1981). "Sharing time": Children's narrative styles and access to literacy. *Language in Society, 10,* 423–442.

Ninio, A. (1980a). Picture book reading in mother–infant dyads belonging to two subgroups in Israel. *Child Development, 51,* 587–590.

Ninio, A. (1980b). Ostensive definition in vocabulary teaching. *Journal of Child Language, 7,* 565–573.

Ninio, A., & Bruner, J. (1978). The achievement and antecedents of labeling. *Journal of Child Language, 5,* 1–15.

Olson, D. R. (1977). From utterance to text: The bias of language in speech and writing. *Harvard Educational Review, 47,* 257–281.

Pellegrini, A., Brody, G., & Sigel, I. (1985). Parents' book reading habits with their child. *Journal of Educational Psychology, 77,* 332–340.

Pellegrini, A. D., & Galda, L. (1991). Longitudinal relations among preschoolers' symbolic play, metalinguistic verbs, and emergent literacy. In. J. Christie (Ed.), *Play and early literacy development* (pp. 47–68). Albany: SUNY Press.

Pellegrini, A. D., Galda, L., Bartini, M., & Charak, D. (1998). Oral language and literacy learning in context: The role of social relationships. *Merrill-Palmer Quarterly, 44,* 38–54.

Pellegrini, A. D., Galda, L., Flor, D., Bartini, M., & Charak, D. (1997). Close relationships, individual differences, and early literacy learning. *Journal of Experimental Child Psychology, 67,* 409–422.

Pellegrini, A. D., & Horvat, M. (1995). A developmental contextual critique of Attention Deficit Hyperactivity Disorder (ADHD). *Educational Researcher, 24,* 13–20.

Pellegrini, A. D., Moshovaki, E., & Meadows, S. (in press). Teachers' affective presentation of stories and young children's affective engagement during classroom story reading. *Discourse Processes.*

Pellegrini, A. D., Perlmutter, J., Galda, L., & Brody, G. (1990). Joint book reading between Black Head Start children and their mothers. *Child Development, 61,* 443–453.

Piaget, J. (1983). Piaget's theory. In W. Kessen (Ed.), *Handbook of child psychology: History, theory, and methods* (pp. 103–128). New York: Wiley.

Schaffer, H. R., & Emerson, P. E. (1964). The development of social attachment in infancy. *Monographs of the Society for Research in Child Development, 29.*

Scollon, R., & Scollon, S. (1981). *Narrative, literacy and face in interethnic communication.* Norwood, NJ: Ablex.

Scribner, S., & Cole, M. (1978). Literacy without schooling. *Harvard Educational Review, 48,* 448–461.

Slade, A. (1987). Quality of attachment and early symbolic play. *Developmental Psychology, 23,* 78–85.

Sorsby, A., & Martlew, M. (1991). Representational demands in mothers' talk to preschool children in two contexts: Picture book reading and a modeling task. *Journal of Child Language, 18,* 373–395.

Suomi, S., & Harlow, H. (1972). Social rehabilitation of isolate-reared monkeys. *Developmental Psychology, 6,* 487–496.

Teale, W. (1984). Reading to children: Its significance for literacy development. In H. Goelman, A. Oberg, & F. Smith (Eds.) *Awakening to literacy* (pp. 110–121). Portsmouth, NH: Heinemann.

Trivers, R. (1972). Parental investment and sexual selection. In B. Campbell (Ed.), *Sexual selection and the descent of man* (pp. 136–179). Chicago: Aldine.

Vygotsky, L. (1978). *Mind in society.* Cambridge, MA: Harvard University Press.

Wertsch, J. (1979). From social interaction to higher psychological processes. A clarification and application of Vygotsky's theory. *Human Development, 22,* 1–22.

Whitehurst, G., Falco, F., Lonigan, C. J., Fischel, J., DeBaryshe, B., Valdez-Menchaca, M. C., & Caulfield, M. (1988). Accelerating language development through picture book reading. *Developmental Psychology, 24,* 552–559.

Wilson, E. O. (1975). *Sociobiology: The new synthesis.* Cambridge, MA: Belknap Press.

15

Parent–Child Storybook Reading as a Complex Adaptive System: Or "An Igloo Is a House for Bears"

David B. Yaden, Jr.
Rossier School of Education,
University of Southern California

> "So chaos theory is all just random
> and unpredictable?" Gennaro said.
> "No," Malcolm said. "We actually find
> hidden regularities within the complex
> variety of a system's behavior. That's why
> chaos has now become a very broad theory
> that's used to study everything from the
> stock market, to rioting crowds, to brain
> waves during epilepsy."
> —Ian Malcolm, in *Jurassic Park* (Crichton, 1990)

In Michael Crichton's best-selling novels *Jurassic Park* (1990) and *The Lost World* (1995), and the latest film sequel, *Jurassic Park III* (Spielberg, 2001), an eccentric mathematician's use of chaos theory serves as both foreshadowing of and explanation for a series of disasters, set in motion by a wealthy entrepreneur who clones various species of dinosaurs from fossil DNA in the hope of opening a theme park filled with live specimens. Warning against this dangerous and foolish enterprise, the character Ian Malcolm invokes one of chaos theory's central tenets, warning that the entrepreneur's attempts to reverse the course of evolutionary history will result in consequences that are entirely out of proportion to the initial effort—in other words, highly nonlinear, unpredictable and, most of all, uncontrollable. And as a great many readers and moviegoers can now attest, the dinosaurs do indeed overcome their initial genetic limitations, reproduce, and—led by the uncannily intelligent raptors—devour and generally run roughshod over their poorly matched human creators.

Interestingly, although general systems theory was introduced over 40 years ago (cf. Lorenz, 1963; von Bertalanffy, 1968, chapter 3), only within the past decade or so has a wide spectrum of scientists and researchers attempted to mesh new scientific discoveries about the complex behavior of large and small systems with our knowledge about the natural and physical sciences (e.g., Bak, 1996; Goldberger, Rigney, & West, 1990; Kauffman, 1991, 1995; Kosko, 1999; Prigogine, 1996; Prigogine & Stengers, 1984) as well as the social (cf. Abraham, Abraham, Shaw, & Garfinkel, 1990; Baker, 1993; Edelman, 1992; Fuhriman & Burlingame, 1994; Guastello, 1995; Vallacher & Nowak, 1994). Despite the diversity of their disciplines, all of the works just cited share the common belief that behind unpredictability—whether of natural disasters (Bak & Chen, 1991), the effects of certain drugs (Sacks, 1990) or the mysterious turnings of a literary figure's life path (Hayles, 1991)—there is still some order present: a nonlinear order to be sure, but nonetheless some "material effectuation ... with spatio-temporal coordinates," to use Foucault's phrase (1972, p. 86).

Many educational researchers have also posited that a systems approach could be applied to subdisciplines such as curriculum theory (Doll, 1989, 1993; Gough, 1994); composition studies (Greening, 1993; Syverson, 1999); educational research (Lindsay, 1989); special education (Guess & Sailor, 1993); learning theory (Ennis, 1992; Lindsay, 1991); teacher education (Patterson, Cotton, Kimball-Lopez, Pavonetti, & Van Horn, 1998); reader-response (Sumara, 2000); and literacy (Robinson & Yaden, 1993; Weaver, 1985; Yaden, 1999a). This chapter proposes that the emergent knowledge of how written language "works," as this knowledge is manifested in parent–child storybook reading, also has some of the characteristics and integrity of a nonlinear, dynamic system, or a Complex Adaptive System (CAS) (Holland, 1995a, 1995b).

The following discussion has three objectives. First of all, it presents several excerpts of parent–child storybook dialogue, not only in order to illustrate the complexity of the stops, starts, interruptions, and disagreements, but also to suggest why the field needs more sophisticated analytic tools to determine how storybook reading conversations contribute to the growth of literacy knowledge. Secondly, it attempts to relate various aspects of the conversational exchange to seven widely accepted dynamic principles (see Cronbach's 1988 review of James Gleick's book *Chaos: The Making of New Science* [1987] for evidence of the applicability of dynamic metaphors to the social sciences). Finally, I present a specific methodology for dynamic analysis of storybook reading discourse, and I describe the possible interpretations that might be formed as a result of this approach.

THE NATURE OF STORYBOOK READING CONVERSATIONS

When Standard Action Formats Do Not Result in Standard Understandings

As Taylor's (1986) ethnographic description of a storybook reading event suggests, home storybook reading events are often punctuated by the interruptions of daily life, by children's "off task" comments, and by frequent incongruities of communication between parents and children. Although the seminal studies of Ninio and Bruner (1978) and Snow (1983) have shown that parents establish regular storybook reading routines through the use of "standard action formats," "semantic contingency," and "scaffolding," a close examination of the published data from these studies shows that children and parents often have very different levels of understanding about the text, both during these routines and between conversational exchanges. For example, a sequence of dialogue between a 31-month-old child and his mother in Snow's (1983) study clearly demonstrates that despite repeated attempts by the parent to "scaffold" via accountability responses, the child persists in his idiosyncratic interpretation of print:

> *Nathaniel:* [pointing to KLM on toy truck] That say airport truck.
> *Mother:* No, that says KLM.
> *Nathaniel:* [insistently] That says de airport truck.
> *Mother:* KLM cargo.
> *Nathaniel:* [more insistently] That says airport truck
> *Mother:* [patiently] In the airport the trucks have to carry the cargo from the planes to other planes, or into the city and that's what this truck does.
> *Nathaniel:* [pointing to KLM] Who's this?

Mother: Where ...
Nathaniel: That says ... de airport ...
Mother: [interrupting] KLM, Nathaniel, this says KLM. (p. 176)

Within these 10 conversational turns, Nathaniel insists during his first three that the cargo truck and its corresponding label (KLM) in the illustration must be identified as "de airport truck." During the sixth turn the mother, rather than correcting the child a third time, simply reads the accompanying text, which identifies the truck as carrying cargo. However, Nathaniel senses that something is wrong and redirects his Mother's attention to the picture of the truck and its label and says, "Who's this?" And before she answers, he exclaims that it says "de airport ..." Finally, the mother, interrupting Nathaniel this time and using his name for emphasis, declares for the fourth time that the label says "KLM."

In this exchange, mother and child spend 80% of their conversational turns disagreeing about how the truck should be labeled. This raises a number of questions about the analysis of storybook dialogue:

1. Even though all of the mother's comments were semantically contingent, was this a successful scaffolding sequence?
2. Why didn't Nathaniel capitulate under his mother's insistence that the writing on the truck "said" something different than what he was claiming?
3. Will this conversation have a residual effect on Nathaniel's future interpretation of text? If so, how?

Snow also provides an interesting example, this time from an alphabet book reading, of a semantically contingent exchange (defined as topic continuation) about letter naming. The exchange does not bring about conventional understanding on the part of the child, even though he is reiterating his mother's exact words:

Mother: "I is for ... ice cream.
Nathaniel: Eh dis a I. I for ice cream.
Mother: Which is the I?
Nathaniel: Dis is de I.
Mother: I.
Nathaniel: E.
Mother: No, that's an I.

Nathaniel: Dat's a I.
Mother: And that's a little I.
Nathaniel: Dat's a little I. Dis is E … dis is de little I.
Mother: No, this is a big I, a big *I*. (p. 178)

Unlike in the first excerpt discussed, here Nathaniel follows his mother's lead very closely in the first four turns, by both repeating the words of her reading and confirming the identification of the letter *I* in response to her directive questioning. The mother even finishes off this first sequence of exchanges with a reconfirmation of Nathaniel's correct identification. However, Nathan's next statement is that the letter is really an *E*. The mother immediately corrects him in turn seven, and in turn eight Nathaniel restates that the letter is an *I*. So far so good. Now, the mother introduces the little *I*, and Nathaniel, while confirming the latter's identification, reverts to his earlier interpretation that the capital letter is really an *E*. Quickly, the mother corrects his statement and reiterates (twice) that the letter is a "big *I*, a big *I*."

Again, one can pose some interesting observations and questions regarding the interpretation of this sequence. First of all, Nathaniel may be identifying the letter *I* as he hears it: /ai/. If so, then his visual identification is actually correct. But his mother doesn't understand that he is using the second part of the diphthong of the name for its identification (cf. Templeton & Bear, 1992, on the use of parts of letter names to represent phonemes). If we speculate that this is so, then his mother's next comment, "No, that's an I," must be confusing to Nathaniel, since that is what he just said: /ai/. Unsure of what to do next, Nathaniel restates his mother's identification of the letter as an "I," something that was never in question in the first place.

Of course, the interpretation could be made that Nathaniel is simply confused by all these letter names and shapes, and that it takes a while to get them all straight. However, from a developmental perspective, what is the meaning of the phrase "it takes a while? "Just how long is "a while?" And then again, "how many" semantically contingent responses or identifications must be made before the letter is no longer confusing to the child? In the preceding sequence of 11 turns, the mother identifies the capital *I* six times (in turns 1, 3, 5, 7, and twice in turn 11). How many more turns will it take? 10? 15? 20? And even when a child confirms a response, as Nathaniel does twice (in turns 4 and 8), that doesn't necessarily indicate that he has developed a conventional understanding of the fact in question. While the child's age—only 31 months—could be a factor, such alternative readings and perceptions persist even among older preschoolers, as the following examples demonstrate.

The following excerpts (from Yaden, 1995) are taken from three consecutive readings of Mary Ann Hoberman's (1982) combination picture story/concept book, *A House Is a House for Me*. In the excerpts, Samantha—who is already highly experienced in storybook reading with both parents—and her mother are looking at an illustration of three igloos. A polar bear stands off to one side, and a speech balloon from the animal's mouth reads "An igloo's a house for an Eskimo." No Eskimos are actually pictured. Samantha is having trouble understanding why her mother doesn't describe the polar bear in the picture as living in an igloo.

First Reading:

Mother: An igloo's a house for an Eskimo. A teepee's a house for a Cree. "That's a kind of Indian." A pueblo's a house for a Hopi, another Indian. And a wigwam may hold a Mohee.

Samantha: And a bear that lives in the dark home.

Mother: A bear that lives in a dark home is called a cave, huh?

Samantha: Yeah.

Mother: [continuing reading] A garage is a house for a car or truck. A hangar is a house for a plane.

Samantha: You forgot that.

Mother: Oh, I read that. An igloo's a house for an Eskimo.

Samantha: An igloo is for a bear.

Mother: A polar bear?

Samantha: Yeah, a polar bear.

Mother: Oh, okay.

Second Reading:

Mother: Okay, well, let's see what it says. An igloo is a house for an Eskimo. A tepee is a house for a Cree.

Samantha: Did you do that one?

Mother: Yeah, I did that one.

Samantha: Well, you have to say, "A bear is a house for igloos?"

Mother: Huh, uh. [i.e., "no."]

Samantha: No, that's a polar bear.

Mother: Right, but an igloo's a house for an Eskimo.

Samantha: Oh.

Third Reading:

Mother: An igloo is a house for an Eskimo.

Samantha: No, for bears.
Mother: For polar bear. Okay.

In this dialogue, even after repeated readings and the mother's correction, Samantha insists that igloos must be houses for polar bears, though the orally rendered text indicates that Eskimos live in igloos. This sequence of readings illustrates some notable inconsistencies on the parent's part as well. As the last line in the first reading indicates, the mother agrees with the child's inference that bears can also live in igloos. However, in reading 2, line 7, although the mother confirms Samantha's prior identification of the polar bear, she also states clearly, "but an igloo's a house for an Eskimo," to which the child seemingly assents ("Oh."). In the third reading, Samantha directly contradicts her mother's claim that igloos are for Eskimos and flatly states, "No, for bears." And, surprisingly, this assertion by the child stands, as the mother agrees for a second time, "For polar bear. Okay."

How is Samantha to process her mother's sequence of *agree-disagree-agree*, in response to the question of who exactly lives in the igloo? Is the mother's waffling confusing for the child? Or does it really matter what the mother says, since Samantha from the very first reading was convinced that polar bears lived in igloos? As in the example of Nathaniel's exchange with his mother, how many corrections will need to take place before Samantha understands that Eskimos, not polar bears, live in igloos? And does the mother's agreement that bears *do* live in igloos merely compound the problem and extend the time it will take for the child to understand the concept?

Another example from Samantha's transcript illustrates that some children not only persist in their own interpretations, but freely import information into the story (cf. Elster, 1995, 1998) and make associations that obviously could not have come from the particular reading in question, thus complicating the storybook conversation even further. In this example, taken from the third reading of McDonald's *Alphabatics* (1992), the mother is explicitly trying to focus Samantha's attention on the sounds represented by the letters *J* and *K*. For the child, however, this repetition of sounds after a few early exchanges calls a song to mind. The reading depicted here happened while the book was open to a two-page spread with the letters *J* and *j* on the left-hand page, and a picture of a jack-in-the-box on the right-hand page:

Mother: [sounding J] /j/ /j/ / /j/ /j/.
Samantha: K, K, K.
Mother: K? No.

Samantha: I know this one's K.

Mother: This is not K. This is a jack-in-the-box ...

Samantha: Jack.

Mother: ... Jack-in-the-box. Now look, this letter [sounding first *J* then K, emphasizing each one] /j/ /k/, /j/ /k/, /j/ /k/, /j/ /k/ ...

Samantha: [joining in with the mother in the middle of the above sequence] ... /j/ /k/, /j/ /k/, [now begins singing] Frere Jac-ques, Frere Jac-ques ... [emphasizing "Jacques" as in the above sounding of the letters].

Mother: [after the full song is over, somewhat resigned] That's the letter, J.

Samantha: J.

Mother: ... and K.

Samantha: K.

At the end of this session, Samantha seems to agree with her mother on the names of the letters. But it is difficult to assess just how successful the mother actually was in helping Samantha understand the distinction between the two. Instead of understanding that the mother's sequence of /j/ /k/ is associated with the two separate visible letters on the page, the child recalls a favorite song with a similar sequence of sounds. As in the previous examples, many questions arise here about what this portion of the storybook conversation actually means to the child. With what unit exactly is she associating the sounds? The visible, graphic representations of the letters *J* and *K*? The phonetic sequence heard in /Jac-ques/? Or perhaps the entire song as a seamless whole? Can it be legitimately construed that the child's insistence in lines 2 and 4 that the *J* is really a *K* suddenly gives way to the insight that her mother is really right about the identification of these letters? I think not.

When the Scaffold Won't Reach

What the preceding examples *do* illustrate is that storybook reading conversations are anything but straightforward. Despite the fact that the emergent literacy field (see Sulzby & Teale, 1991; Yaden, Rowe, & MacGillivray, 2000; Whitehurst & Lonigan, 1998), in particular, has taken storybook reading as the sine qua non of early reading practices (see Meyer, Wardrop, Stahl, & Linn, 1994, and Scarborough & Dobrich, 1994, for some notable exceptions), researchers still know very little about how the actual flow of conversation is converted into conventional understanding. If the preceding examples are representative of how at least some of these conversations actually proceed, then it becomes more difficult to see how traditional analytic notions such as semantic contingency, scaffolding, and use of familiar formats and routines might help researchers decipher the ongoing construction of meaning.

Thus, a primary difficulty for most of the current descriptive schemes of storybook reading analysis—whether they focus on the content of children's talk (e.g., Roser & Martinez, 1985; Morrow, 1988; Yaden, Smolkin, & Conlon, 1989); the linguistic structures that children employ (e.g., Panofsky, 1986; Pappas, 1991, 1993); or the social strategies employed by either child or adult (see DeBruin-Parecki, 1999; Hayden & Fagan, 1987; Kook & Vedder, 1994; Shanahan & Hogan, 1983)—is that the actual sequence of statements (i.e., the linguistic, social and semantic concatenation of propositions spoken in succession) is not taken into consideration. It is one thing to describe a conversation as being comprised of X number of adult questions, Y number of child responses, or Z number of times that "topic continuation" took place, and quite another to determine whether the parent's questions made sense to the child in the first place, whether the child's answers were directed to the same metalinguistic level as the questions, or whether the number of agreements or disagreements between parent and child resulted in confusion, comprehension, or simply went by the wayside.

To be sure, mismatches in the metalinguistic levels of questions and answers, or persistent disagreements between parent and child over the identification of text elements, do not happen during all readings (it bears stating that I know of no research that even speculates on the proportions of questions or comments or any other criteria that constitute an "optimal" storybook conversation about print). However, those disconnections that do occur cannot simply be dismissed as unimportant components of the storybook reading process. Their frequency casts doubt on the "linearity" of parent–child talk and the stepwise accretion of literacy knowledge that the scaffolding metaphor suggests. Even though storybook reading effects are seen across various periods of time (Phillips, Norris, & Mason, 1996; Wells, 1986, Whitehurst, Epstein, Angell, & Payne, 1994), close examination of individual sessions produces questions about how children actually take information away, speech act by speech act, from each reading or rereading.

STORYBOOK READING AND DYNAMIC SYSTEMS: IS THERE A MATCH?

CAS theory offers a perspective on storybook reading that may help account for the types of metalinguistic mismatches and unconventional notions illustrated in the preceding examples. One of the key features of complexity theory is that it seeks to understand a dynamic system as it evolves, whether it does so evenly or not (Nowak & Lewenstein, 1994). In this spirit, the following subsections apply Holland's (1995a, pp. 45–46) seven characteristics of Complex Adaptive Systems (CAS) to the study of storybook reading conversations, to suggest how storybook reading may qualify as a dynamic system.

All Cases Consist of Large Number of Components or Agents That Continually Interact With One Another

Not surprisingly, this feature of dynamic systems is evident in storybook reading. Researchers have identified numerous facets of storybook interaction that affect the style and content of the surrounding talk, including genre type (Smolkin, Yaden, Brown, & Hofius, 1992); repeated readings (Roser & Martinez, 1985; Yaden, 1988); socioeconomic status (Ninio, 1980); story familiarity (Pellegrini, Perlmutter, Galda, & Brody, 1990); parent reading style (Reese, this volume; DeBruin-Parecki, 1999; Haden & Fivush, 1994; Teale & Martinez, 1986); type of picture book illustration (Smolkin et al., 1992); and even attachment bonds between mother and child (Bus, this volume; Bus & van IJzendoorn, 1988), to name just a few. Aside from these "external" variables, the event also seems to be constrained by features of the child's own cognitive development (cf. Ferreiro & Teberosky, 1982; Vernon & Ferreiro, 1999; Yaden, Smolkin, & MacGillivray, 1993). Thus, CAS theory suggests that the overall behavior or series of events in a complex system like storybook reading is an outcome of multiple interactions and must be studied as such. It is not possible to study any one event or aspect in isolation, without continual reference to the other elements impinging upon it.

It Is the Concerted or Aggregate Behavior of These Agents That Must Be Understood

As was stated earlier, when conversational segments are looked at in isolation one is likely to draw the conclusion that children are, a great deal of the time, resistant to their parents' suggestions, and that parents themselves oftentimes acquiesce to their children's insistence on unconventional notions about the text (cf. Samantha's mother conceding that polar bears live in igloos). However, three decades of research (cf. Bus, van IJzendoorn, & Pellegrini, 1995) has consistently found that children who come from homes where there is regular storybook reading increase their vocabulary and language development, learn to read earlier, respond to school instruction more quickly, and are more successful in school than their peers who do not regularly engage in this activity. Thus there seems to be, during the preschool period, a larger, or perhaps deeper, algorithm at work, which guides children through the maze of information laid out by the varieties of print in their environment and the statements that adults make about text.

What, then, can be made of the frequent differences of opinion between parent and child? Do these simply cancel out over time? Through what kind of dialogic exchanges does the child attain more conventional notions of text? Is it simply a matter of repetition? Or do these apparent contrasts in perception contain within them the very seeds of understanding? According to CAS theory, the answers to all of these questions must be sought by looking at the behavior as a whole.

The Interactions That Generate Aggregate Behavior Are Nonlinear, and Aggregate Behavior Cannot Be Derived by Simply Summing up the Behaviors of the Isolated Elements

Although some information about the nature of conversation can be inferred from looking at categories of interaction such as numbers of questions, comments, confirmations, or negations (e.g., Hayden & Fagan, 1987), or examining the content of talk in terms of literacy elements (cf. Morrow, 1988; Yaden et al., 1989), this kind of analysis is unable to track the effects of comments over time, which is, in essence, what a conversation is all about. A nonlinear view of the talk between mother and child allows, in one interpretation, for a repeated piece of misinformation to have a relatively small effect in the child's overall understanding, whereas a seemingly small conventional understanding may have far-reaching effects. Of course, the reverse may happen as well, which might help to explain why some children who find reading difficult tend to persist in unconventional notions about the interpretation of written symbols and text, while others move on easily.

The Agents or Components of a CAS Are Both Numerous and Diverse, Each Having Individual Histories, but Melded Into a Complex Web and Hierarchy of Interconnections

Storybook reading conversations are comprised of many dimensions, of which the following three are most salient here (cf. Spradley, 1980; Yaden, 1993):

1. Actors (e.g., mother, father, grandparent, sibling).
2. The activities performed (e.g., readings of various kinds of text, with varying approaches, at various times).

3. The places where these activities occur (e.g., parents' bed, child's bed, living room, dining room).

The possible permutations of these variables truly challenge any effort toward a definitive research description, since the interactions have a pattern that changes each time a story is read, sometimes subtly, sometimes dramatically. For example, after having read one book, a child frequently "imports" (see Elster, 1995, 1998) a selected bit of information from that book into the reading of another, thereby forging a new connection between the two texts. In storybook reading, patterns form one over the other, pattern upon pattern, new and old over-layered in an ever-evolving learning experience (cf. the meaning of the geologic metaphor in Vygotsky, 1960/1997).

The Diversity of CAS Agents Is Not Just a Kaleidoscope of Accidental Patterns, Since the System Reorganizes Itself With a Cascade of Changes If One Element Is Removed

One of the signature features of dynamic systems is their sensitive dependence on initial conditions (Lorenz, 1993). In other words, each change in the system, large or small, brings about a change in the entire system. Small changes are not always dampened; instead, they may become amplified or send ripples throughout the entire system. Similarly, in storybook reading, children's patterns of interaction vary according to the reader, the type of book read, the number of rereadings, etc. (Smolkin et al., 1992). Interestingly, this type of restructuring may explain the differences between home and school storybook reading. Even though the same books may be read in both settings, the changes are evident in the environment, the identity and number of participants, and the expectations around the reading. Children's responses to storybooks are not uniform across different environments. No part of the system may be changed without influencing the outcome.

The Diversity of the Agents Evolves, With New Niches for Interaction Emerging and New Kinds of Agents Filling Them; Hence, the Aggregate Behavior Exhibits a Perpetual Novelty, Never Settling Down, an Aspect That Bodes Ill for Standard Mathematical Approaches

Another widely noted feature of complex systems is their internal algorithm for change, above and beyond any external influence. What this means for actors engaged in storybook reading is that even though the event is, in essence, an "open system," in which all participants are sensitive to the social interactions between them, some changes within children seem to follow their own internal clock. White (1954) noted long ago that after the reading of a book, her daughter seemed to go through a "simmering and brewing" process, from which questions and comments about the book would emerge sometimes days or weeks later. The examples presented in the introductory section of this chapter also illustrate that parent's corrections can be resisted over time, so that their social inputs, in some instances, have no immediate effect on the child's understanding. In summary, no two storybook readings are ever the same; some aspect of the system is always changing, even through several rereadings of the same work.

CAS Agents Employ Internal Models of a Seemingly Diagnostic Character to Direct Their Behavior: That Is, A Set of Rules That Enables an Agent to Anticipate the Consequences of Its Actions

For some time now, researchers with a developmental perspective (Ferreiro & Teberosky, 1982; Vernon & Ferreiro, 1999) have pointed out that when it comes to interpreting the written symbol system, children's behavior is rule-governed. It seems that parents and children both follow internal scripts during storybook reading. For example, Snow and Ninio (1986) have posited seven "contracts," or rules, that children learn during the course of book reading, including rules that books are for reading, not eating; that the book controls the pace and sequence of the reading; that pictures are for naming, yet pictures are not in real time; and others. One important implication of this rule is that all behavior is purposeful. For example, the children's rejections of their parents' corrections in the preceding examples must be interpreted as adhering to some set of principles which allows for the child's interpretation and not the parents, instead of merely being a piece of misinformation that will be eradicated after sufficient parental correction. Changes in the child's interpretation come *with* changes in the rule system, not before (cf. Piaget, 1975/1985).

MOVING FROM METAPHOR TO METHOD

Creating a "Strange Attractor" or Fractal Image of a Conversation

The advantage of a nonlinear systems approach to storybook reading is that it is possible to preserve the moment-by-moment evolution of the variables selected for analysis, through an analytic technique known as "state space reconstruction," which graphs these interactive, time-series relationships in three-dimensional space (Shaw, 1984). Theoretically as well as mathematically (Vallacher & Nowak, 1994), these shapes, graphed in three dimensions, are equivalent to the shapes or images that would appear if all of the relevant variables that influence the system could be graphed simultaneously. This graphing is accomplished by a mathematical technique known as Ruelle and Taken's Trick Protocol (Greeley, 1990, 1995) or Taken's Theorem (Vallacher & Nowak, 1994), which is now widely used as a reliable method for reconstructing the "shape" of the movement in a dynamic system, as explained later.

The assumptions behind this technique are as follows. First of all, it would be ideal, but nearly impossible, for one to select the exact variables that describe the function of a dynamic system. For example, in storybook reading, what are the most important aspects to be observed or measured? As mentioned earlier, various studies have already looked at the contributions of, for example, parent style, narrative versus expository structure, the content of children's questions, teacher style, genre type, and gender (see Kamler, 1999, and Solsken, 1993, for a discussion of gender's influence on literacy development) to the outcomes of storybook reading. And ideally, all of the aforementioned variables, perhaps with the addition of still others, should be looked at simultaneously to fully understand what constitutes a storybook reading event.

However, the second principle underlying "state space reconstruction" is that the key variables in a system contain a residual trace or reflect the history of other variables. As Farmer (cited in Gleick, 1987, p. 266) has pointed out, "When you think about a variable, the evolution of it must be influenced by whatever variables it's interacting with. Their values must somehow be contained in the history of that thing. Somehow their mark must be in there." Briggs and Peat (1989) further stated that "in a turbulent flow, each element of the flow acts as a contingency for every other part ... measuring one part or aspect [allows] a snapshot of the whole system" (p. 88). Therefore, not all possible variables in the system need to be measured—only those that preserve the dynamic nature of the system.

The state or "phase" space attractor is interpreted visually by looking at the structure of the three-dimensional shape created by the plotting of three time series (the original data sequence and two more derived from it; see Yaden, 1999b, for details on the graphing procedure for this data set). In addition, there are many possible distinct shapes that indicate the presence of a dynamic system. As Gleick (1987) has written, "truly random data remains spread out in an undefined mess. But chaos—deterministic and patterned—pulls the data into visible shapes" (p. 267). An example of one of the classic, dynamic phase plots depicts the pattern of a dripping faucet (Shaw, 1984), as shown in Fig. 15.1.

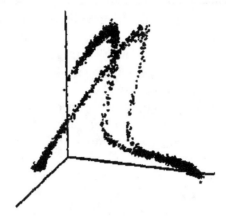

FIG. 15.1. Phase space portrait of water dripping from a faucet (from Shaw, 1984).

3-Dimensional, Fractal Images of Storybook Reading Conversations: Why a Dynamic Reanalysis?

The dynamic systems analysis in this chapter reanalyzes data collected from an investigation of the effects of genre and print format on children's print-oriented talk (see Smolkin & Yaden, 1992, Smolkin et al., 1992, and Yaden et al., 1993, for complete details). In this study, six preschoolers and their parents read nine books three times each over approximately a month's time, in a multiple-baseline, alternating treatment design (with book genres conceptualized as treatments). The nine books were divided into three sets. Two of the sets contained an alphabet book along with a picture book or information book, and the third (control) set comprised only picture storybooks. Each book set was read over a 10-day period, after which the books were collected and another set was given to the parents. The instructions dictated only that each book should be read three times; their specific order was determined by the parent and child. Coding schemes for the classification of questions and comments were applied in two dimensions: one system (19 categories) was used to describe the dialogic interaction (e.g., question, comment, request, answers, etc.); the other system indicated the print content or focus of attention of the utterance (e.g., letter, word, phrase, directionality, metalanguage, act of reading). A total of 17 hours and 40 minutes of storybook reading were transcribed for the six children, including a total of 1,894 comments and questions.

The general findings showed that the type of book used during storybook reading at home had a decided influence on both the types of linguistic exchanges and the topics of conversation in parent–child dialogues. For example, the two alphabet books, *Dr. Seuss's ABC* (Seuss, 1963) and *A Is for Angry* (Boynton, 1983), accounted for over half of the total number of responses: 555 and 420, respectively. *Crictor* (Ungerer, 1986), which has alphabet-book-like characteristics on two pages, generated the third highest number of responses (258). This is in contrast to the numbers of questions and comments for the information book and the five other picture storybooks, which ranged from 56 to 151. Although conversations about letters occurred more frequently in the alphabet books, questions and comments about words, conventions (such as directionality), and the act of reading itself occurred in all types of books with significant regularity.

What these analyses did not show was how the discourse categories evolved in time: that is, how did the conversation flow? How did each speech act connect or not connect with those preceeding and succeeding it? As Taylor's (1986) description so aptly demonstrates, parent–child storybook reading discourse is subject to stops and starts, digressions, gaps of focus and attention on the part of both the child and the parent, as well as a host of other conversational features that interpenetrate, interact, and shape the dialogic style and content of the talk. Without some way of preserving the interconnectivity of these dialogic elements, "the temporal sequence of material is lost" (Rapp, Jimenez-Montano, Langs, Thomson, & Mees, 1991, p. 209). Thus, through the use of an analytic systems scheme such as state space reconstruction, we hoped to recapture the dynamic of this nonlinear dialogue and catch a glimpse, even if only a representational one, of the process of meaning-making as it happened.

The Topography of Conversations During Storybook Reading
Dynamic Analysis Potentials and Caveats

As stated earlier, the emergence of distinct forms strongly suggests the presence of a nonlinear system, while randomized data appears to be undifferentiated (similar to what a scatter plot would look like for a correlation of zero). In addition, the software used to generate the following graphs has the capability of tracking the conversational turn-taking in color, thus revealing the types of comments from both mother and child as they follow one another in sequence. Further, because this image is three-dimensional it can be rotated on the screen and viewed from various angles, allowing a kind of graphic factor analysis.

Subsequently, a visual scan of the multi-colored plot can reveal who is doing the most talking and, depending on the designation of the coding, what they are talking about. Also, any part of the figure—in other words, any portion of the conversation—can be isolated on the computer and those specific data points or sequence of comments examined in more detail. Thus, a state space reconstruction of a phenomenon such as a conversation allows simultaneous viewing of both the broad system parameters "in motion," and the individual components in one glance (see the review by Weitzman, 2000, for other ways of analyzing conversation with more traditional software programs). However, since the images to be discussed in the next section of this chapter can only be printed in black and white, I discuss just the first stage of dynamic analysis, or, in other words, only the overall shape of the phase plot or "fractal" image. Under these circumstances, results of all the six children's storybook reading conversations will not be discussed: for clarity's sake, only the two most distinct and the two least distinct are shown.

Graphic Representations of Four Children's Storybook Talk

The individual graphs in Figs. 15.2a–d and 15.3a–d show the resulting three-dimensional scatterplots and phase portraits of four of the six children's dialogue (all names are pseudonyms). Figure 15.2 shows two pairs of scatterplots and phase portraits—one of each for Alice (Figs. 15.2a & 15.2b) and the other for Carol (Figs. 15.2c & 15.2d). Particularly in the two scatterplots (Figs. 15.2a & 15.2c), an obvious "clustering" of data points appears in certain sections, giving the overall impression of different kinds of snowflakes being formed. These clusters of points, or "galaxies," as Greeley (1995) termed them, represent sites within the conversation where certain sequences of talk occur at regular, albeit nonlinear, intervals. Figures 15.2b & 15.2d represent the phase space trajectories, or phase portraits, that are constructed by connecting the values of the time-series sequentially. Again, the plots of Alice and Carol show a distinct pattern, resembling something like a lopsided six-pointed star, with open areas, or "basins of attraction," in their middle areas.

In contrast to the data for Alice and Carol, Mark and David's scatterplots and phase portraits (Figs. 15.3a & 15.3b and 15.3c & 15.3d, respectively) show little, if any, distinctive patterning.

In both boys' scatterplots (Figs. 15.3a & 15.3c), but particularly in David's, the data points are distributed almost equally across the three dimensions, although the outlying points for Mark are beginning to line up in a more regular fashion. The boys' reconstructed phase portraits (Figs. 15.3b & 15.3d), however, are much less distinctive than those of the two girls, particularly in their centers. Unlike the portraits in Figs. 15.2b & 15.2d, neither Mark's nor David's

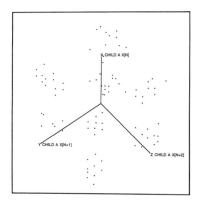

FIG. 15.2a. Scatterplot of the 227 discourse moves of Alice, age 4 years, 1 month.

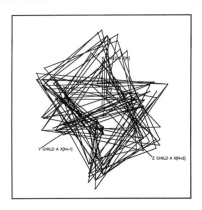

FIG. 15.2b. Alice's phase portrait.

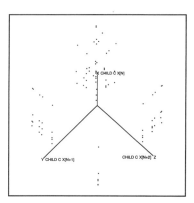

FIG. 15.2c. Scatterplot of the 304 discourse moves of Carol, age 4 years, 2 months (from Yaden, 1999a).

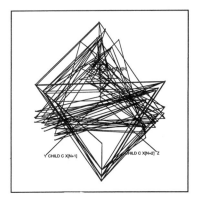

FIG. 15.2d. Carol's phase portrait (from Yaden, 1999a).

graph shows any recognizable open areas or basins of attraction around which the points are clustered.

INTERPRETATIONS AND SPECULATIONS

The following interpretations are a first attempt at understanding storybook reading as a deterministic, nonlinear system by applying some of the methods which have been developed for analyzing complexity (see Yaden, 1999a, for another discussion of CAS theory and patterns of reading difficulty). The discussion focuses

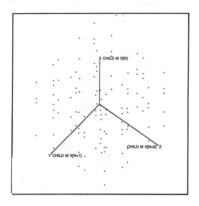

FIG. 15.3a. Scatterplot of the 335 discourse moves of Mark, age 3 years, 9 months.

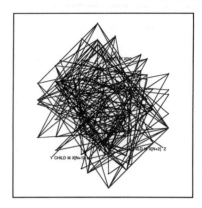

FIG. 15.3b. Mark's phase portrait.

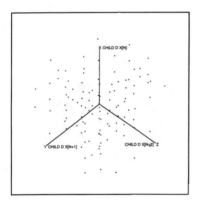

FIG. 15.3c. Scatterplot of the 233 discourse moves of David, age 4 years, 8 months (from Yaden, 1999a).

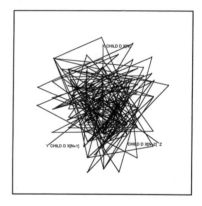

FIG. 15.3d. David's phase portrait (from Yaden, 1999a).

on some general principles of CAS theory as they relate to storybook reading, background information on the children, and inferences about how what is known about early literacy acquisition can be interpreted, and perhaps illuminated, through the use of dynamic terminology and concepts.

Revisiting Standard Nonlinear Action Formats

As Ninio and Bruner (1978) have pointed out, many parents use a "standard action format" in storybook reading, a type of scaffolding which basically involves calling their child's attention to a portion of the book, asking for or supplying a label, and offering some type of feedback, thus implying an emerging, but predictable sequence. However, none of the graphs discussed here indicate a corresponding regularity in the children's behavior. If the children were merely responding in kind or following the parents' lead, then the individual plots would show convergence where each individual child's responses were "pooled"—a steady state, in other words, somewhat similar to a "line of best fit." As can be seen, none of the trajectories show such a convergence. A more colloquial way of explaining this is that parents do not always get answers to their questions, nor do they always respond to their children's comments or requests. Similarly, children often do not wait to be asked for their input, and from early on may actively attempt to participate in the reading, despite the parent's idea of how a reading should be conducted. However, the phase portraits of Alice and Carol show a kind of behavior that can be described as "locally unpredictable, but globally stable" (cf. Kellert, 1993; Stewart, 1989). Assuming that storybook reading involves a relatively small set of operational behaviors (i.e., question/answer, gesture/label, etc.), these behaviors produce a highly complex dialogic pattern. The growth of literacy knowledge, then, must be seen as embedded in the ebb and flow of storybook conversations, and not in a simple scaffolding structure, in which knowledge is assumed to grow by accretion.

"Attractor Basins" in Storybook Reading

What are the "attractors" around which the children's trajectories—particularly those of Alice and Carol—are shaped? And what is to be made of the graph of David's behavior, which shows the least structure of all? One definition of an "attractor" is that it is the state to which a system eventually settles (Lewin, 1992, p. 20) or "some portion of the phase space such that any point which starts nearby gets closer and closer to it" (Stewart, 1989, p. 110). As can be seen from Figs. 2b and 2d, Alice and Carol's phase portraits clearly demonstrate the presence of one or more basins of attraction around which their trajectories of responses are constrained. From a storybook reading perspective, the basin of attraction may be formed by underlying (and implicit) conversational rules operating with something analogous to both centripetal and centrifugal forces. In other words, the conversation between mother and child forms a dynamic but flexible tension in which both partners exert their expectations, and yet "cooperate" such that information flows back and forth between them in a satisfying and productive way, although each person may have different ideas of what exactly the conversation is about (cf. Vygotsky, 1934/1987, and the discussion of the assignment of different meanings to the same words in conversation used by children and adults).

Snow and Ninio (1986) have suggested that children learn seven implicit "contracts" or rules during storybook interactions with their parents. One possible candidate for a storybook reading "attractor" is this rule-governed acquisition of literacy knowledge, which subtly shapes the behavior of both parent and child. The growth of literacy knowledge must be seen as more than just the presence of a book and a willing adult to read to the child; there may be developmental issues shaping the child's behavior, as well as variations in the abilities of parents to provide a sufficient universe of information from which the child can draw.

A preliminary hypothesis is that Alice and Carol's plots may provide examples of how healthy storybook reading conversations proceed. In other words, the conversation is not just a matter of turn-taking, but rather a complex rhythm in which both conversants exhibit a "give and take" between them, and also allow (whether consciously or not) disagreements, misunderstandings and even silences to become part of the overall dialogue, with each phenomenon contributing just as much, perhaps more, or perhaps as little, to the dynamic rhythm of the conversation as any other portion.

In contrast, this rhythm never seemed to develop in either Mark's or David's sessions. Even though David was the oldest child in the sample (4 years, 8 months), his phase space plot shows an almost, if not completely, random dispersion of responses. From the transcripts, it was clear that David's father had a more structured agenda and allowed his son much less freedom to explore various aspects of the book. One interpretation of David's seemingly random response pattern could be that that he may have been uncertain about the "contracts" which he was supposed to learn, and through which literacy knowledge is acquired; hence, his responses did not show the patterned regularity seen with Alice or Carol, for whom the storybook reading environment was more secure and comforting.

CONCLUSIONS

Goldstein (1994), in a paper entitled "So you've found chaos in your data—so what?" suggests two ways of answering his own question. The first is to establish the *sources* of variability or nonlinearity in the data: to ask, in other words, what is driving the system. The second tack is to discover *why* the variability is necessary—or, said another way, to determine whether the dynamic system is useful to the particular network of forces or organism being observed.

Sources of Variability

One source of variability that emerged in this study (Smolkin et al., 1992) was the child's contribution to the dialogue. Variability in this factor was a consequence not only of the child's participation as a regular interlocutor, but also of the type of response given. It derives from the quality of the child's questions, comments, and answers less than it does from the quantity of those responses within the overall interchange between parent and child.

It should also be noted that the phase portraits of the two female subjects show distinct similarities to each other, as do the graphs of the two males. Unfortunately, as contact has been lost with these parents, it is impossible to say for sure whether gender differences were a significant source of variability in the children's learning how to read; but the similarities and contrasts between the phase portraits are tantalizingly suggestive of some underlying pattern, perhaps created by mothers reading to daughters and fathers reading to sons (cf. Solsken, 1993). Overall, this type of analysis may help us sift through all of the factors that have traditionally been suggested as important variables in storybook reading (e.g., rereading, book format, adult gender, reading style), to determine which of these really do have a significant influence on the flow of information between parent and child.

The second question, about how a dynamic system can benefit the organism or system under examination, also offers exciting possibilities for thinking about literacy growth. In fields like medicine (Goldberger et al., 1990), for example, researchers are finding that variations in individual cardiac rhythms act as a buffer, allowing the normally functioning body to survive considerable stresses over the course of its life span. This ability to react to a wide variety of new stimuli has also been posited as the primary survival mechanism for several species in the animal kingdom (Freeman, 1991). It is entirely feasible that a wide variation in responses during storybook time, including the use of unconventional questions, answers, and comments, may be the best way for children to explore the nature of written language and test out their hypotheses, implicit though they may be.

The freedom to explore books and experiment with written forms without undue adult criticism may serve children's literacy development in much the same way that physiological variability enables the body to function healthily. As Goldberger et al. (1990) stated, "The healthy heart dances, dying organs march." As literacy educators and researchers we need to consider whether it may be a diversity of "dances" that leads to healthy reading habits. We must seek out newer and more appropriate ways to conduct our research and analysis—ways that don't slow the growth or the understanding of literacy down to a few unsure, shuffling steps.

ACKNOWLEDGMENTS

I would like to thank Laura B. Smolkin for collecting the data that was used for the constructing the phase portraits. I would also like to thank Lillian Greeley for generating the original graphic portraits on which Figs. 15.2 and 15.3 are based, and for her assistance in interpreting them.

REFERENCES

Abraham, F. D. , Abraham, R. H., Shaw, C. D., & Garfinkel, A. (1990). *A visual introduction to dynamical systems theory for psychology*. Santa Cruz, CA: Aerial Press.

Bak, P. (1996). *How nature works: The science of self-organized criticality*. New York: Springer-Verlag.

Bak, P., & Chen, K. (1991, January). Self-organized criticality. *Scientific American, 264*, 46–53.

Baker, P. L. (1993). Chaos, order and sociological theory. *Sociological Inquiry, 63*(2), 123–149.

Briggs, J., & Peat, F. D. (1989). *Turbulent mirror: An illustrated guide to chaos theory and the science of wholeness*. New York: Harper & Row.

Boynton, S. (1983). *A is for angry: An animal and adjective alphabet*. New York: Workman.

Bus, A. G., & van IJzendoorn, M. H. (1988). Mother–child interactions, attachment, and emergent literacy: A cross-sectional study. *Child Development, 59*, 1262–1272.

Bus, A. G., van IJzendoorn, M. H., & Pellegrini, A. D. (1995). Joint book reading makes for success in learning to read: A meta-analysis on intergenerational transmission of literacy. *Review of Educational Research, 65*, 1–21.

Crichton, M. (1990). *Jurassic park*. New York: Alfred A. Knopf.

Crichton, M. (1995). *The lost world*. New York: Alfred A. Knopf.

Cronbach, L. J. (1988, August-September). Playing with chaos. *Educational Researcher, 17*, 46–49.

DeBruin-Parecki, A. (1999). *Assessing adult/child storybook reading practices* (CIERA Technical Report No. 2-004). Ann Arbor, MI: Center for the Improvement of Early Reading Achievement.

Doll, W. E., Jr. (1989). Complexity in the classroom. *Educational Leadership, 47*(1), 65–70.

Doll, W. E., Jr. (1993). *A post-modern perspective on curriculum*. New York: Teachers College Press.

Edelman, G. M. (1992). *Bright air, brilliant fire*. New York: Basic Books.

Elster, C. (1995). Importations in preschoolers' emergent readings. *Journal of Reading Behavior, 27*(1), 65–84.

Elster, C. (1998). Influences of text and pictures on shared and emergent readings. *Research in the Teaching of English, 32*, 43–78.

Ennis, C. D. (1992). Reconceptualizing learning as a dynamical system. *Journal of Curriculum and Supervision, 7*(2), 115–130.

Ferreiro, E., & Teberosky, A. (1982). *Literacy before schooling*. Portsmouth, NH: Heinemann.

Foucault, M. (1972). *The archaeology of knowledge*. New York: Pantheon.

Freeman, W. J. (1991). The physiology of perception. *Scientific American, 264*(2), 78–85.

Fuhriman, A., & Burlingame, G. M. (1994). Measuring small group process: A methodological application of chaos theory. *Small Group Research, 25*(4), 502–519.

Gleick, J. (1987). *Chaos: Making a new science.* New York: Viking.

Goldberger, A. L., Rigney, D. R., & West, B. J. (1990). Chaos and fractals in human physiology. *Scientific American, 262*(2), 43–49.

Goldstein, J. (1994, February). *So you've found chaos in your data—So what? Scientific explanation in applied chaos theory.* Paper presented at the second annual Winter Chaos Conference, New Haven, CT.

Gough, N. (1994, April). *Chaos and curriculum inquiry: More than a metaphor?* Paper presented at the annual meeting of the American Educational Research Association, New Orleans, LA.

Greeley, L. (1990). *Philosophical spacing: Key to the nonlinear complex dynamics of the attentional system of the cognitive learning process in the philosophical dialectic method.* Unpublished doctoral dissertation, Harvard University, Cambridge, MA.

Greeley, L. (1995). Complexity in the attention system of the cognitive generative learning process. In A. Albert (Ed.), *Chaos and society* (pp. 373–386). Sainte-Foy, Québec, Canada: Presses de l'Université du Québec; Amsterdam: IOS Press.

Greening, M. M. (1993). *The sense of chaos: A dynamical theory of narrative.* Unpublished dissertation, University of California–Santa Cruz, Santa Cruz, CA.

Guastello, S. J. (1995). *Chaos, catastrophe, and human affairs: Applications of non-linear dynamics to work, organizations, and social evolution.* Mahwah, NJ: Lawrence Erlbaum Associates.

Guess, D., & Sailor, W. (1993). Chaos theory and the study of human behavior: Implications for special education and developmental disabilities. *The Journal of Special Education, 27*(1), 16–34.

Haden, C. A., & Fivush, R. (1994). *Consistency and change in maternal reading styles.* Paper presented at the annual meeting of the American Educational Research Association, New Orleans, LA.

Hayden, H. M. R., & Fagan, W. T. (1987). Fathers and mothers reading familiar and unfamiliar stories to their children. *Reading-Canada-Lecture, 5,* 231–238.

Hayles, N. K. (1991). *Chaos and order.* Chicago: University of Chicago Press.

Hoberman, M. A. (1982). *A house is a house for me.* New York: Puffin Books.

Holland, J. H. (1995a). Can there be a unified theory of complex adaptive systems? In H. J. Morowitz & J. L. Singer (Eds.), *The mind, the brain, and complex adaptive systems* (pp. 45–50). Reading, MA: Addison-Wesley.

Holland, J. H. (1995b). *Hidden order: How adaption builds complexity.* Reading, MA: Addison-Wesley.

Kamler, B. (1999). *Constructing gender and difference: Critical perspectives on early childhood.* Cresskill, NJ: Hampton Press.

Kauffman, S. A. (1991, August). Anti-chaos and adaptation. *Scientific American,* 78–84.

Kauffman, S. A. (1995). *At home in the universe: The search for the laws of self-organization and complexity.* New York: Oxford University Press.

Kellert, S. H. (1993). *In the wake of chaos: Unpredictable order in dynamical systems.* Chicago: University of Chicago Press.

Kook, H., & Vedder, P. (1994, April). *Parental book-reading to four- and five-year-old children in Curaçao.* Paper presented at the annual meeting of the American Educational Research Association, New Orleans, LA.

Kosko, B. (1999). *Heaven in a chip: Fuzzy visions of society and science in the digital age.* New York: Three Rivers Press.

Lewin, R. (1992). *Complexity: Life at the edge of chaos.* New York: Collier Books.

Lindsay, J. S. (1989, February). *Chaos theory: Implications for educational research.* Paper presented at the annual meeting of the Eastern Educational Research Association, Savannah, GA.

Lindsay, J. S. (1991). *The chaos pattern in Piaget's theory of cognitive development.* Unpublished manuscript, University of Virginia, Charlottesville, VA.

Lorenz, E. N. (1963). Deterministic nonperiodic flow. *Journal of Atmospheric Sciences, 20,* 130–141.

Lorenz, E. (1993). *The essence of chaos.* Seattle: University of Washington Press.

McDonald, S. (1992). *Alphabatics.* New York: Aladdin Books.

Meyer, L. A., Wardrop, J. L., Stahl, S. A., & Linn, R. L. (1994). Effects of reading storybooks aloud to children. *Journal of Educational Research, 88,* 69–85.

Morrow, L. M. (1988). Young children's responses to one-on-one story reading in school settings. *Reading Research Quarterly, 23,* 89–107.

Ninio, A. (1980). Picture-book reading in mother–infant dyads belonging to two subgroups in Israel. *Child Development, 51,* 587–590.

Ninio, A., & Bruner, J. (1978). The achievement and antecedents of labeling. *Journal of Child Language, 5,* 5–15.

Nowak, A., & Lewenstein, M. (1994). Dynamical systems: A tool for social psychology? In R. R. Vallacher & A. Nowak (Eds.), *Dynamical systems in social psychology* (pp. 17–53). San Diego: Academic Press.

Panofsky, C. (1986, December). *The functions of language in parent–child bookreading events.* Paper presented at the annual meeting of the National Reading Conference, Austin, TX.

Pappas, C. C. (1991). Young children's strategies in learning the "book language" of information books. *Discourse Processes, 14,* 203–225.

Pappas, C. C. (1993). Is narrative "primary"? Some insights from kindergartners' pretend readings of stories and information books. *Journal of Reading Behavior, 25* (1), 97–130.

Patterson, L., Cotton, C., Kimball-Lopez, K., Pavonetti, L., & Van Horn, L. (1998). The shared "AH-HA experience": Literature conversations and self-organizing complex adaptive systems. In T. Shanahan & F. V. Rodriguez-Brown (Eds.), *Forty-seventh yearbook of the National Reading Conference* (pp. 143–156). Chicago: National Reading Conference.

Pellegrini, A. D., Perlmutter, J. C., Galda, L., & Brody, G. H. (1990). Joint book reading between Black Head Start children and their mothers. *Child Development, 61,* 443–453.

Phillips, L. M., Norris, S. P., & Mason, J. M. (1996). Longitudinal effects of early literacy concepts on reading achievement: A kindergarten intervention and five-year follow-up. *Journal of Literacy Research, 28,* 173–195.

Piaget, J. (1985). *The equilibration of cognitive structures: The central problem of intellectual development* (T. Brown & K. Thampy, Trans.). Chicago: University of Chicago Press. (Original work published 1975)

Prigogine, I. (1996). *The end of certainty: Time, chaos and the new laws of nature.* New York: The Free Press.

Prigogine, I., & Stengers, I. (1984). *Order out of chaos: Man's new dialogue with nature.* New York: Bantam Books.

Rapp, P. E., Jimenez-Montano, M. A., Langs, R. J., Thomson, L. & Mees, A. I. (1991). Toward a quantitative characterization of patient–therapist communication. *Mathematical Biosciences, 105,* 207–227.

Robinson, R., & Yaden, D. B. (1993). Chaos or nonlinear dynamics: Implications for reading research. *Reading Research and Instruction, 32* (3), 10–14.

Roser, N., & Martinez, M. (1985). Roles adults play in preschoolers' response to literature. *Language Arts, 62* (5), 485–490.

Sacks, O. (1990). Chaos and awakenings. In O. Sacks (Ed.), *Awakenings* (pp. 351–366). New York: HarperCollins.

Seuss, Dr. (1963). *Dr. Seuss's ABC.* New York: Random House.

Scarborough, H. S., & Dobrich, W. (1994). Another look at parent–preschooler book reading: How naked is the emperor? *Development Review, 14,* 340–347.

Shanahan, T., & Hogan, V. (1983). Parent reading style and children's print awareness. In J. Niles & L. A. Harris (Eds.), *Thirty-second yearbook of the National Reading Conference* (pp. 212–217). Rochester, NY: National Reading Conference.

Shaw, R. (1984). *The dripping faucet as a model chaotic system.* Santa Cruz, CA: Aerial Press.

Smolkin, L. B., & Yaden, D. B. (1992). O is for mouse: First encounters with the alphabet book. *Language Arts, 69*(6), 432–443.

Smolkin, L. B., Yaden, D. B., Brown, L. M., & Hofius, B. (1992). The effects of genre, visual design choices, and discourse structure on preschoolers' responses to picture storybooks during parent–child read-alouds. In C. Kinzer & D. Leu (Eds.), *Literacy research, theory, and practice: Views from many perspectives. Forty-first yearbook of the National Reading Conference* (pp. 291–302). Chicago: National Reading Conference.

Snow, C. E. (1983). Literacy and language: Relationships during the preschool years. *Harvard Educational Review, 53,* 165–189.

Snow, C. E., & Ninio, A. (1986). The contracts of literacy: What children learn from learning to read books. In W. H. Teale & E. Sulzby (Eds.), *Emergent literacy: Writing and reading* (pp. 116–138). Norwood, NJ: Ablex.

Solsken, J. (1993). *Literacy, gender and work: In families and in school.* Norwood, NJ: Ablex.

Spielberg, S. (Director), & Johnston, J. (Director). (2001). *Jurassic Park III.* [Film]. Hollywood, CA: Universal Pictures.

Spradley, J. (1980). *Participant observation.* New York: Holt, Rinehart, & Winston.

Stewart, I. (1989). *Does God play dice? The mathematics of chaos.* Cambridge, MA: Basil Blackwell.

Sulzby, E., & Teale, W. (1991). Emergent literacy. In R. Barr, M. Kamil, P. Mosenthal, & P. D. Pearson (Eds.), *Handbook of reading research* (Vol. 2, pp. 727–757). New York: Longman.

Sumara, D. J. (2000). Researching complexity. *Journal of Literacy Research, 32*(2), 267–281.

Syverson, M. A. (1999). *The wealth of reality: An ecology of composition.* Carbondale, IL: Southern Illinois University Press.

Taylor, D. (1986). Creating family story: "Matthew! We're going to have a ride!" In W. H. Teale & E. Sulzby (Eds.), *Emergent literacy: Writing and reading.* Norwood, NJ: Ablex.

Teale, W. H., & Martinez, M. (1986). Teachers' storybook reading styles: Evidence and implications. *Reading Education in Texas, 2,* 7–16.

Templeton, S., & Bear, D. R. (1992). *Development of orthographic knowledge and the foundations of literacy: A memorial festschrift for Edmund H. Henderson.* Mahwah, NJ: Lawrence Erlbaum Associates.

Ungerer, T. (1986). *Crictor.* New York: Harper & Row.

Vallacher, R. R., & Nowak, A. (1994). *Dynamical systems in social psychology.* Orlando, FL: Academic Press.

Vernon, S., & Ferreiro, E. (1999). Writing development: A neglected variable in the consideration of phonological awareness. *Harvard Educational Review, 69,* 395–414.

von Bertalanffy, L. (1968). *General systems theory: Foundations, development, applications* (rev. ed.). New York: George Braziller.

Vygotsky, L. S. (1997). Genesis of higher mental functions. In R. Rieber (Ed.) & M. J. Hall (Trans.), *The collected works of L. S. Vygotsky, Volume 4: The history of the development of higher mental functions* (pp. 97–120). New York: Plenum Press. (Original work published 1960)

Vygotsky, L. S. (1987). Thinking and speech. In R. W. Rieber & A. S. Carton (Eds.) & N. Minick (Trans.), *The collected works of L. S. Vygotsky, Volume 1: Problems of general psychology* (pp. 39–285). New York: Plenum Press. (Original work published 1934)

Weaver, C. (1985). Parallels between new paradigms in science and in reading and literacy theories: An essay review. *Research in the Teaching of English, 19*(3), 298–316.

Wells, G. (1986). *The meaning-makers: Children learning language and using language to learn.* Portsmouth, NH: Heinemann.

Weitzman, E. A. (2000). Software and qualitative research. In N. K. Denzin & Y. S. Lincoln (Eds.), *Handbook of qualitative research* (2nd ed., pp. 803–820). Thousand Oaks, CA: Sage Publications, Inc.

White, D. (1954). *Books before five.* New York: Oxford University Press.

Whitehurst, G. J., & Lonigan, C. J. (1998). Child development and emergent literacy. *Child Development, 69,* 848–872.

Whitehurst, G. J., Epstein, J. N., Angell, A. L., & Payne, A. C. (1994). Outcomes of an emergent literacy intervention in Head Start. *Journal of Educational Psychology, 86,* 542–555.

Yaden, D. B., Jr. (1988). Understanding stories through repeated read-alouds: How many does it take? *The Reading Teacher, 41,* 556–560.

Yaden, D. B., Jr. (1993). Evaluating early literacy knowledge by analyzing children's responses in storybooks during home read-alouds. In A. Carrasquillo & C. Hedley (Eds.), *Whole language and the bilingual learner* (pp. 132–150). Norwood, NJ: Ablex.

Yaden, D. B., Jr. (1995, December). *Complexity theory and parent–child storybook reading: Exploring the topology of conversation.* Paper presented at the annual meeting of the National Reading Conference, New Orleans, LA.

Yaden, D. B., Jr. (1999a). Reading disability and dynamical systems: When predictability implies pathology. In P. B. Mosenthal & D. Evensen (Eds.), *Reconsidering the role of the reading clinic in a new age of literacy* (pp. 293–323). Greenwich, CT: JAI Press.

Yaden, D. B., Jr. (1999b). *Reconstructing the state space of parent–child storybook reading conversations: A synopsis.* Unpublished manuscript, University of Southern California.

Yaden, D. B., Jr., Rowe, D. W., & MacGillivray, L. (2000). Emergent literacy: A polyphony of perspectives. In M. Kamil, P. D. Pearson, P. Mosenthal, & R. Barr (Eds.), *Handbook of reading research* (Vol. 3, pp. 425–454). Mahwah, NJ: Lawrence Erlbaum Associates.

Yaden, D. B., Jr., Smolkin, L. B., & Conlon, A. (1989). Preschoolers' questions about pictures, print conventions and story text during reading aloud at home. *Reading Research Quarterly, 24*(2), 189–214.

Yaden, D. B., Jr., Smolkin, L. B., & MacGillivray, L. (1993). A psychogenetic perspective on children's understanding about letter associations during alphabet book reading. *Journal of Reading Behavior, 25*(1), 43–68.

16

What Do We Expect Storybook Reading to Do? How Storybook Reading Impacts Word Recognition

Steven A. Stahl
University of Illinois

In *Becoming a Nation of Readers,* a report sponsored by the National Research Council, authors Anderson, Hiebert, Wilkinson, and Scott (1985) claimed that "the single most important activity for building the knowledge required for eventual success in reading is reading aloud to children" (p. 23). By reading to children, they mean a teacher or parent sitting down with a child or a group of children to read a book.

Anderson et al.'s (1985) conclusion was based on an extensive review of literature and a bit of hyperbole. The research on the relationship of parents' reading to children's literacy was based largely on correlation data. Strong correlations do not necessarily imply causality; the correlations could be due to factors such as parents' education, household income, "literacy press," or a general household emphasis on literacy learning and other factors which might influence both the amount of reading that parents do with their children and the children's reading achievement. The purpose of this chapter is to explore the relations between storybook reading and reading, stressing the relationships between teachers' and parents' storybook reading and the child's developing word recognition abilities.

A CONSERVATIVE VIEW OF THE RELATION BETWEEN STORYBOOK READING AND LITERACY

Many of the studies cited by Anderson et al. (1985) were surveys. Such surveys will inherently inflate the amount of reading reported, because reading to children is socially desirable. The relationships are much smaller in observational studies, where surveys are supplemented by on-site observers.

Barr and Dreben (Barr, 1983), Meyer, Stahl, Wardrop, and Linn (1994), and Stallings and Kaskowitz (1974) all used observational data and compared actual observations of adults' (parents' and teachers') reading to children and children's later achievement. In all three studies, the correlations were non-significant and sometimes negative. In Meyer et al.'s study, the correlations between teachers reading to children and reading achievement varied in kindergarten from −.48 (using the Wide Reading Achievement Test, or WRAT, as a criterion) to −.19 (using the Chicago Reading Test, a measure of decoding skill). Positive correlations were found only on the CIRCUS Listening Test, a measure of language comprehension, and not on the reading measures. In first grade, the correlations were closer to zero, ranging from .02 on the WRAT to .07 on the Woodcock Reading Mastery Test comprehension subtest. Reports of parents reading to children were positive, but lower than expected, ranging from 0.11 to 0.18. This suggests that only about 5% of the variance in children's achievement is associated with parents reading to them. Correlations were considerably higher (in fact, double on nearly all measures) between parents' ratings of children's participation in reading and their achievement.

Although this correlation seems low, given the weight of expectations that storybook reading supports reading achievement, the result is in the same neighborhood as findings from two meta-analyses of the effects of storybook reading on reading achievement. Bus, van IJzendoorn, and Pellegrini (1995) and Scarborough and Dobrich (1994) both found that the amount of reading that parents did to their children accounted for approximately 8% of the variance in reading achievement in kindergarten or first grade. Whether this is a lot or a little depends on one's perspective. Factors such as SES or mother's education level account for more variance (Bloom, 1976), but these characteristics are more difficult to modify. Either way, the reality of storybook reading does not seem to live up to the extravagant promises of *Becoming a Nation of Readers*.

A SIMPLE VIEW OF READING

One model that might be useful for understanding the effects of storybook reading on children's reading achievement is the "Simple View" of reading. Gough and Tunmer (1986) proposed that reading comprehension could be explained through two factors—Decoding (D) and Language Comprehension (C)—in a simple equation $RC = D \times C$. In this equation, as a person's ability to decode words drops toward zero, then reading comprehension will also drop toward zero, regardless of the child's language comprehension. If a person's language comprehension drops to zero (as when one is reading a regularly spelled language that one does not understand) then reading comprehension also drops toward zero. Several authors (Carver, 1993; Hoover & Gough, 1990) have generally validated this model. In these validations, the two factors were highly potent: The individual terms accounted for so much variance that there was little left to be explained by the interaction term.

The simple view suggests that there are two, non-intersecting factors in reading comprehension. Storybook reading might have an effect on language comprehension, word recognition, or both. The effects of storybook reading on children's language comprehension are well documented by the other chapters in this volume. The effects on the development of word recognition and other print-related skills are less clear.

WHY WOULD ONE EXPECT STORYBOOK READING TO IMPROVE READING ACHIEVEMENT?

The assumptions underlying the recommendation of *Becoming a Nation of Readers* and others are, wittingly or unwittingly, based on a particular view of the reading process. In this view, children learn to recognize words through exposure, which in turn is achieved through repeated interactions around storybooks. (I use the term *storybook* because narrative fiction is the genre most commonly read to children. Non-fiction is also read to children both in school and at home, as are other genres of text, including alphabet books.) The theory, whether explicit or implicit, seems to be that at least some children will listen to a storybook repeatedly, since children usually request favorite storybooks. They will then try to "read" the book by themselves. At first, the child will make up a story based on the pictures (e.g., Sulzby, 1985). However, with repeated exposure to the story, the child will come to recognize that the words contain the story and will begin to concentrate on the text. As the child becomes better at using the information contained in print, the story re-enactments will get closer to the written text. Sulzby (1985) has documented a progression through a series of stages of emergent text reading, from lack of reliance on the text to nearly accurate text reading (see Sulzby's Fig. 1).

In Sulzby's (1985) model, children's initial attempts at "reading" a storybook are governed by the pictures, not the print. These initial picture-governed attempts involve labeling and commenting on the pictures, without a coherent story. At this stage the child sees each page as a unique entity, disconnected from the other pages. As children develop, they begin to see that written "stories" are similar to those told orally; written language register (Purcell-Gates, McIntyre, & Freppon, 1995) only comes later. According to Sulzby's model, children do not attend directly to the print until relatively late in the process. At first their attention to the print reveals itself in a refusal to read. As Biemiller (1970) found, children will refuse to read once they realize that the print contains the story and that they do not know how to unlock that story because they cannot recognize the words. As they learn about print, they use more and more cues in the text to recognize words, following a developmental path like that proposed by Ehri (1998).

Text reading, in this emergent perspective, can evolve through interactions with adults or knowledgeable others, or through interventions such as fingerpointing during reading, or parents cueing the child to look at the print. But text reading may also emerge through the sheer volume of parents' reading to children. Adams (1990) calculated that she spent at least 1,000 hours reading to her son John prior to first grade, with an additional 1,000 hours spent on literacy-related activities, such as playing with magnetic letters or watching *Sesame Street*. Contrasted to 180 hours of small-group reading instruction in first grade (assuming an hour of such instruction per day), the amount that is learned in each of Adams' 1,000 hours of parent–child reading can be less efficient than each hour of school-based reading and still be quite effective. Indeed, for precocious readers, this process of learning through exposure seems quite sufficient (Durkin, 1966).

Precocious readers, however, are a very small percentage of the population, perhaps less than 1% (e.g., Neuman, 2000). For most children, the exposure model breaks down at two critical junctures. First, children need additional knowledge—most specifically phonemic awareness—to take advantage of exposure to text. Second, most children also need some guidance in reading text, which they obtain through interactions with an adult. Such interactions are rare.

One explanation for the low correlations between storybook reading and achievement in the early grades may lie in the choice of measures used to assess reading in the early grades. In the Meyer et al. (1994) study, reading was assessed using the Wide Reading Achievement Test (a measure of reading isolated words), the Chicago Reading Test (a criterion-referenced measure of decoding), and several standardized group measures, such as the Stanford test. The WRAT and Chicago assessments are measures of isolated word reading; the other, group-administered measures tend to weight word recognition heavily in the early grades. Consequently, what was measured was largely print knowledge.

Thus, it is possible that the low correlations between storybook reading, either by parents or teachers, and achievement may be explained by the fact that storybook reading does not affect children's word recognition. In contrast, storybook reading *does* exert demonstrated effects on children's listening comprehension abilities. This has been shown not only by the Meyer et al. study, but by numerous other studies as well. Children clearly learn word meanings by listening to stories (see deTemple & Snow, this volume), but they also may develop syntactic knowledge (Chomsky, 1972) and general language comprehension (Stanovich, 1998) through exposure to the text in stories.

These low correlations do not mean that it is not possible for storybook reading to affect word recognition, only that it typically does not. The next section reviews a developmental model of word recognition in order to suggest points in the developmental process where storybook reading *could* actually impact word recognition, and then suggests ways of using storybooks to do so.

HOW DOES WORD RECOGNITION DEVELOP?

A number of different developmental models have emerged to describe the growth of different components of early reading. A survey of these models reveals some similarities. Storybook reading has a crucial but developmentally limited role in this process. Because its effects are seen at several critical phases in the growth of word recognition and are relatively circumscribed, global measures of storybook reading are likely to find only relatively small effects on reading.

Growth of Word Recognition

Ehri (1998) described the growth of children's knowledge of words through four qualitatively different phases. At first, children recognize words through distinctive visual features, such as the "tail" in *monkey*, or the two "eyes" in *look*. Ehri (1992) called this stage "visual cue reading." Gough, Juel, and Griffith (1992) described a study in which a group of pre-readers learned a series of flashcards, one of which had a thumbprint in the corner. When given the cards again, this time with the thumbprint on a different card, they tended to misread the thumbprinted card as the one from the first set, suggesting that they were attending to the thumbprint rather than the letters.

As children learn more words, this purely visual system of identification becomes unwieldy (Treiman & Baron, 1983). Once they develop rudimentary phonemic awareness, they begin to use salient letters to identify words. They usually begin this process with the initial letters of words, but sometimes use other letters as cues as well. Ehri called this *phonemic cue reading* or *partial alphabetic coding* (1992, 1998).

As their written vocabulary increases, children need to further analyze words; they therefore need to examine more parts of each word in order to identify it. This leads to *full alphabetic coding*, in which the child examines each letter of a word. This skill may come with instruction in decoding, or children may develop it on their own. Letter-by-letter decoding in turn gives way, with practice, to consolidated word recognition, in which a reader uses groups of letters, either as chunks or through analogies, to recognize words automatically, as proficient readers do (Chall, 1996; LaBerge & Samuels, 1974).

This development does not occur in a vacuum, but rather in conjunction with growth in phonemic awareness and exposure to text of difference types. Phonemic awareness is a part of phonological awareness, which "refers to a broad class of skills that involve attending to, thinking about, and intentionally manipulating the phonological aspects of spoken language" (Scarborough & Brady, 2001, p. 25). Phonemic awareness is that part of phonological awareness which deals with phonemes, rather than syllables or onsets and rimes. My colleagues and I (Stahl & McKenna, 2000; Stahl & Murray, 1998) have suggested that phonological awareness develops from an awareness of syllables, onsets, and rimes into an awareness of initial phonemes, then final phonemes, and lastly vowels.

Although phonemic awareness is related to reading, especially the decoding aspects of reading, the relationship does not seem to be strictly causal. Instead, it appears to be reciprocal, with simple phonemic awareness being necessary (although probably not sufficient) for children to develop rudimentary word recognition skills. After that point, growth in word recognition seems to enable further analysis of spoken words, which in turn enables further ability to decode more complex words (Beach, 1992; Perfetti, Beck, Bell, & Hughes, 1987).

The Development of Spelling

Children pass through a similar set of stages with respect to invented spelling. A number of different scales have captured this development (e.g., Bear, Invernizzi, Templeton, & Johnston, 2000; Gillet & Temple, 1990; Zutell & Rasinski, 1989). Many of these scales concentrate on early emergent spellings. Bear et al., for example, provided a 15-point scale, ranging from pre-alphabetic spellings to sophisticated knowledge of the morphemic structure of derived words.

Initially, a child may spell a word by drawing a picture or scribbling something that looks like writing (Harste, Burke, & Woodward, 1982). As children learn that words are composed of letters, they may use random letters to represent words. Bear et al. (2000) termed this phenomenon *pre-phonemic spelling*. At this point, the writers themselves are the only ones who can decode what they have written.

As children begin to think about sounds in words, their spelling may evolve to represent only one sound in a word—usually an initial sound, and occasionally a final sound. This is called *early letter name spelling*. Sometimes they will represent a word with a single letter or pair of letters, but more often signal a word by using the correct initial letter followed by a random string of letters. For example, one child in our reading clinic wrote *fish* with an initial 'f' followed by six other letters, explaining that "'f' words have a lot of letters in them." As children analyze words further, they may use the names of letters to represent sounds. At this stage, they may represent all of the consonants in a word, albeit often without vowels. For example, they might spell *girl* as "GRL" or *ten* as "TN." As Treiman (1993) pointed out, children use some letter names, but not others, to represent syllables. This phase seems to represent the beginning stage of their analysis of words into phonemes, usually consonants.

As children learn more about how words are spelled they begin to use vowels, and the words they write begin to more closely resemble the actual words they mean, as in the use of "DRAGUN" for *dragon*. Mastery of short vowels usually comes first, followed by long vowel patterns. This pattern may reflect the sequence of instruction, or may be the result of a tendency to favor simpler short vowel codings. Bear et al. (2000) referred to this stage as *letter name spelling*. When a child can consistently spell short vowels, but not yet long vowels, Bear et al. (2000) termed their spelling *within word pattern spelling*. The Bear scale continues beyond this point, but the present discussion is limited to the stages appropriate for exploration of the effects of storybook reading.

Stahl, McKenna, Gatliff, and Hagood (1998) and Stahl, McKenna, and Kovach (in press) found that spelling growth tends to follow growth in word recognition, as might be expected, because spelling is a production task and word recognition is a recognition task. But spelling growth has been used by a number of researchers as a way of assessing growth in children's knowledge of the alphabetic principle (e.g., Morris, 1993).

THE ROLE OF THE ALPHABET

A sketch of the developmental sequence for the growth of phonemic awareness, word recognition, and spelling might begin with knowledge of the alphabet—an important predictor of children's success in reading (Adams, 1990; Chall, 1967). Although children do not need to know every letter of the alphabet in order to learn to read, knowledge of the alphabet supports growth in word recognition, spelling, and phonemic awareness.

The effects of alphabet knowledge on spelling and word recognition should be obvious; however, the effects of alphabet knowledge on phonemic awareness are no less important. Stahl and Murray (1994) found that nearly all children who could segment an initial phoneme could also name at least 50 upper- and lowercase letters. No child who had not mastered the alphabet could segment an initial phoneme. This suggests that knowledge of the alphabet is necessary, although not sufficient, for children to segment initial consonants. Letters of the alphabet contain the phoneme they represent, and the majority contain it in the initial position (e.g., *t, d, v, z*). Worden and Boettcher (1990) found a developmental sequence for the recitation of the alphabet (usually the ABC song), the naming of individual letters, the printing of those letters, and the identification of letter sounds.

Treiman, Tincoff, Rodriquez, Mouzaki, and Francis (1998) found that children learn letter-sound information more easily if the represented consonant is found in the initial position of the letter name, suggesting that letter name knowledge seems to lead to letter sound knowledge. This was true regardless of whether the consonant was a sonorant or an obstruent, a stop or a continuant. Letter name knowledge may also mediate letter sound knowledge through exposure to alphabet books, as is discussed next.

Alphabet Books

The relationship between letter name knowledge and phonemic awareness may be mediated by exposure to alphabet books. Children who are read alphabet books may develop the insight that one can think about words as containing sounds. In closely observing children as they were read alphabet books, Yaden, Smolkin, and MacGillivray (1993) found that at first children could not make sense of why "M" might stand for "mouse." Through interaction with their parents, the children began with the assumption that there was an arbitrary association between the letter and the picture. For example:

Father: What letter is that [pointing to the O]?

Miriam: P, P. [Looking at the P on the facing page]

Father: What's this one? Let's just do this one. What is this? [Still pointing to O]

Miriam: P for pig! [Still looking at the P]

Father: That's right. It is P for pig, and that says pig. It's also for playful.

Miriam: And O is for mouse.

Father: That's not—mouse doesn't start with an O. That's an opossum.

Miriam: Possum, him looks like a mouse. (Yaden et al., 1993, p. 52)

At this point, Miriam has not yet grasped the alphabetic principle that letters can stand for sounds. Nor does she seem to see words as being decomposable into sounds. Her father is trying to provide that teaching by helping his daughter make sense of the book itself.

In their observations of two young children, Yaden et al. only observed the beginnings of abstract thought. Smolkin, Yaden, Brown, and Hofius (1992) found that alphabet books elicited significantly more print-related responses from children in one-on-one readings. This suggests that children attend to the print during these readings. Each book was read three times. For the alphabet books, the number of print-related responses increased with each reading, a pattern not found in most of the other picture books. (Children's print-oriented responses did increase with each reading of a predictable book, however. Such books are discussed later in this chapter.)

Van Kleeck (1998), observing storybook reading sessions of 2-, 3-, and 4-year-old children with their mothers, found that alphabet books were the only genre that elicited any maternal utterances related to the form of words. The number of form-related utterances increased with age. For 2-year-olds, mothers tended to treat alphabet books as a form of expository text. For 3- and 4-year-olds, the majority of maternal utterances focused on the letters. Van Kleeck replicated this basic finding with an observational study of children 3½ to 4 years old.

In alphabet books, print-related responses lead to greater awareness of print. Alphabet books have competing purposes: The child's purpose is to engage the story; the parents' purpose is to teach the alphabetic principle. These purposes are not mutually exclusive, however, and it seems clear that children do gain alphabetic insight through interactions with alphabet books.

In an experimental study, Murray, Stahl, and Ivey (1996) found that reading alphabet books to young children significantly improved their phonemic awareness. Working with a group of at-risk 4-year-olds, they compared the effects of reading three types of books to children for 10 minutes per day for 6 weeks. One class was read conventional alphabet books with a "B is for bear" structure, such as *Dr. Seuss' ABC* (Seuss, 1960). A second class was read books that contained the alphabet, but did not stress the sound values of letters, such as *Chicka Chicka Boom Boom* (Martin, 1989). In this book, the letters are recounted in order ("A told B and B told C / Meet me on top of the coconut tree"), but the book tells a story rather than identifying the sounds associated with the letters. A third class was read quality children's stories, which were brought into the class for this study. The class receiving the alphabet books with sound values made significantly greater progress on a measure of phonemic awareness.

This study, although fairly modest, indicates some causal link between alphabet book reading and phonemic awareness. Although alphabet knowledge surely influences children's recognition of words (see Adams, 1990, for a review), it also affects their awareness of phonemes. This effect is evident first with letters whose names begin with the phonemes that they represent (*b, c, t,* etc.) and later with consonants whose names end with that phoneme (*m, n, l*). As children learn about the relationship between letters and sounds, even in a rudimentary way, they can use this knowledge to identify words. This beginning letter-sound knowledge is the hallmark of Ehri's "partial alphabet cueing" phase, in which children use initial consonants as cues to identify words.

Although children may learn about the alphabet from a number of different sources, alphabet books seem to play an important role in the development of knowledge of written words. The studies supporting this premise have all been small in scale, however, and are thus far not definitive.

THE CRUCIAL ROLE OF FINGERPOINTING

Fingerpointing, also termed "concept of print in text" (Morris, 1993), is one of the most obvious interactions between storybook reading and word recognition development. Children differ in their ability to accurately point to words as they are being read—a skill known as print-to-speech match (Clay, 1991). This skill seems to be related to children's ability to use initial (and possibly final) letter cues to recognize words. Morris (1993), measuring phonemic awareness through invented spelling, found that children who could provide an initial phoneme in their invented spellings—what Bear et al. (2000) called "early letter name spellers"—were better able to fingerpoint than children who could not provide the initial phoneme. Ehri and Sweet (1991), using a segmentation task as their measure of phonemic awareness, found that children who could segment were also better able to fingerpoint. Uhry (1999), in turn, found that letter identification, as well as the use of final consonants in spelling, also contributed to children's fingerpointing ability.

Morris (1993) observed kindergarten children every 2 months over the kindergarten year. He found that for roughly 90% of the children in the study, the ability to segment beginning consonants preceded the ability to fingerpoint. Fingerpointing ability, in turn, preceded full segmentation, which itself preceded the ability to recognize words in isolation. Ehri and Chun (1991, cited in Uhry, 1999) found that training in letter sound knowledge also facilitated fingerpoint reading.

The ability to track print seems to be the nexus of storybook reading, alphabet knowledge, phonemic awareness, and the development of word recognition. Once children have mastered the alphabet and developed an awareness of initial sounds, then they can use initial consonants to identify words, both in isolation and in context. These identifications lead to further analysis of words, and eventually to full segmentation and alphabetic decoding.

It is unclear whether children's ability to fingerpoint is a result of word identification growth or whether it can develop independently. Using a multiple baseline design, Pierce (2000) modeled fingerpoint reading for three children and found that the modeling led to more accurate fingerpoint reading. This modeling was done individually: It is unclear whether the same practice would be effective in groups, as proposed by some (e.g., Holdaway, 1979), or whether it would be effective when a child is not developmentally ready.

Predictable Books

Many authors have suggested that emergent reading might begin with predictable books (e.g., Holdaway, 1979). Predictable or patterned books contain a repeated linguistic pattern that children can use to support their reading. An example would be "Brown bear, brown bear, what do you see? / I see a redbird looking at me / Red bird, red bird, what do you see?" and so on (Martin, 1983). Such books usually carry the pattern throughout, until it is finally broken at the end. Patterns can be more or less complex, and the books' predictability can come from text placement, the amount of support given by the pictures, or the familiarity of the content, as well as from linguistic patterns (Peterson, 1991).

Educators such as Holdaway suggest that predictable books allow children to concentrate on the words, using the text as a support. These books are typically read to the child in shared reading situations. As the book is re-read, children are expected to take more of the responsibility for reading onto themselves.

Such books are read for the purpose of learning to read more accurately, rather than for enjoyment of a story. Although they are more clearly intended for instruction than for pleasure, the actual reading exchange between adult and child is similar to that seen with conventional storybooks.

Smolkin et al. (1992) did find that children made a large number of print-oriented comments when reading predictable books, and that the number of such comments increased with multiple readings. This suggests that, at least for the given book, children were concentrating on the text. However, the results from word-learning studies are not as clear. Bridge, Winograd, and Haley (1983) found that first graders could learn sight words from predictable books more efficiently than from pre-primers. Their study, however, involved not only repeated readings of the predictable books, but also the use of word cards to isolate words from the text. Bridge and Burton (1982), who studied kindergartners without using word cards, failed to find significant word learning from predictable texts. Johnston (1998) examined first graders' word learning from predictable books and found significantly more word learning from the use of predictable books in combination with a word bank, than from re-reading by itself. McKenna, Stahl, Duffy, and Vancil (1996) found in one study that children learned more words from a book that was not patterned than from a book with a strong linguistic pattern. In another study, however, using more elaborate instruction, they failed to replicate that finding (Duffy, McKenna, Stratton, & Stahl, 1996).

One reason for this inconsistency may be that books cannot be easily divided into predictable and non-predictable types, but instead vary along a continuum of predictability (Peterson, 1991). Relatively predictable books may have a single, simple pattern, in which the words are well-supported by pictures. As children become more proficient, they can read books with multiple and more complex patterns, whose content is not supported by the pictures and may be out of the child's experience. As children use increasingly less predictable books, they need to concentrate more on the text. In Reading Recovery, this move from attention to the pattern to attention to the print is gradual (Clay, 1991). Even the most highly patterned texts eventually break their pattern, usually at the book's end. This break forces the child to attend to the print, at least for the duration of a single word. For example, in *Brown Bear, Brown Bear* (Martin, 1983), the pattern goes "[color] [animal], [color] [animal], what do you see? / I see a [new color] [new animal] looking at me," until the end, at which point it first changes to "Teacher, teacher what do you see? / I see children looking at me." Then the text lists all the animals that the children have seen, thus recapitulating the story. This simple break is signaled by the pictures and usually causes minimal disruption. However, Reading Recovery teachers suggest that such breaks do require children to concentrate more on print information, leading to development in word recognition (Stahl, Stahl, & McKenna, 1999).

Predictable books may have a small but important effect on word learning. Children may use the patterns to support their memorization of text. For the most part, memorization may draw attention away from the print, especially for younger children. The exception to this tendency is the break in the pattern, which requires children to return their attention to the print. As children gain in reading proficiency, the books they read should be less and less predictable, forcing them to attend more closely to the print throughout.

The print cue used in early, highly patterned books is usually an initial consonant. It is rare to see a pattern break cued by a medial vowel or final consonant. Thus, highly predictable books may be most appropriate at the stage when children are moving from visual cue reading to partial alphabetic coding. As they become more proficient in word recognition, they will benefit more from less-predictable texts (see Table 16.1).

INTERSECTIONS BETWEEN DEVELOPMENTAL SEQUENCES

I have, in this chapter, discussed developmental sequences for four aspects of early reading: storybook retelling, knowledge of the alphabet, word recognition, and spelling. There seem to be two points of intersection among these aspects. The first is the concept of the consonant. In storybook reading, recognition of this concept occurs at the break between picture-governed reading and print-governed reading, and is signaled by the beginning of accurate fingerpointing. In word recognition, it occurs when children move from visual cue reading to partial alphabetic coding, at which point they begin to use some phonemic information to match print to speech. I propose that the process of learning about consonants begins with learning the letters of the alphabet, possibly with the aid of alphabet books. From their knowledge of the letters of the alphabet, and the ways in which those letters relate to words, the children develop the rudimentary phonemic awareness needed to enter the world of print. Once a child is tracking print, this awareness is refined through shared storybook reading.

The second important intersection is the concept of the vowel. Given that consonants are folded into vowels in speech, and that vowels are not a universal feature of orthography (indeed, only alphabetic languages use them [Gleitman

TABLE 16.1
Developmental Trajectories of Various Aspects of Early Reading

Storybook Reading	Alphabet Knowledge	Word Recognition	Spelling
Picture governed—no story formed			
Picture governed—story formed (oral convention)		Pre-alphabetic—pictures	
Picture governed—story formed (written language conventions)	Knows ABC song		Pre-alphabetic—scribbles
	Can identify letters		
	Fingerpoints	Visual cue reading	Pre-alphabetic—random letters
Print-governed—refusal to read (not knowing written words)	Knows letter sounds	Phonetic cue reading	Early letter name (initial letters)
Print-governed—aspectual	Knows many words	Phonetic cue reading	Early letter name (initial and final letters)
Letter name			
Print-governed—strategic		Full alphabetic coding	Within word
Independent reading		Automaticity of word reading	Within word (and later stages)

& Rozin, 1977]), vowels are the last phonemes of which children usually become aware (Liberman, Shankweiler, Fischer, & Carter, 1974). As a consequence, children understandably have the greatest difficulty reading and spelling vowels (e.g., Shankweiler & Liberman, 1972).

The concept of the consonant seems to be phonological; but in children's word recognition and spelling the vowel concept may come from print, since vowels are difficult to conceptualize phonologically. Thus, vowel concepts may come from children's joint reading of storybooks. As children make their own attempts at reading and writing text, they need to attend to more parts of the word, especially the medial vowels. Much of this learning comes from instruction, but some of it comes from interaction with storybooks.

WHY THE LOW CORRELATIONS BETWEEN STORYBOOK READING AND READING SKILL?

Revisiting the question that began this chapter, I propose that storybook reading plays a small but crucial role in developing children's word recognition skills. This small role may be expressed in small correlations, especially with measures of word recognition.

Two special genres of text—alphabet books and patterned texts—have particular roles to play in children's learning about print. As pointed out earlier, alphabet books may lead children to the realizations that letters represent sounds, and that words can be thought of as collections of sounds—the beginning of both the alphabetic principle and phonemic awareness. Patterned books can also play a role at this juncture, once children begin to use initial consonant cues to aid in word recognition.

The effects of conventional storybooks are likely to be more diffuse. Studies show that neither parents nor teachers generally emphasize print while reading (e.g., Dickinson & Tabors, 2001). Although fingerpointing has been discussed in the professional literature, it is unclear how much either parents or teachers model it in practice. Instead, adults tend to stress the story. Some parents and teachers do augment the story with discussions of word meanings (see the chapters by deTemple and Snow, and Reese, both in this volume). But few use storybook reading time as a venue for teaching about the construction of words. Children, for their part, also tend to focus on the story rather than the words during storybook reading time, even with alphabet books (e.g., Yaden et al., 1993).

With the exception of books especially constructed or chosen for learning about print, such as predictable books or basal reader stories, the vocabulary of children's storybooks is too diverse, and too rarely repeated (Hoffman et al.,

1994), to help children learn words effectively. Hayes and Ahrens (1988) found that the density of "rare" words in children's books—a measure of vocabulary difficulty—was greater in children's storybooks than in conversations between two college-educated adults or in "educational" television shows. Storybooks also tend to contain more complex syntactic structures than are usually heard in everyday speech, even among college-educated adults (Chomsky, 1972).

Word recognition growth, however, seems to be aided by repetition (Chall, 1967; Hiebert, 1998). Thus, conventional storybooks may be a wonderful source for language development, in terms of both vocabulary and syntax; but the same characteristics that make them useful for oral language development, vocabulary diversity, and complex language probably impede growth in word recognition.

Those studies that have found strong relationships between storybook reading and print-related skills may actually be confounding the effects of storybook reading with those of a home or classroom with a high literacy press. For example, a recent large-scale survey conducted by the National Center for Educational Statistics (Nord, Lennon, Liu, & Chandler, 2000) found that children who were read to at least three times a week were significantly more likely to know all the letters of the alphabet, to read or pretend read a book, and to write their own name—all early indicators of emergent literacy. But the same survey found that children who were read to three or more times a week were more likely to be able to count to 20. One can hypothesize a path from sharing storybooks to literacy; the relation to counting is more difficult to imagine. More likely, the relationship to counting, and probably to literacy, is largely explained by the fact that children who are read to often are more likely to be in homes with a strong academic press, where literacy and numeracy activities are more numerous and more common. It is this type of home, of which frequent storybook reading is just one characteristic, that gives some children an advantage in literacy learning.

Dickinson and Tabors' (2001) findings are more problematic. They observed 3- and 4-year-old children around a storybook reading event in their homes and classified the talk around the book as either "immediate" or "non-immediate." They found that 43% to 60% of the talk was immediate, meaning that it involved labeling of pictures or words in the text. Considerably less of the talk—11% to 18%—was non-immediate, meaning that it used the text to talk about personal experiences or the use of general knowledge to make predictions or draw inferences. The study found moderate negative correlations (–.28 to –.32) between the amount of immediate talk used at ages 3 and 4 during storybook reading and an emergent literacy measure, including such print-related measures as writing concepts, story and print concepts, sounds in words, and environmental print. They found positive correlations of the same magnitude between the amount of non-immediate talk and emergent literacy measures in kindergarten. Normally, one would expect that non-immediate talk would draw children's attention away from the print, and thus cause *lower achievement,* rather than the higher achievement found by Dickinson and Tabors. It could be, however, that non-immediate talk is another characteristic of homes with a high literacy press.

Given that neither parents nor teachers nor children tend to focus explicitly on print during storybook reading time, it is not surprising that the correlations between storybook reading and print learning are so small. As a practical matter, one can encourage parents and teachers to fingerpoint, since modeling fingerpointing may encourage children to do more of it themselves during their own interactions with books (Pierce, 2000). We also might recommend increased use of alphabet books, since reading alphabet books may improve children's early word learning, as well (Murray et al., 1996).

One series of studies examined the effects of print orientation during storybook reading on children's acquisition of print concepts. Ezell and Justice (2000) and Justice and Ezell (2000) found that a videotape demonstration of print-oriented storybook reading (including fingerpointing, tracking of print, comments, questions, and requests about print) produced an increase in these behaviors among parents and children, as well as an improvement in children's knowledge of literacy concepts. Justice and Ezell (n.d.) extended this work to Head Start teachers and found that, in an 8-week training program, the use of print-referencing behaviors during storybook reading led to improvements in print recognition, alphabet knowledge, and phonological awareness, but not in basic print concepts, letter orientation, and use of literacy terms. The lack of effects on measures of print concepts is somewhat surprising, since presumably many of the adult interactions would be directed toward those concepts. This work is promising, but still in its preliminary stages. It is unclear whether short interventions would have long-term effects on such culturally mediated and ingrained behaviors as storybook reading.

In summary, reading books to children can improve their language skills, and language comprehension is essential for reading comprehension (Gough & Tunmer, 1986), but storybook reading is not a panacea for children's literacy. Instead, storybook reading should be part of a total instructional program that also includes direct instruction in print-related skills.

REFERENCES

Adams, M. J. (1990). *Beginning to read: Thinking and learning about print.* Cambridge, MA: MIT Press.

Anderson, R. C., Hiebert, E. F., Wilkinson, I. A. G., & Scott, J. (1985). *Becoming a nation of readers.* Champaign, IL: National Academy of Education and Center for the Study of Reading.

Barr, R. D. R. (1983). *How schools work*. Chicago: University of Chicago Press.

Beach, S. A. (1992). *Toward a model of the development of reader resources in the emergence and acquisition of literacy skill*. Unpublished doctoral dissertation, University of California at Riverside.

Bear, D. R., Invernizzi, M., Templeton, S., & Johnston, F. (2000). *Words their way: Word study for phonics, vocabulary and spelling instruction* (2nd ed.). Upper Saddle River, NJ: Merrill.

Biemiller, A. (1970). The development of the use of graphic and contextual information as children learn to read. *Reading Research Quarterly, 6*, 75–96.

Bloom, B. S. (1976). *Human characteristics and school learning*. New York: McGraw-Hill.

Bridge, C. A., & Burton, B. (1982). Teaching sight vocabulary through patterned language materials. In J. A. Niles & L. A. Harris (Eds.), *New inquiries in reading research and instruction: Thirty-first yearbook of the National Reading Conference* (pp. 119–123). Washington, DC: National Reading Conference.

Bridge, C. A., Winograd, P. N., & Haley, D. (1983). Using predictable materials vs. preprimers to teach beginning sight words. *The Reading Teacher, 36*, 884–891.

Bus, A. G., van IJzendoorn, M. H., & Pellegrini, A. D. (1995). Joint book reading makes for success in learning to read: A meta-analysis on intergenerational transmission of literacy. *Review of Educational Research, 65*, 1–21.

Carver, R. P. (1993). Merging the simple view of reading with reading theory. *Journal of Reading Behavior, 25*, 439–455.

Chall, J. S. (1967). *Learning to read: The great debate* (1st ed.). New York: McGraw-Hill.

Chall, J. S. (1996). *Stages of reading development* (2nd ed.). Fort Worth, TX: Harcourt-Brace.

Chomsky, C. (1972). Stages in language development and reading exposure. *Harvard Educational Review, 42*, 1–33.

Clay, M. M. (1991). *Becoming literate*. Portsmouth, NH: Heinemann.

Dickinson, D. K., & Tabors, P. O. (2001). *Beginning literacy with language*. Baltimore: Brookes.

Duffy, A. M., McKenna, M., Stratton, B., & Stahl, S. A. (1996, December). *Tales of Ms. Wishy-Washy: The effects of predictable books on learning to recognize words*. Paper presented at the annual meeting of the National Reading Conference, Charleston, SC.

Durkin, D. (1966). *Children who read early*. New York: Teacher's College Press.

Ehri, L. C. (1992). Reconceptualizing the development of sight word reading and its relationship to recoding. In P. Gough, L. C. Ehri, & R. Treiman (Eds.), *Reading acquisition* (pp. 107–143). Mahwah, NJ: Lawrence Erlbaum Associates.

Ehri, L. C. (1998). Grapheme-phoneme knowledge is essential for learning to read words in English. In J. L. Metsala & L. C. Ehri (Eds.), *Word recognition in beginning literacy* (pp. 3–40). Mahwah, NJ: Lawrence Erlbaum Associates.

Ehri, L. C., & Sweet, J. (1991). Fingerpoint-reading of memorized text: What enables beginners to process the print? *Reading Research Quarterly, 26*, 442–462.

Ezell, H. K., & Justice, L. M. (2000). Increasing the print focus of adult–child shared book reading through observational learning. *American Journal of Speech-Language Pathology, 9*, 36–47.

Gillet, J. W., & Temple, C. (1990). *Understanding reading problems* (3rd ed.). Glenview, IL: Scott-Foresman.

Gleitman, L. R., & Rozin, P. (1977). The structure and acquisition of reading I: Relations between orthographies and the structure of language. In A. S. Reber & D. L. Scarborough (Eds.), *Toward a psychology of reading* (pp. 1–53). Mahwah, NJ: Lawrence Erlbaum Associates.

Gough, P. B., Juel, C., & Griffith, P. L. (1992). Reading, spelling, and the orthographic cipher. In P. B. Gough, L. C. Ehri, & R. Treiman (Eds.), *Reading acquisition* (pp. 35–48). Mahwah, NJ: Lawrence Erlbaum Associates.

Gough, P. B., & Tunmer, W. E. (1986). Decoding, reading, and reading disability. *Remedial and Special Education, 7,* 6–10.

Harste, J. C., Burke, C. L., & Woodward, V. A. (1982). Children's language and world: Initial encounters with print. In J. A. Langer & M. T. Smith-Burke (Eds.), *Reader meets author: Bridging the gap* (pp. 105–131). Newark, DE: International Reading Association.

Hayes, D. P., & Ahrens, M. G. (1988). Vocabulary simplification for children: A special case of "motherese." *Journal of Child Language, 15,* 395–410.

Hiebert, E. H. (1998). Text matters. *The Reading Teacher, 52,* 552–566.

Hoffman, J. V., McCarthey, S. J., Abbott, J., Christian, C., Corman, L., Curry, C., Dressman, M., Elliott, B., Matherne, D., & Stahle, D. (1994). So what's new in the new basals? A focus on first grade. *Journal of Reading Behavior, 26,* 47–73.

Holdaway, D. (1979). *The foundations of literacy.* Sydney, Australia: Ashton-Scholastic.

Hoover, W. A., & Gough, P. B. (1990). The simple view of reading. *Reading and Writing: An Interdisciplinary Journal, 2,* 127–160.

Johnston, F. R. (1998). The reader, the text, and the task: Learning words in first grade. *The Reading Teacher, 51,* 666–675.

Justice, L. M., & Ezell, H. K. (2000). Enhancing children's print and word awareness through home-based parent intervention. *American Journal of Speech-Language Pathology, 9,* 257–269.

Justice, L. M., & Ezell, H. K. (n.d.). *Print awareness intervention in Head Start: An experimental evaluation.* Unpublished manuscript.

LaBerge, D., & Samuels, S. J. (1974). Toward a theory of automatic information processing in reading. *Cognitive Psychology, 6,* 293–323.

Liberman, I. Y., Shankweiler, D., Fischer, F. W., & Carter, B. (1974). Reading and the awareness of linguistic segments. *Journal of Experimental Child Psychology, 18,* 201–212.

Martin, B. J. (1983). *Brown bear, brown bear, what do you see?* New York: Henry Holt.

Martin, B. J. (1989). *Chicka chicka boom boom.* New York: Simon & Schuster.

McKenna, M. C., Stahl, S. A. Duffy, A., & Vancil, J. (1996, April). *Tales of Ms. Wishy-Washy: The effects of patterned language books on the learning of sight words.* Paper presented at the annual meeting of the American Educational Research Association, New York, NY.

Meyer, L., Stahl, S. A., Wardrop, J., & Linn, R. (1994). Effects of reading storybooks aloud to children. *Journal of Educational Research, 88,* 69–85.

Morris, D. (1993). The relationship between children's concept of word in text and phoneme awareness in learning to read: A longitudinal study. *Research in the Teaching of English, 27,* 133–154.

Murray, B. A., Stahl, S. A., & Ivey, M. G. (1996). Developing phoneme awareness through alphabet books. *Reading and Writing: An Interdisciplinary Journal, 8,* 307–322.

Neuman, S. B. (December, 2000). *A portrait of precocious early readers: An empirical analysis.* Paper presented at the annual meeting of the National Reading Conference, Scottsdale, AZ.

Nord, C. W., Lennon, J., Liu, B., & Chandler, K. (2000). Home literacy activities and signs of children's emerging literacy: 1993 and 1999 (Report NCES-2000-026). Washington, DC: National Center for Educational Statistics. (ERIC Document Reproduction Service ED 438 528).

Perfetti, C. A., Beck, I. L., Bell, L., & Hughes, C. (1987). Phonemic knowledge and learning to read are reciprocal: A longitudinal study of first grade children. *Merrill-Palmer Quarterly, 33,* 283–319.

Peterson, B. (1991). Selecting books for beginning readers. Children's literature suitable for young readers: A bibliography. In D. E. Deford, C. A. Lyons, & G. S. Pinnell (Eds.), *Bridges to literacy: Learning from reading recovery* (pp. 119–147). Portsmouth, NH: Heinemann.

Pierce, L. E. (2000). *Fingerpoint modeling: Effect of picture-governed readers' visual tracking*. Unpublished doctoral dissertation, Brigham Young University, Salt Lake City, UT.

Purcell-Gates, V., McIntyre, E., & Freppon, P. A. (1995). Learning written storybook language in school: A comparison of low-SES children in skills-based and whole language classrooms. *American Educational Research Journal, 32,* 659–685.

Scarborough, H., & Brady, S. (2001). *Toward a common terminology for talking about speech and reading: A glossary of the Phon words and some related terms*. Unpublished manuscript.

Scarborough, H. S., & Dobrich, W. (1994). On the efficacy of reading to preschoolers. *Developmental Review, 14,* 245–302.

Seuss, Dr. (1960). *Dr. Seuss' ABC*. New York: Random House.

Shankweiler, D., & Liberman, I. Y. (1972). Misreading: A search for causes. In J. F. Kavanaugh & I. G. Mattingly (Eds.), *Language by eye and by ear* (pp. 293–317). Cambridge, MA: MIT Press.

Smolkin, L. B., Yaden, D. B., Jr., Brown, L., & Hofius, B. (1992). The effects of genre, visual design choices, and discourse structure on preschoolers' responses to picture books during parent–child read-alouds. *National Reading Conference Yearbook, 41,* 291–301.

Stahl, K. A. D., Stahl, S. A., & McKenna, M. C. (1999). The development of phonological awareness and orthographic processing in Reading Recovery. *Literacy, Teaching and Learning, 4*(3), 27–42.

Stahl, S. A., & McKenna, M. C. (2000). *The conjoint development of phonological awareness, word recognition and spelling*. CIERA Archive Report #01-07. [On-line]. Available: http://www.ciera.org/library/archive/2001-07/200107.htm.

Stahl, S. A., McKenna, M. C., & Kovach, J. J. (in press). *The development of word recognition, spelling, and phonological awareness*. CIERA report.

Stahl, S. A., McKenna, M. C., Stahl, K. A. D., Hagood, M., & Gatliff, J. (1998, December). *The development of word recognition, spelling, and phonological awareness*. Paper presented at the annual meetings of the National Reading Conference, Austin, TX.

Stahl, S. A., & Murray, B. A. (1994). Defining phonological awareness and its relationship to early reading. *Journal of Educational Psychology, 86,* 221–234.

Stahl, S. A., & Murray, B. A. (1998). Issues involved in defining phonological awareness and its relation to early reading. In J. Metsala & L. C. Ehri (Eds.), *Word recognition in beginning literacy* (pp. 65–88). Mahwah, NJ: Lawrence Erlbaum Associates.

Stallings, J. A., & Kaskowitz, D. H. (1974). *Follow through classroom observation evaluation* (Report No. SRIURU7370). Menlo Park, CA: Stanford Research Institute. (ERIC document Reproduction Service ED 104 969).

Stanovich, K. E. (1998). *Literacy experiences and the shaping of cognition*. Paper presented at the annual meeting of the American Educational Research Association, San Diego, CA.

Sulzby, E. (1985). Children's emergent reading of favorite storybooks: A developmental study. *Reading Research Quarterly, 20,* 458–481.

Treiman, R. (1993). *Beginning to spell: A study of first grade children*. New York: Oxford University Press.

Treiman, R., & Baron, J. (1983). Individual differences in spelling: The Phoenician-Chinese distinction. *Topics in Learning and Learning Disabilities, 3*(3), 33–40.

Treiman, R., Tincoff, R., Rodriquez, K., Mouzaki, A., & Francis, D. J. (1998). The foundations of literacy: Learning the sounds of letters. *Child Development, 69,* 1524–1540.

van Kleeck, A. (1998). Preliteracy domains and stages: Laying the foundations for beginning reading. *Journal of Children's Communication Development, 20,* 33–51.

Uhry, J. K. (1999). Invented spelling in kindergarten: The relationship with finger-point reading. *Reading and Writing: An Interdisciplinary Journal, 11,* 441–464.

Worden, P. E., & Boettcher, W. (1990). Young children's acquisition of alphabet knowledge. *Journal of Reading Behavior, 22,* 277–295.

Yaden, D. B., Smolkin, L. B., & MacGillivray, L. (1993). A psychogenetic perspective on children's understanding about letter associations during alphabet book readers. *Journal of Reading Behavior, 25,* 43–68.

Zutell, J., & Rasinski, T. (1989). Reading and spelling connections in third and fifth grade students. *Reading Psychology, 10,* 137–155.

Author Index

Note: Page numbers in *italics* indicate pages on which full bibliographical references appear; *f* indicates figure.

A

Abbott, J., 377, *381*
Abraham, F. D., 337, *358*
Abraham, R. H., 337, *358*
Abramson, S., 215, 220, *227*
Adams, C., 59, 65, 87
Adams, M. J., 290, 291, 294, 301, 304, *311*, 366, 370, 372, *379*
Ahrens, M. G., 29, 31, *34*, 378, *381*
Alexander, E. I., 6, 8, *15*, 59, 71, *91*
Alexander, P., 298, *313*
Allen, J., 159, *175*, 236, 237, *251*
Allen, P., 42, *55*
Allington, R. L., 124, *136*
Altwerger, A., 59, 63, 86, 145, *156*
Amerman, J. D., 74, *89*
Anastasopoulos, L, 101, 102, *113*
Anderberg, M. R., 44, *55*
Anderson, A., 206, 207, 223, *229*
Anderson, J., 203, 204, 206, 207, 214, 215, 222, 223, 225, 226, *227*, *229*
Anderson, R. C., 17, *33*, 115, *136*, 363, 364, *379*
Anderson-Yockel, J., 283, 284, *311*
Angell, A. L, 20, 26, 36, 41, 54, 56, *57*, 130, 131, *139*, 177, 178, 183, 184, 185, 186, 187, 188, 189, 192, *199*, *200*, 297, 305, *320*, 344, *362*
Anno, M., 128, *139*
Anthony, J. L., 96, *112*, 305, *315*
Aram, D., 59, 86
Armstrong, M., 72, 86
Arnold, D. H., 20, 26, 36, 41, 54, 56, 178, 181, *197*, 278, *311*

Arnold, D. S., 97, *111*, 130, 131, *139*, 184, 185, 186, 187, *197*, *200*
Ash, G. E., 127, *137*
Au, K. H., 237, *250*
Auerbach, E., 225, *227*
Auerbach, S., 53, 55
Axelrod, R., 330, *333*

B

Baddeley, A., 304, *314*
Bailey, L. M., 19, *34*
Bak, P., 337, *358*
Bakeman, R., 302, *315*
Baker, C. D., 233, 238, 239, 248, *250*
Baker, L., 4, *13*
Baker, P. L., 337, *358*
Ball, E., 304, *311*
Bandura, A., 181, *197*
Barnes, S., 177, *200*
Barnes, W. E., 4, *15*
Barnett, S., 109, *111*
Barnhart, J., 144, *157*, 222, *227*
Baron, J., 367, *382*
Barr, R. D. R., 364, *380*
Barrera, R. B., 253, *267*
Bartini, M., 298, *316*, 331, *334*
Barton, D., 204, *227*, 240, *250*
Barton, M., 19, *35*
Bashir, B., 59, *91*
Bates, E., 18, *34*, 277, *313*
Battle, J., 116, 129, *137*, 258, *266*
Bauer, E. B., 260, 261, 263, 265, *266*
Baumann, J. F., 116, *136*
Beach, S. A., 368, *380*

385

Subject Index

Note: *f* indicates figure; *t* indicates table.